ON STAFFING

ON STAFFING

Advice and Perspectives from HR Leaders

Editors

NICHOLAS C. BURKHOLDER

PRESTON J. EDWARDS SR.

LIBBY SARTAIN

WILEY

JOHN WILEY & SONS, INC.

For general information on our other products and services please contact our Customer Care Department within the United States at (800)762-2974, outside the United States at (317)572-3993 or fax (317)572-4002.

Wiley also publishes its books in a variety of electronic formats. Some content that appears in print may not be available in electronic books. For more information about Wiley products, visit our web site at www.wiley.com.

Library of Congress Cataloging-in-Publication Data:
Burkholder, Nicholas C.
　　On staffing : Advice and perspectives from HR leaders / Nicholas C. Burkholder, Preston J. Edwards Sr., Libby Sartain.
　　　p. cm.
　　Includes index.
　　ISBN 0-471-41069-1 (cloth)
　　1. Human capital.　I. Title.

HD4904.7.B87   2003
658.3—dc21

2003041122

Printed in the United States of America.

10 9 8 7 6 5 4 3 2 1

To the staffing professional—past, present, and future

The core of human resources, staffing is the most fundamental and critical driver of organization performance. The goal of staffing is to optimize human capital performance. Staffing includes workforce design and structure as well as the acquisition, development, assessment, and retention of human capital. Today staffing may include employees, contingent workers, contractors, consultants, and outsourced operations working around the world.

Contents

About the Editors and Contributors

Current information on the editors and contributors is available at www.staffing.org/onstaffing.

Editors

A global authority on human capital performance, Nick Burkholder is the founder and President of Staffing.org. His management experience includes virtually every aspect of workforce design and management with organizations that include Johnson & Johnson Worldwide Family of Companies, CIGNA Corporation, The Vanguard Group, and the U.S. Army. He has personally filled over 800 key positions in 48 countries and directed the recruitment of over 124,000 worldwide. Since 1998, Burkholder has helped hundreds of organizations worldwide to measurably optimize their human capital performance.

Burkholder is an adviser to state, national, and international organizations regarding current and long-term human capital challenges. He is also a member of the World Council of the World Association for Cooperative Education and a long-term Director of the Employment Management Association. Burkholder led the development of the Wall Street Journal School Business Partnership Awards Program. He is also a recipient of the Donald Sweet Award for exceptional and sustained contributions to the Employment Management Association of the Society for Human Resource Management (SHRM).

He frequently speaks and writes on staffing issues and routinely presents at conferences worldwide. The Human Capital Blueprint, a cutting-edge tool developed by Burkholder, is the culmination of over 20 years of research and development. The Blueprint integrates every aspect of human capital, including the ultimate measure, organization performance, and provides a holistic framework that enables organizations to make the best decisions, now and for the future.

Preston J. Edwards Sr. is the CEO of iMinorities, Inc., a publishing and Internet company that merged with Black Collegiate Services, Inc., the 30-year-old publisher of the *Black Collegian* magazine and *Black MBA* magazine and two web sites: IMDiversity and The Black Collegian Online.

Edwards was previously employed as Local Vice President for the Interracial Council for Business Opportunity; Regional Manager of Affirmative Action for the Great Atlantic and Pacific Tea Company; Assistant Professor in the College of Business at Southern University; and Assistant Cashier for Citibank in New York. With a BA degree from Dillard University and his MBA degree from Atlanta University, Edwards was awarded the Honorary Degree of Doctor of Humane Letters from Livingstone College. He also received the Employment Management Association Foundation President's Award for outstanding service, the Employment Management Association's Pericles Award, the CEBA "Pioneers of Excellence" Award, and the Phi Beta Sigma African-American Male Image Award.

Edwards is a member of Xavier University's Cluster and its Business Advisory Council. Previously, he served on the boards of the Council on Career Development for Minorities (CCDM), Junior Achievement of Southeastern Louisiana, the Urban League of Greater New Orleans, the Central Business District Historic Landmark Commission, the Employment Management Association Foundation, and the Orleans Private Industry Council (OPIC).

With more than 20 years of experience in human resources management and formerly Board Chair of the Society of Human Resource Management, Libby Sartain is Senior Vice President, Human Resources, and Chief People Yahoo, at Yahoo! Inc. Sartain is responsible for leading Yahoo! Inc.'s global human resources efforts and managing and developing the human resources team. She also focuses on attracting, retaining, and developing Yahoo!'s employees who promote and strengthen the company culture, as well as represent the powerful Yahoo! brand.

Before joining Yahoo!, Sartain served as Vice President of People for Southwest Airlines, where she received the 1994 President's Award for Annual Outstanding Employee and the 1998 Heart and Soul Award for Outstanding Employee. She has been an active member of SHRM for over 13 years, serving as both Vice President-at-Large and as Vice Chair of the board before being named Chair in January 2001. Sartain has been instrumental in the organization's legislative initiatives, frequently testifying on Capital Hill on SHRM's behalf. She was also chair of the SHRM Compensation and Benefits Committee from 1995 to 1997.

Sartain is active with SHRM on local levels as well. She served as President of the Board of Directors of the Dallas Human Resource Management Association and has held several positions for the State of Texas SHRM Conference, including Executive Director. She is a fellow of the National Academy of Human Resources, and has earned lifetime certification as a Senior Professional in Human Resources (SPHR) from the Human Resource Certification Institute, an affiliate of the Society for Human Resource Management.

Contributors

Lou Adler is a veteran recruiter and is CEO and founder of CJA—The Adler Group (1978), a major executive search firm headquartered in Southern California. Adler is also the CEO and founder of POWER Hiring, a consulting and training organization.

Nancy Ahlrichs manages her own speaking and consulting practice, EOC Strategies, LLC. She has written guest columns for a variety of newspapers, technical journals, and online resources.

Kathy April Barr has 12 years of recruitment experience. She is currently the Director of Executive Search for The Stump LLC, a diversity consulting and recruiting firm located in Chicago, Illinois.

Karen Bloom is the principal of Bloom, Gross & Associates, Inc., an executive search firm based in Chicago. She serves on the board of directors of both the Employment Management Association and the Employment Management Association Foundation.

Joseph A. Bosch has been Chief People Officer of Human Resources for Pizza Hut in Dallas since July 1997. His career has included numerous HR positions with PepsiCo and Pizza Hut.

Kim Burns is Executive Director of Staffing.org. She played a key role in organizing the first national meetings on HR metrics. Kim directs Staffing.org's web-based operations including the Resource Center.

Harvey Burstein is a Professor of Security, College of Criminal Justice, Northeastern University, as well as a security management consultant to various Fortune 500 companies. He was previously a Federal Bureau of Investigation special agent, as well as Chief, Foreign and Domestic

Investigations, Physical Security, and Security Surveys, U.S. Department of State.

Gerry Crispin, SPHR, writes, speaks, teaches, and consults internationally on the growing role of emerging technology in employment strategies and processes. He is the coauthor, along with Mark Mehler, of *CareerXroads*, a best-selling annual directory of job, resume, and career management web sites on the Internet.

Bernie Cullen is a founder and partner of Cambria Consulting, a Boston-based HR consulting firm that works with executive teams to address strategic human resource issues through implementing new technologies.

Annette Merritt Cummings is Vice President and National Director of Diversity Services, Bernard Hodes Group. She consults with clients nationally to help recruit and retain a diverse workforce.

Jim Dalton is the Content Director of ERE and managing editor of its online publication, the ER Daily. ERE also hosts the ER Expo conference series on recruiting and workforce management topics.

Ron Elsdon specializes in the workforce development and career fields through organizational consulting, individual coaching, career counseling, publishing, and lecturing. He is a Principal in New Beginnings: Career and College Guidance.

Bruce Ferguson is Vice President, Talent Acquisition Solution (TAS) for Exult, Inc., a provider of eHR, a comprehensive, Web-enabled integrated service designed to manage the entire human resources department for Global 500 corporations.

John Flato, an expert in the field of campus recruiting, is the National Director of University Recruiting at Ernst & Young.

Michael Foster is Chairman and CEO of AIRS, the global leader in recruitment training, and a leading provider of recruitment software tools and media services.

Peter J. Franks has been associated with work-integrated education his entire adult life. He was the first Chief Executive Officer of the World Association for Cooperative Education, Inc., and recently completed a two-year term as President of the Employment Management Association Foundation.

Cheryl Fry is Vice President, Human Resources, for the North American region of BBDO Worldwide, a major international advertising and communications organization.

Bill Gaul is President and CEO of The Destiny Group, an Internet-based recruiting tool that utilizes the latest patent-pending technology for organizations to use to source men and women departing the military services.

Tim Gibbon is President and Chief Executive Officer, JWT Specialized Communications, New York. He joined JWTSC as a Managing Partner of the Employment Communications Group in 1996, and was appointed to his current position in January 1997.

Raj Gnana-Pragasam is Vice President of Recruitment Services, North American Division, Compass Group.

Daniel Guaglianone is Senior Director Recruiting for Merck's Research Laboratories. He was previously Vice President of Global Recruiting for Unisys Corporation.

Carl Haacke is an economist and consultant to The New York Times Job Market.

Heather Hartmann is the Executive Director of the Human Capital Metrics Consortium, an independent nonprofit hosted by Staffing.org to establish standard, universally comparable human capital metrics. She has more than 16 years of staffing experience including key positions at Accenture and Cap Gemini Ernst & Young.

Row Henson, instrumental in human resources and human resource management systems for the past 30 years, retired in July 2000 as Vice President of HRMS Global Product Strategy at PeopleSoft. She is a PeopleSoft fellow and consultant.

Laura Herring is President and CEO of The IMPACT Group, a global career/life transition assistance firm based in St. Louis, Missouri, which has assisted employees and their family members of over 200 companies and organizations worldwide.

Elizabeth Hoane is coleader of IBM Global Learning Solutions and Performance.

Elwood F. "Ed" Holton III, Ed.D. is Professor of Human Resource, Leadership, and Organization Development in the School of Human Resource Education at Louisiana State University.

Gary Hunt is the Vice President of Human Resources for OMI, Inc., responsible for all aspects of OMI's equal opportunity and affirmative action programs, contracts compliance, employee relations, negotiation, labor relations training, organizational development, recruitment and retention, and other staffing issues.

Gail Hyland-Savage is Chief Operating Officer for Michaelson, Connor & Boul, a real estate marketing and management company in

Huntington Beach, California. She is President of the Employment Management Association.

Kent Kirch has led recruiting worldwide for Deloitte since June 2001. He works with country leaders to develop strategies, tools, and programs to enhance recruiting efforts globally.

John G. Kitson, an expert in the area of mergers and acquisitions, is Senior Vice President and Chief Human Resources Officer for FirstBank, Inc., a privately owned bank holding company.

Tony Lee is Editor in Chief and General Manager of The Wall Street Journal Online Network, which includes CareerJournal.com, StartupJournal.com, RealEstateJournal.com, CollegeJournal.com, CareerJournalEurope.com, and CareerJournalAsia.com.

Yves Lermusiaux is President and founder of iLogos Research, a RecruitSoft company that produces data on industry trends, best practice methodologies, and benchmarking information with a focus on metrics and business analytics.

David Lowry is Vice President, Social and Community Affairs, and Human Rights Compliance Officer for Freeport-McMoRan Copper and Gold Inc. He is also President of the Freeport-McMoRan Foundation.

David Manaster is the President and founder of Electronic Recruiting Exchange, Inc. (ERE), which hosts a web site providing daily articles, online networking opportunities, and premium research reports for the recruiting profession.

Lou Manzi joined SmithKline Beecham Consumer Products as Manager, Government and Public Affairs in 1985. He is currently with GlaxoSmithKline Corporate Staffs and leads the Global Recruitment function, with responsibility for coordinating all U.S. Human Resources Shared Services initiatives.

Debbie McGrath founded HR.com in August 1999, committed to establishing the most helpful knowledge hub, community, and marketplace for human resources on the Web.

Barbara Mitchell is a principal with The Millennium Group International, LLC—a Washington, D.C.–based innovative human resources and organizational development consulting practice that focuses on helping client organizations attract and retain the talent to succeed.

Robert Morgan is President of the Human Capital Consulting Group of Spherion Corporation, a provider of recruitment, outsourcing, and technology solutions.

Arthur (Arte) Nathan is Senior Vice President/Chief Human Resources Officer for Wynn Resorts.

Rob O'Keefe is Vice President, Marketing Resources for TMP Worldwide Advertising and Communications.

Elaine Pavlow is a Management Recruiter for Wal-Mart Stores, Inc. and a founding member of the Human Capital Metrics Consortium.

Steve Pogorzelski is President of Monster North America, responsible for the daily operations of Monster North America, which include Monster.com, Monster.ca, and other Monster entities.

Lawrence J. Quartana, Ph.D., is a management and organizational consultant with over 20 years experience in the public and private sectors. He is a member of the adjunct faculty of the Wharton School of the University of Pennsylvania and was the Manager of Organizational Development for the City of Philadelphia during the Rendell Administration.

Keiko Saito, President of ILCC, Co., Ltd., founded ILCC almost 30 years ago and continues to specialize in all forms of written and oral communication. She is a recognized leader in work-integrated learning in Japan.

Allan Schweyer is Senior Researcher at HR.com.

Nicholas Scobbo is a Human Resource Information Systems Analyst with Mitre Corporation.

Barry Siegel is President of Recruitment Enhancement Services (RES), an Omnicom Group Inc. company that is a leading provider of Total Outsourced Talent Solutions. He is also President, Interactive and Staffing Solutions, of Bernard Hodes Group, a world leader in recruitment communications and staffing solutions.

Dr. John Sullivan is a well-known thought leader in HR and author of the "World-Class Way" series of books on emerging HR issues. He is a Professor of Management at San Francisco State University, and was once called the "Michael Jordan of Hiring" by *Fast Company* magazine.

John Sumser founded interbiznet, Inc. in 1993 as a platform for defining and managing the growth of the electronic human capital marketplace. He writes a daily column for the *Electronic Recruiting News*, interbiznet's flagship newsletter.

Richard A. Swanson is a recognized authority on organizational change, human resources development, the analysis and evaluation of work behavior, and financial benefit analysis.He is director of the Human Resource Development Research Center at the University of Minnesota and senior partner of Swanson & Associates.

Bruce Tulgan is widely recognized as a leading expert on generational difference in the workplace, and in particular young workers. He is the founder of RainmakerThinking, Inc. in New Haven, Connecticut, and the author of many books on managing different generations in the workplace.

John Vlastelica is director of Recruiting Programs for Amazon.com. Previously, he was the founding consultant of Recruiting Toolbox, a specialized recruiting service which helps organizations improve their in-house recruiting and retention performance.

Garrett Walker and Elizabeth Hoane lead the IBM Global Learning Solutions and Performance organization. They manage the $1 billion annual investment IBM makes in internal employee education and actively align business and learning strategy for the greatest business return on that investment.

John Wentworth founded The Wentworth Company, Inc., which develops expert system recruiting management software that automates, among other things, progressively richer candidate pools and continuous improvement of selection criteria and workforce performance over time.

Kevin Wheeler is the President and founder of Global Learning Resources, Inc., a leading provider of human capital acquisition strategies and development processes.

Dr. Wendell Williams is Managing Director of ScientificSelection.com, LLC, a company that develops hiring tests that minimize turnover, reduce training expense, and maximize personal productivity.

Preface

The editors and contributors of this book consider the job of staffing—finding and developing the talent needed to deliver the highest-quality products and services—to be one of the most important and critical roles in any organization. We also believe that the systems, tools, and processes to support and measure effectiveness of talent acquisition and development initiatives are value-added investments. Thankfully, we have come a long way since the mid-1980s, when only a few enlightened organizations had started to improve their practices and processes as they recognized the critical nature and strategic value of staffing. At that time, "employment" positions were the lowest-paid in corporate HR, and external recruiters garnered little respect. Johnson & Johnson, Southwest Airlines, and The Vanguard Group were among the first organizations to recognize not only the importance of staffing but also the looming war for talent. These companies set out to fundamentally improve recruiting and best posture themselves for the challenges ahead. Ultimately, McKinsey coined the phrase "war for talent," and wrote the book on it: *The War for Talent* by Ed Michaels, Beth Axelrod, and Helen Handfield-Jones.

Most organizations now recognize that having great people is the only way to create a sustainable, competitive advantage. And yet staffing remains a core strategy for only a few notable organizations that have, not coincidentally, a reputation for acquiring top talent and delivering better return for their stakeholders. Despite the progress we've made in this direction, staffing is not universally regarded as a strategic, valuable HR function. Positions in staffing are often filled internally or as entry-level positions with no training provided; there is often no clearly articulated recruiting or talent strategy; and there's rarely a deliberate process to identify, assess, and develop top talent or to measure the effectiveness of talent acquisition and development programs. Workforce planning is often done as part of a budget planning process rather than an overall talent, inventory, and forecasting effort. The technology that supports excellent recruiting and staffing initiatives is not always seen as a worthwhile investment because the business case has not been made to justify the expense. An emerging trend for some organizations is to separate the talent management function from HR so that it can be more strategic. Other organizations have considered staffing to be noncore, so the entire function is outsourced—often to the lowest bidder—without thoughtful regard for the level of service quality. Some of these approaches may be the right thing to do in certain organizations for strategic reasons, but not for the sole purpose of cost cutting or efficiency, and not because the staffing profession is not up to the task.

There are many bright spots on the horizon. Organizations that have made hiring great people a top business agenda item have brought about many positive initiatives. These new initiatives have transformed the way we tackle staffing—not to mention the way we bring real value to both the marketplace and our external stakeholders. As in any war, the war for talent drove rapid development in methodologies, practices, and technology. As this book is being written, we are in a slump in the economy. Shortsighted thinkers will be tempted to conclude that the war for talent is behind us. But most of us know that it will soon rage again—the simple demographics of available talent in the near and mid future are irrefutable. The economic and demographic challenges we face at the next turn of the economic cycle will make creative, innovative, and world-class staffing techniques and philosophies indispensable.

We have learned a tremendous amount during the last employment boom. And it's essential that we capture the wisdom, insights, and strategies so that we can build on what has gone before, not start all over again. And so, we offer you this book.

To gather the absolute finest content from this era's most powerful staffing thought leaders, we handpicked an exclusive, carefully assembled list of HR practitioners and consultants and invited them to contribute their expertise in the form of sharply focused essays. From that list, only the most powerful, content-rich pieces were chosen to build this offering of the best of the best information on staffing. We are all indebted to the contributors for sharing their expertise, from which we can all learn.

Nick Burkholder
Preston Edwards
Libby Sartain

You may e-mail us at editors@onstaffing.org.

Introduction

John Kitson and Lou Manzi

L et's get one thing straight from the start: Staffing is the most important function in any organization. And while this evolving function itself takes many forms and is performed by many different people, it remains true that to get the job done effectively, you have to have the right person doing the job.

Staffing has changed significantly over the past several years. Staffing used to be about hiring people, short and simple. Today, staffing is so much more. It's about conducting research and sourcing candidates from places that until recently either didn't exist or were never even thought of as potential staffing avenues. It's about assessing skills and placing people in jobs where they will succeed. It's about coaching and providing career paths. It's about implementing programs that retain top performers and show nonperformers the way out the door. It's about determining the human capital requirements of the organization and making certain that the appropriate people are in place. And staffing is about ensuring that the human capital engaged to conduct the organization's business has the talent needed to meet performance expectations.

A lot has changed in the world of work, too. Consider:

Workforce composition and employees' skills, attitudes, and perspectives on relationships with employers have been dramatically revised, as the work world moved from a "career-for-life" mentality to one that embraces change and multiple career paths and opportunities. The Internet and highly sophisticated software implementation in organizations are changing the fundamentals of how employees and their companies work together. In addition to creating more opportunities for communication, the Internet has also increased the speed and quantity of information exchange so employees can access greater amounts of information in very little time and from virtually anywhere in the world. New technology also means that companies are outsourcing more tasks. In fact, analysts predict that outsourcing will continue to grow. Globalization means that organizations throughout the world are expanding their geographical reach so that global business skills and a global way of thinking will be key for success. In today's world of work, there's a lot more competition—competition for customers and competition for employees. We're all aware that the demand for workers continues to outpace supply; regardless of economic conditions, we will experience labor shortages for the next 15 to 20 years. At the same time, workers must constantly learn new skills as a result of the increased demand for better-trained and better-educated employees. The attitudes, motivations, and needs of the emerging workforce are noticeably shifting, which means that the definition of the employer-employee relationship will continue to evolve.

All of these developments present an incredible array of challenges for organizations that manage people and for people who must manage their careers within and across organizations. And that's why the staffing profession has changed so dramatically. How we address the challenges of an evolving and dynamic workforce directly impacts the success of the organizations we serve.

Today's staffing professionals must not only understand and intuit the needs of organizations but be prepared to shift priorities and responsibilities as those needs change. We have to be business and financial analysts, sales and marketing specialists, strategic planners, coaches, and mentors. We have to be creative in sourcing practices and more targeted in staffing selection as we recruit for performance, not just competencies. Our recruiting processes have to operate faster and with greater flexibility. And we have to measure our own results.

We are also called upon to be leaders within our organizations and among other staffing professionals. Because as technology and competition continue to level the playing field, human capital performance will become the only sustainable advantage an organization has over its competitors. Once we've hired the right person for the job, we have to have the compensation and benefits packages, development programs, and retention strategies in place that will keep that individual on board. That means turning our organizations into learning organizations, turning our managers into coaches and mentors, minimizing barriers to entry, and closing most of the exits so our competitors don't benefit from attracting the best people first or luring them away. We have to train for the project, not a lifelong commitment, and create as many career paths as we have people.

Unquestionably, staffing has evolved into a profession all its own. And the impact staffing professionals can have on the success of organizations will continue to grow.

On Staffing: Advice and Perspectives from HR Leaders is a compendium of staffing knowledge, an outstanding collection of essays from some of the most highly regarded people in our profession today. It is insightful, thought provoking, and full of innovative ideas. But more importantly, it offers you the knowledge and expertise that only people who share incredible enthusiasm for the staffing profession can bring to you. In a world that constantly demands more and demands it better and faster, we must continuously assess our skills and performance, drawing from every available resource in order to improve. With *On Staffing: Advice and Perspectives from HR Leaders*, we have a new and remarkable resource. We have no doubt that this book will positively impact the contribution you make as a staffing professional.

The Revolution Continues

Steve Pogorzelski
President, Monster.com

"If you want to do something new, you have to stop doing something old," says Peter Drucker, noted business management author, professor, and lecturer.

The result of any successful revolution is drastic change—a complete overthrow of established thinking, practices, and approaches. With the advent of the Internet, employee recruiting experienced its equivalent of the Boston Tea Party, Bastille Day, and fall of the Berlin Wall all rolled into one. And with this sudden and dramatic paradigm shift already largely behind us, there are still new challenges and tests ahead for online career management and recruiting that will keep the revolutionaries pressing forward.

In the Beginning: Defeating Defeatism

To appreciate just how far career management and recruiting have come, just look back to five or six years ago. Most of us can recall (with a collective groan) the pre-Internet process of finding a job. This process usually ranked right up there with doing your taxes and suffering through a series of bad blind dates.

First, there were the countless Sunday afternoons spent scanning the "Help Wanted" ads for anything that closely resembled a match to your skills, industry, desired location, and the companies you admired. Then, after circling your choices, you found yourself at the local copy center formatting your resume, printing cover letters, and buying envelopes. If you were really on the ball, you had enough postage stamps on hand to mail your cover letter to the nameless, faceless, colorless, and odorless post office box provided in the ad. Often, you could apply in person at a large corporate employment office that possessed all the warmth and ambiance of your local Division of Motor Vehicles. It was, at best, a discouraging and defeating process that left you feeling overwhelmed and underequipped to wage the battle of finding a job.

On the corporate side, human resources (HR) professionals would find themselves under pressure to fill positions, only to be held captive by a snail's-pace process: placing an ad, waiting weeks for applicants to reply, and then spending more weeks combing through stacks of resumes to find the right mix of experience, skills, salary requirements, and career goals. Whole businesses were winning and losing in the marketplace based on their ability to respond quickly and efficiently to changing market needs. HR departments were often hamstrung and struggling to maintain corporate trust in their ability to deliver business value.

Then came the Internet.

Taking Up Arms: Empowerment and Efficiency Found Online

Virtually every human resource practitioner today agrees that the Internet has revolutionized the job/candidate search process. This revolution has put millions of job opportunities just clicks away for the average applicant, while providing employers with robust databases of potential employees, lowering their cost-per-hire and time-to-fill statistics, and improving the quality of candidates who reach their desks.

Take my own company, Monster, as a proof point for the Internet's impact on the human resources industry. Monster grew in just eight short years from being the 454th registered site on the World Wide Web to being the 16th most visited site in the world (*Media Metrix*, May 2002), with close to one million jobs and internships listed at any given time.

As yet another proof point, classified "Help Wanted" advertising dropped 50 percent in 2001. By June 2002, nearly $2 billion worth of "Help Wanted" advertising revenue had completely disappeared. The concept behind the revolutionary rise of the Internet in general, and of career sites in particular, is simple: The consumer is in control. Companies like Monster recognized in the mid-1990s that a power shift was under way. The Internet was giving consumers greater access to information and empowering them with tools to share ideas, likes, and dislikes. The human resources market began to experience its own power shift between the employer and employee as labor shortages began to become more acute, baby boomers got older and approached a period of mass exodus from the workforce, and the economy began to heat up. At the same time, Internet adoption curves accelerated, search engine technology matured, and software agents were invented. Suddenly, employees sensed that they didn't have to stay in the same dead-end jobs and there was a whole world of opportunity open to them.

Coincidentally, and perhaps even ironically, employee empowerment worked to the benefit of employers as well, energizing their workforces, streamlining their hiring processes, and increasing staff productivity.

Winning the Fight on New Fronts

Despite tremendous paradigm shifts in the recruitment process for both candidates and employers, the revolution continues as online recruiting is tested by new challenges and a new set of market dynamics. Given today's weakened economic environment, the public's distrust of corporate institutions, and the government's mandate for greater corporate responsibility, the next phase of the online recruiting revolution will be defined by how it responds to five key market changes:

1. Skills shortages.
2. The death of the resume.
3. The rise of employer branding.
4. The critical role of career networking.
5. The explosion in hourly staff recruiting.

SKILLS SHORTAGES AND THE DEATH OF THE RESUME

The looming skills shortages and the death of the resume are inextricably linked. The new economy and the resulting rise in highly specialized disciplines, coupled with employers' needs for highly structured, standardized, and searchable databases, mean that the traditional resume is as archaic to today's online recruiting environments as punch cards are to IBM. As a result, the industry will need to move to profiles based on the U.S. government's Standard Occupational Classifications, enabling employers to conduct much more detailed and precise candidate searches. With this detailed employee information, the industry will be able to create better online assessment systems, which will further increase the productivity of employers' recruitment processes and enable them to quickly address employee skill deficits. For consumers, profiles will allow individuals to assess their skill set against future aspirations using new online "gap analysis" tools. These tools provide more than assessment; they will link employees to training and learning courseware that will help them fill any gaps while managing their own careers.

RISE OF EMPLOYER BRANDING

Since the recession of the early 1990s, influential human capital experts such as Dr. Peter Cappelli in his book *The New Deal at Work* (Harvard Business School Press, 1999) have traced a major shift in consumer attitude from "being loyal to a company to being committed to a career." Given the unfulfilled promises of the dot-com era and the public's continued mistrust of corporate America, employer branding—that is, a company's brand value to its employees—will become more important than ever. But employer branding cannot be achieved and measured by driving candidate traffic to the corporate web sites. People who go to a corporate web site are already familiar and comfortable with the brand. More important in building the employer brand will be the use of third-party sites, such as Monster, that can reach a large and growing audience of consumers not yet comfortable with a company's brand from the employee's perspective. Advances in rich media content will enable companies to create experiences through these partner sites that utilize streaming video and other technologies to enhance their brands in the eyes of candidates.

CRITICAL ROLE OF CAREER NETWORKING

The structure and behavior of people networks as they exist on the Internet will begin to have profound impacts on the nature of online recruiting. In his book, *Linked: The New Science of Networks* (Perseus Publishing, 2002), Albert-Laszlu Barabasi formulates the role of networks in the job search process. Citing research in Mark Granovetter's paper "The Strength of Weak Ties," Barabasi explains that when it comes to finding a job, our weak social ties are more important than our cherished strong friendships. In fact, managerial workers are more likely to hear about a job opening through weak ties (27.6 percent of the cases) than through strong ties (16.7 percent). Internet recruiting hubs will need to act as network facilitators between these links and add one more layer of functionality to the job search process.

EXPLOSION IN HOURLY STAFF RECRUITING

The near future will also see revolutionary changes in the recruiting of hourly and skilled trade workers. From a consumer perspective, the protypical method of finding a job is demeaning and inefficient. The old method—taking time off from work, moving from location to location while filling out different applications at each stop, and then having to wait to be interviewed and/or tested—creates an unproductive process for both the worker and the employer. Although conventional wisdom dictates that hourly and skilled trade workers are not Web-enabled, a test market survey conducted by Monster in the first half of 2002 found the opposite to be true. Monster launched a Cincinnati job matching service at http://tristatejobmatch.com in an effort to determine how to best recruit hourly and skilled trade workers. Thousands of candidates left their profiles on tristatejobmatch.com. Each was given a choice on how to complete their profile: via the Internet, on paper using the traditional application to be subsequently uploaded to the Internet, or via a phone-based IVR system. Fully 90 percent of the workers who wanted to leave their profiles did so using the Internet. Given that hourly and skilled trade workers outnumber white-collar professionals (it is estimated that more than 70 percent of the U.S. labor market is comprised of nonexempt workers), the opportunity to revolutionize this aspect of recruiting may have a greater impact than any other online recruiting efforts to date.

Changing demographics, acute skills shortages, and shifting attitudes toward large employers will certainly keep the online recruiting revolution rolling on for the next several years. This new era may contain changes that are greater than anything we've seen thus far. The Internet's capacity to deliver increasingly greater levels of innovation and efficiency for both the employer and the consumer will be limited only by the boundaries of connectivity, the employer's tolerance for experimentation, and our own industry's willingness to "do something new" and "stop doing something old."

Managing Your Workforce

Allan Schweyer

Senior Researcher, HR.com

Deb McGrath

CEO, HR.com

Managing Your Workforce

In most organizations, human capital can be broken down into four segments, with the needs of each currently addressed by different technology platforms. Consider:

Current staff	Human resources information systems (HRIS).
Contingency staff	Vendor management solutions systems.
Ex-staff/alumni	Alumni systems or HRIS.
Applicants to your firm	Applicant tracking systems or talent management systems.

To improve the processes associated with hiring permanent staff, large employers have for years been using applicant tracking systems or talent management systems (TMS). When it comes to hiring and managing temporary and contract workers, the less mature vendor management solutions (VMS) industry has recently sprung up. HR.com research shows that managing your contingent workforce is a critical issue for large organizations.

The Case for Total Workforce Management Solutions

Why is managing your contingent workforce critical? There are about 12 million contingent workers in North America, representing a roughly $75 billion industry. Employers' use of contingent labor and workers' willingness to be free agents are both on the rise. As we all know, the contingent labor force is usually the first to boom when an economy is coming out of a recession.

With the streamlining and centralizing of functions like billing, tracking, and performance monitoring for temporary workers, vendor management solutions systems can automate these processes and show significant savings. The same is true for organizations that contract with managed service providers (MSPs). In these cases, a VMS will aid in the selection, cost management, and administrative functions in much the same manner. Staffing firms have developed an interest in VMS over the past couple of years. As increasing numbers of organizations look to contingent labor as an area to increase efficiencies and lower costs, progressive suppliers have been quick to offer their customers managed vendor solutions.

Kelly Services, Inc. for example, manages centralized contractor acquisition programs and centralized vendor management solutions for its clients. Sue Marks, vice president of Kelly HR Solutions Group, a business unit of Kelly Services, Inc., says, "All of our new programs are powered by Web-based technology, and our existing clients are migrating to them. We find that once clients get used to the changes in process—they order online instead of over the phone—they are very happy with the reduction in administrative activities, the real-time reporting, the 24/7 access, and the increased speed. Contract labor is usually an organization's largest indirect spend, yet it remains one of the most loosely managed. A strong program, coupled with the new vendor management solutions technology, makes significant savings and production improvements possible. Finally, at the end of the day, these Web-enabled programs help companies acquire the best talent at the best price."

Advantages of Combining Vendor Management Solutions with Talent Management Systems

Organizations are saving significant time and money with both VMS and TMS systems, but much greater efficiencies are possible by combining the two. Chris Colbert, human resources technology manager at Siemens, agrees. "An integrated talent acquisition system would provide greater ROI [return on investment] by reducing the number of point solutions needed to build a complete workforce," he says. "Reporting and workforce planning would also be enhanced by having tools for vendor management and permanent recruiting in one system."

Some TMS providers claim to offer vendor management modules. What these modules typically do is allow hiring managers and recruiters to post their requisitions to preferred staffing vendors and independent recruiters. Some give vendors a secure window to the TMS, so they can submit candidates for consideration, communicate, and generally collaborate with internal staff to fill positions. This is where they tend to stop, however.

True vendor management solutions offer contingency workforce management tools, and this is where the majority of ROI is realized. Integrated recruiting (including resume tracking, prescreening, and matching) of the temporary workforce—coupled with time and expense tracking, vendor and candidate quality monitoring, approvals, consolidated billing and attendance—round out what's necessary. "Total workforce acquisition" solutions would allow an organization to use one system to post a requisition for permanent, contract, or temporary workers. This would include the flexibility to hire a combination of permanent and temporary workers under one requisition.

How an Integrated Approach Would Work

Suppose a company is looking for five technical writers; two will be full-time and the other three will be hired on one-year contracts. The hiring manager needs to be able to configure work flows on the fly so that the full-time hires go through their necessary approvals and stages while the temporary hires follow a different work flow.

In an integrated, seamless approach, the hiring manager would select where the requisition is to be distributed for the full-time hires (i.e., intranet, corporate career site, job boards, recruiters, etc.) and the organization's approved staffing agency vendors for the temporary hires. The hiring manager should also be able to use the system to hire someone into the job temporarily and quickly (through a staffing agency) while the lengthier process of filling the position permanently is launched at the same time.

The applicants and the candidates submitted by staffing firms would come back to the hiring manager appropriately flagged, prescreened, and ranked. The system would facilitate notes and communications between the hiring manager and vendors where necessary. It might also promote price/service competition between vendors, and, at the very least, inform hiring managers of the benchmark prices for temporary, hourly, and contract workers in their areas for the position in question. The system would track both permanent and temporary candidates through the process—including interview scheduling, tracking correspondence, decisions, and so on. Permanent and temporary candidates would route to different parts of the integrated systems for payroll, time sheets, attendance, performance pay, and so forth.

The VMS portion of the integrated tool would consolidate invoicing to the vendors and handle automated payments to contractors and consultants. For reporting, it would be possible to benchmark against other similar organizations to compare vendor rates, contingent worker salaries, and process efficiencies. As with TMS, the VMS portion of the system should track related budgets and use alerts to warn procurement or HR managers when, for instance, contracts are expiring or diversity targets are not being met.

ROI calculators should be capable of determining time and cost savings on a continuous basis. The system should contain an element of vendor and worker evaluation. All permanent and contingent worker data would merge at the back end for complete workforce statistics, analytics, ad hoc reporting, affirmative action planning, workforce planning, and cost/ROI information.

This is the second major benefit of integrated TMS and VMS—a much more holistic and complete view of the entire workforce. A "total workforce management" solution would connect equal employment opportunity (EEO)/diversity systems and workforce planning components with VMS and TMS (including internal staff and alumni) seamlessly. This, along with performance and learning management, might give organizations the first automated 360° view of their entire workforces. It might allow them to:

- Monitor performance against diversity targets, time-to-fill and cost-to-hire goals, and retention efforts.
- Track skills and competencies.
- Determine which positions are better to staff full-time versus with temporary staff.
- Assess the performance and quality of staffing agency vendors as well as the candidates they refer.
- Determine training and development needs.
- And, in effect, properly align corporate objectives to available human capital once and for all.

Who in the Organization Owns Total Workforce Management?

Though at least two different parts of the organization need to be involved in administering and owning the software, their different interests might actually aid in the process. The procurement/purchasing function cares about contracts, prices, and legalities; the HR function, on the other hand, cares more about people, quality of hire, and best fit. Neither is usually interested in doing the other's job. Therefore, as Jim Grundner, vice president at Peopleclick, states, "Both functions' strategic goals can be achieved while eliminating the conflicts caused by operating two disparate systems."

It is becoming clear that workforce management decisions should be reshaped to maximize the total workforce. Whether you are in the market for a TMS or a VMS, it would be prudent to ensure platform integration down the road. A few human capital solutions providers are currently making efforts to combine tools that help organizations recruit and administer their permanent and contingent workforces. The first generation of fully integrated TMS/VMS tools are in the works. Further integration with workforce and affirmative action planning tools and then performance and learning management must follow.

Generational Shift

Bruce Tulgan

RainmakerThinking, Inc.

R ight now, there are four generations working side by side, each with differing perspectives, needs, and expectations. As the aging workforce moves closer to retirement, the younger generations are quickly becoming the majority of the prime-age workforce. This generational shift is going to reshape the numbers, values, and norms of the workforce in ways that every business leader focused on staffing strategy must consider.

The four generations now working through the most profound changes in the economy since the industrial revolution are called the silent generation, the baby boomers, Generation X, and Generation Y. This civilian, noninstitutional workforce breaks down into these categories:

GenYers (born 1978–1986)	14%
GenXers (born 1965–1977)	30%
Baby Boomers (born 1946–1964)	45%
Silents (born before 1946)	11%

Since 1993, we at RainmakerThinking, Inc. have been conducting in-depth interviews to study the attitudes of the different generations and the impact of generational differences on workplace issues. While it is dangerous to make vast generalizations about tens of millions of people, it is very valuable to look at the overall trends in generational attitudes. Each generation comes from a different perspective, is going through different life and career stages, and has different needs and expectations. Let's look at a brief snapshot of each of the generations in the workplace right now.

Silent Generation Perspective

Born before 1946; as of 2002, roughly 11 percent of the workforce. Years of experience have taught "silents" to rely on tried, true, and tested ways of doing things, and many would still agree, "If it's not broken, don't fix it." Silents still favor established systems, policies, and procedures. They like the old rules. After years of working under command-and-control management, silents are experiencing a radical change in the new workplace. Silents respond best to leaders and managers who respectfully assert their authority and demonstrate a clear track record of success. The message silents want to hear from employers: Welcome to the family. Give us your best every day, and we'll do our best to take care of you.

Baby Boomer Perspective

Born 1946–1964; as of 2002, roughly 45 percent of the workforce. Boomers generally feel they have paid their dues and climbed the ladder under the old rules and now find themselves operating amid constant downsizing, restructuring, and reengineering. Boomers still pride themselves on their ability to survive sink-or-swim management, but fewer today are willing to keep up the frenetic pace. Boomer women led the charge for workplace flexibility, and now many boomers have caught on to the free-agent mind-set. Boomers respond best to leaders and managers who listen attentively to their input and include them in decision making, while challenging them to keep growing. The message boomers want to hear from employers: Welcome to the inner circle. We want to put your skill, experience, and wisdom to work for our customers and clients.

Generation X Perspective

Born 1965–1977; as of 2002, roughly 30 percent of the workforce. When Generation Xers hit the workforce in the late 1980s, they were typecast as disloyal job-hoppers who didn't want to pay their dues and wanted everything their own way. But by the mid to late 1990s, it was clear that Xers formed the vanguard of the free-agent workforce. Now Xers are growing up and moving into positions of supervisory responsibility and leadership, but they are not settling down. Xers remain cautious and they know their security rests in staying on the cutting edge. Always in a hurry, Xers will often sidestep rules as they push for results. They're willing to take risks to keep learning and innovating. Xers respond best to leaders and managers who spend time coaching, clarifying the day-to-day bargain at work, and giving credit for results achieved. The message Xers want to hear from employers: Here's the deal—you get lots of work done very well every day, and we'll pay you more and give you more control over your schedule.

Generation Y Perspective

Born after 1978; as of 2002, roughly 14 percent of the workforce. This is the first wave of the "echo-boom" or the "millennial" generation. Coming of age during the most expansive economy in the past 30 years, GenYers are the children of baby boomers and the optimistic, upbeat younger siblings of GenXers. The first cohort of truly global citizens, they are socially conscious and volunteer minded. GenYers have been told by parents, teachers, counselors, and churches that they can do anything—and they believe it. They are poised to be the most capable and the most demanding generation in history. GenYers respond best to leaders and managers who respect them as individuals and keep them engaged with speed, customization and interactivity. The message GenYers want to hear from employers: Come here and be a superstar on our winning team. You work hard to make a difference for our customers and clients, and we'll treat you like a professional.

Generational Shift

Each of these generations is a significant force in today's workplace, and those of every generation play critical roles in most organizations. It is imperative, however, to look ahead to the major impact that will be caused by the generational shift that is under way. Every single year—for the foreseeable future—the generational shift will reshape the numbers, values, and norms of the workforce.

THE NUMBERS

The demographics of our workforce are undergoing a dramatic change of historic proportions. At one end of the spectrum, the population is aging, so the workforce is aging. As we have seen, already 11 percent of the active workforce are over the age of 56. As the baby boomers age, that percentage will grow steadily. Every day, 10,000 baby boomers turn 55. Most organizations are poised now for the steady departure of huge numbers of their most experienced people. The real problem is that there are simply not enough people in the younger generations to fill the positions that are being vacated. On the heels of the aging baby boomers, the much less populous Generation X will provide a shrinking pool of prime workers. And even with the modest increase in population among Generation Y, the numbers are simply not enough to fill the void that will be left by retiring baby boomers. Initially, the most significant impact will be a serious shortage of skilled prime-age workers. Employers and companies had better prepare for the real talent wars. The late 1990s were just a dress rehearsal.

THE VALUES

The new free-agent attitude—the one we've seen spreading across the workforce among people of all ages—will become status quo as Generation X and Generation Y begin to dominate the prime-age workforce. Already, very few employees of any age trust employers to provide them with any real job security. The idea of a traditional long-term career in one company will soon be entirely obsolete. Employees will come to accept that they must take responsibility for their own success and fend for themselves as best they can. That means that the most successful people will be focused on learning marketable skills, building relationships with decision makers who can help them, and selling their way into career opportunities. The problem, however, is that there will be a growing tension between the goals of employers and the needs of employees. Most individuals will feel an increasing amount of pressure to work longer, harder, smarter, faster, and better. In response, workers will become much more assertive about getting their workplace needs met—primarily flexibility—one day at a time.

THE NORMS

Employment relationships will be much less hierarchical and much less formal. Relationships between employers and employees will become much more short-term and transactional. Individual careers will be much more fluid and self-directed. Most communication will be just-in-time oriented, tied to the growing availability of information through easy-to-use technology. The pace of everything will continue to accelerate; long-term thinking and planning will be much less relevant. Managers will have to discard traditional authority, rules, and red tape and become highly engaged in one-on-one negotiation and coaching with employees in order to drive productivity, quality, and innovation.

Best Practices and Strategies

The challenge posed to leaders and managers will be tremendous. Most organizations will soon be facing a serious shortage of skilled prime-age workers. Because this shortage is driven by this great demographic shift, it will last for the foreseeable future. Due to the change in world affairs, immigration will not be a viable solution to the staffing shortages to come. Already in crisis are employers in health care, government, education, transportation, nonprofits, and manufacturing. You will have to gear your organization to succeed with much leaner core staff levels. How will you do that? Following are some of the best practices we've seen in organizations that have responded to this challenge.

Create an organization structure that is lean, with lots of flexible staffing options. As your core group of traditional employees shrinks, you'll have to grow your fluid talent pool: Create a large reserve army, a proprietary talent database of former employees, temps, independent contractors, outside firms, part-timers, some-timers, flex-timers, telecommuters, and so on. Develop solid working relationships with a wide range of vendors who can be counted on for outsourcing.

Because your prime-age workforce will shrink, your ability to leverage an older workforce will be key to maintaining your core staff as well as building a growing flexible staff. How? First, engage older workers in career planning dialogues early and often, so they are thinking about the next stage of their working lives instead of the first stage of retirement. Second, support semi-retirement whenever feasible and appropriate by accommodating flexible schedules, locations, and conditions. Build giant reserve armies of older former employees and let them be the ones to finally teach you to support flexible work arrangements. Third, create programs to capture and transfer as much knowledge, skill, and wisdom as you possibly can from one generation to the next.

You will have to prepare GenXers (and also younger boomers) for positions of supervisory responsibility and leadership. The infamous free-agent rule breakers are ascending to their prime working years, but GenXers will always be in short supply and full of attitude. Xers want status, authority, and rewards. They should be ascending to positions of supervisory responsibility and leadership. But many are resisting traditional management positions. Create new paths to leadership and develop this next generation to take on new kinds of leadership roles. How? First, teach transferable skills— such as communication, negotiation, conflict resolution, strategic planning, critical thinking, and problem solving—to those Xers with high potential. Second, create ad hoc leadership opportunities for high potentials, such as project leader roles. Third, encourage high potentials to create their own paths to leadership.

Tap into the high-maintenance, high-performance talent of Generation Y and beyond for important roles. Relying on employees to do more at younger ages will be a critical piece of the staffing puzzle. Human resources specialists and hiring managers will have to recruit new employees at younger ages, get them up to speed faster, and trust them with critical tasks and responsibilities. We'll have no choice.

You're going to have to get more work and better work out of fewer people, consistently. Having hired like crazy in the frenzied seller's market of the late 1990s, business leaders found themselves downsizing even faster throughout 2001 and 2002. They are not going to make the same mistake again of hiring every warm body in sight. Rather, the pressure will be on to hire the best person for every role at every level—and then manage every person aggressively to reach higher levels of productivity. That means there will be great pressure to make dramatic improvements to your systems for attraction and selection.

Commit to fast-paced, intense, mission-driven training on day one and every day thereafter. Gear the training of individual contributors for the specific tasks, responsibilities, and projects they are going to be working on in the very near term. Put new contributors through your own boot camp style of orientation. Get them up to speed very quickly so they can start adding value right away. Then create just-in-time training opportunities that can support ongoing, as-needed learning.

Move toward real performance-based pay, in place of long-term fixed salaries. Short-term pay-for-performance agreements require all the elements of a well-negotiated purchasing contract: Managers and employees will have to agree on measurable individual performance benchmarks. Every step of the way, clear deliverables should be defined for every contributor, with concrete rewards tied directly to those deliverables. Managers and employees will have to regularly establish clear expectations about the relationship between specific individual behaviors and specific rewards. Managers will have to monitor regularly and closely the performance of every individual, keeping good, contemporaneous records. The key to making real pay-for-performance work is ongoing communication about the process between managers and individual contributors.

Because managing people will be so high-maintenance, you'll have to turn supervisory managers into hands-on coaches. That means leaders will have to commit to requiring highly skilled and effective behavior on the part of managers. You'll have to consider interpersonal communication skills as a key criterion in promoting people—which means you'll need to provide much more training in those skills. You'll have to audit those in supervisory positions and be honest about their communication skills. And you'll have to hold managers accountable for how they manage people.

Finally, be prepared to create custom work conditions for every person—in exchange for increased performance. That means figuring out ways to give people more of what they need in the workplace. Based on our research, what most people say they need is more flexibility when it comes to when they work (schedule); where they work (location); what they do (tasks and responsibilities); who they work with; and what they are (or are not) learning on the job. You won't be able to give everybody everything they want. But the most flexible employers will be the most successful at recruiting, motivating, and retaining the best people.

CHAPTER

4

Positioning Success from the Start: Strategic Employee Assessment and Assimilation Practices

Robert Morgan

President, Spherion Human Capital Consulting

If Alan Greenspan's career path had not led to a four-term tenure as chairman of the Federal Reserve Board, where might it have taken him? Maybe his music studies at Juilliard would have landed him in the New York Philharmonic or a New Orleans jazz band. What if Sir Isaac Newton had chosen to manage the estate he inherited—farming rather than solving great scientific riddles through mathematics and physics?

In every life, hundreds of factors influence where we go and how we get there. In cultivating a talented, high-performance workforce, businesses need to consider the factors that influence how employees are introduced into the human capital life cycle of an organization. Are skills and talents well matched to jobs? Are employees given tools to succeed from the start? Are physicists asked to farm? Are economists playing the clarinet? How good is the organization at putting the right talent in the right place?

These are vital questions to ask in a competitive business environment where workforce productivity is essential to success. In its 1998 study—*The War for Talent*—McKinsey and Company estimated that high performers generate 40 percent to 67 percent greater productivity than low performers. Such dramatic differences highlight the importance of cultivating a high-performance workforce. The process of doing so begins with assessment and assimilation—the two elements of the human capital life cycle that largely determine job success.

Without reliable assessments, organizations risk matching talented people to the wrong jobs—missing opportunities to nurture and develop high-potential performers. Without thorough assimilation, organizations do not equip employees for success. To develop talent, leadership, and innovation within the workforce, a business must assess employees to ensure the best match to both the job and the company. Equally critical is the process of assimilating employees to ensure successful integration into the workplace, the company culture, and specific roles and responsibilities.

Good assessment practices promote smooth assimilations. In new hire situations, the right-match employee who receives a comprehensive introduction to the organization, and his or her role in it, is better equipped to succeed. As an employee succeeds in one role and completes the training and development needed to move on, the assessment and assimilation dynamic repeats. Such recurrence throughout an employee's career is the fine-tuning of talent cultivation that provides a foundation for growth and helps organizations develop future leaders and innovators from the very beginning of the human capital life cycle.

The Two Roles of Assessment in Talent Acquisition

Assessment should occur in several places within the human capital life cycle. First, it is a key component of recruitment. Assessments are used to prescreen job applicants to ensure they have the right skills and experience to enter into interviewing and hiring consideration phases. HR professionals use prescreening assessments to manage the chaos that can ensue when hundreds of resumes and applications are submitted for one job. They narrow the applicant pool to the top candidates whose skills and experience most closely match the requirements for the position.

Next, assessment resides in the selection phase, where its purpose is to go beyond an evaluation of basic skill requirements to behaviorally and culturally match candidates and employees to the right job. People have the potential to succeed in multiple roles. After all, Michael Jordan is a stellar athlete who excelled at baseball, basketball, and football in his youth. But it was on the basketball court where he became the best in the world. By analyzing a candidate's fit with the specific job environment and requirements, assessment can help match employees to roles that nurture their talents and provide them with the best opportunities to become star performers.

Assess Beyond Skills and Experience

The Saratoga Institute's annual human capital benchmarking survey of American companies reveals that an average of 18.7 percent of all exempt employees quit within the first year of joining a new organization. For nonexempt employees, the rate jumps to 36.8 percent. HR professionals face a daunting reality: They can expect approximately one-third of their new hires to walk out the door before their first year is out.

High numbers of early departures are a signal that organizations need to do a better job of assessing and matching new talent to the right jobs. Assessment can help reduce high new-hire turnover by matching employees to jobs that are so well suited to their temperament and abilities that they will be reluctant to leave. To do this, assessment processes must analyze more than a candidate's skills and experience. Exploring how individual work habits, career goals, and preferred management styles align with an open position is another important role that assessment plays in ensuring employees can perform well, find job satisfaction, and succeed within the organization. To be placed in the right role, a person must be assessed based on what is known about the job environment, the existing management structure, and future career opportunities.

Can the candidate thrive in this working environment?

Is there a growth path available to the candidate?

Will the management structure and culture foster the candidate's talents or create roadblocks?

While it may seem that matching the right skills and experience is the greatest hiring hurdle, the true test is finding a candidate who can quickly adjust to the existing workplace, make a significant contribution, and grow to meet changing business demands. Growth, a primary focus in assessing individual job fit, must be assessed on two levels:

1. Can this person grow within the job role?
2. Can he or she grow within the company?

If not, turnover will continue to decimate the talent development program; management bench strength will be depleted; and human capital costs will soar. Leadership roles cannot be filled from within without a firm commitment to finding and placing people who have the potential to grow with the organization.

Business Benefits of Assessment

In addition to giving employees the right starting point, good assessment practices reduce HR costs and improve bottom-line business numbers. According to Spherion surveys, employee prescreening assessment can dramatically reduce hiring time by as much as 11 days in some organizations. It also has been shown to reduce turnover by 25 percent to 45 percent, helping organizations shrink hiring costs as they retain talent and intellectual capital within the company. The Saratoga Institute reports that cost per hire for a nonexempt employee averages nearly $4,000. For an exempt employee, it averages $6,400. From the very start, a business is heavily invested in each and every employee hired, spending thousands to get new talent in the door. Without rigorous assessment processes to ensure the best job matches, there is a sizable risk attached to that investment. To demonstrate how good assessment practices can lower turnover and hiring expenses, Spherion conducted a study with a large national retailer. More than 200 eligible candidates underwent prehire assessment, and then all were hired, regardless of job match status.

Candidates assessed as best match for the job showed a turnover rate of less than 18 percent.

Candidates assessed as marginal match had a turnover rate of 57 percent.

Candidates assessed as least match turned over at a rate of 69 percent.

A tremendous eye-opener, this short-term experiment proved how hiring only best-match employees can save employers thousands of dollars by reducing turnover and decreasing hiring expenses.

Case Study: Prehire Assessment Success

Organization: One of the nation's largest gas suppliers and convenience store chains.

Challenge: High cashier turnover in the convenience stores was costing the company hundreds of thousands of dollars annually. The position was extremely difficult to fill, and most new hires did not perform up to company standards. Those who did perform well did not stay long.

Solution: A customized assessment was designed to screen applicants for cashier positions nationwide. Not only did the assessment screen for job skill, competency, and experience, it also was designed to analyze employee match with specific job realities—long hours working alone, dramatic fluctuations in stress and activity levels, and constant customer service responsibilities.

Results: By introducing assessments to the recruitment process, the company reduced its cashier turnover by nearly 11 percent and increased tenure 33 percent within one year.

Creating a Development Path

Employee assessments are also the first step in employee development, another critical phase in the human capital life cycle for nurturing high performers. Through the assessment process, employee strengths and weaknesses are identified and evaluated, building an early framework for each individual's development program. Assessment results give HR professionals and business managers the critical knowledge they need to help employees assimilate into the organization, while outlining current or future training needs. For example, consider how an organization that needs to hire help desk representatives might prepare and develop employees for their new roles. For less experienced candidates whose assessments reveal high potential for success, training could be customized to emphasize communication techniques for stressful situations, how to document interactions, and when to bring in a manager. For those with lots of successful call center experience but less technical knowledge, training geared to the new technology tools they will use daily may be just what is needed to speed proficiency in their new roles and help them more quickly meet productivity goals.

Post-hire assessments evaluate suitability and readiness for advancement into roles of increasing responsibility. Moreover, they can aid managers as they make judgments about an employee's learning agility and potential to serve the organization in different ways. And post-hire assessments can also be used to identify potential leaders and management candidates.

Assessing throughout the Human Capital Life Cycle

By clearly defining the competencies and performance standards required by an employee who aspires to a leadership role, organizations can more quickly identify and assess candidates for management development. True, many organizations concentrate their leadership assessments on upper management and executive levels. But there is significant value in providing employees and managers at all levels with a clear set of standards to judge leadership potential. Not doing so gives rise to uneven leadership quality. Individuals are often promoted into management for various reasons rather than for meeting specific performance goals and demonstrating traits identified as essential for leadership success within the organization. In addition, promotion into management roles is left to the discretion of leaders within the organization who themselves were not required to meet defined leadership prerequisites.

When employees do not understand the parameters for advancement and the behaviors and actions that will lead to success in the organization, they become frustrated and seek career advancement elsewhere. As voluntary separations increase, organizations are forced to recruit appropriate talent outside of the company, further alienating internal talent.

In a competitive employment market, a business cannot afford high turnover at any level. As the demographic profile of the American workforce undergoes substantial changes, the employment market can only get tighter. The prime source of talent feeding the American workforce has traditionally been people aged 25 to 54. From 1980 to 2000, the number of people in this age group grew by 35 million. According to a Harvard University study, this age group is projected to grow by only 3 million from 2000 to 2020. This tremendous shortage of incoming talent means businesses must nurture high performers, leaders, and innovators from the internal talent pool. They must create processes for identifying, assessing, developing, and pulling go-getters up into the organization so that the business can endure future talent struggles, supported by a talented management team and a committed workforce.

Case Study: Internal Assessment Success

Organization: Large U.S. retailer.

Workforce: 20,000+ employees.

Size: 600 locations.

Challenge: The company had a comprehensive program for assessing and developing assistant managers for management positions. But there was no standardized process for assessing and developing individual contributors looking to move into assistant management roles—the very positions that fed the management identification and training program. Due to the lack of a consistent assessment and development process, managers provided employees with hundreds of answers to the question "How do I become an assistant manager?"

Solution: Using the required competencies for store managers as a foundation, the company defined and executed a process to qualify hourly associates for managerial roles across the entire organization. The process utilized development activities that placed individual contributors in the shoes of a manager and allowed the company to:

- Identify, screen, track, and develop management candidates and those with leadership potential.
- Create a national pool of skilled, endorsed employees.
- Provide a consistent and long-term career development path.
- Provide employees with a realistic portrayal of managerial roles and responsibilities.

Results: Availability of internal leadership and management resources increased in all locations (in some markets the percentage of management positions filled by internal employees went up 30 percent).

External recruiting costs were significantly reduced.

Time to fill management roles was decreased.

The process served as an effective recruiting tool by giving candidates perspective on the company's formal career growth and development strategy.

The Role of Employee Assimilation

Assimilation is the second key element in the human capital life cycle that is critical to job success. Assimilation is the process of successfully integrating new employees into the organization. Assimilation helps employees understand their roles, adapt to the working environment, and learn how to be productive and successful. When implemented well, assimilation consists of formal orientation and training as well as informal information sharing and peer interactions. Together, these assimilation practices provide new employees with cultural insights (the ins and outs, dos and don'ts), communication pathways, and operational protocols that reduce the stress and confusion typical of a new working environment.

Unfortunately, the assimilation process in many organizations today is akin to dropping someone on a treadmill going 100 miles per hour. A new employee must rapidly absorb overwhelming quantities of information and perform new job tasks with neither a cultural context nor a comfort zone in which to operate. In many organizations, assimilation is taken for granted, with individual departments and managers overseeing the process without any standardized practices. To effectively assimilate employees takes deliberate intervention on the part of the hiring organization, whether the employee is new to the company or just new to the role. A streamlined and successful assimilation process designed to most efficiently integrate new employees consists of:

- An orientation that clearly defines the operating culture, the business environment, and the organizational policies.
- A clear explanation of the path to success so each employee understands expectations and how to grow within the organization.
- Executive-level sponsorship in which higher-level managers demonstrate visibility and interest in new employee participation, productivity, and success.
- Peer-level coaching to help ease employees into their new roles and guide them as they begin working with new colleagues.

- Role clarification (manager, individual contributor, etc.) so that employees understand how they fit within the greater organization.
- Multiple checkups by managers and peers to ensure that employees are getting a good start.
- Job-specific training in order to ensure the job is done correctly and skill gaps are quickly managed.
- Timely and constructive performance feedback and coaching to help employees continuously improve their performance and increase productivity.

Successful Assessments, Successful Assimilations

When employees have been well assessed for the job, assimilation is simple. The assessment process supports and informs the assimilation design, revealing if and where knowledge or skill gaps exist. Job match assessments also will identify what workplace issues may need to be addressed in the assimilation process.

Is this a new management style for the new employee?

Is this more or less collaboration than the worker is accustomed to?

An informed assimilation process that builds on the knowledge gathered in the assessment allows employees to more quickly become contributing and valued members of the work environment.

Establishing a Comfort Zone

The assimilation process helps employees become more productive more rapidly—primarily because it helps new employees establish a comfort zone within the work environment. Interaction with peers and management, as well as detailed information on processes and operations, helps workers adjust to their roles and mitigates the stress of being the new employee on the block. The more quickly employees are comfortable in their work environments and able to function, the more likely they are to find contentment in their jobs. Job satisfaction, another workforce building block, increases retention and gives businesses an opportunity to build employee loyalty and develop managers, leaders, and innovators from within their own talent pools.

Trends to Consider

In every organization, the caliber and the satisfaction of internal talent grow in importance as the workforce shrinks and the demand for skilled employees increases. The rapidly changing demographics of the American workforce promise to have a profound impact on many organizations. Year 2000 U.S. Census data indicates that a large portion of the workforce is aging quickly. By the end of 2002, nearly 6.5 million baby boomers turned 55 and became poised for early retirement. Combine this with fewer people entering the workforce—over the next 15 years there will be a 15 percent decline in the 35-to-44-year-old population—and the recruiting challenges of the future look severe.

Skilled workers are in short supply as well. According to the U.S. Bureau of Labor Statistics, 75 percent of the jobs of the future will be knowledge-based jobs, yet 21 percent of the current adult population has only basic literacy skills. A recent study by the John J. Heldrich Center for Workforce Development at Rutgers University revealed that 4 out of 10 employers surveyed who are unable to fill specific positions cite the lack of workers with high-level skill requirements as the primary barrier to filling jobs. Yet, today's organizations depend more than ever on a well-trained workforce in order to compete effectively.

Add to talent shortages the rising costs to hire—as well as the expenses related to replacing outgoing employees—and the importance of retaining the right employees is starkly evident. The Saratoga Institute 2001 human capital benchmarking report cited a 40 percent increase in cost per hire since 1997. The report also showed that the cost to replace a nonexempt employee averages six months of the worker's pay. For exempt employees, the cost to replace is anywhere from six months to one and a half years in pay. Steep hiring and replacement expenditures are not the only high costs employers face. When critical job functions are not filled, business productivity and profitability suffer as well.

These workforce realities underscore the importance of hiring and retaining the right employees. Businesses today need to assess, assimilate, and retain employees who can grow into greater roles and contribute to future business innovation and success. The talent pools that businesses cultivate within their own walls are quickly becoming the most important, cost-effective, and skilled source for recruiting future management and organizational leadership. By better assessing and assimilating employees as they move through the human capital life cycle, organizations with higher satisfaction and retention rates are cushioning themselves from impending talent struggles. As they grow, they are able to leverage the talent and leadership strength within their highly satisfied and committed internal talent pools.

The Framework of Talent Development

When assessment and assimilation processes are properly integrated within the human capital life cycle, they provide the framework for successfully developing the right employees at the right time. Managers and future leaders are put in roles that will enhance their skills and offer new challenges. Innovators are placed with teams that foster creativity. The organization is able to grow organically, nourishing its management and development needs with well-trained, well-experienced, and well-placed insiders.

The most important result of optimizing both assessment and assimilation is that employees are positioned to achieve from the start, whether it is in a new job or a new role. Assessment delivers employees who can succeed, while assimilation equips them with the organizational tools they need to succeed. Together assessment and assimilation are a powerful force within the human capital life cycle, cultivating a highly skilled workforce to fuel business innovation, performance, and profitability.

The Critical Role of Recruiting—Strategic Hiring

Dr. Wendell Williams

Managing Director, ScientificSelection.com

Recruiting is one of the most complicated, misunderstood, and mismanaged of all organizational activities. If line managers or technical professionals knew as little about their technologies as recruiters do, they would have very short careers. Indeed, recruiting skills are to employee performance what purchasing standards are to quality. Using a Total Quality Management term, out-of-control hiring practices always produce marginal overall performance.

State and Federal Law

In the United States, both state and federal laws address the need for organizations to present fair and equal employment opportunities to applicants regardless of race, religious belief, gender, disability, or age. As of this writing, the laws do not force employers to hire unqualified people. The laws merely want employers to: (1) clearly establish business need and job relevance; (2) use only validated tools backed by formal studies showing scores predict performance; and (3) continually search for new tools that have the least adverse impact on protected groups. These standards were clearly outlined more than 22 years ago in the Department of Labor's Uniform Guidelines on Employee Selection Procedures.

Mutual Goals

State and federal laws are not intended to hamstring organizations; they are intended to stand for best practices. After all, the goals of defining business needs, proving job requirements, using tools that accurately predict performance, and searching for ways to increase applicant pools are in perfect alignment with organizational objectives as well. When position objectives are clearly defined in measurable terms, recruiters and hiring professionals have clear targets against which to assess applicants. Using only hiring tools that are proven to predict performance produces uniformly qualified applicants.

Hidden Costs of Recruiting

Recruiting costs are much greater than the combined expense of placing ads, paying referral fees, and absorbing turnover. Recruiting costs are buried deep inside the organization where people are expected to be productive. Researchers compute these individual performance differences in standard deviations. When performance is plotted along a bell curve, the standard deviation is estimated based of the number of people who are clustered around the average. One standard deviation is the number of people who produce 66 percent of the overall product.

Experts estimate that differences in productivity (i.e., standard deviations) are worth about 19 percent of the average salary for semiskilled workers, about 32 percent for skilled workers, and 48 percent for managers and professionals. Translated into dollars, this means that differences in personal productivity for managers or professionals who are paid $60,000 amount to about $28,800 per year per person. It does not take a rocket scientist to compute how fast these numbers can add up.

Build a Performance Taxonomy

A truly professional recruiter will use a performance taxonomy that considers the whole job and the whole person. Again drawing from the research, performance in all jobs tends to fall into four different areas. These are:

1. Cognitive ability (the ability to think, problem solve, learn, use technical knowledge, etc.).
2. Planning ability (the ability to plan, organize, sequence, etc.).
3. Interpersonal ability (the ability to get things done through others, coach, sell, resolve problems, etc.).
4. Attitudes, interests, and motivations (likes and dislikes associated with the job).

Every job has certain needs that fall into each area. If a recruiter skips any area, an applicant's skills in that area will be left to chance. For example, technical managers and technical recruiters tend to place heavy emphasis on technical skills (i.e., a cognitive ability) but readily admit that technical people tend to "crash and burn" more often based on poor interpersonal skills—an area the technical recruiters seldom measure. Or consider customer service representatives who work in call centers. Call center recruiters tend to skip measuring motivational fit, but customer service representatives tend to turn over because they do not like the nature of their work.

Exact Measurement

Using a "whole job" performance taxonomy as a guide to recruiting is only the first step. Next, the recruiter must use tools that accurately measure applicant skills.

Every method used to separate applicants into two piles (i.e., not qualified and "looks okay") is a test. Most people think of tests in terms of pencil and paper. They are surprised to learn that resumes are tests, application forms are tests, and interviews are tests because they all separate people into two piles.

The purpose of any test used for hiring is to predict performance. Table 5.1 summarizes the most recent research about the approximate accuracy of each commonly used test.

It is obvious from this table that a professional recruiter should use the

Table 5.1   Test and Predictability

Test Type	% Predictability
Handwriting analysis	0
Age	0
Interests	1
Amount of education	1
Job experience	3
Reference check	7
Conscientious tests	10
Biographical data	12
Assessment centers	14
Traditional interviews (unstructured)	14
Integrity tests	17
Job tryout	19
Prior job knowledge	23
Peer ratings	24
Structured interviews (behavioral or situational)	26
Mental ability tests	26
Work samples	29

Adapted from an article by Schmidt and Hunter, *Psychological Bulletin*124 (1998), copyright 1998 by the American Psychological Association. Percentages have been rounded. "% Predictability" refers to the percentage of variance accounted for based on meta analysis.

right tests for each position, or the wrong people will be hired and individual productivity will suffer. Yet many recruiters tend to rely on surface-level hiring tests (i.e., resume screen, interview, and background check). The overall result of using these hiring practices is that the recruiter gets to know the applicant but seldom measures hard skills. That leaves performance triage to the hiring manager and the training department.

It is a trite analogy, but the recruiter is an organization's talent scout. Like the talent scout for any good sports team, a recruiter who is only 50 percent right is doing serious harm to the team's overall productivity.

Validation

Validation is the key to good hiring. It means statistically comparing the data gathered from a hiring tool and deciding whether scores predict performance.

Seldom do recruiters take time to learn whether the tools they use have anything to do with performance. They tend to borrow tests from training, believe vendors' recommendations, treat group averages as validities, or fail to understand the basics of a validation study. This oversight means recruiters tend to provide hiring managers with little or no correct data on which to make hiring decisions. As a consequence, hiring managers think variable performance is an everyday part of the job.

Solutions

No one expects a recruiter to become an expert in hiring technology overnight. Entire graduate programs are devoted to the subject. If a recruiter cannot define job requirements and accurately measure applicants, he or she needs to find a trustworthy industrial psychologist to do the work for him or her. Industrial psychologists are trained in developing competencies, validating tests, and training organizations to use them effectively.

Examples

What does a high-performance team look like? Start by thinking about the high performers in your organization. Now imagine that they are the norm, not the exception. Or put yourself in the shoes of a major electronics organization that became profitable within one year instead of two years; consider a major auto manufacturer that outproduced its Detroit competitors by almost three to one; envision a manufacturing company that completed its start-up in six weeks instead of six months; think about an employment agency that reduced its turnover 70 percent, increased productivity 25 percent, and decreased training time by half.

Magic? No. These organizations just identified the superstars before hiring.

Employer Branding—The Last Legal Advantage in Winning the War for Talent

Tim Gibbon

President and CEO, J. Walter Thompson

It's a Tight Labor Market—and It Will Get Tighter

Anyone involved in employment remembers that the late 1990s boom was a nightmare. Trying to find qualified people became ever more challenging. Dot-coms threw outlandish bonuses, stock options, and perks at candidates—particularly impressionable college students. Candidates would renege on offers when counteroffers came from their current employers. The wait for permanent work status visas for skilled alien professionals stretched into years.

So now, with the economy slow, dot-coms gone, and unemployment higher, the pendulum has swung back in favor of the employer, right? Not exactly.

Though there are more qualified applicants for many positions, there are also positions—and employers—still going begging. If even the conservative estimates prove right, we are likely in for another recruiting war that will make the prior one look like a skirmish. The underlying cause of the upcoming "war for talent" (as a famous McKinsey study dubbed it) is neither technology nor the economy but rather a shift in demographics. And, like global warming is to the ecology, this demographic change is gradual, inexorable, and—once manifest—probably too far gone to solve anytime soon.

Studies by both the U.S. Census Bureau and the United Nations assert that the supply of workers 25 to 44 years old will decline 15 percent over the current decade. That means there will be far fewer prospects to recruit for midlevel jobs—the core of the workforce.

The problem isn't just an American one, either. *Executive Talent* magazine reported that "the 2001 Conference Board and Accenture survey of more than 500 CEOs around the world shows that competition for talent is the number one management challenge in Europe, and number two in North America."[1]

Aggravating this demographic crisis is the attitude of workers, or what marketers call psychographics. Whereas baby boomers and their parents grew up believing that jobs were scarce and, once obtained, should be tightly held onto, younger workers have a very different view. Over 60 percent of 5,000 North American workers surveyed in 2001 by Towers Perrin stated that there is no appropriate amount of time to stay in any one job; only 10 percent surveyed felt one should stay three to five years.[2] The same study found that 12 percent were actively looking or had already found another job, and 44 percent were open to discussing other opportunities. In other words, over half—56 percent—of workers are either actively seeking or passively considering different employment at any given time.

This GenX point of view has seeped into the psychographics of not only their successors, but also the mind-sets of the baby boomers. Since this mind-set is transgenerational, those who subscribe to it are known collectively as "the emerging worker."

The emerging worker is heavily influenced by brands. This is in part due to upbringing: From the boomers on to today, people are subject to market-

[1] A. McKenzie and S. Easton-Leadley, "Branding for the Long Haul," *Executive Talent*, Spring 2001.

[2] Towers Perrin, "Today's Workforce Realities," March 19, 2002.

ing from infancy through every phase of life, up to and including the end of it. Boomers grew up on TV; GenX, on MTV. And the sheer weight of media bombarding consumers in the developed countries forces them to seek the security of reference points to make sense of all the clutter. Those reference points are brands—names and symbols that stand out because they are known and trusted.

Despite predictions that the Internet would destroy brands (the argument was that the transparency of prices on the Net would make brands irrelevant), the opposite occurred. Brands became more important because people need help in deciphering all of the offers available to them. And now there is evidence that brands influence people's choice of employers and vice versa.

According to a recent study, a company's brand has a direct influence on people's perceptions of that company as an employer.[3] Millward Brown runs a global brand equity study that has examined more than 15,000 brands across the world—the BRANDZ study. This study measures the equity of these brands versus competitors and validates the results against sales performance.

JWT Specialized Communications asked Millward Brown to add an employment question to its 2001 BRANDZ study. The question was:

"I would like you to think what the companies on your list would be like to work for. It doesn't matter whether you work in the industry or not, or don't work at the moment; it is just your impressions we are interested in. So do you think _____ (BRAND) would be a very good, good, poor, or very poor place to work?"

Millward Brown selected 1,317 brands that had common brand and company names—companies like McDonald's, Bank of America, or Nokia. (Brands such as Dove or Prozac were not covered because the company does not have the same name as the product brand.) Over 35,600 people were personally interviewed across 16 countries and 18 product and service categories. Each respondent looked at a list of the key brands in the category and answered for every one with which he or she was familiar.

The results showed that the better known a company was, the better it was perceived to be as a place to work. When the results were adjusted for cultural differences and companies were compared to their competitors,

---

[3]P. Walshe and N. Purdie, "'I Like Your Brand—Gi' Us a Job': Evaluating the Assets of Your Company," Millward Brown Research, March 13, 2002.

better-known brands were perceived as a "very good place to work" (+9.5) by a wide margin over lesser-known brands (−6.6).[4] An interesting facet of this finding was that the brands/companies known for low prices were less likely to be perceived as good places to work (−4.1) than brands/companies known as being expensive (+2.7). The report concludes:

> Companies with attractive brands are surely attractive companies. The "first date" with the company is not so blind if there is already a relationship via the brand. Conversely, if the initial encounter is via a poor brand, there may be more courtship necessary.
>
> What about companies that do not share their corporate name with one of their brands? This suggests they might be well advised to play on the strengths of their brands and make some connection with the corporation by ensuring that there is clear reference to them in recruitment communications.[5]

The Millward Brown BRANDZ results correlate with a study JWT Specialized Communications did for a high-tech client in 1999. We asked 371 software engineers in Northern California to answer this question: If you were actively looking for a job, how would you go about doing it? Their top choice was networking with their friends and acquaintances. Second, however, was "A company's web site." This ranked far above "Online job boards" (fifth) and "Newspaper classified help wanted ads" (eighth). The implication is that, faced with finding a job, these highly prized professionals would go to a shortlist of companies they already had in mind and shop their opportunities online. Conversely, if your company is not on their shortlist, the only hope you have of attracting them is if there is nothing available for them at one of their shortlist employers. Companies in this second tier are, in effect, living off of the crumbs that fall from the first-tier companies' tables.

What Is an Employer Brand?

A brand is marketing shorthand for the complex relationship that exists between an organization and its stakeholders. In product sales, the brand dis-

---

[4]These are indexes based on a number of factors; a score of 0 would indicate a company is perceived as no better and no worse than its competitors.
[5]Walshe and Purdie, "I Like Your Brand."

tinguishes one type of laundry detergent, for example, from another. But while Tide promises to get out stains, Cheer says it works in all types of washers and water. One pledges to solve your laundry challenges; the other offers energy savings and flexibility. Countless others entice the shopper with fabric softeners, color-safe bleach, or fragrances. But each has a relationship with its buyers, current and potential.

Tide loyalists, for example, have been trained to look for the familiar orange-and-blue/black box. And their choice of Tide is reinforced with product advertising, sponsorship of a NASCAR racing team, a web site with stain-removing tips, a customer help line, and in-store promotions. Buying one of the new, energy-efficient washers that use little water? Tide has a version formulated especially for you. Chances are your new washing machine came with a complimentary sample box of Tide.

Procter & Gamble—the makers of Tide—understands that in order to keep your loyalty, it has to have a presence at every touch point that relates to you and your laundry. P&G wants you to have a consistent, positive image and experience of Tide no matter what your laundry needs.

Likewise, employers have a brand, one that also is influenced by all of the employment touch points that exist between an organization and its employees, current and potential. Your employer brand is the complex relationship you have with all these people. Even if there is no direct connection (as is the case with nonemployees), people have an image of your organization. As we saw from the 2001 Millward Brown BRANDZ study, corporate image can influence employer image, if not shape it altogether (e.g., the finding that companies known for low-cost products were perceived negatively while those known for high-priced products were perceived favorably).

But the employer brand goes far beyond the intangible concept of image. It is also derived from very real facets of the relationship such as compensation, the location of your facilities, advancement opportunities, development programs, and internal communications. It is strongest when your internal policies and procedures directly support your external branding and sales efforts. It is weakest when an employer says one thing, then does another.

The Decision-Making Process

One way of visualizing the touch points between an employer and employees is represented in the Thompson Total Employer Branding

(TTEB) Hiring Pyramid (Figure 6.1). TTEB is shorthand for a body of branding expertise and techniques adapted from the seminal work done by J. Walter Thompson Co., one of the world's preeminent branding agencies. The same ideas and practices that have helped make Ford, Nestlé, and Kraft household names throughout the world now generate similar results for employers as varied as the U.S. Marine Corps and Microsoft. (See Exhibit 6.1.)

Students of marketing theory will recognize it as the familiar pyramid used by marketing strategists. The journey a prospect or employee goes through begins at the bottom of the pyramid and wends its way to the apex of commitment.

"Trigger" is a catalytic event that prompts the person to think about changing jobs. It could be a bad day at work, a rumor of pending layoffs, or a merger. Whatever it is, it gets people thinking about change.

"Consider" is the stage when they begin to think about what it is they want from a new job—more opportunities for advancement, more flexibility, less travel, and so on. It is at this phase that prospects begin to formulate their employer shortlist—which employers offer what they are looking for?

"Search" is where prospects begin to examine employer web sites. If your organization is not well known, this is where you begin to suffer a competitive disadvantage to better-known organizations. Even if you are a household name in one field, people in another may not think of you as

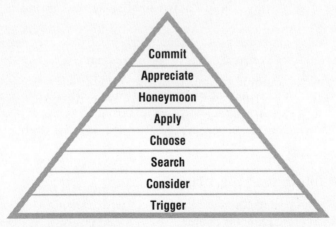

Figure 6.1   TTEB Hiring Pyramid.

TTEB stands for Thomson Total Employer Branding, a proprietary employer brand strategy technique adapted from the proven methodologies of Thompson Total Branding (TTB). TTB, first articulated in the early 1970s, has helped global marketers such as Ford, Kraft, Unilever, Nestlé, and others build powerful consumer brands for decades. TTEB uses the same cycle of questions as its antecedent:

- *Where Are We?* What is the client's current situation in its market?
- *Why Are We Here?* Insights into forces framing the client situation.
- *Where Could We Be?* What is the defined brand vision?
- *How Will We Get There?* What steps are needed to achieve the brand vision.
- *Are We Getting There?* What metrics will we use to measure progress?

Once the cycle is complete, it begins anew. After all, business is changing. Brands are in flux more than ever, and require constant monitoring.

Exhibit 6.1   What Is TTEB?

an employer. One automotive client of ours was extremely well known for its vehicles, but our research demonstrated that no one thought of the company as a place to work. If you recruit information technology professionals and you're a hospital or a hotel chain, you're not as likely to be on IT specialists' radar screens as are banks, insurance companies, or IT specialty firms.

"Choose" is the phase where prospects become applicants and begin drafting their resumes and cover letters, talking to people they may know at a target employer, and doing research on the organization. This is where your current employees can make or break you. If they validate your employment communications (i.e., recruitment advertising, employment web site, job postings, brochures, etc.), then the prospect feels encouraged to proceed. If they negate those efforts by bad-mouthing your organization, then only the most needy and desperate job seekers will continue the process.

Do you promote and reward employee referrals? During the late 1990s boom, Cisco Systems chairman John Chambers publicly praised the Cisco "Friends" program that connected prospects with current Cisco counterparts via the Web. Chambers claimed that 64 percent of Cisco's engineering hires in 1998 came from the "Friends" program.

"Apply" is the most emotional portion of the journey. This is where prospective applicants have second thoughts about leaving their current coworkers and are afraid of being caught out by their current boss during their interviewing process. What do you do to assuage their anxiety?

Is your employment lobby discreetly located and comfortable for waiting? Do your hiring managers meet prospects promptly and give them undivided attention? Do they respond quickly to questions about the compensation package or benefits? Are candidates given VIP treatment, with preferential parking or deluxe (not opulent) hotels and car service to and from the airport? If you can't answer "yes" to all of these questions, stop for a moment. Reflect on the negative impression you're making on the talent you've already spent thousands of dollars to attract. Then go back and talk with all of the people who have declined your offers in the past year and see what a difference it would have made to treat candidates as customers and not like supplicants begging for indulgence.

If you are deficient in any of these areas, you need to determine where the gaps are and how to close them. Tools such as "secret shopper" programs (where professional candidates go through and evaluate your recruiting process unbeknownst to anyone but you), process mapping, and incremental interviews have helped employers dramatically improve their recruiting ROI. By improving the ratio of acceptances to offers, these employers are getting the maximum yield from their employment investment.

"Honeymoon" is the period immediately after the candidate becomes an employee. In most cases, it is a time when the new employee sees the new workplace through rose-colored glasses. Smart employers leverage this by making sure that the first days delight rather than dismay. The new employee's workplace and equipment are waiting, business cards have been printed, and orientation covers exactly the topics of most interest to the employee. Often, the CEO or president will personally appear at orientation to endorse the new team member's decision to join.

Again, if your organization is not doing these things, you run the risk of the relationship getting off on the wrong foot. The enthusiasm the new employee brings to your environment is dimmed by a perceived lack of care or sound processes. Doubt begins to cloud the employee's view of the enterprise. And, before you know it, he or she has resigned, and you're back to square one.

"Appreciate" is a phase when employees begin to question whether their efforts are recognized and valued. Its timing varies between industries, but within disciplines it can be remarkably predictable. Registered nurses, for example, reach this phase somewhere around the sixteenth month of their employment. They've had enough time to learn all that's good and bad about where they work, and now they begin to wonder if there may be better opportunities elsewhere (almost back to a trigger event). If the institution has done a good job of recognizing and publicly lauding good performance as well as keeping staff fully informed about the status of the institution, that feeling of "Do they appreciate me?" can be softened. Conducting incremental interviews, either one-on-one or in focus group format, can surface underlying concerns and tensions and allow the nurse to vent, as well as the institution to respond with developmental programs or shift changes.

In cases where clients have followed a regimen of well-planned and executed internal communications as well as proactive research, turnover has been reduced by as much as 50 percent. And, obviously, every employee saved is one less to recruit.

"Commit" is, of course, the ideal. We all want committed employees who will give 110 percent effort. One cannot take that commitment for granted, however. A change in top management or a merger can mean all bets are off, and even the most committed long-timers will reassess their relationship. Such events can be disastrous if handled improperly. You need to have thorough plans for communicating with your employees and their families about the changes and what they mean.

American Airlines has a formula that says that any major change affecting employees will be communicated to them a minimum of nine times using different channels (e.g., the airline's intranet, newsletters, direct mail to employees' homes, postings in employee areas, multicasts, videotapes, etc.). During 2001, between the horrifying events of September 11 and the acquisition of TWA, American had a lot to communicate to its employees. By having plans in place designed to deal with everything from commonplace work rules to human tragedy, American was able to weather a challenging year successfully.

The TTEB Hiring Pyramid helps you visualize what your prospective or current employees are thinking, feeling, and doing at every stage of their relationship with you as an employer. Effective employer branding demands that you have a plan for addressing each stage of the pyramid, from advertising designed to cast a wide net to catch those at the trigger phase, to research and programs designed to probe employees' feelings and attitudes.

A *Harvard Business Review* article discussed employer branding in terms of a dynamic process involving three major elements: vision, culture and image.[6] The vision portion is just what its name implies—the ideal that management establishes and points everyone to.

The culture is the environment created to allow people to pursue the vision, or, as the authors put it, "the organization's values, behaviors and attitudes—that is, the way employees all through the ranks feel about the company."[7]

The image is the public perception of the enterprise. And the "public" includes the media, investors, analysts, community leaders, suppliers, political figures, and many others along with the all-important customers.

The authors go on to point out that many of the public perceptions are shaped by contact with employees, those presumably who know the organization best. If your people don't understand or aren't living up to the vision of management, then the entire brand is degraded. (Imagine meeting a Tide employee wearing dirty clothes, for example. How would that affect your brand perception?) A study by MOHR Research found that 20 percent of customers will immediately leave a store upon receiving bad service; 26 percent will tell their friends and neighbors about it. McDonald's estimated it lost 11 percent of its global customer base in 2000 due to poor service—a staggering $785 million in lost revenue.

So, you already have an employer brand—whether you've consciously cultivated it or not. People already have an opinion of what it's like to work for your organization if they know anything about it at all. If they do not know anything, then their opinion will be one of suspicion.

Why Is Your Employer Brand Worth Cultivating?

Branding is a central concept for today's emerging worker, given the trends in demographics and psychographics. Even if your organization is downsiz-

---

[6]M. J. Hatch and M. Schultz, "Are the Strategic Stars Aligned for Your Brand?" *Harvard Business Review*, February 2001.
[7]Ibid.

ing, you need to do whatever you can to protect and enhance your employer brand in order to keep surviving workers motivated and aligned with your corporate brand and vision.

Simple logic supports this view. If your customers are buying less, then every point of contact you do have with them has to count for much more. Your employees have to perform at their utmost in order to: (1) keep customers coming back for more; (2) convince customers to spend more each time they do return; and (3) get them to come back more often. If your employees disappoint, however slightly, it's all too easy in today's fluid economy for the affected customer to switch brands or reduce consumption.

Case in point: Southwest Airlines. The spunky low-frills carrier is known for very selective hiring and thorough orientation. Their flight attendants adopt a folksy yet professional demeanor to put leisure passengers (Southwest's core market) at ease flying. In the wake of September 11, Southwest was one of two carriers that did not lay off anyone. Southwest employees volunteered to take unpaid time off or perform unpaid volunteer work such as landscaping headquarters in order to help the airline.

Southwest returned to pre-9/11 load levels much sooner than any other carrier. And the market cap of Southwest (NYSE: LUV) is greater than that of American, United and Delta combined ($14.17 billion as of April 1, 2002). While its low fares are a big attraction for businesses and families looking to cut costs, other major carriers slashed fares dramatically in the fourth quarter of 2001. Most analysts credit the Southwest staff, with their combination of cost cutting and delivering on the brand ("It's fun to fly") for the recovery.

Even if your organization does not have direct contact with the end user, keeping your employer brand aligned with your overall corporate brand can yield major dividends. Microsoft has had an admittedly difficult past couple of years, with negative publicity surrounding charges from the U.S. Department of Justice and several states' attorneys general. Those allegations helped fuel the perception that Microsoft was no longer cutting-edge.

The prescription was to leverage the corporate tag line, "Where Do You Want to Go Today?" as well as the familiar Microsoft palette and typography, in a campaign targeted at very specific venues such as airport frequent-flier lounges (to capture consulting techies) and the BART station in San Francisco serving Silicon Gulch, that city's high-tech development neighborhood.

One result was widespread publicity about the campaign. Pieces on ABC's *World News Tonight*, in *The Wall Street Journal* and local newspapers, as well as on the Web, not only were complimentary but also added hundreds of thousands of dollars in additional exposure. Salon.com, the online journal of commentary, observed, "Maybe someone should mention this to all of those dot-com companies that spent well over $1 million on forgettable Super Bowl ads."[8]

Another result was a doubling of traffic to the Microsoft employment web site and consequent increase in both applicants and hires. The company began to appeal to technology's best and brightest by making sure the messages coming from product marketing and employment had the same tone as well as the same core idea: Microsoft gives you the freedom to do your best, as a user or as a developer/enabler.

Where Do You Begin?

Cultivating and nurturing your employer brand is a challenging, but rewarding, endeavor. The starting point is to understand what your employer brand is. You need to design a research plan for evaluating your current employer brand and how to achieve consensus on what it should be.

If you're an HR executive, you need to begin doing it soon. According to a study conducted by the Conference Board in 2001, twice as many marketing communications executives identified the need for a strong employer brand and plan to budget for it versus human resources executives.[9] If HR does not take the role of employer brand steward, marketing communications will gladly do it for them. While the two should always collaborate, and marketing communications by definition sets the corporate brand, abdicating responsibility for employer branding means less control over the entire recruiting process. As recruiting becomes increasingly defined by marketing concepts such as value proposition and segmentation, HR runs a very real risk of being marginalized unless it steps up and takes a leading role.

According to the *International Journal of Advertising*, "Employer advertising will grow in importance exponentially . . . to the point where it is a pri-

[8]Salon.com, "Station Domination," October 1999.
[9]Conference Board, "Engaging Employees through Your Brand," February 2001.

mary business objective to simultaneously attract new staff and retain existing employees. Indeed, in many situations, it may be far easier to find customers . . . than it will be to employ the skilled individuals to deliver on these offerings.

"The struggle to recruit suitable knowledge workers probably eclipses the traditional marketing problem of acquiring customers."[10]

[10]Michael T. Ewing, et al., "Employer Branding in the Knowledge Economy," *International Journal of Advertising*, World Advertising Research Centre, Henley-on-Thames, England, March 2001, pp. 11–12.

Building a Global Employer Brand in Five (Actually More) Lessons

Rob O'Keefe

Vice President, Marketing Resources, TMP Worldwide

Developing any brand has its potential pitfalls. Developing an employer brand has even more. Heading down the path of a global employer brand can be fraught with infinite opportunities for missteps—ranging from fragmented brand strategies to disenchanted global teams.

But why learn from your mistakes when you can learn from someone else's? It costs less, reduces those embarrassing explanations to the CEO, and may actually result in endless accolades about your foresight and inclusiveness.

Lesson Prelude: Get Your Relationships in Order

The concept of an employer brand is now an accepted concept in human resources departments throughout corporate America. The result has been an increasing debate among the corresponding marketing departments as to its relationship to the corporate brand. For those with no real corporate

48

brand, developing one is often seen as the first step toward an identity that supplements the organization's product or service brand focus. For those with an established corporate brand, an employer brand is sometimes seen as a simple extension, developed for a particular audience. For still others, however, the idea of an employer brand is seen as unnecessary and problematic, redundant at best and fragmented at worst.

To understand why this dynamic tension exists, it is important to be familiar with the distinction between brand and branding. When marketers refer to brand, they are addressing something larger than the name of the company or its associated products and services. They are referring to an idea about the organization that encompasses its values, culture, mission, financial standing, and offerings. They seek to create a host of positive associations about the corporate brand in the minds of various constituencies: investors, customers, communities, and employees. And while there may be a differentiated value proposition for each target, there is a common essence that ties all propositions together.

Branding, in contrast, tends to be about the act of communicating brand attributes. In the employment sector, branding took hold as a means to be noticed in an increasingly competitive and undifferentiated market. For many companies, this simply meant an image advertising approach that creatively demonstrated one or more aspects of the employment experience. Others, however, became more sophisticated—after realizing that merely communicating a creative and differentiated message was not enough. Their message needed to align with the actual offering, leading some companies to define the employment experience in marketing terms as the "employee value proposition."

Whether an organization chooses to develop an actual employer brand or wishes to communicate one aspect of its corporate brand through employer branding is a matter of philosophy. Either approach is fine—as long as the fundamentals of marketing and brand strategy are adhered to.

Lesson 1: What Did You Just Read?

Ensure that marketing/brand management and human resources are on the same page. Does everyone agree that you are looking to develop an employer brand? Or are you really looking to add employment context to an existing corporate brand? These are two very different issues that require individualized approaches and expectations. When this key point is not defined during initial stages, a good deal of resources must be applied to re-align the global initiative.

Lesson 2: Could I Have a Definition, Please?

Clearly define what you mean by a global brand. For some organizations, a global brand means a universal strategic platform that gives equal weight to all cultures and must be adopted by everyone. For others, a global brand means an umbrella approach with room for localization. And for others, it is simply a means to promulgate one dominant view (usually the view held by the home office country). Whatever the underlying motivation is, it should be shared up front with global stakeholders so that they understand their place in stewarding the final strategy. When this expectation is not set, stakeholders become reluctant (sometimes indefinitely) to adopt the final approach. There is nothing less rewarding than a global brand strategy that is adopted only by one country.

LESSON 2A

Rigid uniformity is not the same as consistency. The former leads to the fulfillment of a false premise: One size fits all. Brands must allow for localization without sacrificing the broad-based strategy. When this approach is not taken, the result is either lack of effectiveness or local rejection.

Lesson 3: *Qu'est que c'est?*

Articulation of the brand across borders is more than a matter of translation. Each culture has its own nuances that must be considered. Utilization of a transliteration or transcreation process achieves brand relevance without compromising desired brand attributes.

Here's something that's hardly a surprise. Really clever headlines in one language that rely on wordplay are usually just obscure and meaningless in any other language. No matter how brilliant that new word you created from the name of your company appears to be in English, it will just leave them shaking their heads in French. In China, they'll be wondering why you are making disparaging remarks about family members.

Lesson 4: Have We Met?

Brand strategy must address the appropriate means of introduction. A one-time global brand rollout may be appropriate for some organizations, while a phased country-by-country or business-by-business approach may be right for others. During assessment and development, make a determination as to the correct approach. Expediency does not guarantee effectiveness.

Lesson 5: Can You Spare Some Change?

Are you prepared for any ensuing change management? Developing a global employer brand often uncovers key operational issues that affect the employment experience. Many of these issues result from the natural outgrowth of the challenges faced by a multinational organization. However, any discussion of these issues typically results in the following: If employees provide input, they want to see the resulting change. When employees are not given clear parameters regarding the scope and expected outcomes of the employer brand endeavor, the risk of employee disillusionment is high.

Bonus Lesson: Research Your Research Approach

Not all brand development begins with research. Some brands are created with the idea of instilling a perception in the market. This is hard to do with employer branding because the brand is based on an actual—not perceived—experience that the target market will eventually encounter. As such, research becomes an important aspect of development. But not all research methods are universally effective. The focus groups that uncover amazing insight in a country known for the extroverted character of its people aren't going to get you much in a culture that respects consensus and uniformity of thought.

Case Illustrations

Now, three lessons from the "It really happened" archives.

YOUR MOMENT

The projector is still humming. You have just finished presenting your global employer brand strategy. Your boss is present, along with the requisite division heads and thought leaders of your company. You think to yourself, "This is my moment!" as you prepare to open the presentation for discussion. Then you get the first question. It's from the marketing director. "Can you explain why we invested in this project when we already have a brand?"

Maybe you can explain, but it really doesn't matter. For all intents and purposes, this project has ended—and let's hope that's all that has come to a conclusion. Review Lessons 1 and 2 in an effort to determine what went wrong.

NAME RECOGNITION

You want to achieve name recognition in a new market in Asia. It turns out that your company name can be interpreted to mean something related to cleaning shellfish. That would be fine for a seafood restaurant, but you're branding a technology company.

Obviously, you can't change your name. The execution components of your global brand should no doubt rely heavily on clarity and explanation. The emotional connection with your brand can wait—at least until the tide goes out.

PANDORA'S BOX

Everyone from your worldwide locations is excited about the global brand initiative—especially the internal focus groups (see bonus lesson above). Participants are lined up well in advance, and do they ever participate! You uncover lots of important insights regarding the employment experience. But you also discover that there is a serious disconnect between how corporate understands the market and the mission and how one of the company's most important local teams understands them. In many ways, this is like the classic Pandora's box in employment marketing: You have a problem that exceeds your mandate, combined with a constituency that believes change was the inevitable outcome of being heard (because no one told them otherwise). Opening that box, so to speak, encourages people to bring up issues that go beyond your goals and mandate.

The Last Lesson

There is something innately appealing about creating a global employer brand. It's all so neat and tidy in concept—exactly the opposite of the makeup of most global companies. Just because yours is a global company, however, do not assume that the development of a global brand is the only approach. Should you determine that it is, remember these five (actually more) lessons.

CHAPTER

8

Cross-Cultural Communication

Keiko Saito
President, ILCC Co., Ltd.

Two Stories of Lost Cross-Cultural Communication

A luxury apparel shop sold several thousands of dollars worth of merchandise to an Indonesian family visiting the city. Two days later, the family returned to the store and happily shopped again, spending several thousand dollars more. In appreciation, the store sent a fruit basket to the hotel of their "new favorite customers." And, sure enough, the Indonesian customers returned in a couple of days to buy more clothes. The staff greeted them as old friends and began showing them the latest fashions. In a gesture of friendship and a sense of "being part of one family," one salesperson brought out the store mascot, an adorable dog who immediately scampered around the customers seeking a pat on the head. The Indonesians appeared flustered and immediately gathered their belongings and hurried out of the store, never to return.

A large U.S. manufacturer was running into problems with its Germany subsidiary. The U.S. staff felt they were not respected by their German counterparts because, as they explained, "the Germans are always asking for

54

trivial details that don't matter. And they want the information instantly. They are impatient and feel their project is more important than anything else." The German contingent, on the other hand, described their American colleagues as "not caring about doing things correctly. They keep secrets and don't tell us everything. And they are always late and don't pay attention to schedules." What began as a polite, cooperative, and mutually beneficial relationship had deteriorated into a situation of frustration, distrust, antagonism, and unproductive efforts.

In both of these cases, communication broke down. And breakdowns in cross-cultural communication are the number one reason for the deterioration and eventual collapse of international ventures and relationships. More than cutbacks in funding, political issues, or changes in the marketplace, "a failure to communicate" causes the majority of problems in international business, whether that business is conducted across national borders or within house with international staff or at one's desk with overseas vendors.

Sometimes the collapse is sudden and huge; sometimes it is a gradual erosion of trust and respect that eventually results in a complete breakdown. But in the end, international business—which is, in actuality, *any* business in today's global economy—cannot survive without effective cross-cultural communication and understanding.

An example of communication breakdown is the difficulty faced by Daimler and Chrysler as they undertook the merger of the two automotive giants. Major issues were dealt with, but basic cultural understanding and awareness were neglected. Minor misunderstandings were ignored. Gradually, what understanding there was began to erode. In the end, as reported in media, the two organizations disagreed on even the smallest details, such as the layout of business cards.

Small companies and large conglomerates face similar problems. As an example, a small but rapidly expanding biotech company experienced turmoil in the ranks when dealing with a multicultural staff. Chinese-national scientists worked effectively in the labs, but were reportedly "not pulling their load" in meetings when confronted and challenged by their more aggressive Western European colleagues. The complaint was that "they just sit there and won't argue with us—and after the meetings they are very cool toward us." In both cases, the basic assumption—transplant people and they will magically and immediately remold themselves to match the new culture—was wrong. It takes time, training, and adaptation on both sides for effective communication to take place.

In today's world, all business is international. It may be business-to-vendor or customer or supplier; business-to-subsidiary; employing an international workforce; or receiving and sending expatriate employees. Making a multinational, multicultural staff work—really work, not just exchange courtesies and be polite—is critical. And because all communication is culturally based, bridging cultural gaps, resolving conflicts, curtailing deteriorating conditions, and shoring up weak situations fall to the human resources staff.

There are tomes of research, volumes and volumes of written material, and numerous workshops that focus on both specific and general issues. All of that information and training can be boiled down to four basic areas:

1. Recognition and acknowledgement of problems.
2. Cultural knowledge.
3. Specific skills and tactics.
4. Training, training, and retraining.

Human resources experts must deal with multicultural situations and problems day in and day out. Analyzing these four basic areas is by no means all-inclusive, but it is a very good place to start thinking and planning in order to recognize multicultural issues in your company.

Recognition and Acknowledgment

An American company with a Japanese subsidiary ran into serious trouble when it assumed all was well; after all, when senior managers visited Japan, they were entertained well and were invited to drink and socialize with the staff. What they failed to deal with was an undercurrent of frustration, resentment, and misunderstanding.

After the Americans went home, the Japanese would shake their heads and apologize for the faux pas committed by the visitors, and then repair any damaged customer relationships. The Americans returned home equally frustrated by the lack of decisive action by their partners. What they failed to understand was that Japanese make decisions by consensus, and that requires time and patience. Procedures must be followed: Masses of data will be considered and reconsidered, and everyone up and down the ranks must be informed and consulted, often several times. An American executive of a U.S. subsidiary of a Japanese automobile manufacturer once complained, "They can't make a decision." Well, of course they can. If they couldn't, the company would be out of business. But the pace of the decision-making process is slow by U.S. standards, and complex. The Americans felt the Japanese were procrastinating; the Japanese felt the Americans were pressuring them and were not being thorough. But no one said anything. Neither side acknowledged the problem for fear of offending someone. As the frustration grew, it slowly evolved into resentment and finally outright hostility, with the false conclusions: "They can't make a decision." "They are not thorough." Had both sides merely acknowledged that a problem existed and described it in a nonjudgmental way that did not find fault, they could have resolved the issue while it was still able to be resolved.

Once a problem is recognized and acknowledged, you are ready to develop a strategy that will remedy the situation.

Cultural Knowledge

"Knowledge is power." A relevant variation would be: "Knowledge is the first step toward resolution." Once the problem is recognized and acknowledged, the cause or source of the problem will be soon become evident. It is important to separate the real from the presumed. The cultural conflict, and thus the cultural communication problem, could be rooted in history, misinformation, misunderstanding, cultural values, personalities, cognitive patterns, or even geography.

If you understand the history of a country, you understand a good portion of its culture. Human behavior and the resulting business behavior and practices are formed in large part by history. The head of an international agricultural company, who was doing a great deal of business in Eastern Europe, once commented about hiring people for overseas placement: "Give me people who understand the history of an area. I can teach them about selling my widgets, but they need to know what political and historical occurrences have shaped and influenced the behavior and attitudes of their customers and colleagues."

One of the greatest errors people make when communicating is to assume they have succeeded. At ILCC, we always tell our clients, "Do not assume you have delivered your message successfully. Do not assume you have been understood correctly." Not getting your message across is often the source of misinformation and misunderstanding. How many people base their knowledge of Indian culture on movies? How many people believe they have an understanding of Japanese culture because they eat sushi? That may seem an extreme example, but (and we are not making this up) we had a client who told us, "I understand a great deal about Japan. I have seen all of Kurosawa's movies and I love chicken teriyaki." Or even worse, how many Europeans and others base their impressions of America on what they've seen on TV and in movies? While visiting New York, a Japanese businessman refused to take the subway, despite horrendous traffic jams. Why? Because the in-flight movie on his trip to New York was *Die Hard with a Vengeance*, which featured explosions in the subways.

A trip to any travel store or large bookstore will yield volumes on cultural values. The resources are many, because the cultural differences are many. Even something as simple and as fundamental as the concept of time differs from culture to culture. In one Indian culture, a favorite expression is "You are hurrying to your grave." In contrast, many American businesspeople live by the creed "Time is money." Another example of even more dramatic differences: When invited to a dinner party at 7 P.M. in the United States, what time should you arrive? Though 7 P.M. is fine, 7:15 P.M. is better. If the party is held in Sweden, you would probably arrive a few minutes early and wait outside until ringing the bell at precisely 7 P.M. If the party is held in Brazil, don't even think of arriving before 9 P.M. These may seem simple, but a basic understanding of the concept of time in a specific culture can help enormously when planning the pace of a project or when anticipating responses.

Meetings offer a dramatic example of cultural differences in business. We train our clients to know that understanding the purpose of a meeting—and, therefore, what takes place at a meeting—is critical to an effective session. For example, in America and Western Europe, a meeting generally means a debate and airing of issues and opinions. The result of most meetings is resolution of a problem or an action list (Americans love action items). In Japan, most of the work—the debate, the gathering of information, the resolving of issues—takes place before the meeting in a practice called *nemawashi* or "preparing the soil for planting." The purpose of the actual meeting, therefore, is to confirm what has already been decided. You can imagine the confusion and frustration when an American walks into a Japanese meeting prepared to debate or a Japanese walks into an American meeting and finds his colleagues embroiled in an energetic discussion.

One of our clients, an international law enforcement officer, was called to the scene of a kidnapping in an Asian country. On arrival, he asked the local police if there was any evidence. "No," he was told, "no evidence." He then surveyed the scene and found, among other things, a bloody rag, a knife, and an empty wallet. Astonished, he inquired about what he had found and was told, "Those aren't evidence. Those are souvenirs!" Our client related this story to us and said in amazement, "They just don't think like we do." Voilà! That was the beginning of successful cultural understanding—a recognition that cultures differ in the way they think or process information.

Often our company is asked to teach business etiquette and protocol to clients on both sides of the Pacific. We can and often do that, but we warn our clients that in such cases "a little bit of knowledge is a dangerous thing." We can teach how to present a business card, but that is only the first step. Unless you know how "they" think and process information, the second step is subject to polite courtesies but no real action or progress. And then, the third and subsequent steps are probably doomed to failure. It's knowing what to do after presenting your business card that means the difference between success and failure. Knowing how to present information in a way that will be understood, knowing how to develop and implement an effective negotiations strategy, knowing what to say and how to say it are critical to establishing and maintaining a cross-cultural business relationship.

Even the geography of a culture is important to know when working cross-culturally. For example, countries that are islands tend to have more orderly and formal societies. Countries that are geographically isolated tend to be more insular in their thinking and not as open to outside opinions and information. It may seem a statement of the obvious, but geography can offer important, and often overlooked, clues to understanding a culture.

Having recognized the extent of a problem, and armed with knowledge of the specific cultures, it is important to acquire the skills necessary to bridge the gaps, increase awareness, and apply the knowledge. There are a myriad of skills to learn, and once learned they must be refined and adapted for application to each situation. Three of the most critical skills are (1) adapting communication to cognitive patterns; (2) demonstrating commitment to the business relationship or project; and (3) maintaining relationships.

Cultures differ in the way they learn or process information. Failure to adapt to those differences is the cause of much misunderstanding and frustration. It is the responsibility of the sender of the message to adapt the message to the communication pattern of the receiver. These are very simplistic and certainly there are individual exceptions, but the following general rules go a long way toward successful communication.

- North Americans and Western Europeans tend to communicate in a linear pattern: The message starts at point A and moves straight to point B and so on. New information is presented at the beginning, followed by supporting details.

- Mediterranean cultures tend to communicate in a looping pattern: The first point is made and then the message is softened with related information, then the second point is made and its message is softened, and so forth.
- East Asian cultures tend to communicate in a pyramid pattern. They begin with a foundation of the history or background, then narrow the information until the final detail, usually the newest information, is stated last.

It is easy to imagine the confusion and frustration that occurs when a "pyramid communicator" sends a message to a "looper." Therefore, it is important to think before writing the memo, making a presentation, or even opening a discussion: Should I state, perhaps again, the background of the situation? Am I too direct in this message? Do I need to soften the message?

A more specific example of this occurs in oral presentations. An American businessperson who is presenting to a Japanese audience needs to begin with a complete background or history. You need to set the stage for the new information. If the American begins with the new information and moves directly from point to point, he or she will quickly lose Japanese listeners who are trying to place the new information in context. The reverse is also true. A Japanese businessperson who begins a presentation with a long history soon loses an American audience, who is waiting for the crux of the speech, the new information. In both examples, the speaker failed to adapt the message to the cognitive pattern of the audience—and the message was lost.

Demonstrating a sense of commitment requires knowing the culture of your partner. It means knowing and demonstrating that you know and respect cultural practices. We tell our clients that when they approach or negotiate with another culture, "They will look you over. They will talk you over. And they will work you over." Your commitment (and your patience) will be sorely tested; but once established, that relationship is solid and trusted.

An example: A building equipment company sent one of its female managers to India to finalize the negotiations on a major sale. At their request, she waited in her hotel room while her customers considered the terms of sale. She waited over 24 hours. Finally, they came back with total agreement to all of the terms. And, from that point forward, future business went smoothly and easily. Her commitment, and the commitment of her company, had to be demonstrated and, in this case, tested. She succeeded because she persevered and "stuck it out." The reward was a sale, a strong relationship, and future business.

Once a business relationship is established, the work has just begun. All too often, relationships flounder and subsequently fail because of neglect. Care in cultivating and nurturing the relationship must continue as that relationship grows and matures. When working with Asian partners, you must reestablish the relationship each and every time you communicate. Each memo and letter, each phone conversation and message, each e-mail communiqué, and each meeting *must* begin with a brief episode of small talk that serves to renew and strengthen the relationship.

Training, Training, and Retraining

International business relationships that succeed and prosper have one common trait—the entire staff received and continues to receive cross-cultural training. The training begins while the relationship is forming, before problems arise. Once the relationship begins functioning, training is available on a crisis-to-crisis basis. When a problem arises, it is recognized, acknowledged, and dealt with before the stress escalates to frustration and resentment. Finally—and this is the key factor but one that is often ignored—cultural retraining must take place again and again, perhaps as often as every two years. Cultural retraining most often occurs when new people join the team, or when it's time to renew and rejuvenate. And cultural retraining can be initiated simply to remind people that things work better when there is fundamental understanding of how people communicate, how people think, and how people carry out business practices across cultural borders.

Becoming a Great Recruiter

Dr. John Sullivan

DrJohnSullivan.com

Over the years, I have trained thousands of recruiters, and most turn out to be pretty good at what they do. But a select few strive to and eventually become great recruiters. What sets these great recruiters apart from the rest of the pack? When I tried to answer that question, I began to recognize that there were some patterns in every great recruiter's career. I call those patterns "Eight Simple Rules for Recruiting." And if followed, they can lead to greatness in recruiting.

When Learning

1. *Read everything.* Scan everything you can get your hands on that relates to (1) recruiting, (2) your industry, (3) business in general, and (4) HR in general. It will make your conversations with prospects richer and your candidate assessment questions more productive. But most importantly, it will provide you with names of key leaders and up-and-comers that you can use for referral sources.

2. *Build a learning network.* Identify a few other recruiters who want to become the best in their field. Together, build a learning network to

share ideas and best practices. Take advantage of technology to make it work with recruiters from around the world.

3. *Use metrics.* Great recruiters follow the numbers in order to continually improve. They track precisely what works and why. You, too, should track the best sources, tools, selling techniques, and learning sites. Treat recruiting as a business and track your business impact and ROI every day.

4. *Get a mentor.* Identify other great recruiters and excellent managers. Then ask several to mentor you. Recruiting is one field where it's hard to grow without contacts.

When Recruiting

5. *Rely on referrals.* In a fast-changing world, you can't keep up with the latest changes and the key players on your own. Great recruiters rely on others (referrals) as their primary "finding" tool. Once you realize that top performers always know other top performers, you are home free.

6. *Recognize that you are in sales.* Finding the very best candidates is only half of the game. Selling candidates (on the job and on your firm) and convincing managers (to read resumes, to interview rapidly, and to trust your judgment) are what separates the best recruiters from the rest. Take a sales class and build relationships with top salespeople to learn how to get candidates to listen to you and accept your offers.

7. *Do your market research.* You can't sell anything if you don't know what candidates and managers expect. Hold surveys, interviews, and focus groups to identify what candidates and managers want. Research is the key to any recruiter's success. You absolutely must know is when top performers are ready to shift jobs, and what it will take to get each top performer to change jobs (in other words, their job-switching criteria).

8. *Focus and prioritize.* There isn't time to do it all, so focus on top-performing candidates who are currently employed. These candidates are harder to land, but worth the effort. Next, focus on top-performing managers, filling key jobs, and top-performing business units. This will increase your impact, visibility, and learning speed. Do not, under any circumstances, listen to anyone who tells you to focus on the average. Focusing on the average will just make you average.

Follow each of these rules religiously and you will be a top recruiter.

Leadership and Recruiting

Kevin Wheeler
Global Learning Resources

A Recruiter in Crisis: A Case Study

Mark is in crisis. A middle-aged recruiting director, Mark suddenly finds himself faced with a situation that many in HR routinely confront: increased work levels with decreased staff. Mark has recently downsized his staff of 20 recruiters, and now only has five senior-level recruiters and two support people left. Yet the number of resumes Mark's recruiting office receives has actually gone up considerably from the pre-downsizing days. They have fewer requisitions, but more demanding searches from ever more demanding hiring managers.

This essay will review how recruiting managers like Mark often confront crisis within their departments, typically because they're still thinking like twentieth-century recruiters instead of twenty-first-century recruiters. Translated? Mark needs to rethink his whole approach to recruiting. For too long, Mark's approach to recruiting has been focused on "resume" and "requisition." In today's complex world, this simplistic approach no longer works. Mark needs to rethink his whole approach to recruiting. Here's how.

Background

Mark is a typical recruiting director has been in the recruiting business for more than 15 years. Previously he was an HR generalist, and he has a fairly broad background in human resources.

His academic life has been undistinguished, but adequate. He graduated from a state university with an arts degree—history, actually—and leveraged that into his first personnel job in the mid-1980s. He likes working with people and feels that being a recruiter is a positive way to help people and the company he works for. His only formal training in recruiting has been a series of seminars and short courses in interviewing skills, a basic course in recruiting for HR, and a series of Internet search courses he took a few years ago. A few senior-level recruiters he has worked for at other companies mentored him; they gave him coaching and assistance in developing his current skills. He considers himself to be well above average in his knowledge of recruiting techniques and in his understanding of the talent marketplace.

Two years ago, Mark's department put out a request for proposal (RFP) and finally selected an applicant tracking system (ATS) vendor to help them deal with the volume of resumes they faced. Unfortunately, they experienced many implementation problems with the vendor, and the system took almost a year to become fully operational. And it still isn't satisfactory. The recruiters find the interface difficult to use; its limited reporting capabilities have made it very time-consuming for Mark to provide management with much hard data on how his department is doing.

Mark's team has been struggling to keep up with sourcing and screening for the number of requisitions that need to be filled. Mark has personally been doing interviews and sourcing to take some of the load off his recruiters. All the recruiters are frustrated with overly demanding hiring managers and inadequate resources.

The Crisis

Yesterday, the company's vice president of human resources and Mark's boss let him know that she is not happy with his department's performance. She acknowledged that she has received many complaints from hiring managers about the quality of the candidates they have been seeing, as well as the long periods of time between submitting the requisition and getting candidates to review.

She gave Mark an ultimatum: Make improvements in one quarter, or she will have to take some other action. Mark understands that unless he and his staff show substantial improvements, he will probably be fired.

Solutions

Here are four specific strategies that Mark can—and should—follow in order to make some progress and give himself time to make more substantial changes.

DEVELOP A COMMUNICATIONS STRATEGY

Mark has obviously not had enough contact with either his boss or the hiring managers. If he had, he would have already shared conversations with his boss about the lack of resources and the growing frustrations among his own staff and the hiring managers. If there had been adequate communications and a communication strategy for when things go wrong, the hiring managers would have talked directly to him and his recruiters—instead of venting to the VP of HR.

It's simply a good HR practice to be in constant communication with the hiring managers and put recruiters in physical proximity to the most important of these managers. Centralized recruiting departments that keep recruiters clustered in one area away from their clients are rarely successful—and then only under special circumstances. Mark should distribute his staff and establish a regular time to personally meet with each hiring manager.

ESTABLISH A BENCHMARK AND A STANDARD SET OF METRICS TO REPORT

Obviously, Mark also needs to track how successfully or how unsuccessfully he and his fellow recruiters are performing. I would recommend that he adopt a standard set of metrics, such as those developed by Staffing.org, a nonprofit organization devoted to measuring human capital performance that advocates the use of staffing metrics such as quality of new hire, time to fill, and cost per hire. Mark can assess his organization against these metrics, and use the results as part of his overall communications plan and as possible leverage to get the manpower and software resources he needs to make recruiting an efficient and successful operation. The use of metrics will help him focus and prioritize his improvement efforts on those areas where he and his recruiters are performing poorly.

PRACTICE PROACTIVE TWENTY-FIRST-CENTURY RECRUITING

Overall, Mark needs to rethink his whole approach to recruiting. He is definitely a twentieth-century recruiter. By this I mean that his approach to recruiting is to think "resume" and "requisition," and then practice a matching mentality. In today's complex world, this approach is far too simplistic. Candidates, hiring managers, and jobs are multidimensional; it is the overall mix of skills and attitudes and capabilities that makes for success. This complex mix cannot be determined by a resume search on keywords, or in a 20-minute telephone screen. Mark's recruiting technology is no doubt inadequate, as is his overall recruiting philosophy and approach. Reactive, retroactive recruiting is dying quickly. Mark needs to develop a talent strategy and take into account existing internal resources, as well as promotional and development possibilities for his staff.

SIX EMERGING KEY SKILLS FOR RECRUITERS

Mark needs to focus on developing and making sure his staff members possess the six emerging key skills for recruiters. Nowadays, recruiters need to be able to:

1. Create an image and a brand for their organization.
2. Market and sell the organization and the functions within it.
3. Become masters of identifying and tapping diverse sources of talent.
4. Understand the power of competitive intelligence.
5. Focus on relationships and candidate experience to build talent pools or communities.
6. Measure the impact of what they do.

Conclusion

Mark may not survive, and many other twentieth-century recruiting directors won't, either. Change is difficult and the path is never perfectly clear. Success, however, lies in embarking on the journey with the realization that the map is less than perfect. The only certainty in this story is that the hiring managers will figure out a way to get the people they need—one way or the other. Mark has no choice but to join them in this search by acquiring and embracing the skills and tools necessary to be a recruiter in the twenty-first century.

Top 10 Secrets to Effective Networking

David Manaster and Jim Dalton
Electronic Recruiting Exchange, Inc.

The set of skills that a recruiter needs to be successful has evolved over the past few decades. What many once considered little more than an administrative position, tasked with placing classified ads and reading resumes, has now become a profession that requires the investigative skills of a researcher, the persuasion and closing skills of a salesperson, and the assessment skills of a psychologist.

But one thing hasn't changed, even with the advent of the Internet and the ubiquity of applicant tracking systems. Networking is still the heart and soul of the recruiting profession. And it is effective networking that sets the top recruiters apart from the merely average.

In 1998, our company built an online hub of networking and information for recruiters called the Electronic Recruiting Exchange. Back in those days, it seemed inconceivable that a group of natural-born networkers like recruiters didn't have a place they could come together and exchange ideas online. Now there are a number of recruiting communities online, where recruiters from across the globe come to share resources and debate best practices.

But when recruiters network, it's not just with other recruiters. It's with everybody. And that's how the best recruiters succeed: by building a professional network with roots that literally extend everywhere. It's difficult, but not complicated, expensive, or mysterious. In fact, for most top recruiters, networking is one of the most enjoyable facets of their job.

But there are a number of rules to be followed, and certainly some secrets that are employed by the best recruiters. We'd like to share just a few of these with you here. And we guarantee that if you keep these points in mind, you'll quickly find yourself with more (and better) candidates, more clients (if you're a third-party recruiter), and more hiring managers who can rely on you to deliver results.

Here, then, are the top 10 secrets to effective networking for recruiters.

1. *Think long-term.* A good deal of your networking efforts will rely on laying the groundwork and not necessarily reaping immediate benefits. Not everyone you network with will be the ideal candidate for the requisition you have open now, but down the road a solid network can become an efficient pipeline for qualified candidates.

2. *The world is your network.* Often, the most fruitful contacts come when you are least expecting them, perhaps at a wedding, your child's soccer game, or other social functions. Network with everyone you meet, because you never know who will lead you to—or turn out to be—the star employee that you've been searching for!

3. *Always get names.* Ask everyone you talk to give you the names of friends and peers that may be top candidates. If the people they introduce you to don't turn out to be who you're looking for, ask those people for names. Your network will never run dry if you can consistently follow this rule.

4. *You can meet almost anyone in the world over the Internet.* Explore online forums in the profession you're recruiting for, and you'll quickly meet qualified candidates and other people who can lead you to them. One of the best parts about forums is that you can identify the people who really know their stuff by their contributions. Just make sure to respect the societal norms of the community and keep your contributions constructive. Posting a job description on a public forum is not networking!

5. *Get involved in the community.* Attend events in your local community, such as those hosted by your chamber of commerce, rotary club,

or perhaps your own religious organization. Particularly if you're recruiting for local positions, this is a great way to meet candidates. Better yet, have your company sponsor a local event. You know your community better than anyone. Generate ideas for events that have local interest, and get your company involved.

6. *Use e-mail to stay in touch and form ongoing relationships.* You'll meet many qualified people within your network, for whom you may or may not have a job opening today. But the great thing about e-mail is that it allows you to keep in touch regularly without an overwhelming amount of time and effort. A great way to maintain a relationship with a large group of people is to start a monthly newsletter, which can be compiled and sent at relatively little cost.

7. *Network with other recruiters.* You may be tempted to perceive other recruiters as your competitors. But the fact is you have much more to gain from your relationships with them than you have to lose. Other recruiters can be some of the best sources of ideas and knowledge you'll find. Get involved with your local recruiting organization (there is at least one in almost every city) or join any of several online recruiting communities. Like any profession, there is an extensive body of knowledge out there, but the only way to receive it is to get to know its greatest practitioners and experts.

8. *Make a name for yourself.* If you're well known in your industry, candidates will find you. They'll also respect your expertise and listen to your advice. Instead of just attending conferences, speak at them. Become a leader in the organizations you're involved in. Publish articles. You'll vastly expand your network and you're likely to open up new career opportunities for yourself as well.

9. *Follow up on referrals in a professional manner.* If you don't you'll never get another reference from that person! If people you're referred to aren't interested in what you have to offer, thank them politely. If they aren't qualified for the position you're recruiting for, let them know respectfully. Obeying these simple rules of etiquette and others like them will help you maintain a solid, lasting network.

10. *Always deliver value.* People want to professionally network with others who can help them (don't you?). If you can offer something of value—an introduction, a bit of information, or some helpful advice—you'll have a much easier time becoming a part of your target

business community. Nobody wants to listen to a salesperson. Of course, there are times when selling is what you'll need to be doing. But the more you can find ways to deliver value to those in your network, the more respect for yourself you'll earn and the more results you'll see from it.

If you enjoy making friends and talking to lots of people, then you've certainly chosen the right profession. Every expert we've talked to agrees that networking is the single most important activity for any recruiter to pursue. It's a far better way to find candidates than posting on job boards, even better than much-touted Internet search techniques.

Get out there and start building a strong network today, and we guarantee your hiring managers, clients, and even your own career will benefit immensely.

Reversing the Brain Drain: Strategies to Bridge the Corporate Recruiting Skills Gap

Mike Foster
CEO, AIRS

Overview

Technology can move digits and documents, but it can't find, evaluate, and sell your company's value proposition to top performers with the precise skills, experience, and cultural perspectives you need; only well trained, articulate recruiters and managers can do that.

As a result, the quality of the people you attract to your organization is often a simple function of the skill, professionalism, and character of your recruiting and interviewing teams. A corporate recruiter is often the first point of contact for many of your prospects—and whether it's fair or not, a strong perception of your company will be shaped by that recruiter's professional behavior.

So, how sharp are they? How knowledgeable? How skilled in the really critical recruiting competencies—not placing ads, searching job boards, or sorting through resumes, but rather building relationships and networks and being a strong and attractive sales representative for your organization and culture?

After two years of downsizing, do you have enough skilled recruiters tucked away to train the next generation fast enough? As importantly, do they have the right skills today? This essay looks forward to a market where corporate recruiters are scarce, and real recruiting skills are even scarcer. It urges HR and recruiting leaders to take stock, evaluate their options, and act now to rebuild and retool. It also offers a snapshot of the skills corporate recruiters must acquire to roll back third-party fees, speed up the cycle, and hire the very best people going forward.

Recruiting Knowledge Will Be the Next Killer App

As human resources and recruitment leaders brace themselves for the next wave of the talent wars, employers are in danger of repeating one of the most expensive lessons of the last boom.

The current economic downdraft notwithstanding, experts agree that the dominant business problem over the next two decades will be talent acquisition—not an excess of unqualified applicants. Just over the trailing edge of the current recession is a steep labor shortage that will rival or outstrip the competitive market of the late 1990s. Yet, most companies today are focusing on the short-term pain of an overabundance of candidates—while their hard-won recruiting knowledge evaporates.

Over the next 36 months, the market will rebound, the two million or so downsized job seekers will be reabsorbed, and many employers will be exactly where they started a decade ago. They will have new, state-of-the-art applicant tracking systems—but no applicants to track. Worse, they will have lost a knowledge base of creative recruiting experience they paid dearly for in the previous candidate shortage.

Today, more than 60 percent of the 30,000 recruiters who attended AIRS training between 1998 and 2001 have simply disappeared. As they are being laid off, these experienced corporate recruiters are not moving to similar jobs with third-party firms—they are leaving the recruiting profession entirely. In fact, as their clients downsize, search firms are shedding tens of thousands of experienced recruiters, too.

What will happen when the cycle returns from bust to boom? The companies best positioned to aggregate the best talent fastest and at the lowest cost will leap forward again, while their competitors scramble to keep up. And that means a deep bench of experienced, well-trained recruiters will soon replace automated resume filtering as the most important link in your recruiting chain.

Are you investing in experienced recruitment professionals now, at the bottom of the market, and/or equipping your remaining recruiters with new skills? You should be. The alternative is familiar to those who rode the last wave down in the late 1980s, and back up again over the next decade. Starting now, the killer app is recruitment training. It is time to get ready for the next wave—and to craft recruiting strategies that keep your staffing costs and time to hire as low as possible, for as long as possible through the next upswing.

Protect Your Knowledge Base

When we began to teach AIRS e-recruiting techniques to early adopters like Microsoft, Cisco, and Amazon.com back in 1997, most employers could not fathom the idea that they would actually recruit from their competitors in an open marketplace. That doesn't mean they never approached people who worked for their competitors—it simply means they used third-party recruiters to do it for them.

This paradigm is one of the reasons employers threw hundreds of millions of dollars in fees at third-party search firms in the early 1990s. These employers saw their recruiting costs explode, as job seekers disappeared, newspaper ads became irrelevant, and more job openings were handed off to contingency and retained search firms every month. It took several years for many companies to realize that competitors were eating their lunch—and that as they paid search firms big fees to find candidates one at a time, they were losing ground to companies that aggressively fielded their own recruiting teams.

The first wave of Internet-ready corporate recruiters focused on developing mass candidate pools through job postings, augmented with active search where necessary. Their mission was to replace with the company's own candidate funnel the huge numbers of middle-tier openings that were being filled by third-party recruiters. The employers who moved fastest and most creatively were very successful—and this model resulted in much lower costs and a faster hiring cycle.

In the process, these employers also learned a series of valuable lessons, including:

- The power of a strong employment brand—and how to establish one.
- How to turn a simple career center into a 24/7, always-on recruiting platform.
- Which recruiting functions to centralize, and which should be locally driven.
- How to lower job posting costs by working with niche boards and communities.
- How to use advanced Internet search tools.
- How to organize, staff, and equip sourcing and search teams.
- To quickly screen, test, and assess candidates on the Web.
- To link sourcing, search, applicant tracking, and hiring into a smooth work flow.
- How to build candidate communities for just-in-time recruiting.

If your company has already paid the price to absorb these and other key recruiting lessons, don't let that knowledge slip away. Although they've downsized considerably, market-leading companies like Dell Computer, Sapient, Siemens, and Cisco are redeploying key recruitment leaders, to be reactivated when the time comes. In fact, Corning has deployed its recruiters as outplacement specialists—not only to help departing workers, but also as a creative way to encourage boomerang hires.

It's important to keep the DNA of your corporate recruiting team intact, so it can grow again—or invest now to learn the basics, if you haven't already. Bottom line: Your company will have three options to keep pace with your hiring needs once the market turns. First, use more third-party recruiters; second, outsource your hiring completely; or third, retrain and grow your own staff again, quickly.

The Expertise to Find the Best Candidates

By the end of the last boom, there was really only one recruiting imperative: Find more candidates. As a result, most recruiters who joined the workforce after 1997 were taught to do that, and only that.

An entire generation of recruiters has been trained to post jobs on the big job boards, and search resume banks every day looking for new job seekers. That's a great way to find commodity candidates (most companies are experiencing the dark side of that strategy now, as they battle their way through a flood of ridiculously unqualified resumes coming from the same big boards today), but no way to find great people.

The best people are hidden away inside your competitors' companies. They are being treated very well and have no reason to leave. That's your recruiter's job—give them a reason to leave! If your own staff isn't savvy enough to find them or articulate enough to sell them, then you'll have to pay a 30 percent premium for a third-party recruiter to do it for you—or simply settle for lesser contributors.

In the next cycle, the brightest companies already understand that their staff recruiters must acquire the next level of headhunting expertise. To deliver quality—in other words, to find, assess, attract, and hire the best people—corporate recruiters need to develop better skills across the entire recruitment life cycle.

Headhunting Skills for Corporate Recruiters

As AIRS consultants help our corporate clients prepare for recruiting in the next wave, similar areas of weakness commonly appear. It's interesting that many recruiters are conversant with Internet recruiting tactics, yet are unclear that recruitment is not merely mining data and processing resumes; it is sales. And that their sales objectives should be to find, vet, and persuade top performers to join the team. Today, it is essential to strengthen these basic recruiting skills, in order to close better candidates and break free of third-party fees.

CANDIDATE DEFINITION

There is a sense of mistrust and tension between recruiters and hiring managers in many organizations. The managers report being irritated by the high number of unqualified candidates forwarded to them, and recruiters are frustrated in their attempts to understand what the manager really wants.

This problem cuts both ways, of course, but it is ultimately the corporate recruiter's responsibility to understand the needs of the client (the manager) sufficiently to deliver the right candidate the first time—not just pass along resumes that look close. In so doing, the recruiter will create trust by truly solving the manager's problem, instead of unwittingly creating more work and confusion for them.

The best third-party recruiters take pride in the fact that they can deliver the one or two candidates who will be a solid fit, every time—a skill that impresses busy managers, and compels them to take their searches outside.

Much of the professional headhunters' success has to do with the diligence of their initial profiling process and the fact that they invest significant effort in defining the manager's needs and the attributes a candidate must bring to the table to answer them. This is a complex process, and most corporate recruiters (and the recruiting systems that support them) simply don't apply the discipline or allocate the time to mine and assimilate the most important characteristics of the search, up front.

NETWORKING AND PHONE SKILLS

Headhunters rely on their networks to generate leads, candidates, and hires. Though recruiters today have access to a free database of 350 million people on the Internet, nothing beats a personal network of friends, associates, and acquaintances who are motivated to help.

Networks are built on communication and trust—the more you communicate, the stronger the trust. But today, many recruiters pluck names from the Net, send a bulk e-mail, and call it a day, because that's how they've been trained to reach a mass audience. Headhunting the best candidates is best done one contact at a time, over the phone. To reach and build relationships with the right people, many corporate recruiters need to be retrained to use their headsets and grow their interpersonal skills.

SOURCING

There are over 40,000 niche job boards and communities filled with candidates on the Web, yet 85 percent of corporate recruiters are competing with each other every day for job seekers at the three major boards.

Why? Mostly because it's easier than tracking down, testing, and measuring hard-to-find, sometimes sketchy niche boards—and because many recruiters equate a high number of resumes with recruiting success. Well, there certainly are a lot of resumes at the big boards.

But a small percentage of savvy recruiters are tapping into a much larger pool of great passive candidates on the Net. Corporate recruiters need to learn how to break away from the crowds and stop trying to find a hundred candidates at once. Instead, find one or two really great candidates in niche boards; then use networking skills to meet their friends and coworkers.

GETTING TO THE HIDDEN CANDIDATE

The best candidates aren't in any job boards, of course, because they're not looking for a job. In order to find them, recruiters must be able to get into the company, get past the gatekeepers, and ring right into their office or cubicle.

Many headhunters still accomplish this by fooling the front desk into thinking they are an employee from another office or an old family friend, and then calling every desk they can in an attempt to map the company. Another common tactic is to rely on black market company directories for this information.

But corporate recruiters can aggressively headhunt, using ethical strategies and information widely available in the public domain. Any good researcher can build an organization chart with names, titles, and phone extensions right from the Web. Why run from cubicle to cubicle, when you can simply find your candidate's direct line on the Net?

QUALIFICATION AND ASSESSMENT

This stage is the complement to deeply understanding the hiring manager's needs. To make a match the first time, the recruiter must be certain that the candidate is qualified in all respects, will fit well in the culture (and on the manager's team), and is eager and excited to join the company.

Headhunters are trained to move quickly through a pack of prospects, keeping them all interested, while they methodically sort, sift, and zero in on the very best one. The ability to triage quickly and make accurate decisions about a candidate's value and motivations is critical in the recruiting process.

CONSULTATIVE SALES SKILLS

Recruiting is sales, whether you are on a corporate staff or in a search firm. In fact, it is one of the most rigorous sales jobs anywhere. As a result, third-party recruiters are steeped in sales lore and taught to build networks, position their client, and sell the opportunity—or move on quickly to new prospects.

Sales fundamentals, such as goal setting, personal motivation, time management, cold calling, relationship development, and problem solving are critical requirements for all recruiters. But the most important sales skills are critical examination and listening. These techniques help recruiters better understand their internal client's priorities and match them to success factors in the candidate.

Unlike headhunters, surprisingly few corporate recruiters regard themselves as true salespeople. This is a nonproductive attitude from the days when in-house recruiters placed ads and hired search firms, but never actively recruited anyone themselves. To be competitive moving forward, corporate recruiters must learn to listen, articulate your company's vision, and persuade the right people to sign up for the ride. In short—sell!

What Happened to Internet Recruitment?

Internet recruiting has evolved to include a broad palette of activities—from building an employment brand to building a recruiting web site, and from posting jobs to searching for passive candidates on the Web. Internet recruiting is a mainstream activity today, and should be baseline knowledge for all recruiters.

But the Internet is simply a tool set that can streamline, automate, and accelerate your recruiting process, for better or worse. If you recruit badly, now you can recruit badly even faster.

At AIRS we believe tools should be selected to leverage your recruiting objectives, not the other way around. That means if your objectives are to acquire the very best people possible, rather than lots more people faster, you may have to reevaluate how you are using the Net. Do job boards really serve this purpose?

In any case, it's time for corporate recruiters to integrate the lessons they've learned about e-recruiting with the more fundamental relationship-building, networking, and sales skills that headhunters have been refining for decades. As we look forward to the next wave of labor shortage, these skills can be a powerful lever to move us toward lower costs and better staffing.

CHAPTER

13

A Primer on Internet Recruiting

Tony Lee

Editor in Chief and General Manager,
The Wall Street Journal Online Network

It crosses geographic boundaries, reaches millions of job candidates, and works at the speed of technology. The Internet, in theory, should be one of the recruiting industry's finest tools. And yet studies show that Internet recruiting is difficult to master. Some recruiters are achieving no better than a 4 percent to 8 percent return when sourcing candidates online, a statistic that would surely cost them their jobs if it were the sole criterion on which they were judged.

The challenge to using this dynamic medium is to take advantage of its strengths and overcome its weaknesses. While the Internet is a valuable tool, viewing it simply as a tool is insufficient and may only increase, instead of streamline, your workload. Consider what happened in Denver, Colorado. Hoping to build on an already successful web site, the city government decided to ask candidates to apply online for jobs. Initially, it appeared to be a great success; the number of online job applications boosted the candidate pool by 33 percent. But the only change Denver made was to collect applications online; there were no additional mechanisms in place to process them, and the online applications were simply printed out and routed the same way as all other applications. The result was an increased workload without an increase in staff or a change in processing, which soon overburdened the human resources department.

Instead of using the Internet to simply automate traditional recruiting, an Internet recruiting program must be well planned and executed, from initial posting to final offer. And if done so effectively, its potential could be staggering. In the United States alone, approximately 133 million adults (66 percent of the adult population) have access to the Internet at work or at home. And that's a lot of potential candidates for your Internet job pool.

Objectives, Strategies, and Process

The objectives of an Internet recruiting campaign are the same as a traditional program: reach, inform, and attract job candidates. What the Internet adds, however, is speed and ease of use. Therefore, its specific objectives are to reach more qualified candidates in expanded geographic areas, to communicate meaningful information faster, and to ultimately attract a more talented pool.

There are multiple strategies for reaching these objectives, and these vary depending on corporate philosophy. Recruiters can post open positions to job boards large and small, general and niche. They can use search engines to scour the Web, tapping into resume databases and bulletin boards for candidates who may meet their requirements. They also can develop their own web sites to advertise jobs, promote their companies, and accept online applications.

These strategies must be supported by a communications system that prompts timely processing and follow-through. For instance, the Internet can be programmed to automatically e-mail a generic response to candidates who submit online job applications; due to the nature of the medium, online candidates often expect fast responses. Online technology can also be used to check references, set up job interviews, and review company policies with potential candidates. In-house, intranet strategies and resources can help track candidates and issue internal reports on how many have applied per job. Resumes and applications can be quickly routed to appropriate people, and the hiring process can be prompt.

Advantages and Success Stories

The Employment Management Association has calculated the average cost per hire in Internet recruiting at $377, while print ad recruiting averaged $3,295. This dramatic difference is obviously a success of the medium. But it's not the only success.

The Internet offers recruiters the opportunity to find the ideal job seeker—namely, the passive candidate who is happily employed but willing to consider a better opportunity if it emerges. In essence, the Internet is a remarkable tool for career self-management. For the first time, employees can take control and chart their own course in a career, at their own pace.

Consider the case of a chief financial officer working at a Chicago-based manufacturer. The CFO frequently visits online sites to review news reports, trends in his industry, sports updates, and new job listings in his field. When asked why he reviewed job listings even though he was satisfied in his job, he explained that it's for the same reasons he looks at listings for vacation homes and sports cars for sale: It's fun, and may eventually lead to something real.

One day, an online job agent created by the CFO on CareerJournal.com delivered a particularly interesting job listing via e-mail. The CFO researched the company's information, and then decided to apply for the job. In less than a month, he was interviewed by the company's recruiters and top managers, was offered the job, and accepted this different CFO position that offered better opportunities for future growth and compensation. And the total cost to the company for sourcing him online had been minimal.

Challenges, Developments, and Trends

The future of Internet recruiting is bright. It will be an integral part of standard candidate searches, and will continue to save companies time, effort, and recruiting dollars. A few of the key trends to expect in the next few years include:

- Reviewing candidate skills and interests online will evolve into a more sophisticated model. There will be better prescreening, and hence more efficient hiring.
- As the Internet evolves, online applications will become the norm and will be used instead of fax or postal mail.

- As Internet access spreads among diverse populations, and federal oversight strengthens, recruiting minority candidates will gain even greater focus. In addition, companies will recruit wherever the talent is, despite potential language barriers in foreign countries.
- There will be more niche recruiting sites online. As recruiters target their online searches more effectively, the sites that attract specific audiences will gain in popularity.
- Legal protections will intensify, forcing companies to modify how they collect and keep candidate background data. This will limit access to such data for recruiters.
- Demographics will continue to play a role in the importance of Internet recruiting, as the leading edge of the baby boomers turns 55 this year and the shortage of 20-somethings entering the workforce continues.

Conclusion

The Internet must be manipulated carefully to produce efficient recruiting results. As with any emerging technology, becoming educated about the resource will help you use it to your best advantage. As Internet use continues to grow, however, simply using the Internet doesn't set your company apart from the thousands of others recruiting there, and having an online presence doesn't present a competitive advantage. The determining factor will be the quality of your online presence, and the professional approach you use to interact with potential candidates.

Despite its technology focus, the Internet is inherently a human activity. If you let this focus drive your recruiting activities, you will see results.

14

Integrating e-Recruiting and HR Processes

Bernard J. Cullen

Partner, Cambria Consulting

Overview

The first Internet-driven revolution in HR is over, but the real one has only just begun. At last count, 91 percent of *Fortune*'s Global 500 companies have an e-recruiting page on their corporate web sites. The first revolution—putting recruiting and career sections on the Internet—is over. The real revolution—building fully integrated HR processes—is just coming into focus.

While most large companies have career pages on their web sites, there are huge differences in how e-recruiting has been implemented by different companies. The Corporate Executive Board, an organization of senior executives who pursue innovative business strategies, conducted an excellent review of employment web site features and noted:

Like all online phenomena, employment web sites have undergone a rapid evolution. In fact, the speed of their elevation from "nice to have" is paralleled only by the rate at which their users have grown more sophisticated, leading to the rise of a "second generation" of employment web site development.

They go on to note that employment web sites are key elements in the ongoing "war for talent":

In practice, this means that the employment web site is now both an opportunity and a threat: companies that "get it right" can gain much-needed leverage in the "war for talent," while companies that provide an inferior online employment experience will differentiate them negatively.

Companies have been busily trying to ensure that their employment sites are competitive. When we first looked at 131 employment sites in 2000, we noted the following best practices:

- A design that emphasizes accessibility, logic, ease of navigation, and visual appeal.
- Availability of background information on the company and work environment.
- Clear, concise, and compelling job descriptions.
- Search tools that facilitate the rapid search of available job opportunities.
- Flexible and easy-to-use mechanisms for sending resumes.
- Ability to apply online for specific positions.
- A "job cart" that enables candidates to apply for more than one job at a time.
- Tools to help candidates prepare resumes.

Since 2000, many of these features have been integrated into the more powerful software packages and, in turn, implemented on many companies' employment web sites. Most of these improvements represent technical fixes that make it easier for candidates to use employment sites.

This candidate-centric focus assumes that the war for talent has the same dimensions that it had during the tight labor market of the late 1990s. The market has changed, though, and the nature of the war for talent has shifted. We now need a more balanced and holistic perspective on the scope of e-recruiting.

That means employment web sites must now be more than candidate friendly. They must also provide significant process enhancements to reduce the burden on recruiters of being inundated with thousands of qualified and unqualified applications. The problem of sourcing candidates has expanded to include the screening and assessment of candidates. (See Exhibit 14.1 for an overview of the recruiting and selection process.) At this point, those responsible for employment web sites still have to be ready to incorporate and customize the latest innovations visible on the best e-commerce sites, namely eBay, Amazon, Orbitz, and so on. In addition, they must also be prepared to tackle the much tougher issues of developing viable application, screening, and assessment tools and integrating them into the recruiting and selection process.

One best practice that has not experienced widespread adoption is the improvement of job descriptions. As noted in Exhibit 14.1, effective job descriptions are part of the requisition process step, an earlier phase of the selection and recruiting process. Our contention is that the slow introduction of more effective job descriptions reflects significant structural issues within HR that will need to be addressed before this best practice can be implemented. These structural issues include the organizational separation (i.e., silos) of HR processes and the lack of standard methods and frameworks for evaluating jobs and individuals that are common across different HR processes. For example, there are few companies that use the same set of individual attributes or competencies for selection, performance management, staffing, succession planning, and development. The slow development of more powerful screening and selection tools reflects these same structural issues and the technical (plus legal) challenge of creating valid, candidate-friendly assessment tools.

Integrating these new advances into the recruiting and selection process will have significant ramifications for both recruiting and selection and for other HR processes, especially performance management, succession planning, and assignment processes. Ultimately, the building of more technology-enabled recruiting and selection processes will precipitate the need for fully integrated HR processes.

We will use the evolution of e-recruiting tools and the need to develop more effective job descriptions to make three basic points:

1. The development of application, screening, and assessment tools will force companies to come to grips with the complex task of systematically defining jobs and job requirements. This will require developing

Process Step	Function and Focus	e-Recruiting Processes Implications
Requisition	Identification of position requirements, documentation of key hiring parameters, and planning of recruiting and hiring process.	Requisitioning processes largely focused on meeting administrative requirements (i.e., form completion). Fully enabled process requires high-quality job descriptions. Quality of job description dependent on quality of interaction between recruiter and hiring manager.
Sourcing	Locating, attracting, and encouraging applications from qualified candidates.	To date, key focus is on branding employment site and making it candidate friendly. Major outstanding issue is quality of job descriptions.
Application	Gathering of critical information from qualified candidates.	Largely resume-based with limited number of qualifying questions. Few companies require completion of online assessment tools as part of application process. Most application forms designed independently of HRIS information requirements.
Screening	Identification of applicants who are technically and administratively qualified and who have realistic salary and job expectations.	Screening either manual or via key word searches of resumes. Some sites have used simple self-assessment procedures to provide more powerful sorting mechanisms.
Assessment	Evaluation and ranking of candidates in terms of technical skills and competencies.	Non-U.S. sites have introduced online tests to evaluate basic skills. These types of tests can trigger legal issues in the United States. Assessment still primarily through face-to-face interviews. Some effort to automate interviews as initial assessment step.
Checking	Verification of key employment information and capabilities by former supervisors/colleagues.	Numerous packages exist to provide background checks. Possible to generate e-mail reference checks, where references supply standard information.
Offer	Generation and positioning of competitive employment offers compatible with existing HR policies and procedures.	Most packages provide for some automated generation of offer letters and tools to track responses.

Exhibit 14.1 Recruiting and Selection Process.

approaches and tools that allow the unique aspects of a job to be specified within a well-defined framework that is in ways employer and candidate friendly. For most companies, their approaches to generating job descriptions will be inadequate.

2. The integration of these tools into an organization's recruiting and selection process will have major implications for those responsible for making selection decisions. Until now, the Internet has largely changed only recruiter and candidate behavior, whereas the next generation of online tools will affect recruiter and hiring manager behavior in far more fundamental ways.

3. Technology-enabling recruiting and selection processes beyond the sourcing of candidates will have significant implications for other HR processes. In the 1980s, the introduction of standard accounting packages and the technology enabling of different finance functions inevitably led to the introduction of Enterprise Resource Planning (ERP) and the reengineering and integration of financial and nonfinancial business processes. Today, HR and recruiting and selection processes are just complex and pervasive enough to trigger the reintegration of core HR processes.

We can illustrate these three points by examining the nature of current Internet job descriptions and the implications of what happens when the generation of these job descriptions themselves is technology enabled.

Job Descriptions in an Internet World

Ideally, recruiting and selection processes should access preexisting job descriptions. However, in most companies—even those with the latest ERP-level software packages from software developers like SAP and PeopleSoft—suitable job descriptions do not exist. As a result, recruiters tend to write and rewrite job descriptions for recruiting as openings occur. The resulting job descriptions frequently contribute little to making the recruiting and selection process more efficient or effective.

Effective job descriptions for recruiting and selection have distinctive characteristics. These characteristics hold whether we are describing job descriptions in *The Wall Street Journal*, an Internet job board, or a company's internal job posting site.

- Clear and widely recognized job titles.
- Accurate descriptions of what candidates are expected to do.
- Requirements that allow or even require unqualified candidates to quickly screen themselves out.
- Requirements that allow recruiters and hiring managers to sort candidates into fully, partially, and unqualified categories.
- Reusable content: similar jobs have similar job descriptions.
- Concise but including all relevant information.
- Compelling but realistic.
- Standard but flexible format.

Many job descriptions on the Internet do not meet these standards. In 2001, as part of an extended analysis of corporate recruiting web sites, we actually evaluated the quality of job descriptions from 245 global recruiting web sites. For this study, we based our evaluation on four criteria:

1. *Clear job titles*. Job titles that immediately communicate the content of jobs and make them sound attractive.
2. *Complete job requirements*. Clearly stated requirements (including travel) that allow candidates to quickly determine if they are qualified or are interested in the position.
3. *Concrete description of tasks*. Easy-to-read, well-organized concrete descriptions of responsibilities and actual tasks. Clear indicators of the level or type of experience needed.
4. *Compelling description*. Description that emphasizes key benefits and attractions of job and company.

These ratings were combined to give an overall rating, with "Effective" defined as fully meeting three of the four criteria, "OK" defined as having no problematic ratings on any criteria, and "Problematic" defined as having one or more problematic ratings.

Our ratings, summarized in Exhibit 14.2, indicated that:

- Few companies (roughly 11 percent) appear to fully meet at least three of the four criteria.

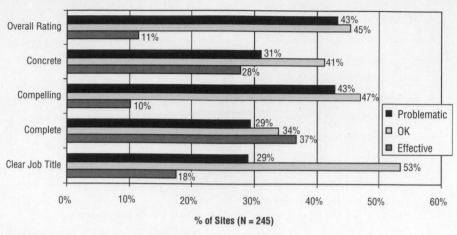

Exhibit 14.2   e-Recruiting Job Descriptions.

- Nearly 43 percent of companies have significant problems in at least one area.
- Few companies (10 percent) provide compelling job descriptions, with many job descriptions being too vague and/or too long to be useful.

Case Examples

Actual examples from the Internet will illustrate that this situation probably has not changed in the past 15 months. Exhibit 14.3 is a commodity manager job description from one of the most highly rated recruiting sites powered by one of the most sophisticated software packages.

What is quickly apparent is that this particular job description is not helpful to candidates, recruiters, or hiring managers. The job title, at a minimum, is confusing to individuals doing exactly the same job at IBM, HP, Sun, Dell, or Cisco. Much of the job description focuses on what the company does in general, not what the job involves. The single paragraph labeled "job description" is incomprehensible—it is completely context free. Does it make a difference what types of process improvements are being considered? The list of requirements boils down to whether or not the candidate has ISM or APICS certification, has a bachelor's degree,

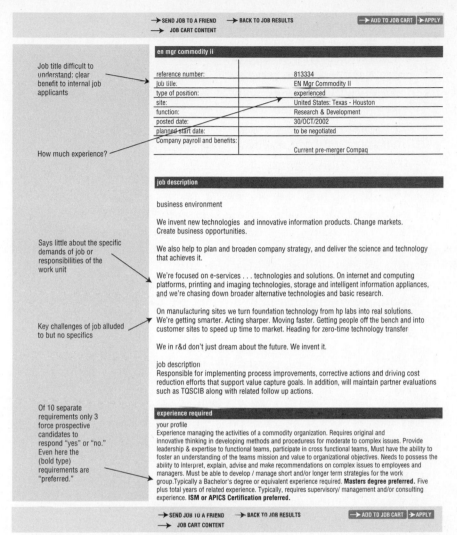

Exhibit 14.3 Sample Job Description.

and has been working for five years. Few candidates who meet these requirements will see themselves as not capable of "original and innovative thinking," providing "leadership & expertise to functional teams," or being "able to develop/manage short and/or longer term strategies." The mind boggles at the range of resumes that this job description is likely to generate.

Equally importantly, what tools and process created this job description? It is hard to imagine the conversation between the hiring manager and recruiter that could have produced it. Clearly, there was no basic template here, yet the process of building compelling job descriptions simply cries out for a standard procedure. Practically speaking, it makes sense to build a library or database of job descriptions that hiring managers and recruiters can customize to meet the specific needs of a particular position and be the basis for screening and assessing candidates.

Contrast the first job description with one for what appears to be a similar job in Exhibit 14.4. It meets far more of our criteria for a good job description, though it could certainly be less wordy and more compelling. Nevertheless, it is a significant improvement over the first example and serves to illustrate that there is an underlying structure for effective job descriptions. With a few edits, this job description could be reused for any commodity manager position at the company. Moreover, it could be constructed from a template that asks the hiring manager to simply state:

- Key technical knowledge and skills, including methods and processes and associated level of expertise.
- Key activities and experience level with each.
- Key indicators of scope of responsibility (e.g., dollars under control and number of people directly supervised).

Exhibit 14.5 illustrates a position requirements form based on the second job description. The requirements could be amended to reflect specific requirements of any commodity-related job at the company. (See, for example, the items in italics.) With a few standard phrases and grammar rules, this completed form could be translated automatically into a job description for an employment web page. Note that this form could, in fact, be used by the hiring manager at the first company and the same basic template could be used for a wide range of positions. These types of tools and libraries of job descriptions already exist and are certainly not hard to build. They simply have not become part of the recruiter's toolbox, in large measure because writing job descriptions is the responsibility of another function within HR for most large companies.

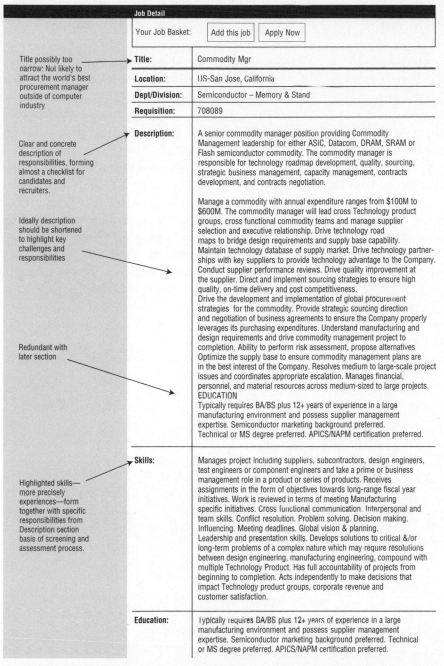

Exhibit 14.4 Sample Job Description.

Implications

A framework like the one presented in Exhibit 14.5 has implications beyond the construction of more effective job descriptions.

First, it provides a basis for screening potential candidates. A number of e-recruiting packages already offer the option of asking candidates to self-assess on key skill areas. The addition of this functionality to an application process will permit recruiters to automatically sort through large number of applicants and resumes, verify the accuracy of self-assessments, and generate lists of technically qualified candidates. This is a far more powerful sorting device than key word matches.

Second, this type of explicit requirements process supplies recruiters with a procedure for ensuring that hiring managers provide realistic assessments of what is actually required to fill a job. At the same time, recruiters receive a more concrete understanding of what the job requires. This is no small achievement. Our experience is that recruiters have a difficult time getting hiring managers to sit down and think through how best to fill an open position. Exhibit 14.3 is a perfect illustration of what happens when hiring managers and recruiters fail to think through what a position actually entails. Whether face-to-face or via the Web, recruiters can increase the involvement of managers in systematically and concretely defining job requirements.

Third, the explicit nature of position requirements and target skill levels and the virtual deconstruction of a position establishes the focus for assessing technically qualified candidates. Using our commodity manager example, those involved in the hiring decision need to determine what candidates actually did when they "evaluated suppliers" and how they did it. Did they demonstrate the competencies referred to in the original job description (cross-functional communication, interpersonal and team skills, conflict resolution, problem solving, decision making, influencing, meeting deadlines, global vision and planning, leadership and presentation skills)? Note that these competencies or individual attributes are not part of Exhibit 14.5. They are superfluous to a job description or screening process based on self-assessments because individuals are unlikely to realistically or accurately rate themselves on these qualities. However, they should be part of the discussion with the hiring manager and definitely should be specifically identified in order to ensure an effective job/person match.

Requisition #: *708089*
Position: *Commodity Procurement*
Level: *Manager*

Part 1: Technical Skills and Experience

Instructions

The following represent a set of technical skills and work experiences that have been found useful for this role. Some of the skills and experiences are not directly relevant but make it easier for someone to acquire the core technical skills and experience. Add and rate other specific skills and the requirements you believe are particularly relevant for this position. Please rate the level of skills needed for the open position. Candidates will not be strong or have experience in all areas.

Ads and screening interviews will be based on this information. Please be realistic with your ratings.

Skills Rating: *Please use the following rating scale.*
1. No or minimal experience.
2. Familiar with basics—formal training in area and/or less then 12 months' experience.
3. Moderate (12 plus months) experience completing various assignments under others' supervision.
4. Extensive (more than 3 years) experience completing difficult assignments with little supervision.
5. Expert—sought out by others to identify and solve complex or unusual problems with no supervision.

Knowledge and Skills		Methods and Processes		Activities	
ASIC	4	Developing technology road maps	4	Coordinate requirements of multiple commodity teams	4
Datacom	4	Defining technical and quality requirements	4	Evaluate suppliers	5
DRAM	4	Planning and managing capacity	3	Procure commodities on global basis	4
SRAM	4	Formulating and negotiating multi-year contracts	3	Manage suppliers to achieve delivery and quality requirements	5
Flash Memory	4	Building and maintaining commodity databases	3	Resolve conflicts between manufacturing and design requirements	5
		Assessing and managing risks *including foreign exchange*	4	*Implement major process improvement*	4

Education and Certifications		Related Experiences	
Bachelor's degree	**Yes/** No	Managed budgets > $100M	4
Relevant master's degree	**Yes/** No	Manage project teams > 25	3
APICS/NAPM certified	**Yes/** No	Extensive global travel	3

Exhibit 14.5   Position Requirements Form or Template.

And fourth, the job descriptions developed for recruiting and selection have implicit linkages to other HR processes including staffing, succession planning and promotions, performance management, compensation, and training and development. *This* is why the effective implementation of a technology-enabled selection and recruiting process is so significant. Technology that enables the recruiting and selection process can act as a catalyst for driving the introduction of tools and processes that create standard job descriptions, which in turn will confront HR organizations with the need to reintegrate its different functions.

This is the real revolution.

CHAPTER

15

When Less Is More: Eight Basic Essentials You Must Know about HR Business Process Outsourcing

Bruce Ferguson

Vice President, Talent Acquisition Solution, Exult, Inc.

Overview

It's ironic. As the staffing function continues to build prominence and attract both respect and interest among stakeholders as a promising factor in the company's competitive strategy, it has also become a target for those who would say, "Okay, let's see how much more you can get done with just a little (or significantly) less in your budget next year (or quarter)." Now that staffing is finally being acknowledged for its strategic potential, it's also feeling the added pressure of performing to and even beyond its limits.

In response, HR executives are increasingly turning to a fundamental principle that has its roots in basic evolutionary theory: specialization—letting those who do it best and most efficiently do it. That way you can save *your* energy and resources for those activities that *you* do best. You get to have more, with less direct, personal involvement—and less investment. Since the dawn of time, species have been discovering that the more they share the job of surviving and thriving with others with the necessary specialized skills, the more smoothly their world runs. And each creature gets the aggregated benefit without having to work quite so hard. In other words, get more benefit with less investment. Sound familiar?

While Charles Darwin certainly never heard of business process outsourcing (BPO), the great naturalist himself would probably appreciate the elegance of the practice's response to the evolving business environment. The principle is basic: Devote your resources, attention, and talent to what you're expert at and what keeps you thriving (your core business). And then pass on the more tangential—yet essential—activities to the professionals who specialize in those. The objectives are met or exceeded (whether it is survival of the species or business viability and profitability), and the entire ecosystem is well taken care of and healthy, with extreme efficiency and very little waste.

There are, obviously, many differences between the specialization of species that evolve over millennia and business management innovations that evolve over the span of, say, a decade. For the purposes of this chapter one of the most important distinctions is that the participants of business evolution can actually impose a mindful approach to taking full advantage of all the new possibilities that business process outsourcing offers the organization. With evolution we have to work with what we get. With business process outsourcing, we have the power to make what we get work to its greatest potential—namely, enhancing HR capital productivity, reducing HR costs, and providing superior HR services—all achievable through specialization.

Another distinction between business process outsourcing and evolution is that by and large evolution isn't generally subject to criticism. Again, we get what we get. But the practice of outsourcing has attracted a small amount of critical commentary based primarily on a lack of understanding of how outsourcing promotes the vigor of the core business. To relinquish day-to-day control over the minutiae that come as part of company's people function does not mean you also give up control over the quality of service or the expense associated with providing your valued employees with great service. Early adopters of business process outsourcing were among the first to discover that outsourcing HR services to the experts provides those quality and expense benefits, all the while releasing the HR function to join the rest of the company in doing what it should have been doing all along: contributing to the organization's core business. And, because there is a single point of accountability between the corporate client and the outsourcer, the client still maintains the ultimate power—while letting go of the day-to-day details.

In a January 2002 report entitled "Business Process Outsourcing at the Crossroads," Rebecca Scholl wrote,

> The BPO market continues to show strong growth despite the economic downturn. Worldwide, BPO will grow from $119 billion in 2000 to $234 billion in 2005, at a 14.4 percent compound annual growth rate (CAGR) . . . the strong growth will pick up in 2003 as a new wave of "megadeals" is announced and as the midmarket begins to adopt the BPO model. BPO adoption will accelerate as providers begin to offer cheaper, more standardized, Web-based business services following the business service provider (BSP) model.

Terming the U.S. labor market as the nation's largest and quite possibly the least efficiently administered market, a November 2002 study from Wachovia Securities estimates that the administrative costs are between $1,300 and $1,600 per employee, totaling more than $244 billion annually. As companies experience the combined pressures of competitive staffing (attracting and retaining essential talent in volatile economic and demographic times) and the need to make every dollar of every investment perform, Wachovia predicts that business process outsourcing will become an increasingly important component in a company's human capital management (HCM) plan: "We project that the growing trend toward outsourcing noncore HR functions will accelerate as companies seek to not only save on expenses, but also seek to free HR resources to address areas of strategic importance. We believe that successful companies will try to upgrade their HCM systems in a manner that is similar to how companies upgraded their manufacturing, supply chain, and customer relationship management (CRM) systems." (Wachovia Securities, *A Guide to the Approaching Boom in Human Capital Solutions*, Second Edition, 2002.)

Because business process outsourcing is still very much an emerging HR management tool, its potential is at this point not completely understood by the HR community overall. So in this chapter I have outlined the basic knowledge you must have about outsourcing so that you can take control over its ultimate value to your company's objectives, even to your own career.

Business Process Outsourcing Responds to a Company's Big-Picture Strategic Initiatives

HR decision makers who dismiss business process outsourcing as merely a tactical decision are missing the most important aspect of the value that outsourcing can bring to an organization. As we've already established, outsourcing allows the company to focus on its core business: what services *it* delivers to its clients and customers and what products *it* makes. Most companies are not expert at HR services, nor do they have the economy of scale that outsourcing services enjoy to provide the best array of HR services at the best possible cost—and in the most professional, consistent manner. So, at the very least, outsourcing this particular area frees up the company's time and intellectual capital to focus on what it really does best.

Additionally, world-class employers recognize that their reputation as being a great place to work supports their competitiveness. They can attract and keep great talent, which ultimately attracts even more great talent and provides great service and products. And, for their part, great and expert talent expects great and expert service. Outsourcing provides that great and expert service, delivered by professionals who are directly recognized and rewarded for the way they deliver *their* core business, which, in this case, is HR services.

Finally, the outsourcing company is your partner in productivity and profitability. In times of staffing uncertainties, when you must ramp up or ramp down at a moment's notice, scalability is a vital asset. Your outsourcing firm can respond to your staffing demands that may change as a result of acquisitions and/or divestitures. In fact, by outsourcing your HR business processes, you position yourself to be better able to retain your core talent, all the while keeping your employee service quality first-rate—and likely at a lower cost.

You can build flexibility into the contract to allow for ranges of volume, recognizing from one year to the next the business needs that will present themselves within that range. If it goes below or above a certain volume, there is a process in place to renegotiate the impact of those changes. The best relationships in outsourcing are partner relationships, rather than vendor relationships; therefore the conversation and the terms of the agreement should always be responsive to the moment and the future—not the past and mistaken predictions. There is no contract that will accommodate every contingency that comes along, for either side, but contracts can be designed with the necessary mechanisms to address unforeseen changes.

Business Process Outsourcing Supports the Company's Internal Branding Objectives

As the people contribution of a company has gained prominence over the past years—especially when the war for talent and the demand for innovation coincided—many of the most progressive companies concluded that it wasn't enough to just be a "best employer." It was also important to have a distinctive internal culture that truly set it apart from its competitors. For this reason, the skeptics have assumed that outsourcing the company's people function would condemn the company culture into a one-size-fits-all model, and that it would be impossible for an outsider to assume the highly tailored and unique cultural nuances of its client companies—that is, relating to their employees with that certain flavor and flair that uniquely represent the company's overall personality.

Even in the best of companies, however, those cultural nuances are designed primarily to support and celebrate the excellence of those employees who directly contribute to the core business. The support employees—especially those who can't be directly tied to a company's year-end profit/loss performance—continue to be treated like, well, back-office employees regardless of the company's much celebrated employee relations philosophy. Case in point: When was the last time you called payroll and thanked them for getting your check out on time and accurately?

When the internal branding message of a company is "all our employees are vital to our success," the outsourcing company can help the client employer demonstrate that value. The professionals hired by the outsourcing company provide excellent service to your valued employees. In its excellence, the service quality itself is a demonstration and reinforcement of the company's internal brand as best employer.

The best way an outsourcing company can help employee branding is by giving exceptional service and being as transparent as possible in the process. Outsourcing companies are capable of this and should be held to that standard.

Business Process Outsourcers Attract, Retain, and Train High-Quality Employees

Few would actually admit it, but employers, especially those whose staffing resources are stretched to the limit, may be tempted to undervalue support employees because they do not directly service the corporate profit imperative. And so, human nature being what it is, they are most at risk for downsized resources, training cutbacks, layoffs, and so on. That reduction in quality the service employees experience will eventually show up in lower quality of service the employer's core business employees will experience.

But for the outsourcing company, those service employees are the core business employees. No longer are they relegated to back-office status. In the outsourcing world, they are the much-valued revenue producers. And outsourcing companies use the more progressive and aggressive ways to attract, motivate, and promote those very people who may have once been undervalued or overlooked.

And their performance is measured accordingly. It's vital that the outsourcer's employees fully understand that they have moved from being in a support organization to being a *service delivery* organization. That requires an entirely different, almost entrepreneurial, mind-set. Not everyone can successfully make that transition. And it's up to the outsourcing company to be able to spot the ones who can versus the ones who can't.

The same expectations apply to the outsourcing organization as a whole. The outsourcing provider itself should be constantly testing the system to see if it delivers the same services better, faster, cheaper. The outsourcing company must subject itself to constant improvement. That's the way it provides the best array of services in a marketplace that's only going to become more competitive over the years.

Clients Retain Control over Quality and Efficiency

Critics will tell you that outsourcing is an unproven business model—empirical at best, at worst a sales job of empty promises polished to a high gloss. While the world of business process outsourcing continues to evolve and refine itself, we have been players of the outsourcing model since before we were even born when our parents outsourced prenatal care to a doctor. Our toys were outsourced to Hasbro and Mattel. Our education was outsourced to a variety of schools. And, now that we are adults, we outsource our entire food supply to a central source of quality control, services, and supply—and at a substantially lower expense of time, effort, and potential failure should we be forced to grow, harvest, and butcher everything in our backyards. The neighborhood supermarket: Such is the beauty of outsourcing.

That's an outsourcing model we're familiar—and therefore comfortable—with. And even with this consumer-level model, we can exercise control over the quality of the product we get. If we don't like it, we ask for a replacement or a reimbursement. And if we're still not satisfied, we can outsource our grocery shopping elsewhere. Likewise, business process outsourcing agreements have imbedded in them a series of carefully considered protections for the clients. In fact, because of the state-of-the-art performance metrics available in this relationship, clients have even more control over their employees' experience than they would have were they to keep this service in-house.

Key performance indicators (KPIs) are critical pass/fail markers that establish whether the outsourcing company is delivering the promised service. These KPIs would include such essential values as payroll accuracy, the average time it takes to recruit and hire, how long it takes to resolve problems, and overall customer satisfaction—all of which is quantifiable and trackable. Should the outsourcing company fall short of the agreed-upon standards, real financial penalties kick into action. On the other hand, while service level agreements (SLAs) may not carry the same financial leverage, outsourcing companies and their clients devote a tremendous amount of time and energy identifying such elements that measure the quality of the employees' experience as they reach out for service from HR. Both SLAs and KPIs are taken very seriously by the client companies and the outsourcing companies as quality indicators. As the client of the outsourcing company, *you* drive the quality and level of service you want your employees to experience when they seek out help from the HR department. Depending on the particulars of the agreement you reach with the outsourcing company, you can receive statistical reports on the company's performance throughout the life of the contract.

Clients of Outsourcing Companies Benefit from Being Associated with a Larger Group

Critics of outsourcing say that the larger the outsourcing company, the higher the likelihood that service quality is going to get lost among the sheer numbers of the outsourcing company's own profit motive. To the contrary: Outsourcing companies offer their clients efficiencies that come with the experience of successful process design, as well as economies of scale that come with the ability to negotiate more attractive arrangements from vendors.

With outsourcing, standardization is actually a good thing. Outsourcing companies should focus on driving their processes toward 80 to 85 percent standardization and only 15 to 20 percent customization. The right outsourcing model says that strategy and policy stay with the client, and the outsourcing company handles everything below that line—which is the supporting processes and transactions. The years of experience and expertise that an outsourcing company offers its clients are reflected as highly refined processes. They're experts at doing what they do best, and they know what processes provide the best results. It's all they do, so they focus on innovation and leverage of technology in ways any single traditional company cannot afford to.

Additionally, the more clients the outsourcing company has, the more each client company is able to enjoy the benefits of the aggregated spend. The outsourcer can gather the collected buying power represented by all the companies it represents, and then go out to the marketplace and get a better price for the HR service than any of its clients can get individually. Outsourcers are interrupting the supply chain for HR services and are driving new levels of service integration and radically new pricing.

Outsourcing Helps HR Link Itself to Larger Corporate Strategic Interests

When outsourcing has assumed the routine, standardizable people processes, it also frees internal HR to be a more active player in more substantial, forward-moving corporate initiatives. At the very least, HR now has the time to deal with issues concerning organizational development, professional and personal development, incentives, promotional opportunities, and any other area that directly enhances the company's position or benefits those who work for the company. But if HR is constantly absorbed with payroll issues, policy problems, benefits, and other time-consuming interruptions, how can it concentrate on more value-adding projects?

In this same vein, when HR is about to responsibly off-load 80 percent of its time-consuming activity to outsourcing, it also takes a big step toward marketing itself as a valuable strategic partner with the rest of the company. Over the decades HR has been laboring under the bad rap of being so absorbed with low-end minutiae that it hasn't had the time or capability to contribute to high-level discussions. With the additional time and focus capacity that outsourcing offers HR, the company's people function can demonstrate by its actions to the rest of the organization just how much it truly is able to contribute to the big-picture discussions.

The downside of this scenario is this: Now that HR executives have the time and freed-up intellectual bandwidth to focus on the larger, more substantial issues, they will actually be expected to provide more substantial contributions. There will indeed be some who will discover that they aren't up to the new challenges and opportunities available to HR after outsourcing has taken over the routine tasks. It's vital that senior HR leadership assess the skill sets of their people leaders to make sure they're up to the fresh challenges and opportunities. There will be those who are up to the new expectations but merely need some additional development opportunities to rise to the occasion. And they should receive any training they need. And then there will be others who discover they don't have the aptitude or interest to upgrade their capacity to contribute in the HR arena. It's better that you know now.

Business Process Outsourcing Can Become a Promising HR Career Path

It's perhaps natural to assume that business process outsourcing can be a haven for employees who are comfortable with routine and prefer back-office living. But that assumption would be wrong. Over the next few years HR outsourcing will emerge as an exciting career path for high-potential HR careerists who want to be valuable players in an aggressive business model built on profitability, productivity, and high service levels. There is plenty of opportunity for HR professionals to demonstrate their acumen in an exposed environment where HR service is the product line.

Choosing a career in HR outsourcing allows you to work in an organization that is revenue-producing; requires that you perform by the same rules and regulations as other service providers; emphasizes constant process improvement; is highly measurable; allows you to attain deep content knowledge in one specific area and then offers you the opportunity to move on to other functional areas to build additional knowledge; and which then allows you to one day enter the corporate environment as a seasoned HR executive—that is, if you want to. For many people who work in the outsourcing business, it will be difficult to walk away from the rewards that come with performing in a revenue-producing role.

Considerations Are More Complex Than a Simple Lowest-Bidder Scenario

The lowest bid is not necessarily the best way to choose an outsourcing company. Cost savings is definitely an important item, but you may be spending more money later in wasted time, frustration, poor service, or a bad relationship that is strictly oriented toward the bottom line. Even more important than the issue of cost are the two questions: Can this outsourcing company provide the service it says it can? And are its people the kinds of people you would want to work with every day?

As we've already discussed, the ideal client/outsourcer relationship should be a partnership, rather than a customer/vendor relationship. With an ongoing, shifting emphasis on what is reasonable, what's fair, what's most appropriate to the client's changing needs, and what's win/win, the actual dynamics of the relationship itself extend far beyond the question of who will come in with the lowest bid.

In any services that you want to procure, consider capability; references and relationships with the outsourcer's previous clients; and the outsourcer's rapport and style compatibility with the rest of the team. You work with people, and need to get to know and understand the people you would be working with. The teams on both sides should be able to come together, work on issues, and problem solve collaboratively from the very beginning.

Are they easy to work with? Do they help you solve your problems? Do they constantly refer back to the contract? Or are they comfortable inside the gray areas of uncertainty and opportunities for creative solutions? Would you want to have a long-term relationship with these people individually and with the company as an organization?

Conclusion

The evolution of business management has always been driven by responding to and making the most of the changes that surround us—economically, socially, technologically, and by industry. Only recently, particularly as a result of the added emphasis on technology and innovation, has the role of staffing truly emerged as a key contributor to a company's vitality and prospects.

In today's business world, every single person should count toward a company's achieving its strategic objectives. The emergence of business process outsourcing offers more than just a solution to problems faced by HR today. It is a dynamic and proactive tool to prepare for the opportunities as they evolve in the future.

16

Contract Recruiting

John Wentworth
The Wentworth Company

Overview

Time was, not too long ago, when recruiters came in only three categories: human resources department employees, contingency employment agencies, and retained executive search firms. But in the 1970s, a Boston search firm began to "rent" recruiters. It sent them all over the country to live inside clients' offices to burn off job openings.

Contract Recruiting Was Born

Contract recruiting usually means that a company hires or rents a recruiter to sit inside their offices and recruit. The person can be paid in a variety of ways: by the hour; by retainer plus a per-hire bonus; or only if a hire is made. The contract recruiter can work from inside the company or from the recruiter's home. Some contract recruiters are independents, while others belong to loose associations that provide a clearinghouse for assign-

108

ments. Some work for a job shop that also provides an assignment clearinghouse function. Some work for generalist human resources consulting firms and alternate between recruiting and writing policies. In a few cases, they work for a real recruiting consulting firm that takes responsibility for standardizing the work process and the quality of the product.

The challenges of contract recruiting are the same as with any other recruiting: to get jobs filled with the correct candidates—on time, on or under budget, through a process that makes everyone comfortable.

It's probably no surprise that the quality of contract recruiters varies tremendously. Some contract recruiters are superb recruiters and equally superb at managing the relationships with their clients and applicants. Others are good recruiters and very transaction-oriented, but not very good at relationships. On the flip side, some contract recruiters are better with relationships than they are at recruiting. And then some contract recruiters just aren't good at either relationships or recruiting. One wonders how they stay in business.

Objectives, Strategies, and Process

WHAT SHOULD YOU LOOK FOR?

At the Wentworth Company, one of the most interesting and puzzling observations we have made is how low our expectations are for contract recruiting. How else can you explain the consistent absence of work measurement and the number of marginally productive individuals who earn their livings as contract recruiters? Somebody is paying them. But why?

When buying other services, strict cost/benefit standards traditionally apply. For instance, if you buy steel, you want to know the type, price, and delivery time. If you buy loss prevention services, you want to know how much the company had caused losses to drop for other clients. If you buy collection services, you want to know how much the receivables have been lowered for clients. If you buy product representation, you might not insist that the person representing your product be warm and pleasant—but I'd certainly think that you would.

But when many companies buy contract recruiting services, they do not ask for a history of time-to-fill, cost-per-hire, interview-to-offer rates or acceptance rate accomplishments. They think metrics are not important.

But metrics are a strong indicator of the effectiveness of the recruiting you will get. And metrics can debunk many of the misconceptions that exist when it comes to contract recruiting.

MYTHS OF CONTRACT RECRUITING

Many believe that hard-driving, fast-talking recruiters are the best. They are not. More and more research tells us that how a candidate is treated by a company significantly influences whether he or she accepts an offer from that company. A fast-talking, hard-driving recruiter sends a pretty impersonal message and probably does not help your chances of closing candidates you want.

Many people do not believe that recruiting can be done well. It can. You can expect a good contract recruiter to:

- Learn your company environment and quickly establish genuine and productive relationships.
- Quickly establish which jobs are open and in what priority they should be filled.
- Interview the hiring managers, build a complete understanding of the requirements, and establish a partnership with the hiring manager about candidate sources and how the search will proceed.
- Start delivering qualified candidates in a week or so.
- Guide candidates and the hiring managers through the process.
- Thoroughly check out candidate backgrounds and get jobs filled with qualified and productive new employees.

IMPORTANT CRITERIA

Some individual contract recruiters are very good, and do their jobs without supervision. The problem a company faces is quickly knowing whether or not it engages one of these gems or a pretender. To evaluate a contract recruiter, consider the following 12 criteria:

1. *Ability to read/understand information and ideas presented orally, in writing, and on computer.* A recruiter needs to be able to understand a new company and its jobs quickly.

2. *Ability to drive and move recruitment process from inception to close.* Recruiting needs to go at a pace that is dictated by both the pace of the company and the pace of the labor market. If either the company needs people quickly or the labor market is tight and good candidates get lured away if they sit too long, the recruiter needs to be able to respond quickly and make the process work quickly.

   Virtually every force in an organization works against recruiting efforts. An effective recruiter anticipates and pushes (nicely) her or his way through the obstacles.

3. *Time-management skills.* If you are paying hourly, you are wise to be assured that you will get good productivity for your money.

4. *Effective creativity in recruitment.* The operative word is "effective." Lots of people demonstrate creativity, but it does not work. And sometimes the old, tried and true ways don't work, either. The effective recruiter figures out what does not work, stops doing it, and then figures out what will.

5. *Ability to embrace your corporate culture and operational philosophy.* Contract recruiters who are one-trick ponies are useful only in companies where they happen to blend in. Recruiters who are stylistically and methodologically inflexible cannot go from company to company successfully. One way or the other, you want a recruiter who is comfortable working your way and representing who your company is.

6. *Proven ability to match the tone of your company, to build credibility and respect with your hiring managers, and to become educated about your company.* In other words, the recruiter not only must be able to work within your system, but must also seem like one of you—to your hiring managers and candidates alike.

7. *Administrative skills and proven ability to submit and maintain organized documentation.* A recruiter's files, electronic or paper, need to be sufficiently organized so that another person can step in and take over the search without losing a beat.

8. *Ability to build relationships—with candidate, hiring managers, client human resources department, peers, and others.* Let me give you an example of what I'm talking about. We had one of those hard-charging, fast-talking recruiters call us for a job the other day. He dominated the conversation, talked only about himself, never asked whether we were hiring or not, and, as best we could tell, talked for a full five

minutes without taking a breath. Recruiters like that cannot build relationships, and recruiting is all about relationships.

9. *Proven computer literacy.* Demonstrates ability to apply sourcing techniques on the Internet. Demonstrates ability to grasp concept and technical implementation of recruiting/research tools. The day is coming that the computer-illiterate recruiter will have nowhere to work.

10. *Energy combined with leadership and management skills in a fast-paced, changing environment.* The reason companies are drawn to the hard-charging, fast-talking recruiters is that virtually every force in a company works against recruiting getting done. The ability to drive the process—which the fast-talking recruiter has in spades—is required much of the time. But these skills need to be paired with good relationship skills, and that's where the unskilled recruiter will come up short every time.

11. *Integrity.* Recruiting presents many ethical temptations. If you lie in the course of doing business, then hiring a recruiter who lies in order to discover candidates or get them interested in your jobs may not present a problem. And don't think it can't happen to you. When I was first taught to recruit in a contingency employment agency, I was taught to lie. And one recruiter whom I recently interviewed for our firm asked rhetorically, "How can you recruit with*out* lying?"

    It goes without saying, however, that we think that honesty is not only morally right but also a much better business practice than dishonesty. If you care, ask.

12. *Proven professional demeanor.* After all, recruiters represent you and your company.

HOW SHOULD YOU PAY CONTRACT RECRUITERS?

How a recruiter is paid has an effect on her or his motivation. You want to motivate recruiters to do a good job in every way, not just to fill jobs. But you also want them to fit in, follow the rules, and fill jobs with good candidates, on time, on or under budget.

If you pay primarily for when hires occur (like a contingency agency fee), you will get behaviors only related to filling the job. Translated? Recruiters will be most concerned with getting hires and less concerned with whether they are good hires, whether the rules are followed, and whether relationships are tended along the way. This is true even if you pay a monthly retainer with a per-hire bonus.

If you pay a salary, you need to set goals and measure performance against those goals. And you need to be willing to let a recruiter who is not meeting the goals go. If you pay hourly, you also need to set goals in order to help the recruiter resist the temptation to run out the process in order to run up the bill.

The trick to compensating contract recruiters is to use the flow of the money to get everyone in the game. If you set goals and are willing to fire a recruiter who does not meet them, the recruiter will want to perform for you. If you pay hourly, and combine this with reporting cost per hire and other metrics, then whoever pays the recruiter's bill will be in the game, wanting to keep the costs down and performance up.

Good recruiting is focused, disciplined, and orderly. If you do not see your recruiter working productively, grinding it out, step by step, your jobs will not get filled. And you are wasting your money.

HOW TO MEASURE RECRUITING

Contract recruiting, like all other recruiting, needs to be measured and the results published regularly. The key measures are:

Cost per Hire

Over the years, the academics have made this harder than it has to be. Cost per hire can reasonably be the cost of the recruiter plus all other hard costs you pay for postings, mining fees, ads, agency/search firm fees (although you should not pay any if you are paying a contract recruiter), list or other candidate source generation, and so on.

Cost per hire should be expressed *only* as a percentage of salary. A $12,000 cost to fill a job is good for a $120,000 per year job (or 10 percent of salary), but not good at all for a $60,000 per year job (20 percent of salary). One highly respected staffing metrics organization, Staffing.org, reports an average cost per hire of $3,997.

Cost per hire is also most useful when applied to the smallest group of jobs possible. Individual position cost per hire is best. The more granular the data, the better the analysis that can be derived from it.

One important note: Your goal should be the best cost per hire that still produces the *right* candidates. The lowest cost per hire probably will result in less than adequate candidates. If the cost is too high, you are wasting money. And remember that cost per hire can vary widely by region and industry.

Time to Fill

In an organization, jobs should be filled on time. If on time is slow, then jobs should be filled slowly. If on time is yesterday, then the job should have been filled then.

The labor market has a pace, however. During labor shortages, making offers to candidates quickly is often necessary, or they will go somewhere else.

But candidates have a pace, too. Moving too quickly may paint you as desperate to a candidate. Or a candidate may need to finish a project before moving to your company.

Start date goals should be set job by job. Recruiters should be measured against meeting those specific goals.

Interviews per Offer

How many interviews does your hiring manager have in order to find a candidate to hire? Your answer to this question actually measures how well a recruiter understands the job, finds and recognizes the right candidates, and screens in only the ones who match. We think this is a pretty core measurement. And it also measures how much of your hiring manager's time is being taken up by the recruiting process.

An average of two-and-a-half to three candidates per offer extended has emerged over the years as a good standard. Fewer than this number and the hiring managers begin to feel gypped: They did not see enough candidates to make a choice of their own. More than that and hiring managers begin to grumble that the recruiter was not listening when the requirements were discussed or cannot recognize a good candidate when they see one.

Offers per Acceptance

No hiring manager likes to go through the entire selection process and become invested in a final candidate only to discover that the candidate is not going to take the job.

The recruiter's job includes making sure that happens as infrequently as possible. I constantly argue for 100 percent acceptance. My recruiters and managers tell me that I'm being unrealistic—but I continue to keep the goal.

Management of Contract Recruiting

If you have not managed recruiting well up to now, you will not do any better at managing contract recruiting. Clarity about this is crucial to knowing what sort of person to engage and how to manage her or him.

If you have an honest-to-goodness strong track record of successfully managing recruiting, then:

- You will have a good cost-per-hire average.
- You will have a good time-to-fill average.
- You will have a good interview-to-offer average ratio.
- You will have a good offer acceptance average rate.
- You will need a contract recruiter only because you have more jobs than your recruiting staff can fill on time.

If you have *all* of these qualifications, you probably know enough to pick a contract recruiter and manage him or her successfully. But if you do not have all of these factors in your favor, you probably have not managed recruiting well enough to manage a contract recruiter any better. In this case, you probably want to pay more and engage a managed recruiting service instead of an independent recruiter. A managed service will set goals and report progress against goals and take responsibility for the completed process.

Challenges, Developments, and Trends

At the Wentworth Company, we are doing everything we can to influence the purchases of recruiting services and to help the purchasers understand that recruiting can be more than just art. No doubt there is art involved, as there is in selling. But no sales professional will tell you that the best way to sell is just to start calling people randomly, hoping for good chemistry. Effective selling involves a process. And although recruiting has resisted being systematized, procedures and software have been developed by professionals like ourselves that can guide recruiters and companies through the recruiting process.

I admit, when I was a new recruiter, I thought that setting goals for recruiting was crazy. Too much happened that was random. But today, we set detailed goals for all of our work, and meet the goals most of the time. Though we recognize that art in recruiting is sometimes good, it's also not enough. We know that an effective process makes recruiting more productive and reliable.

Combining disciplined and orderly process with highly qualified recruiters who are warm and professional ambassadors for your company will get your jobs filled with the right candidates, on time, on budget. This is the future of recruiting. It's here.

Outsourced Recruiting

Barry Siegel

President, Recruitment Enhancement Services

Overview

Today, HR professionals are almost certainly faced with the possibility of outsourcing the recruitment and hiring process, or at least part of it. How should you go about determining what, and when, to outsource? What steps should you take to ensure the desired outcome? And most importantly, why is now a good time to consider outsourcing in the first place?

Despite a steep slowdown in the national economy at the time this chapter was written, the recruiting and retention of talent remains a top priority at the highest executive levels. So, if you work in the recruiting function, you're operating under a microscope. Just like everyone else involved with the bottom line, you're expected to continuously strive to do things better, faster, and cheaper, while ensuring that the experience is highly satisfying to all participants. As a result, you may need to resort to outsourcing in order to achieve the status of what we like to call a world-class recruiting organization. World-class recruiting organizations are those that are consistently able to perform above a certain level—those that are able to hire the strongest talent, quickly and for the lowest cost, by leveraging the best practices in technology, marketing, and recruitment.

What is recruitment outsourcing? It's simply delegating part of the recruiting function to a third party. You already use recruitment outsourcing if you:

- Ever use an employment agency or search firm.
- Ever use contract and/or temporary labor and/or staffing companies.
- Use a third party for drug or skills testing.
- Use an ad agency to place recruitment ads.
- Use a third party for reference checking and/or background investigations.
- Use a third party to host your web site.

Chances are, you said "yes" to one or more of these options. The next questions are: Should you be considering going further with your recruitment outsourcing? Should you consider delegating the majority of your hiring process to a third party? This means that a third party, beginning with requisitions from your hiring managers, works the entire recruiting process seamlessly through to hire. To distinguish this expanded form of recruitment outsourcing from the more elementary models, I'll refer to this broad range of integrated services as Total Outsourced Talent Solutions (TOTS).

TOTS can help you do things better, faster, cheaper, and with greater satisfaction for all the participants involved. There are many circumstances when TOTS makes sense. For example: What happens when you get a flood of new requisitions? Can you handle them with the same efficiency that you apply at the present time? What happens if the flow of requisitions dries to a trickle? Under such circumstances, are you in a position where you can afford to maintain your existing staff? And when it comes to areas of specialized recruiting, do you have the expertise in-house to recruit for all types of very specific requirements?

If you are unable to realistically answer any or all of the following questions, or if you are less than satisfied with the answers you get, you are a good candidate for TOTS.

- What are you spending for recruiting?
- What is your ROI (return on investment)?

- How do you rate the quality of your new hires, and what are poor hires costing you?
- What is it costing you when jobs go unfilled?
- What is your cost per hire?
- How satisfied are hiring managers and candidates with your hiring process?

Let's examine how to begin determining the answers to these and other related questions, and what results and improvements you can expect from TOTS.

Becoming a World-Class Recruiting Organization

Just like anything else in life worth doing, improving the recruiting function does not come easy. To succeed, you need the commitment of top management, the proper tools, and the talent to make it happen. This essay will begin by reviewing how the shortest route to acquisition of the finest tools and talent requires a partnership with a leading TOTS provider. Once you have access to the main ingredients, all you need is a formula that can produce ongoing improvement. If you're able to sustain this improvement, you'll be well on your way to becoming a world-class recruiting organization. The formula, outlined next, revolves around a five-step process: assess, strategize, implement, improve (or tweak), and measure.

ASSESS

The first step to achieving world-class recruiting status is to perform an in-depth assessment of all aspects of your hiring process. Ideally, the audit should be performed by a highly qualified third party. The purpose is to determine initial benchmarks that will serve as a road map on your journey to excellence. The assessment should encompass a wide range of areas, including:

- *Requisition management.* How many and what categories of requisitions are open now? How many have been filled within the past 12 months? How many of each category do you anticipate over the next 12 months?

- *Commitment to talent.* How committed is top management to winning the war for talent? How committed is your organization not only to recruiting the best, but to keeping and upgrading existing talent?

- *Position as an employer.* Why do people join your company? Why do they leave? Who's your competition? How do candidates view you as a potential employer?

- *Culture.* How would you define your actual culture? Is that definition what you'd like it to be? Are you aligning all staffing activities with the culture you seek to achieve?

- *Hiring process.* What are the plans and strategies for making the best hires in the shortest time, at the lowest cost? Who are the players and what are the components of your hiring process? What level of satisfaction does this process produce among hiring managers as well as candidates?

- *Technology.* Are you equipped with automated systems that combine state-of-the-art functionality with user-friendliness? What are your expectations of technology—do you expect technology alone to do the vast majority of the work?

- *Promotions.* What's your employment branding strategy? (If you have one!) Does it align with the company's overall product/services marketing message? Do you have a state-of-the-art career web site? What print, interactive, and/or electronic advertising techniques do you utilize? How well are these various components working, and how consistent are your messages? Do you maintain a proactive campaign, or just a reactive one? Do you have an active public relations effort dedicated to staffing?

- *Metrics.* What do you measure? How accurate are your measurements? What would you like to measure? How do you stack up against the competition when it comes to cost, speed, quality, and satisfaction with your recruiting efforts?

Upon completion of your audit, you will have a report card that identifies where you stand and what is needed for improvement. Most likely, you'll conclude that you have a great deal of work to do, and you need some additional expertise to help you answer questions brought up during the assessment. To reach world-class recruiting status, you almost certainly will need to establish a partnership with a supplier of TOTS.

STRATEGIZE

Following assessment, you'll want to develop strategies for achieving your goals. World-class recruiting organizations set themselves apart through their ability to attract and retain champions. Your initial strategy on the road to excellence should focus on becoming an employer of choice.

Begin by asking yourself the following two questions, which are quoted from the book *Finding and Keeping Great Employees* by Jim Harris and Joan Brannick (AMACON, 1999):

1. "Does your company avoid policies and procedures that make it difficult to find and keep the kind of employees it wants?"
2. "Does your organization allocate the time, money, and additional resources needed to find and keep great employees?"

You are not an employer of choice if you can't answer with a definite "yes" to both questions. Today's HR professional can achieve a transformation to an employer of choice by adhering to the following four recruiting guidelines: (1) engage in market-driven behavior; (2) formalize the process through marketing and automation; (3) develop apostles; and (4) leverage the power of employer branding. Let's briefly examine each of them.

Engage in Market-Driven Behavior

Five to 10 years ago, companies often assumed a position of advantage in job interviews, forcing candidates to sell their qualifications to the company. But conventional laws of supply and demand have forced changes in employer behavior. In today's labor market, despite the temporary economic slowdown, it's often the employers who must do the selling, not the potential employees. Otherwise, candidates that a company can't afford to lose may walk.

Top talent isn't on the market for long, regardless of economic conditions. Candidates have a high expectation level for companies that are employers of choice. To compete, your company needs to be available 24/7. A good corporate web site enables you to do just that.

Pervasive Internet capabilities heighten the need for around-the-clock access to recruiters, as well. The most successful recruiters make themselves available on evenings and weekends to answer candidates' questions via e-mail, by telephone, or even in person. Recruiters are continuously aware that if they don't reach out to candidates, someone else will.

Are you equipped to engage in market-driven behavior on your own?

Formalize the Process through Marketing and Automation

Today's employers of choice are no longer paper-driven. They must be Internet-enabled and, to a large degree, automated.

Being automated doesn't translate into sitting back and watching the process take care of itself. Great job candidates don't just come knocking anymore. Today's recruiters must make it happen. They must be proactive, instead of reactive.

An automated recruitment process should be systematized in such a way that many administrative recruiting responsibilities can be easily and efficiently handled. The task of responding to a job opening, for example, should leverage automation to allow for online response forms that are customized to match each individual online job posting. Candidate databases need to be structured to permit entry and tracking from a wide variety of sources including advertisements in any medium, resume mining and networking, employee referrals, internal mobility systems, career fairs, third parties, and so on.

An effective, automated process produces valuable benefits: speed, efficiency, reports, and metrics. Top recruiting organizations can generate data in nanoseconds. But automation alone will not be effective. It must be combined with the human touch of marketing. Recruiting remains a people business.

Are you capable of formalizing your company's process through marketing and automation on your own?

Develop Apostles

This guideline is simple, short, and sweet. Happy campers spread happy news, or a cheerful noise. That's why so many successful organizations have gone to such great lengths to convince the world that they're excellent places to work.

One great thing about apostles is their avowed loyalty, a trait that can produce handsome dividends. According to a report by HR consultant Watson Wyatt Worldwide, more than half of 7,500 workers surveyed recently said they felt committed to their employers. Those companies with high worker commitment had a 112 percent three-year return to shareholders, versus a 76 percent return for firms with low worker commitment.

Growing numbers of employers are leveraging the proselytizing power of apostles through employee referral programs and internal mobility systems. If an organization exhibits the right behavior, uses an efficient recruiting process, and does effective public relations, it, too, will produce believers and preachers.

Is your organization equipped to develop apostles on its own?

Leverage the Power of Employer Branding

Many companies won't hesitate to spend tens of millions of dollars to project the right image of a product to consumers. But they have a tough time parting with a dollar to project the image of the company itself as a great employer.

I believe they've got it backwards. If consumers are aware that Company A is a terrific place to work, they will naturally assume that Company A produces great products. In fact, consumers will believe Company A makes great products simply because it's a great place to work.

How does one create awareness that Company A is a terrific place to work? By building a brand. A brand is a feeling, an aura, an image, an impression, a perception that becomes embedded through repetition, consistency, reinforcement, and confirmation, thereby becoming a reality. An employment brand centers around the creation of a great career web site. This is a site that is able to stand on its own, not as something six clicks removed from the general corporate site. This is where you sell yourself as an employer, spell out opportunities, talk about employees, list jobs, and establish ongoing relationships with potential candidates. All marketing efforts should drive every potential candidate to this web site.

There is no one magic bullet that builds your brand as an employer. You need a mix of a variety of promotional outlets. More importantly, you need to measure the effectiveness of your recruitment marketing messages as well as media selection so you can determine which ones to emphasize, which ones to change, and which ones to eliminate.

Are you equipped to build an ideal career web site and drive traffic to it on your own? Your brand as an employer does not end when a potential candidate arrives at your web site. Reinforcement of your "employer of choice" message must be given throughout the entire hiring process. In fact, this is the area that separates so-called employers of choice from true world-class recruiting organizations.

IMPLEMENT

By now you can probably see how your company could benefit from the selection of a top-notch TOTS provider. Ideally, your TOTS partner can help you become a world-class recruiting organization by providing the following four services:

1. Completion and analysis of your assessment to clearly establish benchmarks, goals, and projections.

2. Installation and utilization of technology that will get everyone on the same page. This is best accomplished through the creation and implementation of a complex series of integrated web sites, which provide different views and functionality for candidates, hiring managers, general employees, human resources, and third parties.

3. Provision of a wide range of talent to provide the following services:
   - Project manager(s) dedicated to the success of your account.
   - Project coordinators to work with hiring managers and candidates.
   - Cybrarians (Internet researchers).
   - Marketing-oriented recruiters with various areas of expertise, who are available at the candidates' convenience (evenings, weekends, etc.).
   - Recruitment marketing experts to develop creative and media strategies to fill the pipeline (resume database).
   - Programmers and IT support personnel to provide and maintain user-friendly technology.
   - Administrative personnel to ensure overall efficiency of the process.

4. Implementation of a hiring process, utilizing the best practices of the cycle of response and responsiveness, similar to Figure 17.1.

By partnering with an experienced TOTS provider, employers of choice have access to marketing efforts specifically targeted to the employment function, recruiting expertise from multiple areas, a variety of HR process reengineering models, and cutting-edge technology.

IMPROVE—TWEAKING

Einstein once said that the idea is to "make things simple, not simpler." I have tried to make navigating the road to world-class recruiting sound simple, but the journey is complex and difficult. I feel compelled to once again state that recruiting is essentially a people business. Wherever there are people, there are personality conflicts coupled with skepticism and reluctance to change. So no matter how well you have done your assessment, strategy, and implementation, your efforts will fail without the preparation, flexibility, and willingness to properly navigate your way through the obstacles ahead. Improvement, or tweaking, is all about doing anything and everything to secure hiring manager buy-in for what you're trying to accomplish. It involves a great deal of patience, communication, and training. This area is also where

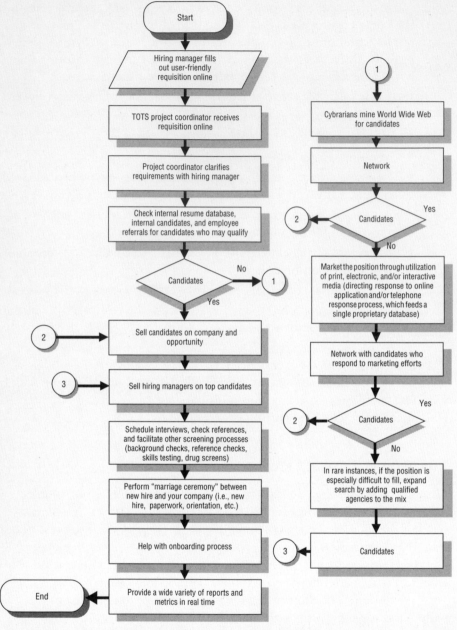

Figure 17.1   Best Practices—Cycle of Response and Responsiveness.

your commitment and that of top management will be tested. I'll deal more with tweaking in the Kellogg Company case study to follow.

MEASURE

On August 21, 2001, Robert W. Baird gave a presentation entitled "Emerging Platforms of Opportunity in Human Capital Management" at the Second Annual HR Partnership Summit. This comprehensive presentation explained that "The war (for talent) is still hell. . . . Companies are rapidly awakening to the fact that they don't know how much they spend on their greatest asset (human capital), or much else about it."

Do you know what to measure, and how to measure it, on your own? Installation of the proper technology and adherence to a specified hiring process will give you measurable results. Success will be obvious as you increase quality and satisfaction, and reduce time and costs. In fact, the mere fact that you begin to measure anything will indicate a major step forward. The following case study provides a more in-depth look at the measurement aspect of recruiting.

Success Story

In 1998, cereal and convenience foods manufacturer Kellogg Company had a vision to improve its recruiting function by implementing a strong vendor relationship and fully outsourcing all recruiting. This was very much breakthrough thinking in 1998. There were very few companies that had taken this step, and there weren't many suppliers with demonstrated competency in providing a broad of scope of outsourcing services.

Kellogg Company was looking for a vendor that could:

- Introduce technology to improve operating efficiency.
- Provide recruiting specialists with specific areas of expertise.
- Improve factors such as timeliness, quality, diversity, reporting capabilities, and management of fluctuations in hiring volume.
- Reduce overall recruiting costs.

Based on the model previously described, this case study illustrates how Kellogg Company developed a successful partnership with outsourcing vendor Recruitment Enhancement Services (RES), an Omnicom Group Inc. company.

STEP ONE: ASSESS

Kellogg Company's HR leadership believed that success in the future would require that they rethink the recruiting process. Leadership understood the value of talent to Kellogg, and developed a vision that would result in improved confidence in the company's ability to acquire the very best people. Due to a company-wide restructuring toward the end of 1998, there was a general mandate to reduce head count. As a result, most of the recruiting staff was reassigned or released. As the company realigned and hiring needs increased, Kellogg Company began to look for a partner that could handle a variable hiring volume, provide superior technology for the recruiting function, and improve the overall effectiveness of the recruiting efforts.

When the decision was made to outsource the entire recruitment function, a strategic selection process was implemented. The RFP was narrowed down from an original list of 14 potential vendors to RES, whose unique scope of services and superior technology met Kellogg Company's selection criteria. Cydney Kilduff, director of staffing at Kellogg Company, recalls: "We weren't looking for an add-on. We were looking to replace an entire internal recruiting function with a supplier solution. I honestly believe that we were blazing a new trail in looking for a *total* outsourcing solution, not just an enhancement."

Outsourcing presented an avenue to reduce head count while also delivering a significant improvement in quality. According to Kilduff, "Cost savings were not the primary issue in the decision to outsource; rather, we wanted the benefits of quality improvement, with the best recruitment services possible. And we wanted to get it up and running quickly."

As RES conducted its assessment of Kellogg Company's recruitment practices, it identified inconsistent processes and limited use of technology. Hiring managers around the country were using over 80 different agencies to fill open positions. Paper requisitions were still being used, and often these would not be completed until after hires were made. Reporting data was incomplete, which made it difficult to deliver consistent metrics and measurements.

After determining which areas needed the most attention, RES and Kellogg Company moved on to the next stage of the outsourcing process.

STEP TWO: STRATEGIZE

Kellogg Company was seeking the following deliverables from RES, as determined by the assessment:

- Integrated recruiting technology.
- Recruiting specialists with highly developed competencies.
- Improved overall function effectiveness, as measured by key metrics.
- Reduction in overall costs.

In deciding to outsource, Kellogg Company questioned whether traditional recruiting roles were still relevant for their organization. The skills of an Internet sourcer, or "cybrarian," are very different from those of a traditional recruiter. Recruiters need to be marketing-oriented and free to focus on candidates at the candidates' convenience. As a result, it is also necessary to introduce "relationship managers" as part of the recruiting team who focus primarily on training and working with the hiring managers. "It was clear that we needed to rethink traditional roles," said Kilduff. "And one of the big advantages of outsourcing is the flexibility, the agility to respond to an organization's variable hiring needs." This ability, plus technology that was already in place at RES, laid the foundation for the outsourcing plan.

RES offered numerous advantages to Kellogg Company in developing a more holistic approach to managing the staffing function, including:

- An internet-based applicant management system that automated a broad range of recruitment activities (RES' proprietary system, ROAM).
- An integrated system to interact with Kellogg Company's own technology for employee referral and internal application processes.
- Development of a "Careers" area on Kellogg.com.
- On-site support staff to interact with hiring managers and human resources.
- An employment branding campaign.
- All recruitment-related activities, from posting ads, sourcing resumes on the Internet, and networking to candidate screening to hiring manager contact.
- Improvement of administrative processes, such as applicant tracking, report generation, and other metrics.
- Creative services for all recruitment marketing efforts.

STEP THREE: IMPLEMENT

All of the areas listed so far were implemented as part of the outsourcing solution, from one single source. RES and Kellogg Company took a number of steps to ensure a smooth transition, including:

- Providing information to the end-user in several forms (intranet, printed materials).
- Soliciting feedback from users and acting on feedback quickly.
- Promoting the benefits of outsourcing with internal champions.

Training was a key component of the implementation process. Initially, RES conducted training in group sessions at Kellogg Company facilities. However, it quickly became apparent that managers who did not have current hiring needs did not make learning about the new system a priority. To assist with the learning curve, RES developed a just-in-time training package that went to managers as new hiring requests were made (detailed under Step Four, Improve).

The timetable for implementation was planned to last approximately three months. This time frame proved to be too ambitious. Although communication pieces (such as the "Staffing Gazette" informational web site, brochures, virtual postcards, promotional items including a training video, etc.) were ready to go on time, software development had not been completed and management support was not fully in position when the launch date arrived.

STEP FOUR: IMPROVE (TWEAK)

Initially, Kellogg Company hiring managers questioned the prudence of the new model. They were accustomed to using outside recruiting agencies and following their own processes. In addition, the original implementation timetable proved unrealistic once the full scope of the requirements was uncovered. This discovery further contributed to more technology customization and enhancements, which took longer than originally planned.

And there were other problems. Despite well-intentioned efforts across the board, hiring managers' expectations were not being met, and overall, hiring goals were not being reached. Kellogg Company and RES were determined to make the partnership work. An action plan emphasizing the partnership between Kellogg Company and its chosen vendor was developed. The focus had to be as much on the human side of problem solving as on the technology of the solution. Placing quality under a microscope, it became obvious that the original recruiting team had to be enhanced, and in a couple of instances team members had to be replaced. RES made the necessary changes and additions. Then Kellogg Company stepped up to the plate. Even though the activities of recruiting had been outsourced, Kellogg Company decided that the internal acceptance of the program would require a stronger joint effort that acknowledged and addressed user concerns. Cyd Kilduff decided to make an addition to her team. An internal champion, Andre Goodlett, was hired to oversee the project and to support it from the top down.

Another major problem was the fact that not all hiring managers were reviewing candidates submitted by RES in a timely manner. Kellogg Company and RES jointly reached out to the hiring managers by implementing a one-on-one training program. This enabled each manager to get comfortable with the technology and RES, without being observed by an audience of peers.

Once the managers were trained on the system, a report was developed to ensure that candidates were being reviewed promptly. If candidate information is not reviewed within five days of receipt, a "no review" report is automatically generated and sent to that hiring manager as well as Andre Goodlett and the RES program managers. This keeps the lines of communication open among candidates, hiring managers, HR, and RES, and ensures that top talent doesn't get lost while waiting for their information to be reviewed.

Although Kellogg Company recognizes the value of outside search in many situations, the extensive use of search firms also had to be addressed. RES and Kellogg Company worked together to formulate policies and develop a methodology to integrate search firms into the overall process. Kellogg Company notified all 80 search firms with whom they had previously worked that they would have to work within the ROAM system (RES' Internet-based applicant management system) in order to remain eligible for future assignments. RES submits information, handles all communications, sets up one-on-one training, and continues to manage all third-party relationships of this type. The end result is that Kellogg HR is now able to track search firm activity and authorize payment within the same overall hiring management system in those rare instances where outside search continues to be utilized. (Note: RES is primarily responsible for positions below the director level. Kellogg continues its partnerships with many fine search firms who work on a variety of levels, but most particularly for positions at director and above.)

Today, recruiters continue to train as needed while building solid relationships with hiring managers. Changes continue to be made to the technology components of the program as new ideas and better methods emerge. Relationships have become stronger with the support of management on both sides of the partnership. Previously skeptical departments and managers have been won over on a case-by-case basis by fulfilling their hiring needs. It is a long-term improvement process.

STEP FIVE: MEASURE

Clearly, selecting RES as an outsourcing provider has been a success for Kellogg Company. By October of 2001, 95 percent of jobs available at Kellogg Company were being filled by RES, versus only 10 percent at the start of the implementation in 2000. Time to fill had gone from 67 days to just 39 days. And perhaps most impressively, cost per hire was reduced by over 60 percent.

Metrics are tracked with a series of reports (25 different reports are available online, in real time), and by conducting regular customer satisfaction surveys with hiring managers. Satisfaction is measured on the process and the RES staff, the level of service provided, and the quality of candidates submitted. The range is 1 to 5, 5 being the highest. Results are based on each requisition, so individual recruiters are reviewed as well. RES runs these reports on each recruiter to see where the levels of service lie with each individual. Satisfaction is high, with scores typically in the 4.25 to 4.75 range.

LESSONS LEARNED

As you can see, any successful outsourcing process takes time, lots of cooperation, and most importantly, constant communication between all the parties involved. RES and Kellogg Company are still working on continuous process improvements. And if I had to do it over again, I would make four adjustments:

1. Limit head count reduction until the outsourcing capability is in position and functioning at the basic levels.
2. Be as flexible and generous as possible in establishing a time frame for rollout, training, technology customization, and overall implementation of the program.
3. Identify a project manager on the client side at the inception of the process, whose primary responsibility is to serve as liaison with the outsourcing partner and act as an advocate of the program.

4. Identify key internal customers, and focus a pilot program on their needs. This would offer the opportunity for tweaking before introducing the program to the company as a whole, and it would create internal champions in areas that need the most help from the outsourcing partner.

THE FUTURE

Now that the Kellogg Company/RES outsourcing program has become an established success, what's next? Kilduff predicts, "We want to get to the point where we're measuring results rather than just efficiency. How do we ensure delivery of value-added services? How can we make sure we are getting the best-qualified candidates, who stay with us? We want to improve retention, and in our next phase of working together, we plan to develop an online tool to measure quality of our new hires' first year."

To do this, RES plans to work more closely with hiring managers in developing job requirement criteria. A system for follow-ups throughout a new hire's first year will then see how well they are meeting these criteria.

The most important goals of the outsourcing program—efficiency (cost), speed, satisfaction, and quality—are continually being improved upon. As Kilduff says, the biggest benefits of outsourcing for Kellogg Company are: (1) the ability of an experienced vendor to bring in new technology quickly and (2) the ability to bring more resources to bear on a variety of different issues, and have them all related to each other through the outsourcing vendor. "Most importantly, we need agility to respond quickly, effectively, and nimbly to shifting needs," she says. "Every part of our business must be able to respond quickly to change! RES, as an outsourcing partner, has truly given us the agility to address a huge variety of hiring needs."

Challenges, Developments, and Trends

In the future, I believe more companies like Kellogg Company will look to outsourcing as the most effective means to improve their hiring processes. The war for talent will only escalate, and companies will be forced to adapt in order to retain status as employers of choice. According to the U.S. Bureau of Labor Statistics, by 2006 two workers will exit the workforce for every one entering. Workforce growth will decelerate each year from now until 2020. And the 25-to-44 year-old age group will decline by 15 percent over the next 15 years.

What this means is that the hiring climate of 1997–2000 will eventually return as the norm. What about the recession of 2001–2002? I believe this will be remembered as a new kind of recession, one in which many companies hired new talent while simultaneously conducting layoffs. And though unemployment rates increased, they still remained lower than those of previous recessionary times. Look at the figures compiled by a Towers Perrin survey from 2001; these things just don't happen in a traditional recession. Survey results show that:

- Talent remained hard to find.
- Seventy-three percent of companies experiencing layoffs were hiring simultaneously.
- Fifty-six percent of U.S. workers were in the job market, with 12 percent actively seeking other jobs.
- Forty-two percent of companies experiencing layoffs simultaneously developed targeted programs to retain top performers.

And this means that you can forget a return to the "good old days" when jobs got filled by newspaper ads, employment agencies, and osmosis. Metrics, web sites, front- and back-end work flow solutions, automated hiring management systems, employee referral programs, internal mobility systems, sophisticated branding strategies, online testing, job postings on 40,000 sites, recruiting as a marketing and sales function, Total Outsourced Talent Solutions, hiring process reengineering—these are no longer theories and/or luxuries; they are necessary tools for survival. They are necessities to compete in the war for talent and to become an employer of choice—in short, a world-class recruiting organization.

So what's an HR director to do? The answer is simple. Find a way to get with the program. Do it yourself, do it through outsourcing, or do it through a combination of the two. Failure to act compromises the future of your company and your own career. I predict that HR operations that fail to upgrade the efficiency of their staffing processes are likely to see the function taken away from them and placed in the marketing department. Outsourced recruiting *can* work for you. Let it help your organization win the war for talent, both now and in the future.

The Partnering of Staffing Relationships from an External Recruiter's Perspective

Karen Bloom

Bloom, Gross & Associates

As an executive recruiter, one area in the human capital cycle that obviously requires more of my expertise than others is the process of talent acquisition. In reality, there is no defined science to this very important function, a function that all companies go through on a daily basis. For the most part, companies engage in talent acquisition in a very disorganized and disjointed manner. No doubt we've all heard about the few who are doing it well. They speak at conferences on "best practices" and "metrics" and the audience members go back to their companies and try to duplicate the models. But for every company who "gets it," there are hundreds, maybe even thousands, who don't. For them, hiring the right people at the right time remains something of a mystery.

The need to understand recruiting and how to acquire talent has always been important to businesses. But it's actually become something of a business prerogative within the last decade. When the recession of the early 1990s ended in 1994, it resulted in something nothing short of miraculous: the technology boom, which created an enormous demand for talent. Those executive recruiters who had weathered the tough days of the early decade now found themselves in demand as well. Whether companies wanted to or not, they found that it was necessary to partner with an outside source to help them identify talent. At the time, talent acquisition options were limited. Corporate staffing executives usually posted the job internally, and then sourced their own files (before the days of database technology) for potential job candidates. But the only sure recruiting options left were to run some well-placed ads and call the local external recruiter.

The tech boom, however, created more search options for in-house staffing professionals—the most exciting of which was the Internet and all of its many job posting sites, services, and niche recruiting capabilities. Resumes can how be "captured" and job candidates can be found as readily as they once called to inquire about a position. Which means that as we emerge from this current recession, corporate staffing professionals have many more options to consider when planning their acquisition strategies.

Of course, in tight times costs drive many of those decisions. While recruitment efforts from an outside source can still be the most effective way to identify talent at certain levels, many companies now turn to that option only after they have exhausted their in-house options. Generally, we are now called in to complete a search that has been open for many months; in this scenario, the hiring manager is angry with the corporate staffing professionals, and the staffing professionals are at their wits' end. They have already: posted the job on a number of Internet job boards and on their own company web site; run a few well-placed ads in newspaper employment sections; looked internally; and asked for employee referrals. Their enthusiasm for filling this job on their own has completely bottomed out. By the time they call an external recruiter, they are looking for not only help but a miracle. Their greatest hope is that the external recruitment partner can deliver the perfect candidate or slate of candidates within days—or even hours.

In many ways, outside search help has become the dirty little secret of our current decade. At almost every conference or professional meeting I have attended in the recent past, corporate staffing professionals have discussed their need and desire to eliminate working with outside recruitment professionals, and how their companies are moving in this direction. It is very much in vogue to state this intention publicly. So, when it does seem necessary to get some outside help, outside recruiters are engaged with what seems to be resentment and almost embarrassment. Granted, this is a sweeping generalization, as many companies understand the necessity of the partner relationship and use it well. But these few are distinct from the many companies that don't.

In today's confusing human capital acquisition environment, it's important to have some guidelines for engaging an outside recruitment source. This essay will address some important steps that human resource and/or corporate staffing professionals should consider in their efforts to acquire the best talent, particularly when they go outside for help.

Guidelines for Acquisition

Recruiters who are not on your company's in-house payroll have many different names: external recruiters, third-party recruiters, independent recruiters, or outsourced recruiters. Whatever you call them, consider these steps when working with external recruiters:

1. *Evaluate the degree of difficulty in filling the position.* If this is a job you can fill through a job board, your own corporate web site, an employee referral, or an internal hire, go for it. But if the person you are looking for proves to difficult find—and you've done your internal due diligence—turn it over to a recruitment partner you can trust and let them do the work for you.

2. *Truly partner with your outside recruitment source.* A good external recruiter will have many long-term relationships established with a very large and broad-based talent pool. If you want to tap into that, you and the recruiter need to work as a unified team. The external recruiter becomes an extension of your company for the time he or she is working on your assignment. A recruiter becomes your own public relations program—communicating to a specific target audience about the benefits of working for your company. As a partner, the recruiter needs to have as much information about the company and the position as you can provide, and immediate feedback and ongoing communications throughout the process.

3. *Learn from them.* As an outside source, the external recruiter is in the trenches and may know much more than you do. For instance, it's their job to know what is going on at your competitors' organizations;

they know how potential candidates in the marketplace perceive your company; and they know which companies are employing best practices and what those are. A good outside recruiter makes it his or her business to know about the current trends in staffing and to stay abreast of emerging issues.

4. *Communicate, communicate, communicate*. Remember: When you hold back information from a recruiter, you are holding back information from a candidate. You might not want to hire a particular candidate today, but maybe you will one day. And all candidates are potential customers or investors in your company; how they are treated in the recruitment process will dictate their views of your company. Nothing is worse than when the corporate staffing professionals become nonresponsive during a search. Everyone knows that it's because they have information they are uncomfortable sharing about the job or the candidates (perhaps an internal candidate has been found, for example). The anger and frustration that the outside recruiter is left to manage is only going to adversely affect the potential candidate's view of the company, and maybe for a long time.

Case Study

A start-up technology company, located in a small college town in the Midwest, recently asked my firm to assist them in identifying a controller, someone who could eventually be promoted into a CFO position. We were hired by the president of the company, someone who had previously been a division president for a large, established international technology company. She did not have any true start-up experience. And while the company had almost a virtual management team in place, she wanted to hire this finance person from the local geographic area. There was a contract HR person in place to assist with the start-up, but our primary contact was initially with the president. She spent a lot of time educating us about the start-up company but was quite clear from the beginning that she needed a controller, not a CFO, and definitely not someone who had venture capital experience, which would be handled by the CEO. She also explained that the CEO was an international businessman who owned companies abroad and lived abroad.

As we began our recruiting for this position, we were very aware that the true success of this company was going to be dependent on a solid management team. A seasoned finance person was going to be critical to the acquisition of venture capital funds. So we interviewed a continuum of talent from the basic specifications that were offered up to us. We were looking for people who would fit the CFO profile with experience at start-up technology companies. The presentation document explained our reasoning, and we provided four candidates who represented different notches along the continuum of experience.

As we anticipated, the president of this company responded most positively to the more experienced candidates. As we were developing candidates, she was also learning about the company and becoming much more aware of how important it would be for a strong finance person to be on board (especially with an absentee CEO, who was really an angel investor). At first, we did not present all of our candidates; we held back a very senior CFO who had worked on a number of start-ups and who had extraordinary relationships with venture capital groups. We did not feel that she was ready to see someone this experienced, and she had specifically stated that she didn't want someone with venture capital experience.

When we began the interview phase of our search, one candidate rose to the top very quickly and the negotiations to hire began. However, in the end, the candidate declined the offer; he was a bit more risk-adverse than he had been a few years earlier, because he was now married with two small children. But his skill level proved to us that the president had definitely moved up the continuum in terms of experience. Instead of going back to the original slate of candidates, we introduced the very seasoned person we had held back. What someone else might have viewed as a risk, he saw as an opportunity. After a very smooth process of interviews and negotiations, he joined the company.

When we started the process, we were looking for a controller with less rather than more years of experience. When it was over, we had assisted the client in seeing that it was a business advantage to hire the more experienced professional at the CFO level. This decision on her part has moved the company along in its start-up activities, and will undoubtedly secure the future success of this venture.

To be sure, we did not engage in this level of partnering with our client company because we wanted to make her spend more money on the employee or on our fees. We engaged in this level of partnering because we were very familiar with start-up companies and how the good ones have survived. We also spent a lot of time talking with people who had been involved with start-ups and valued their opinions on what the company would need to make it. The learning we gained was invaluable to our client, and it helped her make a better hiring decision. Granted, we could have simply filled her specs and given her a controller, but in the end that might not have satisfied the overall needs of the business. Our ability to engage at a level where we were viewed as a consultative partner—and not just a recruiter—was important for the acquisition of the talent really needed for the company.

Partnering Benefits

When an outside recruitment partner gets to work at the level described in the preceding case study, the amount of pride we take in our work is enormous. If this company is a huge success and the CFO contributes to that success, then we will feel that we are an extension of that. We will have made a tremendous contribution to that company. Yes, we will have earned a fee and that's important. But the factor that actually resonates the longest is the knowledge that we contributed in a way that actually made a difference.

Let's consider a few factors. Had there been an HR staffing person on board, would we have been able to be so creative? That is the question that should hound all of us in staffing. Would that corporate staffing person have restricted our ability to present candidates with a continuum of experiences and skills? Would that person have taken the initiative to communicate with the president about business goals, competitive information, and management roles? How much information would we have been fed in the beginning in order to make some of the business assumptions that we made? In the end, we executed this search from start to finish in a little over two months' time. Would that have happened if it had gone through corporate staffing? I would like to think so. But experience tells me that it is unlikely.

It is time for all of us in staffing, both inside and outside the corporations, to work together as partners.

Fact: Good recruiters are born, not made.

Fact: The economy will get better.

Fact: Demographics don't lie.

Talent acquisition will continue to be a company's most challenging endeavor. And with constructive partnering, the quality of that talent should increase. As a corporate recruiter, you need to be sure that you:

- Pick external recruiters who have good reputations in the areas where you need assistance. Find the best ones for the job.

- Once you find them, develop and nurture each relationship. In the years to come, you are going to need a few good sources who can pipeline talent to you.

- Keep your business objectives clear and communicate openly with your recruiting partners. Be open to their perspectives and encourage them to think creatively.

- Be honest with your outside partner and remember that he or she is your best communication link to some of the top talent you are hoping to acquire. How you treat the recruiting source can trickle down to that talent.

- Don't make the mistake that quantity is better than quality. Too many recruiters working on your jobs can send a negative impression to the talent community.

- Have high expectations for your recruitment sources. Give them realistic deadlines but make them stick to them; ask for metrics on their activities; demand that they give you the best service possible.

And, most of all, remember that the level of satisfaction that a competent external recruiter gets from a job well done is extremely high. External recruiters want to work with you to continue to make your company the best in its field. Talent acquisition plays a major part in that.

The Boutique Search Firm

Kathy April Barr

Director of Executive Search, The Stump LLC

T hird-party recruiters—defined as people outside of a particular organization who are hired to recruit talent—are called everything from
executive recruiters to headhunters to, simply, the independent recruiter. And when the need arises, a company can select a third-party recruiter quickly and judiciously, or spend what seems like an eternity by
issuing RFP (request for proposal) presentations and calling together a
selection committee.

In numerous ways, the top 25 recruiting firms have an unfair advantage
over independent recruiters. After all, their billings, revenue, and often
longevity make them an obvious selection for all the right lists. Their senior
management and partner ranks often consist of a fraternity of Ivy League and
Big Ten alumni. More often than not, they have experience in executive
suites and have spent time in some of the most notable consulting and Fortune 500 firms. Their client list reads like a who's who. Their top recruiters
have followed careers and been associated with many of the same people
they've served and placed over the years. No doubt they run auspicious businesses and warrant the respect and brand recognition they've acquired.

There is, however, an alternative to the expansive executive search firm. In the recruitment business, bigger doesn't necessarily equate to better. Thus, the boutique search firm was created. My purpose here is to dispel myths commonly associated with the smaller executive search firm, and outline the many advantages these smaller firms provide.

Myth 1—Lack of Experience

This is a huge hurdle for a younger firm. I urge you to be clear on what you're evaluating and buying. If the firm is five years old but the combined recruitment experience on the team is 75 plus years, you're purchasing the collective experience of the team, not the company name. If it isn't offered, always ask for a resume of the person(s) working on your particular assignment. After reviewing this information, you may be more impressed with the kinds of recruitment they've done (i.e., technical, college, senior management). A respectable number of newer firms combine the experience of seasoned professionals for a stronger portfolio and marketing tool. It's their insurance policy that they can book, maintain, and execute the business they seek.

Myth 2—Cutting Corners

Small firms have something in common with the big boys: They are in business to make a profit. If you have experience with the larger search firm, you know that their infrastructure supports this. Compensation is directly tied to building and maintaining a healthy book of business. In reality, however, the niche firm can't afford to cut corners. This is the reason they often exercise more diligence during the research and sourcing phase of a search assignment. Interviews aren't left to inexperienced associates, and essentially every factor about candidates is checked and rechecked before they walk through the client's front door. Since clients are a lot less forgiving when it comes to a smaller firm making mistakes, smaller firms try to avoid doing so at all costs. Larger firms are frequently afforded more discretion and grace when a search assignment has failed; in a larger firm, clients often presume that this occurrence is negligible and statistically justified, based on the number of searches they perform. Firms in the minor league generally work harder for clients, simply because they have to.

Myth 3—Length of the Client List

Allow me to share a brief but true story: A colleague recently interviewed with a top firm (ranked in the top five of national executive search firms). She was impressive enough to have gone to the third round of interviews, progressing to finally meet with the senior managing partner of the firm. Having succeeded to this point, she was almost certain of receiving an offer. When the time was appropriate, the partner turned the tables and asked if she had any questions. The two she asked sealed her fate. "Yes," she responded. "With the number of clients you have, how is it possible not to poach or recruit out of companies that you've previously served or are currently serving? Don't you run out of available candidates?" The partner replied, "We have 'A' clients and we have 'B' clients, enabling us to better navigate." Her follow-up question? "Do the 'B' clients know they are 'B' clients?" The partner replied with a pregnant pause, then asked if she had any remaining questions. Are you surprised that my colleague did not get hired?

I share this story, however, not to suggest that the largest, multinational firms are deceiving their clients; by virtue of their size, however, they usually incorporate this kind of client segregation. In contrast, smaller firms have autonomy and more control over the number of their clients, which helps them avoid this dilemma. Their goals, missions, and growth strategies are different and usually don't consist of being the biggest. They'd rather be cited as the best to the clients (regardless of the number) they serve.

Myth 4—Success Rate

Success is built on one completed search assignment at a time, one satisfied client at a time. Any firm you consider hiring should be able to provide references, who will verify its performance. Make sure it is good at matching candidates with your culture and position. And make sure the same language is used when talking about the success ratio. Here, it's definitely quality and not quantity that matters. Whether it's 25 out of 25 or 250 out of 250, they both equal a success ratio of 100 percent.

Myths about success rates exist today because people don't focus on the right questions. In my experience, I've found that only five questions really matter:

1. *What is your philosophy around executive search?* In other words, how will you approach our situation? Let's face it, your assignment is the only one you're interested in. You should hear responses to questions you hadn't thought of yet. If the search firm's approach is to walk into a presentation with ready-made solutions—without learning through dialogue about your current situation and challenges—run for the hills. In a search, the model or template may be the same but there are steps that will have to be altered along the way to meet your specific workplace dilemma or circumstance.

2. *Who will do the work?* How many times will my assignment be delegated? Who will be my relationship person? When can I expect completion, and how often will someone communicate with me about the search progress? Who supervises the work? What happens if you reach an impasse? Ask for the script that the recruiter will be using with candidates. You will want to ensure its accuracy.

3. *Do you have access to the candidates we seek?* Niche firms usually build their business around specialties (i.e., functional areas, minorities, etc.). An enormous amount of research and face time is devoted to ensuring that they have inroads into these target groups. When the time comes for them to place a call, they are much more likely to get a quick response time than firms without a specialty. It is no secret that all firms work with a multitude of directories and databases of key individuals. Making them work for you is key.

4. *Are you capable of filling this assignment?* This is a much better way to ask—and get at—whether or not the firm understands enough about your specifications so that it can comfortably recruit for it. A common question, but the wrong one, is: "How many searches like this have you conducted?" A recruiter worth his salt can in short order use the proper tools and resources to educate himself on the industry. Again, the resources in niche firms are usually more experienced and have done recruiting across industries and functional areas. Take notice of the firm that will decline a job that it can't fill; this says a lot about its integrity. Make a note to go back to that firm with a different job. It demonstrates the stuff you want in a vendor.

5. *How will I be charged?* Simply put, read your contract or agreement, especially the fine print. Understand your payment schedule and the fee structure. This will eliminate any misunderstandings down the road. Don't take advantage of the smaller size of the firm by attempting to

negotiate lower fees or deals if the provider isn't negotiating lower service or quality. These discussions are difficult for the small firm. Be timely with the payment of invoices. An $80,000 search fee is insignificant to a multimillion-dollar firm but can mean two to three months of covered expenses in a small one.

Jack Be Nimble, Jack Be Quick

When all is said and done, there are only two measures that clients care about when they hire search firms: quality and speed, and not necessarily in that order.

A vacancy in any company can result in projects on hold, lagging sales, a lack of leadership, and so on. Many times, when a recruiter gets a call it's in the form of an SOS. But going beyond the speed limit on a search assignment can lead to disastrous results and disappointment on both sides; the so-called successful candidate might later be termed a "bad hire" by the client if there was a rush to fill the vacancy. Be realistic about your expectations, particularly if you are behind the proverbial eight ball. The most sought-after candidates will take time to find.

Now, some final observations to ensure a successful outcome from a boutique search firm:

Be reasonable and direct about expectations. If the recruiter doesn't communicate sufficiently or in the manner you desire, let him or her know. If you develop a problem with how your assignment is being handled, talk about it. Even good recruiters fail miserably when it comes to reading minds.

Be in a position to supply all the tools needed for a successful outcome (i.e., access to the hiring manager, organization infrastructure, compensation components, etc.). If something isn't appropriate for public consumption, share it with your recruiter; he or she will know how to market around this sensitive information. A recruiter should be sensitive to confidential information.

Allow recruiters to do their jobs. After the initial and subsequent meetings to review the specifications, the assignment should be crystal clear. If it's not, ask them to state it. Side calls on your own regarding candidates can backfire, and they are often in breach of contract. At worst, if the unsuspecting candidate learns of this and his or her current position is jeopardized, or a candidate thinks that erroneous or negative information has been shared, you (the client) can be faced with a lawsuit. Smaller firms have the resources to appropriately probe into the backgrounds of candidates.

Remember that no executive search firm, regardless of its size, can offer you a solid guarantee. Expect a reasonable policy around the replacement of candidates for a predetermined time period, or expect a portion of the fees already paid to be returned. There are any number of factors that both the client and the search firm cannot control. Family emergencies, unimaginable counteroffers, and other life events can even cause a candidate who has accepted an employment offer to do an about-face. Don't paint them into a corner by asking them to lie to you. Respect them for their honesty and think twice before hiring.

The tried-and-true adage of not judging a book by its cover applies to firms that don't make the top 25 in billings. Firms are characteristically different in every imaginable way. The small firm experience is a personal one, one that might be welcomed and profitable for your company the next time you need the help of a third-party recruitment team.

CHAPTER
20

Using Quality Processes

Gary Hunt
Vice President, OMI, Inc.

Regardless of the economic outlook, recruitment and retention of valuable employees are now clearly recognized as two of the most important issues facing corporate America. Advantages that arise from opening new markets, improving technology, and even lowering material or labor costs eventually prove to be relatively short-run. In today's business world, one company's long-term advantage over another lies in its ability to attract and retain adequate human resources. This means that the qualities that drive performance excellence—such as initiative, imagination, innovation, motivation, and intelligence—are just part of what we call "human resources."

As business struggles with layoffs, lower consumer confidence, softening commercial investment, disillusioned employees, and a volatile stock market, effective recruitment has moved from the responsibility of the human resources department to that of the boardroom. With today's sharper focus on human capital, employees are no longer considered an expense, but rather an investment. And corporate executive officers are expecting HR and recruiting managers to present clear strategies and directions for staffing their respective organizations. The value of a staffing organization is now measured by how skilled it is in recruiting and retaining key employees.

So how do you build a world-class organization, staff it with the best possible people, and drive it forward? The Baldrige Criteria for Performance Excellence is a great blueprint. The Baldridge Criteria recognizes that an organization's success depends increasingly on the skills and motivation of its employees, and addresses these needs in all seven of its categories, with a special emphasis on leadership, strategic planning, and human resources. Finding the right people, whether you refer to them as human resources, human capital, employees, or associates, is never easy. But if you do one critical thing correctly—namely, hire the people who are right for the company—most of the other human resources processes are much easier.

If you want to identify a model that works, look at the recipients of the Malcolm Baldrige National Quality Award. This award was established in 1987 to help American businesses compete globally. Its total quality management approach has led more than 45 businesses to performance excellence success. The Baldrige criteria help organization focus their efforts on seven vital business processes. Following the Baldrige model requires businesses to take a critical look at how they function, and to develop systems for improvement. It's a model that has helped OMI, a 2000 Baldrige award recipient, tackle its challenges with employee turnover.

OMI and Employee Turnover

OMI believes that to be a great company you need to do four things:

1. Be a company that people want to work for.
2. Select the right people in the first place.
3. Get workers off to a great start.
4. Coach and reward to sustain commitment and loyalty.

OMI does three of these four really well. But that second criterion—selecting the right people—is something we simply don't get to do and helps explain why staffing is one of our most unique challenges. At OMI, we're able to use a traditional selection process on only about 15 percent of our workforce; we inherit the rest. Typically, when we are awarded a project, the existing workforce comes with the deal. So more than 85 percent of the workforce may come to us shanghaied, conscripted, and occasionally kicking and screaming. We have to begin our recruiting process after these employees are notified they have a job with OMI.

While we use the Baldrige criteria in all aspects of our business, we find them particularly useful in our HR processes. We've used the Baldrige criteria to set up an HR system that is part of our strategic planning process, part of our balanced scorecard (or what we call our "Family of Measures"), and integral to our culture.

To be successful with our unique recruiting system, we used the Baldrige criteria to help us develop a process for examining three things: our approach, our deployment, and measuring our results.

APPROACH

We asked ourselves: How do you approach your recruiting efforts? Are these efforts aligned with your firm's mission, vision, and strategy? Do you have a solid forecasting model in place to help you determine staffing needs for the next one to two years?

How do you define your recruiting market? And once you have defined it, how do you make sure you dominate it? Once you have defined it, how do you reach it? How do you know what you are doing is effective?

Do you define your requisitions in terms of strategic initiatives, key business focuses, or some other metric relevant to your business strategy? Does your selection process define applicant fit? Do you target strategic hires from your competitors, going after their best talent?

You have to tell your story. Why is working for your firm better than working for any of the other firms the applicant could work for at this time or in the future? Does you story show that you value people?

DEPLOYMENT

After clearly defining your role in the company's business strategy and developing a staffing plan, you need to deploy your plan.

Develop metrics that show where your best hires come from. This will allow you to increase the effectiveness of your staffing program by focusing resources on those areas where you get the best return.

Include your staff in the planning and deployment process to help facilitate the implementation and ultimate success of your business plan. Training will be a major part of your deployment process. You will need to make sure your staff understands your firm's mission and vision and their role in support of the strategic plan.

RESULTS

With the focus on measuring results and with benchmarking against your industry and national metrics increasing, more firms are now in the business of capturing and reporting human resources and staffing data. In our quality process, we use data from the Saratoga Institute, the National Association of Colleges and Employers, the Society for Human Resource Management, and others to help establish and measure results. We also benchmark with other Baldrige recipients in a number of key areas such as staffing and training.

Have you developed a process to measure and share your success rates? How does the effort you put into the system deliver value, and how do you measure that value? When the annual budget process begins, do your metrics and story give you the information you need to justify the investment you are requesting?

The 1999 Saratoga Institute Human Resources Financial Report stated: "To effectively utilize human capital intelligence, organizations must realize its value and learn how to use industry benchmarks as strategic business tools. By using human capital intelligence data as a strategic business tool, companies can understand how to improve performance, productivity, and the return on investment in their workforce."

You have to be able to show that the ROI for your department warrants the investment of additional resources. Can you measure your success in terms of cost per hire, time to fill, key employee retention, or advance rate? How do the stakeholders within your firm know that you do a good job?

Using the Baldrige criteria as a guide, Texas Nameplate Company (a 1998 Baldrige award recipient) developed a strategy and vision statement with nine long-term goals. High on that list was the elimination of employee turnover by hiring the best, training them well, and keeping them on the job. According to Dale Crownover, president of Texas Nameplate Company, "Turnover kills you. It destroys morale within the company, and there is more chance for error when training new people, which affects quality and impacts customer response."

Recognizing the impact of turnover, OMI developed an initiative to determine why associates were leaving and to reduce turnover. As stated previously, OMI has a unique recruiting situation, and turnover is one of the metrics in our Family of Measures that we use to set our strategy and run our company. We determined that turnover was the result of poor hiring and poor training. To try to change this, we developed and deployed better training for both interviewing and management skills and then measured the results. We dropped our turnover by half and now lead our industry in employee retention. How?

- We first focused our training on our selection process. We saw that there was high turnover in the first year of those employees hired through the standard recruiting process. So our training looked at better techniques for sourcing candidates and better selection methods. By improving our pool of candidates and then doing a better job of selecting them, we were able to decrease our first-year turnover.

- We developed better interviewing skills, which also helped managers and supervisors develop better their overall communication skills.

- We developed training programs to improve skills in preparing and conducting performance evaluations. This included how to use OMI tools to clearly define expectations, how to measure results and tie performance to pay, and then how to link the associate evaluation process to overall project and company success. We saw a steady improvement in our already high employee satisfaction (measured by employee survey) and a continued drop in our turnover.

Obviously, getting the new employee through the door the first day is not the end of the staffing process. To be effective you have to look at your retention rates as well. Hiring the wrong people usually means that you get to repeat the process later, a function that significantly increases your staffing costs.

The Baldrige process requires that you learn to produce and measure clear results of meaningful activities and that you link these activities together. Ideally, these results should help you plan your future activities and make sure that your staffing group is aligned with the rest of your organization. And it means that you eventually move from a reactive recruiting mode to a more proactive process. Alignment with overall strategic goals allows staffing to focus on long-term transformational goals, helping to ensure that your company has the right skills, in the right place, at the right time. For example, in our strategic planning process, we were able to identify that the "big city" market would be expanding. Utilizing this information, our staffing group was able to begin hiring associates with the skills and background to support our entry into the market.

"The best way to organize OMI's growth was to build around quality and service to our customers and our associates," says OMI president and CEO Don Evans. "The Baldrige criteria set out a way to do that, and our associates benefited because they could understand their jobs, their purpose, and the direction of the company." OMI, an employee-owned company, has benefited, too. Revenue has grown by nearly 500 percent in the past 10 years and our turnover rate has dropped by 50 percent.

To start the Baldrige process for your company, try using the Baldrige self-assessment to refine your approach for attracting and keeping qualified employees. It will help you align your processes with changing business needs—including the fluctuating labor market. This helps align your staffing function as a key part of your firm's strategic plan and ensures that human resources and staffing have a seat at the table.

The Baldrige process highlights the following criteria: leadership, strategic planning, customer and market focus, information and analysis, human resource focus, process management, and business results. Baldrige recipients clearly recognize the value of recruiting and retention practices and can help you improve your staffing process.

To find out more about the Baldrige program and to complete an online self-assessment, go to www.quality.nist.gov. A number of states have state quality award programs that can help you get started on your quality journey.

Hiring Is a Process—Not an Event

Lou Adler

CEO, CJA—The Adler Group and POWER Hiring

Here are some basic truths about the hiring process:

- "Hiring is No. 1," the mantra chanted by 90 percent of all top executives, is just lip service. Few companies have actually made hiring a formal business. The investment resources and management attention needed to make hiring No. 1 have not yet been put in place by most companies. That's why companies have so much difficulty consistently hiring top people. Until hiring is a repeatable process with metrics, it will never be No. 1.

- One size doesn't fit all. A company's hiring process cannot be simply morphed from one company to another. For example, a company with a great name has a far easier time finding candidates than an unknown company.

- While hiring needs to be a process, it's not the same exact process for every job within a company. For example, the process used to find plentiful web site designers is not the same process as that used to recruit and hire rare medical technicians.

- "ETDBW—Easy to Do Business With," from Michael Hammer's *The Agenda: What Every Business Must Do to Dominate the Decade* (Crown Business, 2001), should apply to candidates as well as customers. As companies design their hiring processes, the point of view of the best candidate is typically ignored. The best are different from the rest, and everything about the hiring process should be developed from their perspective.

- If you're not an employer of choice, the quality of the recruiter and the recruiting team will directly affect the quality of the people hired.

With this foundation established, I'd like to suggest that developing a formal business process for hiring top talent is not all that difficult. You just need to convince top management to invest the time and money to do it. I believe the reason this investment has yet to be made is that there was never a clear vision of what the formal business process would look like. In this article, I'd like to formulate that vision.

Hiring Can Be a Two Sigma Process

Forget the six sigma stuff: That's a bit too lofty a goal for hiring. Less than one error in a thousand? No way. But a two sigma hiring process is achievable—with some planning and diligence.

Collectively, hiring is the least efficient business process in most U.S. companies today. Crude estimates would put it at .5 sigma—an error rate close to 85 percent! While hiring can never be perfect, something close to an 80 to 90 percent success rate is possible. This two sigma goal of an 80-90% success rate is still quite aggressive, but it's definitely worth shooting for, given the importance to a company's future of hiring top talent.

But getting to that two sigma goal won't be easy, considering the current state of the hiring process. Overblown advertising budgets are hiding basic flaws in the process. These are characterized by weak interviewing skills, lack of real job understanding, recruiters and managers who don't know how to counsel and coach top candidates, burdensome online processing that forces the best to opt out too soon, and boring ads that appeal only to the desperate. (See Exhibit 21.1.)

Here are four performance objectives that I believe *are* achievable for a two sigma hiring process:

1. Hire the best possible person for every job. Quality is No. 1. We want the best possible candidate. I think hiring only the top third is a reasonable and achievable goal. These are all of the "A" candidates, along with the "B pluses."

2. Just-in-time hiring is critical. Time to hire is important. The impact of not having a top person in place is very expensive. In most instances, it's not more important than quality, but it's still very important.

3. Minimizing errors and mistakes while increasing efficiency is important from a process improvement standpoint. You can't afford stupid errors from either a business or legal standpoint. Errors add time, cost, and frustration to an already challenging process.

Exhibit 21.1   Advertising and Sourcing Dollars Wasted.

4. Cost to hire should not be ignored. In building a hiring process, cost must be given its due—but not at the expense of quality, time, and efficiency. Unfortunately, too many HR departments overemphasize the cost objective, since it's reasonably easy to measure. Top management should clearly state that cost is on the list—but not first, second, or third. This way, everyone, particularly HR, understands its ranking in the overall scheme of running a business.

With these objectives in mind, it's important to understand how the top third group of candidates (mentioned in point 1) look for new career opportunities and decide whether to accept an offer. Understanding the needs of the customer is the first step in the hiring process redesign.

The Best Are Different from the Rest

Since hiring the best is the number one objective of the new two sigma hiring process, the perspective of these potential hires must be considered at each step. This is the most ignored aspect of every hiring process I've ever seen. It impacts how ads are written, how web sites are designed, how interviews are conducted, and how offers are negotiated. Every aspect of the hiring process must be based on an understanding that the best are different from the rest. For example, think how you would respond if some recruiter called and asked you the following question:

"Would you be open to evaluating a new career opportunity if it was clearly superior to what you're doing today?"

Few people could say no.

This is what you need to ask top candidates when they're about to consider applying or evaluating a career opportunity with your firm. Do your ads, employee referrals, direct sourcing calls, and networking approaches ensure 100 percent "yes" replies? Most ads are written to attract active candidates who are looking for a new job, which means that they're designed to filter out the worst of this lot—not to attract the best. When the process is designed to eliminate the worst, the best never get into the candidates' pool.

The best candidates are different from average candidates. If a company's hiring processes aren't designed with the unique needs of the best in mind, top candidates could be excluded or inadvertently eliminated every step of the way.

The best candidates always have multiple opportunities, including counteroffers. The best see a new job as a step in a career journey, not as the end of a job search. They tend to consider more variables when deciding to explore a situation or accept an offer. Job content is critical. What they'll learn, do, and become is part of the decision-making process. The company and who they'll work for—and with—are critical. They consult with more outside advisers, and take longer to decide. Most hiring processes at most companies ignore how the best make these important decisions. If you're going to treat your candidates as customers, you'd better understand how they make a buying decision and what information they need in order to make it.

Here are six of the more obvious problem areas that need to be considered to ensure that the best candidates aren't inadvertently excluded.

1. *First contact is dull.* If your ads are boring, the best won't apply (even if they don't have a job). If your verbal pitches to potential candidates or attempts to get referrals are boring, forget about it. You need to describe compelling career opportunities, not jobs. If your posted job descriptions don't describe opportunities that are clearly superior to what the best candidates are doing today, you don't have a chance to hire a top performer.

2. *Ads are dull.* I just read 25 different ads from five different job boards. None stood out as special. They were all look-alike jobs with similar titles and similar copy. Most ads are designed to eliminate the bottom third from applying. In the process, they demean the best. The best will not consider jobs that aren't compelling. This requires engaging titles and copy that describes the challenges and opportunities for growth. You need to treat candidates as customers, and with respect. Most ads treat candidates as commodities. A boring ad is a waste of money. If you're not getting dozens of top candidates for each ad, your ads need to be rewritten.

3. *The web site is designed for candidates looking for a job, not those looking for a* better *job.* While it's getting easier to apply online, there are few inducements for a hot candidate to apply for a job with your company. I just went to a dozen major company web sites to test the experience from a candidate's perspective. Only one—it was an auto rental company—made me want to apply and be part of that company. The others offered just jobs. The best are different from the

rest, and they must be treated that way. Little of the technology built into web sites is designed for attracting the best; it's designed to manage data. If filling these positions is important to the growth of your company, do what I just did. Evaluate your own web site. Rewrite the listed job descriptions and make them compelling and easy to find. Make sure the experience is positive. Ask yourself: If a hot candidate is casually looking for a job and comes to your web site, what is the chance they'll find the job and decide to apply? Then ask, why would they come to your web site? Sourcing is equivalent to marketing, and marketing people should be leading this part of the effort.

4. *Screening process eliminates the wrong candidates.* If you filter out candidates based on skills and years of experience, you'll frequently eliminate top performers from other industries, or those with great potential but who are a little light on experience. Instead, try to use performance or accomplishment filters. Look for awards won, patents filed, articles written, speeches given, and management of budgets and team projects as better filters for separating the best from the rest. A few search engines allow you to do this; validated biodata screening tools are also a fine alternative. Get rid of job specs that demand experience and skills. Instead, describe the challenges and opportunities. Everyone complains about the lack of top candidates. What I've discovered is that companies inadvertently prevent them from ever applying by overemphasizing skills. Remember: It's what they *do* with those skills that matters.

5. *The application process is burdensome.* If a hot candidate gets this far, how long does it take to actually apply to one of your posted jobs? Unless you have some inducements along the way, the best will opt out. Make it as easy as possible to review your job profiles. If these are compelling, a candidate is more likely to submit some type of application. Ask for as little prequalifying information as possible. You might want to add one line for any awards won, recognition received, articles written, participation in conferences, or patents held.

6. *The interview process is unprofessional.* The best candidates want to earn the job; it has more value this way. Do your recruiters and hiring manager switch to sales mode once they meet a hot candidate? This not only cheapens the job, driving some top candidates away, but it also results in making inflated offers. Also, by overselling and

underlistening, the interviewer never knows if the person is really any good until it's too late. Conduct comprehensive in-depth interviews of people you suspect are hot candidates. They'll appreciate your level of professionalism and the respect you're giving to them. Not only will you find out if the person is as good as you suspect, but you'll also demonstrate the type of person, manager, and company you are—one with high standards of performance.

You don't have to be great at everything to hire great people—you just need to be pretty good at everything, and bad at nothing. What I've seen is that people are trying to be great at only a few things, but leaving gaping holes elsewhere. For instance, a great web site with boring job descriptions and a cumbersome application process is a waste. The best applicant tracking system will do little if you're not seeing great candidates, or if hiring managers don't know how to interview and close properly. You just need to fill every gap, and then work on those critical areas that drive top talent to your company.

The POWER Hiring Process

Hiring top people is actually quite easy if you have a great company name and competitive jobs. It's quite hard for companies that don't have the marquee name or are offering more traditional jobs. Yet over the years I've found a number of individual managers and a few companies that consistently hired top people—despite these handicaps. The overlapping themes of what they did became the POWER Hiring process described in my book, *Hire with Your Head—Using POWER Hiring to Build Great Companies* (John Wiley & Sons, 2002). POWER Hiring represents the five principles required to hire one great person.

The Five POWER Hiring Principles for Hiring Great People

Performance Profiles: If you want to hire superior people, first define superior performance. Describe what the candidate needs to do to be successful, not what the candidate must have. Describe the job, not the person.

Objective Evaluations: Past performance is the best predictor of future performance. If you know what you're looking for, it takes just four questions to assess candidate competency.

Well-Developed Sourcing Plans: Sourcing is marketing, not advertising. Treat candidates as customers, not commodities. The best are different from the rest.

Emotional Control: Personality and performance are both critical to job success, but measure performance first. Measure your first impression at the *end* of the interview, when you're less affected by it.

Recruiting Right: Recruiting is career counseling, not selling. Create a compelling career opportunity, make candidates earn the job, and then they'll attempt to sell you.

These POWER Hiring principles need to be considered in the design of any business process for hiring. This is true whether you're planning to hire one person or a thousand.

The Three "C" Strategic Drivers

Understanding the needs of the best in combination with the POWER Hiring principles offers the foundation for designing a two sigma hiring process. Creating a practical hiring process requires an understanding of the three strategic drivers:

1. The candidate supply.
2. The company reputation.
3. The competitiveness of the job.

I call these the three "C" drivers. If you have many strong candidates, a great company, and a great job, hiring top people is relatively easy. But, if you have few good candidates, a little-known or poorly thought of company, and an uninspiring job, then the sourcing and hiring process will be very challenging. These three strategic drivers affect:

1. The actual hiring process used (recruitment advertising, sourcing channels, selection methods).
2. The quality of the recruiting team needed to pull it off.
3. The technology infrastructure to manage and process data (tracking systems, career web site).

Obviously, if you have a great company, great jobs, and a plentiful supply of top candidates, the recruiting team doesn't need to be too strong. If the candidate flow is too high, then the applicant tracking system and career web site need to be first-rate to handle the high volume of resumes. If you have an unknown company, the career site should be first-rate to present the company vision. If you can't find enough candidates or the jobs aren't competitive, you need a top-notch recruiting team.

These are all considerations that must be taken into account as a company designs its hiring process. None are hard or complex, but they are typically ignored. That's why one size doesn't fit everyone. You can't just copy what the best companies do and hope to be successful. Don't be fooled by a slick vendor who's got the next best solution to hiring top people. Every product and service must be integrated with every other hiring product and service based on the three "C" drivers, the needs of the best, and the POWER Hiring principles. Companies can easily go astray unless the underlying system is designed first. Then it's important to select the best product, vendor, and service that meets the system's needs. This is the only way the two sigma hiring process can be successfully designed and implemented. A process that seamlessly links systems, people, and practices can serve as the framework for getting hiring under control.

The performance profile is the first step. My suggestion? *Never hire another person until every member of the hiring team agrees to what the person taking the job needs to do to be considered successful.* This step alone will change everything. By defining job success up front, managers will have a relevant benchmark to assess competency rather than relying on their own biases and perceptions. From the candidates' perspective, the performance profile is what attracted them to the job opening in the first place, and why they decided to accept this offer even though they had multiple opportunities. This now represents a career opportunity, not just another job.

Hiring is a process, not an event. "Winning the talent wars" is a dangerous concept. The implication is that once the war is won, the company can go on to something else. The war is never won. Processes, procedures, systems, and management commitment for hiring top talent must be 24/7. The building of the system might start with a major project and a lot of fanfare, but hiring the best requires an ongoing commitment. It must be part of the strategy, operational plan, daily discussions, and every performance review. In the process, don't forget how to hire one top person as you build systems to hire dozens or hundreds. Each great person is unique. Treat them all this way. The best really are different from the rest.

The Staffing Process—with an Emphasis on Volume Recruiting

Arthur E. Nathan

*Senior Vice President/Chief Human
Resources Officer, Wynn Resorts*

In 1972, when I graduated from the Cornell School of Industrial and Labor Relations, the role of the personnel department related mostly to contract negotiations, administration, and record keeping. Employment regulations were at a minimum and the stature of the personnel function within an organization was negligible. The staffing function then consisted of posting job vacancies, accepting applications, and passing these along to the departments with the openings.

Since the mid-1980s, however, personnel has been renamed human resources (HR). There has been a proliferation of employment legislation and regulations, and the HR professionals responsible for staffing have become an important part of the organizations they serve. During this time, the economy has been impacted by technology, globalization, and low unemployment. It's no wonder that the role of the staffing manager has become more important and challenging. And my overarching philosophy about the staffing process reflects the profession's growth.

The role of HR is to source and refer applicants to the manager responsible for making the hiring decision, and that manager must be given the total responsibility and accountability for making that hiring decision. HR is a full partner in this process and is responsible for ensuring that it is completed in a smooth, expeditious, and legal manner.

As the leader of human resources for Mirage Resorts, I had the responsibility for staffing some of the largest hotels in the world, and have experienced firsthand these staffing challenges and complexities. While these experiences were in the realm of volume hiring, the strategies that were used can be adapted for more regular hiring needs in both large and small organizations.

The ideas included in this chapter recognize that the staffing process is divided into several components: planning, recruitment, application intake and processing, interviewing, selection, and new hire processing. The goal of this chapter will be to define the objectives, strategies, and processes for each.

Planning

While most of us in the HR profession are adept at acting, the skill that is most important is the ability to plan. Before any actions are taken, it is imperative that extensive planning takes place when it comes to a hiring program. The following steps are critical:

Know the demographics of your metropolitan statistical area (MSA). This is the area your workforce will probably come from. This information can be obtained from the Internet, the local library, the state department responsible for employment issues and tracking, local business and HR leaders, the news media, and your own company's history and experience. I found that census information and the Nevada Department of Employment, Training, and Rehabilitation were the most helpful in answering questions about the labor force, the demographics of those who were unemployed, and the resources available to help fulfill our staffing requirements. Additionally, the local business and HR communities were extremely helpful in providing insight from their experiences.

Conduct a wage and benefits survey in your MSA. You need to know the prevailing wages for the jobs in your industry in order to be competitive in recruiting and retaining employees. Use the same contacts you met when researching demographics and ask for additional information related to wages, benefits, working conditions, and other total compensation type issues. If there are local unions that represent workers in positions similar to those in your company, obtain current collective bargaining agreements and study them for this information. You might find that companies are hesitant to share this information directly, in which case you may need to use third parties such as local colleges, the state department of labor, local employment agencies, and local employment attorneys. These individuals can help assemble the data while protecting the identity of the potentially reluctant sources.

Determine how you want to document job content. Many companies have detailed job descriptions that can be used to communicate this information to managers and applicants. I personally do not subscribe to these, as they tend to limit management's flexibility and potentially lead to employees being focused on the job's boundaries rather than the need to get work done. Another issue that needs to be addressed is the drafting of essential functions for each of the job classifications. These can potentially identify the required knowledge, skills, and abilities for each while also satisfying the responsibilities you have toward the Americans with Disabilities Act (ADA). In my experience, these proved invaluable in defining these issues for new hires and helped meet the ADA's requirements.

Conduct a statistical analysis of the number of applications needed to provide a sufficient selectivity ratio. In general, 10 applications are needed for every employee hired. This allows for proper consideration and elimination of applicants through the multiple stages of the employment process, and a withdrawal percentage of those who either can't wait or are subsequently not interested in the position. Understand that there will be a fallout of applicants for a multitude of reasons during the employment process—some you reject, others withdraw their applications, and still others rank lower than the better applicants. I believe that managers should be required to interview at least three applicants for each position vacancy; this allows them to gain a good perspective on the comparative qualities of each, and a sense of the relative depth of the applicant pool. You should enlist the assistance of financial analysts in your company who are experienced in dealing with this type of spreadsheet preparation; their help will ensure that the information is accurate and presented in a format that your executives understand and are familiar with. I will tell you that this was the most difficult thing I had to do, and yet in the end it proved to be the most beneficial tool in helping to guide our planning and actions.

Use the information in your statistical analysis to plan the HR department's staffing needs. The analysis will set guidelines for how many applications, interviews, and so forth you will need. You must then determine the length of time the tasks take and how many HR staff will be needed for each. This analysis will also help to set the time line for accomplishing all of the tasks. In the case of opening a new hotel in Bellagio, we determined that we needed 80,000 applications; that 22 weeks and 30 HR staff were needed to accept all of these; that 10 weeks were needed to conduct 27,000 second interviews (conducted by a rotating crew of 180 managers); and that 12 days were needed to process 10,000 new employees. As you conduct this part of the planning, walk through each step carefully—use role-plays and real-life scenarios—so that you fully understand how the process will work and whether your decisions are appropriate.

Take a look at your employment office through the eyes of an applicant. Is it a pleasing environment? Does it make a positive statement about your company? Is there sufficient room for queuing lines and work space, and is the signage helpful, informative, and visible? Remember, this is the first impression that applicants will have of your company—make it a good one!

Get all the help you can find to develop an effective and legal application, and to plan for how you are going to handle those applications. Know what information you need to have and how to legally phrase each of the questions on the application. It will help if you gather applications from your competition and from sources on the Internet. Get legal assistance to make sure you have met all of the requirements. Determine whether to gather equal employment opportunity (EEO) data on applicants; it is not required unless you are a government contractor, but the EEOC will not be happy if you get a discrimination charge and do not have this data. Decide if you want to have paper applications, or whether you want to embark on implementing an electronic version. Decide if you will accept applications only in your office or whether those submitted via the Internet will be accepted. Will you accept resumes in lieu of applications? Mirage Resorts utilized an electronic application and required all applicants to fill theirs out in the employment office so that a personal discussion could be had with each (this will be described in greater detail later in this chapter). We also decided not to accept resumes—they did not contain all the information or signatures that we felt were necessary to make an informed choice about the applicant. The Society for Human Resource Management (SHRM), the Internet, and your labor attorneys are all resources you should utilize to help research these issues.

In the end, you cannot plan enough. The process of planning and walking through each of these steps and issues will give you a firm understanding of how to meet your goals. And it will help the rest of your company understand the complexities and needs of the HR department in achieving their hiring objectives.

Recruitment

Now that you understand the planning needs related to the hiring process, let's examine the components of a successful recruitment program. The following components were used for the openings of the Mirage Casino Hotel (55,000 applicants, 6,000 employees), Treasure Island (65,000 applicants, 5,000 employees), and Bellagio (87,000 applicants, 10,000 employees). While these were indeed volume hiring projects, the same components were applied to the hotels' more traditional hiring needs after the openings were completed. Here, then, are those components.

ADVERTISING

Traditionally, companies place "Help Wanted" ads in local and regional newspapers. These give the position description along with a list of qualifications required of the successful candidate, and then go on to state the compensation and benefits associated with the position. This assumes that only those who meet the qualifications and salary requirements will apply—which, in my experience, is rarely the case. Applicants are those in need of a job. Once they see that a company is hiring, they will apply, regardless of the specifics listed in any advertisement. If that is the case, then the space needed to include all that specific information might be better used for an alternative message.

Use advertising to promote the fact that your company is hiring and list some other attributes about your workplace. In the case of the Mirage Casino Hotel, we wanted to let applicants know that this hotel was going to be a fun place to work. Thus, one of the first employment ads we placed stated: WE ARE LOOKING FOR 5,000 EMPLOYEES WHO WOULDN'T MIND WORKING IN A TROPICAL RAINFOREST WITH LIVE SHARKS AND A VOLCANO THAT ERUPTS EVERY 15 MINUTES. This single advertisement drew more than 50,000 applicants, all of whom we attracted by the whimsical nature of the advertisement.

Hire for personality and train for skills. Most hiring managers are looking for people with good attitudes and work ethics. A successful applicant with those attributes can be trained for most jobs more easily than a skilled applicant can be trained to have a good attitude and work ethic. This advertising method attracted those types of applicants. These same concepts were utilized for the openings of Treasure Island and Bellagio, and resulted in 65,000 and 87,000 applicants respectively.

These same strategies can be used in other advertising formats such as the Internet, employment agencies, job fairs, and direct mail. Focusing on the positive attributes of the company and the hoped-for candidates will result in a better applicant pool from which to choose your new hires.

SOURCING APPLICANTS

My experience has proven two things:

Applicants are hesitant to relocate for most jobs, and thus local and regional recruitment is the most effective. Research your own employees, and I suspect you will find that they lived within commuting distance when they applied. Your recruitment efforts should be targeted within a geographic area that is a reasonable commuting distance for the employees.

The applicant pool is fixed; that means it is finite and can't be increased by conventional methods. Of course you can lower the qualifications and/or increase the pay rates, but those are both bad options. You just need to get the word out about your hiring needs—advertising, job fairs, billboards, word of mouth, your current employees spreading positive information about your company and its employment opportunities, an effective public relations campaign (media interviews and appearances), presentations at local events (community organization meetings), and presentations in classrooms. All of these should produce an applicant flow of all the individuals interested in exploring employment opportunities with your company.

If these strategies do not produce a sufficient number of applicants, you might consider looking in nontraditional places for additional ones. Several that proved successful for Bellagio include:

Your current employees are a good source of applicants themselves. Does your company have a posting policy to allow all current employees to apply for vacancies? You should post all openings and allow them to apply—this will alert you to their interests and give them opportunities to move around and up within your organization. If you do post these openings, make sure you give your employees a real first shot at obtaining these positions. Many companies make the mistake of posting without making it a policy for managers to give preference to current employees. That creates distrust and can potentially affect morale.

Your current employees are also usually willing to refer friends and relatives. Many companies offer a bonus to the referring employee and/or the new hire, either at the time of hiring or when a probationary period is completed.

Your community is made up of large numbers of employees at other companies whose skills and abilities might help you achieve your hiring goals. Many of these will respond to advertising and word of mouth and apply on their own. Others are happy in their current positions, or could be unaware of your openings, and might need some motivating to help them decide to apply. One strategy that we employed at Bellagio was to offer signing bonuses to those who had specific skills that were needed, which we described in our advertising. Another was to send our managers out to identify individuals whose skills and attitudes matched our search criteria. To these we gave a specially printed card that told them we were impressed with their performance and extended an invitation to come into our employment office for an express interview. Since the best way to assess applicants' abilities is to observe them while they are working, we were able to incorporate these observations into the formal interview. Most of these individuals were offered positions as soon as they applied and turned out to be great employees.

Area schools are an excellent source of applicants. Universities have students looking for internships while they are still in school; internships give both you and students an opportunity to view each other and decide if employment in your company is worthwhile. Internships may be paid or may involve the students working for little or no pay while earning credits for their efforts. Community colleges are also excellent sources of applicants. Their student populations are made up primarily of those who have already worked and are back in the education system to gain or improve their skills. They are usually more mature and have work histories that can be easily checked. There are high school students who choose not to go on to college, and they can also be excellent applicants. Some have regular diplomas, while others have specialized ones that may be of particular interest—in Las Vegas there are high schools that specialize in service and technical degrees. Look for trade schools and apprenticeship programs in your area. These graduate students with highly focused skills like graphics, construction trades, administrative and accounting capabilities, and computer programming.

Every state has a Workforce Development Board responsible for ensuring that a sufficient and qualified labor pool exists for employers. These boards are directed by local business leaders and can be contacted through the state's employment security department—you can look them up in your phone book. They also have special programs to help disadvantaged individuals find employment. These include veterans, welfare recipients, ex-offenders, people with disabilities, senior citizens, youths, and homeless individuals. These boards can help source such applicants and assist with preparing them for opportunities in your company. They control funding for job training of new hires as well as incumbent workers and can advise you whether your company would qualify for this money.

There are also programs in every state to promote welfare to work. These may be coordinated by public or private agencies and assist those who have been on public assistance to prepare for employment opportunities. In addition to welfare clients, others include the homeless, ex-offenders, and youths. Like me, you may have little experience with these populations and be concerned about their ability to fit into the world of work. There are experts out there who can assist you and your organization in understanding their special needs and the strategies that can help make them more successful applicants and employees.

Look to the retired population in your community. In Las Vegas, there were large groups of retired individuals who were able to help us achieve our hiring goals. One advantage they bring is the experience and maturity from their previous careers; they are also usually looking for part-time employment and can help you to fill needs that may be less than full-time.

And last, there are employment agencies that specialize in sourcing and referring applicants to employers. These usually charge a fee to either the candidate or the employer.

All of these recruiting strategies can help you to achieve your hiring goals. No one strategy will suffice, and some are more challenging than others. Remember that your primary responsibility is to have a sufficient pool of qualified applicants to satisfy the needs of the hiring managers. It will take many more applicants than there are available positions to ensure that you get the best ones.

The Employment Process

Now that you understand planning the process and sourcing the applicants, we will conclude this chapter by describing the components of an effective application and interviewing program. How you handle these responsibilities will determine both the caliber and morale of the successful candidates. These components create the first and lasting impressions that these individuals have about your company.

APPROACHING THE EMPLOYMENT OFFICE

Most people fill out applications on impulse. But their experience in the employment office can either reinforce that decision or make them sorry they tried.

- Is there enough parking to accommodate the applicants? If not, you may inadvertently chase them away.
- What does the approach to the office look like? Is the signage sufficient to guide them to the door?
- When they enter the office, are there people or signs to greet them and guide them along? Think of the office as the window on your workplace—much the same as a retail store views its windows and entry. Is the office neat, bright, cheerful, and accommodating? These are all subliminal marketing cues that affect the applicants—make this a place that they feel good about entering!

Decide whether you want applicants to walk in when they choose, be scheduled, or have the option of either. Whenever you post vacancies, the potential for a mass response is great and it may be wise to consider having a scheduling process to control the flow. At Bellagio, we found that some applicants were impulsive and wanted to come only when they chose; others wanted the certainty of shorter lines and quicker service. We allowed the former while providing a schedule to those who needed one. This policy helped show the applicants that we were sensitive to their needs.

FILLING OUT THE APPLICATION

Traditionally, applications have consisted of questions on paper that applicants are asked to complete. The applicant handwrites these answers, and the legibility of that information has always been a problem for those who have to review the answers and enter the information into a database. Because paper is costly to purchase, handle, and store, I recommend that every company consider using an electronic, computer-based application. If you have a PC on your desktop, you already have most of the tools necessary to create an online e-version of your application.

I realize you may not have the technical expertise to attempt this—I certainly didn't when we did this at Bellagio—but there are lots of resources out there to assist you. There are software providers that can do this for you (choose between their version or a customized one especially for you), and local colleges and high schools have computer departments and classes where you can find qualified students to help. This is becoming more commonplace as companies place their applications on the Internet, and there are lots of examples of electronic applications from which to choose. If you elect this option, you will have to design space to include several PCs, decide whether to use keyboards or touch screens, and provide staff to assist with applicant questions. If you choose to use paper applications, make sure you have lots of tables and chairs, pens, phone books to check addresses, and both English and Spanish versions. You will also need space and a process for storage and retrieval.

HR REVIEW OF THE COMPLETED APPLICATION

Once the application is filled out, HR staff should review it for completeness. I recommend that this be done in person so that questions can be answered about job choice and any discrepancies related to dates and information can be corrected. Additionally, you would have an opportunity to conduct a cursory assessment of the applicant. This assessment should be well defined and documented, and the staff should be trained to conduct it. At Bellagio we looked for and rated five criteria:

1. Did the applicant apply for a position for which he or she had experience?
2. How long did the applicant stay in his or her last several jobs?
3. Was the applicant dressed appropriately in relation to the position being sought?
4. Was the applicant able to understand English?
5. What was the overall presentation of the applicant?

Each of these criteria had a set of answers and a numerical value. These answers were determined in conjunction with both department managers (for technical issues) and legal staff (for compliance). The applicant was assigned a numerical rating, and the entire pool was then available to the hiring manager for review. The key to making this work was the fact that the HR staff was not assessing technical competencies, but was focusing on generic attributes that they could understand. By having a well-documented set of criteria, the managers were able to understand exactly what the HR staff meant by each rating.

DEPARTMENTAL REVIEW OF APPLICATIONS

Department managers then have access to all of the applications, along with the ratings given by the HR staff. They should have a list of technical skills and abilities against which these are compared and determine which, if any, should be invited in for an interview. If the HR ratings reflect their own criteria, then they will consider them in ranked order and utilize the list as far as needed to satisfy their requirements.

For example, if the ability to speak and understand English is a job requirement, that would be rated highly; then the manager would look at this rating and weigh it accordingly. The opposite would be true as well, and thus the managers have the flexibility to consider and weigh those attributes according to their needs.

Another example would be if the reviewing manager considered experience in that specific job beneficial—such as for construction trades or computer technology—then the higher ratings relative to previous direct experience would be weighed more heavily.

The department managers should complete documentation that shows their decision, the reasons for it, and the action they wish to take with this applicant. The combination of the HR ratings and departmental review has the net effect of eliminating nearly 50 percent of the applicants from consideration at this point. These eliminated applications would be available for reconsideration if needed in the future.

Note: If it was determined to collect and analyze EEO data on the application flow, HR should now begin to look at the decisions. This would alert HR to any disparities and allow the organization to implement mitigating strategies to correct these.

Department Interview

Once the department manager decides which applicants are qualified, three should be interviewed for each available position. This will give the manager a proper selectivity ratio. HR should assist the manager with developing a list of questions that should be used for each interview; that way, every applicant will experience the same review and be treated equally. This is important for legal considerations. These questions can be either technical, situational, or behavioral, or some combination of all three. To further understand the nature of each type, look for information on the Internet—for example, on the SHRM web site. For each question, I recommend that answers also be developed so that the manager is judging each applicant on the same scale. By creating these questions and answers, you ensure consistency and proper documentation in case subsequent legal challenges are filed by any of the applicants.

At Bellagio, we developed four answers for each question—from best to worst—and assigned a numerical value to each. This way, the applicant was again given an overall rating for this part of the employment process. This—along with the HR review rating—became the applicant's overall score, and thus all applicants could be ranked in numerical order for final consideration. At Bellagio, we conducted 27,000 interviews in 10 weeks; for this or any volume of interviews you should consider scheduling the applicants to help maximize your interviewers' time and productivity.

Note: Again, if you are analyzing EEO data on the application flow, HR should review these decisions for potential adverse impact.

Additional Clearances

Many companies require potential employees to undergo background checks and drug tests. If so, this is when they should be conducted. Decide whether you want internal staff or external contractors to check each applicant's background. Employment, military, and academic information is the most common data checked for this purpose; if you choose to do this, it is required that the applicant provide written authorization for you to conduct these checks. If you choose to conduct a credit check on the applicant, an additional and separate authorization must be obtained from the applicant. You must also provide the applicant with specific notice of your intent to do a credit check and what recourse he or she might have if any adverse decision is made as a result of this check. At Bellagio, we did both of these checks and had the applicants sign both authorizations at the time they filled out their original applications.

For those applicants who pass both tests, and who are in line to potentially receive a job offer, many companies require a drug test. At Bellagio, we chose to take a sample of hair from each applicant and have it analyzed for drug usage during the previous three months. An alternative to the hair test is a urinalysis, which determines drug usage for up to the previous five days. We chose the hair test, which was more expensive but also more difficult for the applicant to defeat.

The Job Offer

After all of the interviews were completed and the final applicants were checked and tested, the department manager was given a list of available and approved applicants. This list was in ranked order, and the manager was required to select in this order as many applicants as were needed to fill the available vacancies. Managers were given the discretion to select out of ranked order if they had a valid reason that was both documented and approved. At this point a final analysis of EEO data would be conducted if you were reviewing the applicant flow for adverse impact.

Written job offers were prepared for each of the selected applicants. Each included the position, rate of pay, start date, and supervisor's name and contact number. The applicant then met with the manager to discuss the offer in person. This way, the manager could describe the offer in detail, answer any questions, and obtain the applicant's response directly. In a mass-hiring situation, you want to carefully plan this process to ensure that the greatest number of successful applicants accept the offer. At Bellagio, less than 1 percent of those who were offered positions failed to show up for their first day of work.

At this point, the applicants who accepted job offers were immediately processed for employment. They filled out all of the paperwork required to put them on the payroll, and they were scheduled for their first day of work. In order to facilitate this process we advised them what to bring for processing at the time they were scheduled for the job offer meeting.

Something Else to Consider

Most good applicants are going to be highly sought after. You need to consider how to motivate them to consider your vacancy over all others. Think of marketing these vacancies in the same way that stores market products to potential purchasers. Let applicants know as soon as possible that you are interested in them and hope that they will wait patiently for the full interview process to be concluded. By sending them correspondence to reinforce this message, you increase the percentages of those who will choose your vacancy. At Bellagio, we started sending cards, newsletters, and other novelty items to qualified applicants when the department review stage began. Even though the process took five months, a majority of the applicants we wanted waited for the process to be concluded.

Summary

An effective staffing program takes planning and careful implementation. The most successful ones also contain creativity and sensitivity to local issues and organizational dynamics. During the past 15 years, I have been involved in the volume hiring campaigns to open some of the largest hotels in the world, and was later responsible for the more regular hiring patterns of an ongoing operation. In both situations, I found that the needs of the hiring managers and the applicants were the same. The manager wanted the best-qualified applicant for the position, and the applicant wanted to be treated fairly and humanely throughout the process.

- Good planning prepared the HR staff for its responsibilities.
- A well-documented process and effective training prepared the hiring managers to confidently and competently perform their duties.
- Good communication and thoughtful treatment made the applicant feel appreciated and wanted.

Using Collaboration to Hire Smarter and Maximize Recruitment ROI— in Any Economy

Row Henson
Fellow, PeopleSoft

Few recruitment departments casually offer positions to underachievers. Few operate from unlimited recruiting funds. Today's quest to recruit top employees both rapidly and cost-effectively means survival of the fittest, requiring shrewd judgment and integration of the expertise of all players in the process.

Only with the right tools can an organization recruit competitively. To locate the best talent, screen candidates well, and make the best hiring decisions, companies must ensure that everyone involved in the hiring process collaborates through Web-enabled applications. Effective collaboration is a best practice for increasing access to high-quality candidates and reducing costs and time to hire.

Key to Smart Hiring

Collaboration brings together all recruiting content, transactions, and analytics and makes them available for informed decision making. Collaboration helps companies "hire smart" because all participants in the recruiting process work together using consistent information from a single data source.

The ideal collaborative solution is a comprehensive, integrated, end-to-end system. Applicants, candidates, HR, recruiting professionals, hiring managers, other corporate participants, and third-party vendors access only the information they need when they need it, promoting a smooth recruitment life cycle. Collaboration addresses all phases of this life cycle: attract, recruit, hire, retain, and train. By leveraging workforce analytics, companies can measure results and optimize effectiveness by tracking the best sources of candidates and analyzing time and cost-to-hire metrics.

Collaboration helps recruiting participants become self-sufficient via role-based, secure access to current data, 24/7. Self-sufficiency can be further increased with delivery via a company portal. Portals and other collaborative solutions can speed the recruiting process with features such as applicant home pages and automated resume processing. Collaboration with third-party services can circumvent unnecessary interviews by securing independent background checks.

Top Recruiting Challenges: A TMG Study

Talent Market Group, Inc. (TMG) is an intellectual capital firm focused on market intelligence in the talent marketplace. TMG builds tactical and strategic models and provides consulting services.

Recently, senior TMG consultants interviewed and surveyed recruiting and hiring personnel across North America, resulting in a listing of the top recruiting challenges. Six of the top 10 challenges can be addressed directly through collaboration. The following describes collaboration's role in facing these six recruiting challenges.

THE QUEST FOR QUALITY CANDIDATES: HOW TO GO BEYOND THE FIREWALL?

Web-based systems let companies collaborate securely, quickly, and effectively with candidates beyond the corporate firewall. Collaboration opens the door for attracting quality candidates and communicating with vendors via an environment that is still secure but extends outside the company.

For example, TurniRound Financials Inc., a midsized financial services firm, needs to quickly fill a position that requires rare skills. Without Web-based collaboration, TurniRound would merely have used its intranet to spread the word internally, combined with expensive conventional advertising for external distribution. Web-based collaboration allows TurniRound to speed its progress by expanding the candidate field, taking recruitment safely beyond the firewall through online postings, searches, and screenings.

MANAGING THE TALENT UNIVERSE: HOW TO EFFICIENTLY USE THIRD-PARTY VENDORS?

Through a vendor-management portal or other collaborative system, companies can address the entire universe of talent. Portals extend recruiting systems to staffing companies and other third-party vendors for secure, role-based collaboration, saving time and increasing exposure to recruitment services.

In the TurniRound example, the company is more likely to fill the position rapidly by communicating with staffing companies and vendors via a collaborative environment. These third parties might have specialized methods of securing candidates with rare skills, and collaboration can tie them in for a mutually effective, efficient platform that facilitates information exchange by all contributors. TurniRound might also subscribe to third-party providers for supplemental information such as salary surveys and skill-set demographics.

THE ROLE OF THE HIRING MANAGER: HOW CAN HIRING MANAGERS TAKE OWNERSHIP?

The interests of a hiring manager might become buried in recruiting processes. However, hiring managers directly participating in a collaborative recruiting system are more likely to have their needs and issues addressed because they can actively own their part of the recruiting process while communicating effectively with other participants. Collaboration helps resolve issues among parties involved in recruiting.

Before Web-based collaboration, Will E. Hirefast, TurniRound's hiring manager, would not have participated in recruiting the new candidate because there was no work flow or technology in place that involved him early in the process. Will felt that keeping up with the details and trying to be heard would not have been worth his time. Will was also frustrated because often the right people were not hired. However, it takes only moments for collaboration to involve Will as a key influencer—all the details are in a single location online, and Will can share ideas with the rest of the team quickly and easily from the convenience of a Web browser. The right collaborative technology facilitates and shortens the TurniRound hiring process, particularly for Will.

TALENT RELATIONSHIP MANAGEMENT: HOW TO INVOLVE CANDIDATES INTERACTIVELY?

Talent relationship management seeks to include candidates in the recruiting process, beginning at the corporate career web site. To do this, a true collaborative recruitment system is required. Web-based interaction integrates recruiting information, candidate transactions, and the involvement of participating individuals in the organization.

Upon receiving an online response, Will qualifies and screens the new TurniRound candidate, Betty Payswell. A two-way process emerges—Will and other participants view Betty's profile and submit any additional questions, while Betty gets answers about the company, job functions, and compensation.

LEVERAGING TECHNOLOGY: HOW TO CAPITALIZE ON EXISTING SYSTEMS?

Often companies use a number of valuable systems that are not integrated. Collaboration solves the problem of disparate systems by extending—not replacing—functionality via data warehousing. Collaborative solutions leverage existing systems and data stores through a single data repository that gathers and sources information.

After evaluating all the candidates, TurniRound decides to make Betty an offer. Aware that other companies are also pursuing Betty's skills, Will first investigates competitive compensation information in the company's data collection stores. Will accesses this information through the integrated online system and receives benchmarking data showing industry standards. He then calculates a competitive salary for Betty without leaving his desk.

EMPLOYER-OF-CHOICE MARKETING VERSUS REALITY: HOW TO MANAGE EXPECTATIONS?

Encouraging candidate collaboration in the recruiting system is a predictable way to manage candidate expectations while maintaining employer-of-choice status. It is easiest for recruiters to keep candidates informed and interested if the candidates have continuous interaction, receive prompt answers to questions, and can provide real-time feedback.

By involving Betty collaboratively, Will and the other participants in the recruiting process are able to extend a fair offer to Betty before any of TurniRound's competitors. Collaboration gives all interested parties a way to exchange information about the unique aspects of the position—including specific compensation details and company information—so a competitive offer could be on the table in a timely manner. Due to the collaborative communication process, Betty is comfortable and enthusiastic about the offer, understands the realities of the job, and can make an informed decision.

Preparation for Implementing a Collaborative System

Laying the groundwork for collaborative recruiting is critical for success. Before considering collaboration, however, a talent management system should be in place to clarify business objectives regarding the existing workforce, talent required, plans for workforce optimization, and enterprise performance.

Audit of Corporate Need

After resolving talent management issues, an organization should conduct an audit of its specific recruiting requirements. Companies that leap blindly into technology acquisitions without an audit of corporate need often fail to reap potential benefits. An audit helps avoid conflict between corporate recruiting objectives and collaborative activity, and can also circumvent the pitfall of a one-size-fits-all solution.

Every department must justify technological investments. By identifying areas ideal for collaboration, the recruiting department can achieve buy-in from top management—and where collaboration is unsuitable, seek an alternative. Prior to implementation, it is important to be able to demonstrate the effect of collaboration on transforming existing recruiting practices.

An audit should examine:

- *People*. Who are the participants—including candidates and third parties—and who will need access to the system?
- *Process*. Do current business processes truly support a recruiting model offering competitive advantage throughout the life cycle?
- *Technology*. What are the gaps in the current architecture, and where is the synergy with a collaborative platform?

Collaboration Snafus

Certain issues are not solved by collaboration. Decisions about work flow and use of the collaborative system are the recruiting department's domain. For example, most companies need to maintain advertisement centralization and avoid an excess of diverse candidate sources—job requisition can appear on the hiring manager desktop, but advertising should be assigned to internal and external specialists.

Collaboration does not create expert recruiters. Companies must separately assess training and education requirements for each participant.

Vendors' Roles

Because recruiting is complex, mapping and integrating core processes require vendors to participate as true partners. Vendor accountability must extend through the life of the system, not just in the purchasing or implementation phases. Top vendors offer features such as system optimization training, strategic management consulting, and role orientation support.

Instead of integrating with other applications, some solutions consist of hiring manager desktops that support candidates through the company's career portal. In light of this, it is critical to select an industry-leading vendor offering fully integrated systems that cover all business processes.

Collaborative systems containing extensions to suppliers allow third-party vendors an insider's view of staffing and recruiting processes. Although preferred vendor programs build strong relationships, companies need to regulate access to information and hiring managers. A system audit helps determine to what degree collaboration will positively impact results.

Increased Efficiency and Cost-Effectiveness

Collaboration transforms traditional recruiting systems into bottom-line contributors to corporate success. In its winter 2000 study, the Corporate Leadership Council found that collaborative applications reduced the average cost per hire by 60 percent—from $8,500 to $3,500. Time to fill jobs declined from 54 to 35 days, a 35 percent decrease.

Self-service within a collaborative system lowers transaction costs and increases ROI while promoting organizational efficiency. Self-service helps eliminate guesswork and decreases the time and resources required for routine tasks. The result is a paperless process for applicants, employees, and recruiters—efficiency increases, and cost per transaction decreases.

For example, a recruiter is opening job requisitions, scheduling interviews, and rating candidates' skill sets. Without collaborative self-service, communicating with coworkers, third parties, and candidates and managing the approval cycle are time-consuming. When role-based, personalized self-service is applied to the tasks, a series of preestablished web pages standardize information, which is quickly viewed and processed by others according to role and work flow planning.

Facing Economic Pressures

Recruiting is qualitative, not quantitative. Finding and retaining that ideal person for the job can be time-consuming and costly. The goal is to locate, screen, and hire the best candidates—the first time. Recruiting budgets are limited, and technological investments must be justified by the ability to produce results. Visible results emerge when recruiting is a consultative, collaborative process, rather than a transaction-based business function. Collaboration individually empowers participants while integrating them as a team.

Collaborative tools increase efficiency, thus making it easier to achieve recruiting imperatives while saving time and money. By solving the problem of employee self-sufficiency, collaboration shapes recruiting into a lean process that can more rapidly and cost-effectively secure the right talent.

System Basics

Every configuration is different. However, certain basic requirements of collaborative recruiting distinguish robust, industry-leading solutions from less-than-adequate choices on the market.

Top vendors include the elements comprising best practices, such as pure Internet architecture, role-based security, scalability, reliability, integration with other systems, global capabilities, and multiple databases connected to the enterprise warehouse. Companies should also look for:

- A hiring manager desktop that integrates requisition building, reports, metrics, workforce analytics, skills inventories, and HRMS data.
- Integrated workforce planning and performance benchmarking at each role desktop for knowledge transfer and improved decision making.
- Talent relationship management modules for support throughout the talent life cycle.
- Support for network referrals and vendor management for the recruiting supply chain.
- Corporate career site support to extend the system to applicants and candidates.

Radical Recruiting: Using Culture, Public Relations, and $0 to Get Results

Nancy S. Ahlrichs
EOC Strategies, LLC

Overview

With constant change, persistent pressure for financial results, and no increases in HR budgets on the horizon, anyone with recruiting responsibilities knows that traditional approaches to recruiting are not delivering results. Which begs the questions: Which nontraditional approaches deliver top talent while not straining either the HR staff or the budget?

Doing more with less has never been easy, but a lack of dollars can actually be the driver for innovation and creativity, the watchwords for this decade and the key to successful recruiting in a recovering economy. Successful recruiting and retention of top talent will be considered the next frontier in the endless search for profitability. When you lead the effort to recruit successfully—by capitalizing on the culture and public relations of your organization while spending no additional budget dollars—you will become known as a "radical recruiter" and a strategic leader.

Radical recruiting requires the mind-set of an entrepreneur. ONEX Incorporated, an Indianapolis-based high-tech solutions consulting firm with offices in the Midwest, grew to more than 200 employees in less than three years. The entrepreneurial approach to recruiting of co-founders Joe Huffine and Sally Huffine Breen resulted in fast growth and profitability. Along the way, their organization received six national, regional, and local business awards[1] and was purchased by Inrange Technologies Corporation, an East Coast storage networking solutions firm. A look at their experience will provide valuable lessons in recruiting. (See case study later in the chapter.)

Ten Assets to Leverage

To attract top talent to their emerging organization, the ONEX executives articulated both the current state of the organization and the future vision. They recognized that every hire is a critical hire, so they leveraged the resources they had at hand—especially their own networks and the networks of their colleagues. By leverage, I mean they magnified, multiplied, and amplified the positive effects of readily available recruiting assets. Here are 10 of those assets—assets that are readily available to nearly every organization:

1. *Leverage your managers—and your culture.* Make behavioral interviewing skills an organizational competency. Use lunch and learn programs to reinforce learning and to keep skills sharp after formal interview training. Help to develop competencies for open positions, and teach managers how to develop questions that uncover candidate experience using specific competencies. Train your managers not only to be better interviewers, but also to deliver a "Wow!" interview experience that makes every candidate more interested in working for your organization than they were initially. Be sure that

[1]Two-time finalists for Ernst & Young Entrepreneur of the Year Award, *ComputerWorld* magazine's "100 Best Places to Work in IT," Indiana University Kelley School of Business "Growth 100 Company," the Indiana Information Technology (INITA) CyberStar Award winner, and the *Indianapolis Business Journal*'s "Fastest Growing Companies."

your managers can articulate positive, powerful answers to questions such as "Why should I work here?" and "Why should I work for you?" Use e-mail to survey candidates about their interviewing experiences, whether they accept an offer or not.

2. *Leverage your employee referral program.* Use focus groups and mini-surveys to uncover the bottlenecks that prevent the enthusiastic use of your existing program, and roll out an upgraded program with much fanfare and promotion. Give business cards to employees that list company values and benefits on the back; distribute brochures that feature the real diversity found at your organization, as well as comments from employees about why they like working there. Be sure to cover benefits, fun, culture, and frequently asked questions (FAQs) so that candidates will be motivated to check out your web site and submit applications. Track employee candidate referrals and aim for at least 33 percent of external hires from employee referrals.

3. *Leverage your internal candidates.* Use the same focus groups and mini-surveys to uncover the bottlenecks in your internal candidate-hiring program. Post all openings and offer resume writing and interview skills training so that internal candidates have equal chances to fill job openings as do external hires. Consider a recognition program for those managers who develop their employees for promotion or lateral internal career moves. Track internal candidate numbers and hires.

4. *Leverage your files.* Files contain a pipeline of future hires—if you keep the right files! Ex-employees whose files are marked "would rehire" can be both referral sources and rehires—for full-time, part-time, or project positions. Pursue your best retirees for similar opportunities. Two of the highest-quality sources of top talent are often tossed in the "circular file": namely, the No. 2 candidates and the "declines." In both cases, the candidates know your organization and may be very interested in another opportunity to work for your organization in the future. Track rehires, the hiring of No. 2 candidates, and the hiring of those who initially declined.

5. *Leverage your relationships.* Business revolves around internal and external relationships. Develop and communicate a referral program that reaches beyond the employee referral program. Teach employees about strategic networking through lunch and learn sessions. Ask for, reward, and track employee referrals from:

- Current job applicants (make sure they know about other open-ings within your organization and be sure to ask for referrals).
- Ex-employees or alumni in good standing.
- Customers and clients who know your business.
- Vendors who regularly hear about individuals who are "looking."
- Interns who can refer other intern candidates as well as employee candidates.

6. *Leverage new hires.* Day one of a new job is filled with possibility and euphoria. Consider spotlighting the employee referral program dur-ing orientation—and offering a special double bonus for referrals during the new hire's first 30 days. Be sure the new hire knows the specific job openings, necessary qualifications, and process. Track the number of referrals from new hires.

7. *Leverage external media—get some PR!* Partner your HR and market-ing department to brand your employment experience by using data from employee surveys and focus groups. If you lack data, conduct a minisurvey of new hires—as well as longtime employees—to ask why they chose your organization, and why they stay. Take photos of employees to submit along with queries for:
   - Local newspaper coverage, appropriate trade journal coverage, and web site coverage about your culture (including the use of fun, mentoring, recognition programs, etc.).
   - Articles about employees and their interesting, unusual hobbies.

   Feature any printed articles on your web site and in a scrapbook that job applicants can review.

8. *Leverage your quality practices, ethics, or employment practices—get even more PR!* Seek awards for individuals, departments, and the en-tire organization as an employer of choice. Feature awards on your web site. Set goals to pursue and win awards. Publicize your employ-ees' accomplishments in newsletters and local media.

9. *Leverage community involvement—get more and better PR!* Track em-ployee involvement in professional, community, and even church activities. Create a spreadsheet of employee names and their in-volvement with the community. Recognize your "super community volunteers" with awards and celebrations. On your web site, feature your employees' volunteer efforts by listing the organizations they as-sist. Pitch an article to the local media on volunteerism and ask that

your employees be interviewed. Offer conference room space for community meetings. Provide branded shirts and T-shirts for community activities such as runs and other fund-raisers. Ask employees to consciously consider outside activities as great sources for great candidates.

10. *Leverage technology.* Use your web site to further brand your organization's employment experience; feature photos, quotes from employees, awards, values, and so on. Streamline the web site application process for internal and external candidates. Reignite your telephone job hot line. Publicize the web site address and hot line number on all available media: newspaper ads, mugs, pencils, invoices, letterhead, paycheck enclosures, newsletters, and so on. Consider using free resume blaster services such as www.resumeblaster.com or www.jobbankusa.com.

The most important thing to leverage is your own knowledge. Track the cost, number, and quality of hires from these different sources. Determine the quality of hire by tracking performance levels at six months and one year after hire. Bring in a free or low-cost intern to analyze results and keep your metrics up to date. Be innovative and then evaluate the results. Adjust your tactics, based on results and the impact to the bottom line. Think like an entrepreneur and use culture, public relations, and $0 for radical recruiting results.

ONEX Case Study

Founded in 1997 by siblings Joe Huffine and Sally Huffine Breen, ONEX, Inc. grew to more than 200 IT consulting employees in less than three years through the use of radical recruiting, culture ("Happy on Monday"), public relations, and $0. They understood that every employee wants to help grow their company and that recruiting top talent is everyone's responsibility. According to Sally Huffine Breen, entrepreneurs "make it fun, have faith in the vision, and hire employees who will 'think like an owner.' "

As someone with both human resources and marketing experience, my role was both to raise the profile of ONEX to our clients and potential hires, as well as to ensure that their fun, responsive, and productive culture continued in spite of fast growth. The goal was for our employees to wake up "Happy on Monday."

We wanted our employees to approach Mondays with the same enthusiasm and energy level that they greeted Fridays. To do that, we involved them in planning monthly fun events (duckpin bowling, playing pool at a club, off-site family picnics, as well as weekly basketball games played by everyone from execs to recruiters). Everything about the company—from the way the telephones were answered ("It's a great day at ONEX!") to the funky, primary colors of the decor, to the availability of scooters as a means of getting from meeting to meeting—conveyed "happy." And that extended to our off-site consultants, who were connected through "high-tech high-touch" means: e-mail newsletters, employee events, big boxes of fresh cookies delivered on birthdays, and congratulations calls or voice mail messages from the founders on their annual anniversaries. Employees were encouraged to contribute ideas, collaborate, and take responsibility as needed—to "think like an owner."

Information about current openings was sent to all employees via e-mail every Friday, and the company founders regularly talked to employees about matching their talented fraternity or sorority friends, roommates, siblings, and others with the openings. One of the most successful recruiting tactics was launched at a quarterly all-employee meeting. Dressed as a cowboy-style sheriff with a big moustache, boots, fringed shirt, and cap pistol six-shooters, I swore in all employees as my "Recruiting and Marketing Posse." Every employee received a silver-star "deputy" pin to wear while reading aloud the "Posse Oath." They promised—among other things—to carry their business cards at all times, and to be on the lookout for future ONEXites at professional organization meetings, parties, neighborhood gatherings, day care, and so on. They were urged to contact fraternity and sorority friends, college and high school friends, spouses' siblings, and others with needed high-tech skills. After the swearing in, the oath was turned over and the group ended the meeting by singing Roy Rogers' famous "Happy Trails."

And our efforts clearly worked. Employee and other referrals accounted for the vast majority of hires. According to recruiting manager Chris Fuller, "Approximately 70 percent of the first 150 employees hired were the result of employee referrals. Our employees were so excited to be part of ONEX that they went out of their way to scour their networks to assist the recruiters to find qualified candidates." At the height of the high-tech frenzy that typically caused up to 35 percent turnover elsewhere in 1999 and 2000, turnover at ONEX was 8 percent annually at a time when there were approximately 200 employees. (ONEX was sold to Inrange in 2001.)

In summary, it doesn't matter what type of organization you run (service or product company, not-for-profit, or even university) and it doesn't matter what the qualifications are for those you need to hire. Your current employees, vendors, customers, and other allies can significantly augment your formal recruiting methods. As long as the qualifications are clear and posted, and the recruiting process is defined, the odds of receiving successful referrals are very high. Referral bonuses complete the formula, but the real reward is the joy of building an organization and surrounding oneself with other top talent.

Low Cost/No Cost Recruiting: Leverage What You've Got Before You Spend One More Dime on Recruiting

John Vlastelica
Director of Recruiting Programs, Amazon.com

I've managed $2 million recruiting budgets and $20,000 recruiting budgets. You know what I learned? The best, fastest hires—even when I had plenty of money to spend on the latest and greatest candidate generation techniques—came from the same low-cost sources: employee referrals, employee Rolodexes, and candidate references.

In this essay, I'll share some best practice ideas that you can leverage to improve the quality of your new hires while reducing your cost per hire. I'll draw from my experiences owning—and experimenting with—a company-wide employee referral program, managing and measuring a 20-person recruiting team, and building no-cost tools to help managers find their own candidates.

Improve Your Employee Referral Program

You probably already have an employee referral program. But, if you're like the recruiting leaders at most companies, you'd like to improve the return on investment from this important source of quality candidates.

Where do most companies spend money and energy to "fix" employee referrals? Unfortunately, they often hire an ad agency to make cool posters to hang in the hallways, or convince the CFO to help them raise the referral bonus amount. Both of these efforts cost money, and don't really address the root issues with most underperforming employee referral programs. So what should you, as a recruiter or recruiting manager, do to improve its return on investment?

BUILD CANDIDATE PROFILES

Do you know what good headhunters do with job descriptions? They usually toss them. The responsibilities, credentials, and required experiences found on a job description are rarely helpful. Instead, they rely on short conversations with the hiring manager and successful job incumbents to convert the description into a candidate profile that will drive their candidate sourcing efforts. You need to do the same for your employees. Make it easy for employees to understand what the ideal candidate looks like, so that they can refer exactly the kind of person you need. Identify the industries and companies your target candidate might work in today, and the job titles he or she might possess. (Note: Job titles vary company to company, industry to industry; do a little research to see what your target companies call the people you need, so your employees can better leverage their network outside of your company.) Then, think about the type of college degree they should have, what associations they might belong to, and the specific accomplishments they should have made in the past two years. Finally, come up with a one-line impact statement that quickly communicates why this job is so important to your company, and include it in this short profile. Describe what you need in plain English, so that employees from all over your organization will know a good referral when they see one (an example of a direct, clear profile is in the next section).

COMMUNICATE YOUR NEEDS WEEKLY

Each week, send out an e-mail that includes the profiles of 25 percent of your most critical candidate needs. Too many companies just post their job openings to their web sites, and ask employees to review the jobs and send HR anyone who seems to fit. That never works. Be specific about the positions needing the most help. Also, by describing your target candidates in terms of what they are doing today—instead of the less useful, but more common practice of describing what they would have to do once they were hired—you'll drastically improve the chances that your referrals hit the mark. I can't recall one phenomenal referral for a senior-level job that ever came in to the recruiting function as a result of a poster on the wall. It's the targeted referrals that get us the great hires, the ones that we receive in response to our e-mail campaigns. But if we don't ask, we don't get.

EXAMPLE E-MAIL FOR A TECHNOLOGY COMPANY

By August 15, we need to hire a new sales leader to drive our product expansion into new markets. This is your chance to help handpick the people we all depend on to drive higher revenue and expand our market. Plus, if your referral gets hired, you're eligible for a $1,000 referral bonus. Do you know someone who fits the profile below? If so, e-mail or call Joe Recruiter in HR right away. He'd be eager to get more info about your referral.

Sales Consultant, New Markets, Pacific Northwest Territory

Impact: This salesperson will get to build out a new vertical market as our company works to bring the automotive sales businesses in the Northwest the same customer analysis tools that the retail businesses have been using to drive up revenue and profits for years.

Our ideal candidates are currently high-performing sales reps selling to the general managers of large automotive dealerships. They're probably selling automotive parts agreements, high-end service equipment, large-scale advertising services (newspaper ads, radio, TV, billboards), lead generation tools, or sales training programs to the top dealerships in the Northwest. They're not selling direct to consumers; all of their recent experience is in business-to-business sales. Our ideal candidates are probably called sales representatives, sales managers, account representatives, or sales consultants, and they probably have a four-year degree in business, marketing, or communications. They need to be tech savvy; probably an early adopter of the cell phone, laptop, and PDA. And they need to have extensive networks and big

Rolodexes, filled with the names of the key managers from all of the auto dealerships in the area. They might also belong to the Society of Automotive Analysts, attend NADA conferences, and read *AutoExec* magazine.

MOTIVATE YOUR BEST EMPLOYEES TO MAKE GREAT REFERRALS

Too many companies believe it's the money that motivates the top employees to refer the best people they know. It's not. While no one will turn down a $500 or $1,000 referral bonus, the key to getting good referrals is to tap into the motivation for longer-term benefits to your key employees. You must emphasize the opportunity for your employees to help handpick the team they work with and leverage the natural motivation all of us have to surround ourselves with smart, capable people we can learn from. When you communicate about your program, literally say things like "Help handpick our key hires." Focus more on long-term benefits (working with great people) over short-term benefits (a cash bonus), and you'll begin to see busy people make the time to refer their colleagues.

STOP REQUIRING RESUMES AND START ACCEPTING STICKY NOTES

Leads are the lifeblood of great recruiters, and calling a candidate who's somehow connected to an existing employee is easy and productive. But so many recruiting teams will do the steps outlined above, only to let these targeted referrals sit there because they weren't submitted as a resume. Happily employed superstar candidates often don't have resumes to share; they're not looking for work, so they don't spend time updating their employment history. So spend the extra five minutes with the next employee who gives you the name and number of "one of the best people I've ever worked with," and try to understand how this candidate might fit the profile. If there's a fit, make the call. Don't wait for a resume; you may never get one.

FOLLOW THROUGH, EVERY TIME

If you get a lead or resume of a great candidate, you cannot sit on it. Targeted referrals are golden. And they get stale quickly. Many employees answer the call of duty, and really dig through their past to refer people who fit your profile, only to see their referral disappear into the black hole of the resume database. The number one way to grind your employee referral program to a screeching halt is to send strong messages to your employees—through your inaction—that they're wasting their time. If you don't follow up with employee referrals, your employee looks stupid to his/her friends, and will stop helping you. Don't embarrass your employees by dropping the ball.

REWARD GOOD BEHAVIOR

Never underestimate the power of public acknowledgment. When you send out your weekly updates, highlighting the current critical needs and profiles, be sure to publicize the recent wins. Thank each employee who made a targeted referral that was hired. And if your company culture is competitive and recruiting is a top priority, you might want to track and publish total employee referrals hired, year to date, from each vice president's group. A little peer pressure can go a long way.

Leverage Your Employees' Rolodexes

I've learned that "A+ people" know other "A+ people." But many recruiters don't take advantage of their employees' networks. Good recruiters ask, "Can you get me the resume of anyone you know who's looking to leave their current job who might be a good fit here?" But great recruiters ask, "What are the names of the five best [engineers/accountants/salespeople] you worked with at your last company?"

You've got to be aggressive when it comes to pulling leads from your employees. I've led a team that generated over 150 engineering hires in a single year by leveraging the employee network. True, I've had recruiters work for me who seemed to do nothing but hire people through search firms and online job boards, while my best recruiters were filling critical jobs with phenomenal people without spending a dime. How'd they do it?

KEEP TRACK OF WHO IS ALREADY ON YOUR TEAM

Go through your files, pull the resumes of the last 100 people hired into your company, and update it each week with new hires. Create a simple spreadsheet that includes columns for:

Name and title.

Prior employer #1 and job title.

Prior employer #2 and job title.

Industry expertise (health care, retail, software, insurance, etc.).

College name and degree.

Professional organization affiliations.

Special certifications (Have they attended any special training that may have exposed them to other experts in this field?).

Prior location (If they relocated, from where?).

Hire source (How did we find them?).

Whenever you're working with a hiring manager, bring along the list. Review the contacts who might be able to help introduce you to good leads at the target company or industry you're hoping to pull from.

ATTEND BUSINESS STAFF MEETINGS

To be an effective recruiter, you must know the business you support. You should definitely attend the staff meetings where your hiring managers describe their business challenges and the people gaps on their team. Obviously, you'll want to solicit leads from the managers on the team. Great recruiters go beyond their hiring managers' meetings, though, and take their needs to other groups in the company. You'd be surprised at how many operations people can tell you about the best engineers at their past companies, or how many finance people can tell you the names of the superstar marketing and sales people they've worked with. Make deals with the other recruiters or hiring managers; if they give you leads, you'll give them leads. Present your needs at staff meetings—in profile format—and make anyone who gives you a lead a personal promise that you'll contact every single person they refer.

GET NEW HIRES TO HELP YOU

I've tried taking employee referral request sheets to new hire orientation, as a way to drum up leads. It just didn't work. Why? New employees weren't prepared with names and numbers and, frankly, many didn't understand yet what we needed; they were too new to understand our business and our profiles, and trust our referrals process. Plus, new hire orientation is an overwhelming experience; so many forms and things to remember! Great recruiting teams do get leads from new hires, though. One very successful program I created involved inviting all new hires from a vice president's group to a special orientation and welcome session, led by the VP, within their first 60 days on the job. Entice new hires with pizza and the chance to meet and hear from their VP, who draws an organizational chart and describes how each person in the room impacts the business. Then, the VP and recruiter can talk about the critical employee needs in their organization, and the profiles of the most successful candidates. That's when the recruiter solicits leads. Pass around a sheet of paper to capture names and job titles, right then and there, of five of the best people they worked with at their last two companies. The idea is to get leads, not necessarily resumes, for great people—whether they are looking for work or not. Make it simple. The recruiter follows up individually with each new hire to get more details. When the new hire knows the potential candidate well, the recruiter arms the employee with a prewritten e-mail to send to the old coworker to see if there's interest. Have the employee copy (cc) you on the e-mail, so you can track responses. If the employee knows the potential candidate only by reputation, the recruiter calls the candidate.

Tap into Candidate References

When you're talking to a candidate's references, you're often talking to high-caliber peers and managers whom the candidate respects. These people represent a significant potential source of other great candidates for your openings. You know, "birds of a feather . . ." At one company I worked with, hiring managers—not recruiters—checked the references of potential new hires. Here is a tool/technique managers used to generate high-quality leads and new hires.

MAKING THE CALL

In the beginning of the reference check, tell the reference a little about the position, how important the role is, how hard it is to find great people, and how you could hire 10 more just like candidate X if you could find them (assuming you only check references on final candidates). Toward the end of your conversation, after the reference has finished giving you a recommendation, ask the reference if he/she might know other folks who might be open to a call about an opportunity at your company. If you're asked, tell the reference you're just trying to network, not trying to recruit them.

You'll find many people—if treated properly and approached correctly—will gladly give you leads. In fact, one in 10 will probably even ask you for more information about the role for themselves, if your passion/energy for the work at your company comes through loud and clear.

FOLLOW-UP

Regardless of the quality of the reference, always thank your contact for his or her time, and ask for an e-mail address. Then, send each one a thank-you note (sample follows) with a copy of the job profile attached, and ask for a reference of anyone he or she might know who meets the specs. Also ask for any suggestions of ways to find more great people like candidate X. You'll be surprised how many people will give you information on professional associations, target companies, specialized web site addresses, and—ideally—the names of great, qualified people.

Build your network in a nonthreatening way. Always ask for leads, ideas, and help. After all, the worst they can do is say "no."

SAMPLE E-MAIL

Dear [Reference],

Thanks again for providing a reference for [Candidate]. I know you're busy. Your feedback is an integral part of our hiring process and I appreciate the time you spent with me on the phone today.

[My company] invests considerably in finding great talent; we're always in the market for high-caliber candidates like [Candidate's first name]. If, in the course of your day, you happen upon another great [Job type] prospect who might be a good fit for [My company], please don't hesitate to call me, e-mail me, or forward my contact info to that person. I'd really appreciate any leads you could pass my way.

Here's a short overview of the kind of person I'm looking for:

[Five bullets describing profile of ideal candidate]

This is a high-impact job, with a lot of interesting challenges and a very competitive compensation package. More info about our company and the exciting road ahead is available at [Company web site].

Thanks again!

[Your name and title]
[Your direct phone number and e-mail]

Increase Your Recruiting ROI

Every HR and recruiting team I've ever worked with has been asked to do more with less. We've got to take advantage of low-cost, high-return candidate sourcing efforts. Improving the employee referral program, actively soliciting our employees for leads, and tapping into quality candidate references can generate great new candidates. In fact, these efforts have generated hundreds of quality hires at companies I've worked with, which proves that hiring great people doesn't have to be complicated or expensive. In fact, the methods outlined in this chapter depend only on a renewed investment in the very people you and your hiring managers come into contact with every day—namely, your existing employees and candidate references.

Building a Strong Workforce through Affiliation

Ron Elsdon

Director, DBM

The strength and success of organizations in the future, in an increasingly information and service-based economy, will be determined largely by the ingenuity, productivity, and effectiveness of the workforce. Human resources and staffing professionals are uniquely positioned to take a leadership role in strengthening the relationship between the employee and the workplace. They are also well positioned to guide executive leadership in recrafting the relationship between individuals and organizations to the benefit of both. This article explores the changing workforce from the perspectives of the external environment, the evolving nature of the relationship between organizations and individuals, the importance of individual development, and the role of the HR and staffing professional.

"I can see the challenges we will have engaging people in our organization in the future. I understand how important this will be. But I am concerned that our managers don't recognize how important this is. I am going to put this subject firmly on our future agenda." These are recent words from the CEO of a large communications company. Clearly, it will not be business as usual for the workforce moving forward, and there are a number of factors driving change. First is the slowing growth of the workforce in developed nations—including the United States—which will lead to a growing shortage of people in the years ahead. Indeed the annual rate of growth of the U.S. workforce has steadily declined since the early 1980s (Elsdon 2003) and is projected to continue this decline through the next 25 years. This becomes critical when economic growth is driven mainly by information and services. Furthermore, the level of trust and commitment between individuals and organizations is dropping in response to the ongoing waves of downsizing and the apparently capricious nature of employee movement in the late 1990s and in early 2000. This is leading to sharp declines in satisfaction at work. According to a Conference Board (2000) study, the percentage of people reporting they were happy with their jobs fell from 59 percent in 1995 to less than 50 percent in 2000; for baby boomers aged 45 to 54, the decline was even more dramatic, from 57 percent to less than 47 percent.

Compound this with the corporate governance scandals and criminal activities of certain highly visible CEOs and their associates and we have a crisis of confidence—not just in organizations as institutions but also in corporate leaders. Here is how William Thomas (Thomas 2002), who runs a publicly traded investment company in Dallas called Capital Southwest Corporation, states it: "The impending takeover of corporate America by self-serving, elitist managers may prove to be far more damaging to capitalism than anything Karl Marx could have conceived." And here is how employees who are alumni of a failed dot-com in Northern California respond in excerpts from a threaded e-mail in 2002 after the dot-com failure: "If I say that I really love your company and your corporate culture, and that I'll do whatever it takes, including giving up my life and the pursuit of my own goals for your bottom line, I'm lying." And "You may now only borrow 40 hours of my life a week—that's all I'm gonna give."

Through these remarks, we see declining levels of satisfaction and trust. Is this the organizational world we want for the future? I think not. In working with leaders and HR groups across the United States, I often ask the question: What relationship would you like to see between your organization and its employees in the future? Some of the words that come up include trusting, exhilarating, stimulating, creative, and engaging. They in turn lead to a productive, flexible work environment that nourishes the individual and creates economic and social value.

In 1963, then President John F. Kennedy made this statement: "And we shall, I am confident, if we maintain the pace, in due season reap the kind of world we deserve and deserve the kind of world we will have." Our challenges and our opportunities are to reap a world that is fulfilling for each of us as individuals and creates value for our organizations. Staffing and HR professionals have an important leadership role to play in creating such a world. Let us explore first the kind of relationship that is needed between organizations and individuals. This relationship has evolved from that of master/servant 100 years ago to a tenuous relationship of convenience in many cases today. When extended commitment is sought by the organization, it is often expressed in terms of retention, which is defined by the dictionary to mean "to hold back, to keep, to restrain, to keep in one's pay or service." This golden handcuffs approach is not an appealing prospect. Indeed, studies linking performance to the nature of employee engagement suggest a decline when the employee remains purely due to a perception of limited alternatives. The relationship that we are seeking in the future is one of affiliation, which means becoming closely connected or associated, to adopt. It is a two-way relationship into which both parties enter willingly, unlike retention, which is a one-way relationship defined by the organization. What is needed to build a relationship of affiliation?

In answering this question, let us explore the implications of changing demographics in the future. As the growth rate of the workforce slows it will become more difficult to find people with needed skills. The balance of power between individuals and organizations will begin to shift more to the individual. This means recognizing the needs of individuals, not just those of organizations. Studies of the factors people consider important— their needs—not surprisingly show variations by demographic elements such as age, years of service, function, and gender. However, some common characteristics include: the importance of career development; recognition and appreciation; and a supportive work environment. Perhaps surprisingly, compensation is not one of the top three factors. Competitive compensation is a necessary but not sufficient condition to build a strong relationship with employees. The primary factors are all closely linked to leadership, and it is here that staffing and HR professionals can have a major impact.

These are thoughts from Max DePree (1992), chairman emeritus of Herman

Miller, Inc.: "From a leader's perspective, the most serious betrayal has to do with thwarting human potential, with quenching the spirit, with failing to deal equitably with each other as human beings." So we see the role of leadership, especially in HR and staffing professionals, as one of enabling each person in the workforce to reach his or her full potential. In doing so, this enhances productivity. Value is created one person at a time. This means recognizing that individual development is just as important as individual performance; each supports the other. But a natural reaction might be to question the commitment of resources to individual development. After all, wouldn't this simply lead to people becoming more marketable and leaving the organization? In fact, the reverse is the case. In studies of the impact of providing career development resources within an organization, the return on investment exceeded 180 percent as people self-selected into the organization when they were given options and choices.

What does this mean in terms of leadership? I recall hearing Lew Platt, who was at one time the CEO of Hewlett-Packard, talk about one of his experiences in a capsule from a panel discussion. Someone he had known for many years, an administrative assistant I believe, called him one day to let him know she was being asked to leave the organization and wanted to speak with him. Lew Platt approached this meeting with some trepidation, expecting that he and HP would be castigated for what was happening. Instead, his associate spoke to him about how embarrassed she was at letting her skills atrophy so that she could no longer function effectively. Platt decided that he never wanted a situation to arise in the future where an employee was left stranded because he or she had not developed needed skills. And almost immediately, he put frameworks in place to support individual career development.

Is it necessary to be the CEO to do this? Absolutely not. One organization I spoke with in the health care sector was experiencing high attrition of nurses. This certainly isn't unusual in a sector that is experiencing severe people shortages, which becomes in many ways a leading indicator for other sectors of the economy in the years ahead. The HR department did a good job listening to the organization and knew that its orientation and integration processes were inadequate. So HR proposed a significant enhancement to these processes. This was greeted with skepticism and concern about costs. So the enhancement was tested with pilot groups. The attrition rate for people in the pilot groups was about half the attrition rate for the general population. The financial savings from this far outweighed the additional costs. The HR team demonstrated courageous leadership, just as Lew Platt did in the earlier example. And there are other examples of a slightly different nature. For instance, Whole Foods Market, Inc. limits the compensation of any officer in the organization to no more than 14 times the average full-time salary of all team members (employees); this is a strong statement about the organization valuing its employees. Other examples of proactive and reactive workforce practices are given by Michael O'Malley (2000), whose recent work focuses on employee commitment: "In late 1995, textile producer Malden Mills burned down. Owner Aaron Feuerstein kept his 1,000 employees on the payroll while the factory was rebuilt. It cost him $15 million to do that. Contrast that with a restaurant chain that lays off workers, without pay, for two to four weeks while restaurants are refurbished. Seriously, for whom would you rather work? The turnover rate at Malden Mills is about 5 percent, and over a 14-year span, revenues tripled (in constant dollars) and the workforce doubled. The restaurant chain experiences from 200 to 300 percent turnover."

Lew Platt, Whole Foods Market, Malden Mills—these are examples of leadership courage. Leadership courage means knowing who you are and then living authentically recognizing this. It means creating and nurturing a sense of purpose in the organization. Leadership courage means creating an environment in which people flourish, balancing both getting and giving. It means living the principles of inclusion internally within the workforce, externally through partnerships, and on a community and global basis. Studies of affiliation (Elsdon 2003) show a direct relationship between leadership's ability to create a sense of inspiring purpose and the strength of affiliation that people feel for the organization.

From a practical perspective, building a strongly affiliated workforce requires that leaders, staffing professionals, and HR address the following steps to build a clear understanding of workforce needs linked to organizational direction:

- *First step:* Characterize the workforce by segment. This may mean specifying segments where full-time employment is preferred and those where a contract engagement is preferable. It is then possible to define the nature of the relationship sought in each segment. There are multiple aspects to this, including whether to seek a transactional or extended relationship. A transactional relationship is an engagement built around completion of a particular project. An extended relationship means the organization invests in the individual, which should enhance both performance and productivity. Building clarity around the relationship makes it possible to frame expectations so that they are clear to both the individual and the organization.

- *Second step:* Understand employee issues by creating mechanisms to gather both quantitative (what is happening) and qualitative (why is it happening) input. There are many possible approaches that include interviews, surveys, or focus groups. Preserving confidentiality of information from each individual—by using a third party, for example—is essential in gathering input that addresses root causes.

- *Third step:* Design solutions that address the issues that surface and create mechanisms to measure and monitor progress. Individual development is likely to be a central aspect that surfaces in the organizational listening process as an issue. It can be addressed by a range of frameworks available today that include virtual, instructor-led, and individual approaches. Creating a seamless selection, integration, and development process is also critical.

In conclusion, HR and staffing professionals can demonstrate leadership courage and build strong workforce affiliation if they:

- Help ensure that the organization's purpose is clear, inspiring, and effectively communicated.
- Create frameworks that characterize the current and needed future workforce.
- Establish systems that provide for effective listening to the organization.
- Advocate for workforce solutions that address identified, root-cause issues.
- Establish quantitative and qualitative systems to monitor progress.

By taking such steps, we will create vibrant organizations and communities. These are communities that honor all connected with them.

Replenishing the Workforce

Heather Hartmann

Executive Director, Human Capital Metrics Consortium

Much has been written about the baby boom generation and its effect on business and the economy. But how many companies have seriously considered the impact this generation of workers will have when they start retiring from the workforce?

In the short term, this may not seem like a big issue. After all, the normal business cycles of most companies include periods of organizational layoffs and downsizing in order to gain efficiencies. The recent recession has forced companies to reduce staff even more dramatically. In the long term, however, organizations are going to face a significant labor shortage, driven primarily by the aging workforce. Organizations should begin sooner rather than later to put together a strategy for replenishing their workforces. Questions to ask include:

- What kind of sourcing strategies has your company developed to accommodate an aging workforce?
- How many of these boomers are employed by your organization? When are they scheduled to retire?

- Have you considered the costs of replacing experienced, skilled workers?
- What impact will this demographic shift have on your companies' bottom line, morale, and work environment?

This essay will examine the issues that surround workforce replenishment. And using one company as an example, it will provide some suggestions for how your organization can begin to build the workforce of the future.

The Labor Issue

By the spring of 2002, business economists and experts were predicting that labor shortages would resurface as the economy strengthens. Why? According to *BusinessWeek*, there is "a looming crunch that will hit as huge numbers of boomers retire and fewer new workers fill the pipeline."

The seriousness of the issue is clearly illustrated through the example of one employer in the mining industry. The company recently recognized this demographic reality while reviewing its succession plans and suddenly realizing that the average age of all employees was 50. The company then examined each mining operation to determine how many replacements would be required in the next three to five years, with special attention given to how many replacements would be internal promotions versus external hires. The answer: 1,000 total replacements would be necessary, a staggering number for an organization with a total workforce of 6,500. In short, 15 percent of the company's employee population would be retiring in the next five years! For an organization with historic turnover of less than 10 percent, this was a wake-up call. In fact, company officials realized that they would have to begin recruiting, a process they had not actively pursued in years.

Finding Workers

While the sheer number of looming retirees seems daunting, the numbers on the other side of the equation are equally bleak: Where are their replacements? The Bureau of Labor Statistics expects the number of people in the labor force ages 55 and older to grow 32 percent by 2010, while those between the age of 35 and 44 will shrink by 10.2 percent. In addition, the

Information Technology Association of America predicted a shortfall of 425,000 skilled workers in 2002. When faced with these considerable reductions in potential working population demographics, where are employers supposed to turn in order to replenish their workforces? The future labor shortage that has been predicted is extremely significant, and daunting. Shortages in specific sectors—like information technology (IT) and engineering—have already been identified, and more are predicted.

Let's look more closely at the mining company example. In order to prepare for its worker shortage, the company began to look at the enrollment figures for mining engineers at traditional mining colleges. The news was abysmal. They found that several schools were considering shutting down their mining programs due to lack of interest in the program by college students. Ironically, the company had decided to incorporate a scholarship program into its recruiting strategy, in order to attract students who would be loyal to the company. However, if there weren't any students entering the program, the company realized, the scholarship program was worthless. Instead, this organization had to start thinking immediately about how it could get students interested in the industry, not just the company. They also had to consider where they would find experienced candidates. The Internet has certainly changed the way most companies source candidates, but would this work for a mining company? Do potential mining engineers hang out on job boards or in chat rooms? Did specific, niche mining sites even exist on the Internet? Historically, the traditional method of recruiting for this organization was to place an ad in a local newspaper. Would this sourcing strategy still be the answer?

Paying the Price

In addition to developing sourcing strategies, organizations faced with a major hiring shift also need to consider the fact that their payrolls are going to increase as they replace their current workforce. For instance, new engineers coming into an organization will demand higher salaries than those who started out 15 to 20 years ago. Not only do companies have to figure out the projected costs, they have to budget for it.

The mining company executives, for example, calculated the number of people who would be retiring, but they hadn't even thought about the additional payroll costs to replace them. And what about benefit costs for those retiring, and for those coming on board? The mining company currently provides medical insurance for all of its retirees; did the company budget for this increase as well? It's easy to see how what was once just a "recruiting" issue now demands to be viewed as a human capital issue, with all areas of human resources involved.

Preparing a Strategy

So let's review. Now that you know you need to replenish the workforce, how do you go about it? That answer varies, depending on the following factors:

- *Industry*. Are you in an industry that is considered desirable? Are positions in your company highly sought after by college graduates? If you happen to be one of the employers of choice in your location, replenishing your workforce may not be that large a problem.
- *Location*. What are the demographics of your location(s)? Are there people with the skills and levels of experience needed within your immediate geography?
- *Commitment from upper management*. Does your CEO understand workforce replenishing issues, and is he/she willing to commit the appropriate financial backing, time, and resources? Is he/she committed to spending money on human capital?

Hopefully, you are in an industry that is desirable and that is located close to a labor pool containing an abundance of people with your targeted skill sets, and your CEO has given you an unlimited budget. But let's be realistic. This is often not the case. For a dose of reality, let's go back to the company in the mining industry.

The mining industry is not considered a desirable industry. Mining is still perceived as damaging to the environment, dangerous to its workers, and creating long-term health risks for its employees. Often, mines are located in smaller towns, requiring long commutes for workers. But in our example, one of the few things going for this mining company is the commitment of the CEO. He clearly realizes that to maintain the company's position of leadership within the industry, the company has to spend money where needed. Right now, that means spending money on people.

The company's strategy? A combination of efforts is required, some initiated by the recruiting staff at the company's headquarters and others initiated at each of the mining operations. Consider:

COMPANY AWARENESS

Since recruiting efforts on college campuses and in local markets have been minimal in recent years, organizational awareness is very limited. At company headquarters, one major initiative implemented is the development of a recruitment-marketing brochure. While this may seem like a recruiting staple to most, this organization didn't have one; its only recruitment tool has been the annual report. The annual report does contain interesting information about the company, but it doesn't give a candidate a clear picture of the career opportunities that exist within the organization. Through the development of a brochure that is focused on employment opportunities, the company can outline job prospects, provide testimonials from current employees, and give realistic pictures of employees performing different functions at the mining operations. Not only is this brochure an important recruiting tool, but the company can also use this same information on an expanded Internet career site that it develops. The company has also stepped up its participation in off-site career fairs—looking not only to recruit potential employees but also to build up awareness of their company within a specific community.

SOURCING

As mentioned earlier, the mining company had initially planned to implement scholarship programs at traditional mining programs in colleges across the country. With enrollments declining within these programs, the company decided to work toward creating a larger pool of candidates from local colleges, from vocational-technical schools, and in each of their communities. An effort is under way for the company to partner with its current mining engineers, to get them involved with each of these educational sources. The company now encourages its engineers to make presentations to various engineering and diversity organizations in an effort to dispel industry myths and concentrate on what a career in mining can offer. For example, when asked why she chose a career in mining engineering, one mining engineer stated that she couldn't see herself working in an office environment because she wanted to be able to work outdoors; working at a surface mine in Arizona allowed her that opportunity. Another mining engineer was interested in the variety of engineering work that a career in mining afforded him; not only is he involved in the development of the mine plans, but he also has an opportunity to work on some civil engineering projects, such as the design of the coal roads. In addition, company officials realize that placing an ad in a local newspaper is no longer going to reach enough candidates with the desired talents. Increased efforts have been made to advertise in varying outlets, including niche Internet sites for mining and engineering. Examples of these include Infomine and Mining USA.

METRICS

With increased sourcing efforts in place, including efforts to increase awareness of the organization, the company decided that it was time to put some tracking systems in place to manage the recruiting process. First, officials identified the need for a very basic applicant tracking system that can be used organization-wide. Second, they identified staffing metrics that are important to the organization: recruiting efficiency, contracted time to start, and total compensation recruited were identified as three key metrics important to the senior management team. They are also beginning to track the quality of new hires. After a new hire has been with the organization for 90 days, the hiring manager is asked to evaluate how the new hire is doing in comparison to the prerecruiting requirements. Each expectation that was determined to be important in the prerecruiting requirements is graded on a scale of 1 to 5. This allows the hiring manager to then provide an overall number for new hire quality.

SUCCESSION PLANNING

Though always important to the organization, succession planning is now a priority. Each area of the company was asked to identify high-performing individuals and what, if any, additional training they would need in order to move up in the organization. As part of the formal performance review process, each manager was asked to communicate these opportunities to individuals identified by the succession planning program. Both the manager and the employee are responsible for making sure that the appropriate training is completed.

Company awareness, sourcing, metrics, and succession planning. In today's business environment, these are four important first steps for any organization to begin to replenish a workforce. And at the mining company, results have already been seen. The expanded sourcing efforts produced several hires from niche mining and energy web sites. To compare, in the first quarter of 2002 almost $100,000 was spent in agency costs. For the second quarter, that number was $0. The additions of an applicant tracking system and expanded corporate careers web site allowed the organization to generate greater awareness through expanded job postings, and pushed candidates to their corporate careers site to apply online. It also allowed them to track which sources are most effective, so they can spend their recruiting dollars more wisely. For example, originally the company had monthly contracts with two major job boards, which cost them approximately $2,000 a month. They cancelled these contracts, and now post to a variety of sites. For the first quarter of 2002 the cost for Internet postings was $7,500, which dropped to $2,500 during the second quarter.

Summary

There are many issues that your organization must consider in order to prepare for a successful workforce replenishing strategy and create your workforce of the future:

- *Sheer numbers.* Begin by identifying the number of people that will be retiring over the next three to five years. Then, figure out what the replacement costs are in terms of total compensation recruited metrics. Determine how many positions will be filled by internal promotions versus external hires.
- *Where will you find them?* Develop a sourcing strategy. Determine what tools you will need to implement your strategy. How will you monitor your success? What metrics are important to your organization?
- *Make recruiting a team effort.* Enlist others in your organization to assist you in the implementation of your strategy. Recruiting is a team effort, involving nearly everyone associated with a company's human capital effort. For instance, make sure to convince your hiring managers to think about how they would go about replenishing the workforce. Your recruiting effort, in partnership with the hiring managers, creates a very powerful dynamic.

The Future Is Closer Than It Appears: Recruitment Marketing to a Multicultural Workforce

Annette Merritt Cummings

Vice President and National Director,
Diversity Services, Bernard Hodes Group

Our self-image as a nation is changing quickly, and the transformation is an exciting one. As the old black-and-white America fades into history, a more ethnically, culturally, and racially varied society is coming into focus, a world in which workplace diversity is the rule rather than the exception. Now more than ever, organizations are acknowledging that they must hire and retain multicultural workforces, treat all employees with fairness and equity, integrate boardrooms, and contract with minority- and female-owned businesses.

Corporations that aspire to be global must value and understand people of different cultures, races, religions, sexual orientations, and genders. It's that simple—and yet it's complicated, too.

The Challenge of the Future—
Reaching a Multicultural Workforce

The 2000 U.S. Census revealed a nation in transition, one that is swiftly leaving behind antiquated business practices. To tap into growth markets and remain profitable, organizations must develop strategies that draw on new assumptions about diversity and how to manage it.

The labor force in the United States will continue its ethnic diversification into the twenty-first century, according to *Workforce 2020*, published by the Hudson Institute. Through the first 20 years of the century, the supply of workers will not meet demand (especially in key areas), and the skill levels of those available will vary widely.

Labor Force Projections

Growth in the U.S. labor force is comprised largely of women, minorities, and immigrants. According to the Bureau of Labor Statistics, women comprise over half of the U.S. labor force. By the year 2020, women will make up more than half of all workers, accounting for 60 percent of the total. Additionally, the Hispanic labor force is on track to grow four times faster than the rest of the labor force between 1998 and 2008. Only 58.6 percent of entrants to the workforce will be non-Hispanic whites by 2008; 16.5 percent will be black, 16.2 percent will be Hispanic, and 8.8 percent will be Asian or "other."

But numbers tell only part of the story. When it comes to managing diversity, the heart of the issue is culture, not statistics. To effectively recruit from today's increasingly multiethnic and multiracial talent pool, organizations must come to regard diversity as a driver of company culture. This includes creating "culturally competent" communications to address our new audiences.

Research-Based Strategies and Tactics

The two professions with the greatest insight into diversity seem to be cultural anthropologists and marketers. Why? Perhaps it is because both use observation and objective data to interpret the past and the present and also to predict the future. The best approach to diversity management is based on research and assessment. Where are you now and where do you want to be? How ready is your organization to change?

Effective diversity recruitment and branding strategies depend on measurable initiatives and objectives. The successful diversity recruitment strategy will begin with research. Through the use of primary and secondary research you can determine how your diverse customers and employees perceive you, and how you measure up against the competition. The primary goal is to assure the development of a diversity recruitment strategy that is integrated into your overall diversity plan.

How will we know when we are successful? Metrics. We measure every other vital business function and its contribution to profitability and productivity. Given that diversity is such an integral part of strategic planning, it should likewise be measured. What are the best practice internal measurements?

- Diversity of the candidate pool.
- Number of interviews.
- Hiring and retention of women and people of color versus majority.
- Diversity of executive team and board of directors.
- Data collection to evaluate strategies and change when necessary.

External measurements include:

- Track success of communications—advertising and public relations.
- External reports—from "best of" lists such as in *Working Mother*, *Fortune*, and *Diversity Inc*.
- Diversity branding success with customers and other stakeholders.

Some best practice companies are now producing annual human resources reports for internal clients. These reports are then posted on the company web sites so that stakeholders may view them.

One Caution: Diversity Initiatives Are Not Affirmative Action Plans

Confusion occurs when business executives mistake diversity initiatives and programs for affirmative action plans. Affirmative action plans are aimed at amending wrongs done in the past to Americans who were not of the majority population. As such, they are legal obligations, based on blueprints, which seek to increase the representation of minorities and women where they were underrepresented.

While many companies are still concerned with affirmative action plans and meeting quotas, others focus on managing the diverse culture of their organizations. Practicing diversity management is vastly different from living up to an affirmative action plan. It involves awareness, education, and the positive recognition of the differences among a company's employees.

Diversity management is much more than just a socially responsible or expedient thing to do. It's also a profitable, strategic business approach that contributes to an organization's productivity, earnings, and shareholder value. Having workers who literally speak the customer's language and live in the same culture can only benefit an organization. Though managing diversity touches on all aspects of business, an organization cannot hope to chart progress unless it attempts to recruit and retain a diverse workforce.

Indications are that more and more businesses are doing just that. A recent survey by the National Association of Colleges and Employers (NACE)—an organization acting as a liaison between college students and more than 1,900 employers—found that slightly more than two-thirds (67.3 percent) of employer respondents have annual diversity goals in hiring. Two-thirds (66.7 percent) said they conduct training in ethnic and racial diversity.

Respondents also reported that an average of 20.2 percent of their recruitment budget is allocated to diversity recruitment. Diversity is clearly on the minds of many human resources executives as they attempt to incorporate the nation's changing demographics into their employee base. Companies are also establishing diversity centers and mounting special campaigns to increase minorities and female representation. Such initiatives are undertaken because employers understand the folly of ignoring more than half of the nation's talent pool. As companies begin to cultivate environments where differences are respected, the change in processes and systems will require:

- Leadership from the top.
- Innovative outreach and recruitment.
- Executive development and training.

- Succession planning.
- Rewards and incentives.
- Mentoring and retention programs.
- Innovative employee benefits.

Strategic Diversity Management and Branding

Much of Bernard Hodes Group's corporate communications work deals with diversity management as a client priority. As consultants, we are involved in all phases of diversity management and communications, from consultation to recruitment advertising. We provide executive briefings, action planning with diversity councils, and minority supplier development. Our services also include public relations and event management, and the development of appropriate collateral materials, including college posters, brochures, and trade show booths.

The 360° Methodology

We apply an inventive, streamlined approach to diversity recruitment communications and staffing solutions: our 360° methodology. Whether you're a small firm or Global 500—and whether you're filling a niche position or reengineering an entire staffing process—our 360° methodology inspires customized solutions.

Here's how the model works:

- *Assess:* In-depth assessment to optimize people, process, tools, and technology.
- *Strategize:* Review assessment to develop integrated solutions to maximize ROI.
- *Implement:* Design, develop, and implement solutions and partner to ensure success.
- *Measure:* Metrics-driven benchmarking to evaluate every strategy and solution.

Putting Diversity into Action

Organizations such as Denny's have eradicated old practices of inequity in favor of progress. In the 1990s, the South Carolina–based restaurant chain was accused of racial discrimination and subsequently sued. The present, however, finds Denny's ranked among the top 10 leaders in corporate diversity by *Fortune* magazine in its annual ranking of "America's 50 Best Companies for Minorities." Additionally, the National Association for Female Executives ranked Denny's 13th in its 2002 survey of the "Top 25 Companies for Executive Women."

Denny's is not alone in such progress. ChevronTexaco Corp., which was also sued by minority employees back in 1996, is now deeply committed to promoting an inclusive business environment for its employees. To accomplish that goal, the company has set up its Supplier Diversity/Small Business program, which works with minority- and women-owned businesses to fuel mutual growth. From 1996 to October 2001, Chevron and Texaco contracted a total of $2.7 billion in products and services with women- or minority-owned suppliers. The company is also a recipient of numerous awards for promoting diversity.

The Future Is Clear

One of the most valuable strategies for diversity management involves developing a clearer perspective on the issue. In an interview with *American Demographics* magazine in March 2001, futurist Ryan Mathews, coauthor of the forthcoming book *The Myth of Excellence* (Crown Books) said: "The problem with how corporations have responded so far to trends in multiculturalism is that they're looking at the new data through old filters. When you look at population growth among ethnic groups through the old filters of fixed mainstream culture, you miss what's going on with the way ethnic and mainstream cultures are evolving. The issue has always been culture, not numbers."

Corporations, more often than not, miss the point that you have to understand values before you can create value. "Organizations need to look at diversity as more than just language differences," said Mathews. "Business will have to conduct commerce in terms of what really matters to individuals." Mathews' analysis is on target. The beauty and power of a successful diversity initiative is that it elevates both the individual and the organization, simultaneously.

To forecast the future in business, a manager must have knowledge of the past and understand the present and its rich diversity of viewpoints. The business case for diversity is rooted in marketing and competitive advantage. Ultimately, those companies that truly understand how diverse viewpoints and talents contribute to innovation and increased market share will lead the way to the new, inclusive workplaces of the future.

As companies roll out welcome mats for multicultural and multigenerational workers, they will be required to discard traditional perceptions of diversity. Companies must not think of diversity as an effort to benefit marginalized people, but as something that will improve the workplace for all employees.

Key Success Factors for Managing Your Campus Recruiting Program: The Good Times and Bad

John Flato

Ernst & Young

Introduction

Campus recruiting is an effective and efficient means of attracting new talent into an organization. I have managed the college recruiting function for organizations in four very different industries: professional services, manufacturing, financial services, and management consulting. By experiencing what works well—and, in some cases, what doesn't—I have concluded that a successful campus recruiting program contains essential elements that transcend all industries. This essay will review those elements.

Essential Elements of a Sound Campus Recruiting Program

There are eight key success factors necessary in order to effectively develop and implement a strong campus recruiting program.

GET SUPPORT FROM SENIOR MANAGEMENT

Campus recruiting efforts are more successful and less complicated if you obtain senior-level support from the CEO's office. The use of resources (both human and financial), the ability to prioritize projects, the development of materials and collateral, and the use of senior executives in the recruiting process are all elements of a robust program. By obtaining bona fide CEO support, you will ensure that you have the necessary funding and management involvement to develop these elements.

When I accepted the position of director of university relations for AlliedSignal in late 1992, Larry Bossidy was the relatively new CEO of AlliedSignal. He had previously been vice chairman at General Electric, a company with a significant campus recruiting program for many years; in fact, Larry was one of their prized campus hires, who rose through the ranks at GE. There was no doubt that Bossidy would support bringing in top graduates. He took an active role in the implementation and monitoring of the success of the college recruiting program.

Similar stories can be witnessed at companies across the country. At the CIGNA Corporation in Philadelphia, there was no lack of senior level support when the company moved to centralize its college recruiting efforts, which had become decentralized, uncoordinated, and unfocused. The top two executives of the company, Wilson Taylor, president, and Jim Stewart, chief financial officer, both were recruited off campus for CIGNA's prestigious actuary development program.

RECOGNIZE THE VALUE OF CAMPUS HIRES FOR THE ORGANIZATION

Newly minted undergraduate- and graduate-degreed employees bring great value to an organization. They are often a company's most enthusiastic employees, in part because they are eager to commence work in order to pay off college debts. They are often the easiest to train, coming directly from an educational environment and still receptive to classroom and Web-based learning techniques. Too, new employees generally are not encumbered with an existing client base or necessary meetings, and they are able to pay attention. They are very loyal, and they're also excellent spokespersons for their employer. They customarily have many contacts still in college, and can help feed the pipeline for the next recruiting campaign. Finally, they are often less expensive labor in comparison to more experienced employees. Companies and firms that are too top-heavy with expensive employees can lose business if they price themselves out of the market.

HIRE STRATEGICALLY, NOT JUST-IN-TIME

Companies with well-managed, strategic campus recruiting programs recognize that there is a six-month lead time to adequately plan for the upcoming campus recruiting season. Campus hiring should not be replacement or just-in-time hiring, because campus hiring requires much more planning than traditional replacement hiring. And yet college recruiting is a very efficient way of obtaining talent. We know that students customarily complete their degrees three times a year—in winter, spring, and summer. We know that most graduating students are looking to be employed. We also know how to access this large pool of job seekers through centralized sources. Essentially, we know when, where, and how to attract these future employees.

I have often counseled my management on the importance of developing a hiring plan, one that's specific but flexible. Granted, managers often complain when asked how many campus graduates they will need 12 to 15 months prior to their start date. But the most efficient and well-managed college recruiting programs have a general understanding of anticipated needs, backed by the goals and objectives of a well-designed hiring plan. Why? Because all facets of the campus program come from the hiring plan—namely, how many brochures and how much merchandise to order, how many schools should be scheduled, how many recruiters are needed, how much training needs to be delivered, and so forth. Companies may use a variety of tools to properly develop a hiring plan—tools such as historic turnover rates (which vary depending on the strength of the economy), the business or financial plan, planned retirements, and annual forced reductions in staff.

Campus recruiting can be designed as a standard process, one that can be replicated effectively year after year. And there's a benefit: Companies that take this standard process approach will have the best reputations on campus, one year to the next.

FOR RECRUITING, USE NON-HUMAN RESOURCES EMPLOYEES

From past experience, I know of one financial services company where we had hundreds of "client-serving" employees on our campus recruiting teams. Some of our most active campus teams were composed of 50 to 80 employees, which is much larger than the typical team size. How did we claim such significant participation? The key element may very well be the "carrot and stick" factor. During the financial company's performance review process for employees, one of the elements regularly assessed is the employee's participation in recruiting activities. The performance review assessed the quantity of events one attended as well as the quality of participation. Included in this evaluation were leadership of events or projects, conversion of assigned advisees into employees, and creative participatory methods in recruiting.

Why was this important? Surveys of campus students have shown that students prefer to be interviewed by senior-level practitioners, rather than human resources personnel. And they don't mean recent hires, either. During their interviews, students want to be assessed by practitioners who are experienced rather than newly employed. This way, they are assured that a satisfactory evaluation of the company, the corporate culture, clients or customers, and career paths can be performed.

There is no doubt that using practitioners in the marketing, assessing, interviewing, and selling aspects of talent acquisition is most advisable. Incentives (beyond expense-paid trips back to one's alma mater) must be in place. If companies can require recruiting responsibilities or talent acquisition into their performance evaluation plan—and tie success or failure of these efforts to the individual's compensation plan—there will be enough volunteers to attend career fairs and other company-sponsored recruiting events. If there are no incentives, however, then the HR staff can only use people who are not essential or fully engaged in work (in consulting, these folks are called "on the beach" staff). Consequently, companies may not be using the companies' best representatives for recruiting purposes. I often advise corporate recruiters to remember that the Hallmark Cards tag line— "When you care enough to send the very best"—reaps benefits in campus recruiting, too.

FUND THE CAMPUS RECRUITING PROGRAM ADEQUATELY

The budget allotted to the campus recruiting function for any one company must adequately support the company's efforts. And while it's difficult to put a figure on that amount, it's a given that it should reflect the level of seriousness the firm has in acquiring campus talent.

Surveys have shown cost-per-hire statistics for undergraduate students are roughly $5,000 to 6,000 per hire, while MBA hires cost roughly $10,000 or more. The problem with comparing cost-per-hire statistics for campus recruiting, however, is that no two firms compile the data exactly alike. For example, some companies figure the time and out-of-pocket expenses of all employees involved in recruiting, while others do not include employee time as an expense. Some will lump together the costs of philanthropic contributions, while others will not. Further, some companies include costs carried by the communications or public relations departments for recruiting images, advertising, and brochures, while others will not. The bottom line is that no two companies fund or analyze the costs of its campus recruiting programs precisely the same.

At many companies, budgets may be allocated to specific campus recruiting teams. And at other companies, each school targeted for recruiting efforts may be given a separate designated budget that ranges from as little as $5,000 to as much as $60,000 to fund travel of recruiters, participation in events and on-campus activities, sponsorships, and other school-specific activities. In today's business environment, where all costs are being scrutinized, the campus recruiting budgets are no exception. The funding levels will no doubt be dictated by the volume of hires and the importance of obtaining the top graduates, especially in labor-intensive industries like consulting and investment banking.

REGULARLY REPORT ON PROGRESS TOWARD THE GOAL, AND KNOW YOUR CEO'S HOT BUTTONS

In my first year at AlliedSignal, I was stopped in the hallway by the CEO and asked how campus recruiting was going. I provided anecdotal information, but I recognized right away that my comments were superficial and not at all reflective of the detailed work going on in my office.

Shortly thereafter, I developed a company-wide monthly report on progress toward our recruiting goals. I included the number of acceptances, broken down by the businesses that were hiring, and included race, sex, school, major, degree, grade point average, and the percentage from the company's targeted schools. The distribution of my monthly report, which included a narrative analysis, went to virtually all of the company's top executives. Since college recruiting was such an important priority for AlliedSignal, you could be sure that there was some internal competition among the business leaders to ensure that the progress against their goals was satisfactorily moving along. Because the report was distributed to everyone, I called this my "in-your-face strategy"—not to embarrass a senior executive but to make certain that company goals were progressing as planned.

Keep in mind, though, that a report can trigger different reactions from different executives, particularly when you account for an executive's key concerns or "hot buttons." One spring day, a senior vice president of human resources came into my office, sat down, and said that the CEO was displeased with the results on my last monthly report. I couldn't understand why, since we were well ahead of the previous year's progress, and I thought we were doing quite well. As it turned out, the CEO's eyes had focused on a column of my report that contained the "Targeted School" percentage. It turns out that we had a goal of hiring 50 percent of the 400+ campus hires from the company's 25 targeted universities; that month, the percentage dipped below the expected 50 percent level. Needless to say, the 50 percent goal was achieved by year's end. And that year, in recognition of how important our "Targeted School" goals are, we implemented a policy that required written approval for all campus hires from nontargeted universities.

Having said that, however, another CEO's attention might be focused on a different column, like grade point average. If your company judges the quality of the incoming recruits by its collective GPA, you'll want to make sure to meet or exceed your GPA goals.

Knowing your key customer's hot buttons is a critical aspect in all phases of business, and campus recruiting is no exception.

DON'T TREAT CAMPUS RECRUITING AS A PASS-THROUGH JOB

In many companies, a campus recruiting job is a first introduction to the human resource department. There is an expectation that campus recruiters will grow out or burn out of the job, due to the extensive travel and demands of the position. But I've found that it doesn't have to be that way. Campus recruiters in the most decentralized firms can create their own community or family in order to help one another, sharing what worked and what didn't across the national markets where everyone has offices.

When assessing performance, companies should not lump together competencies for all recruiters. I have successfully argued that the key competencies for campus recruiters differ significantly from those who recruit experienced candidates. Team building, relationship building, planning, creative thinking, public speaking, and communication skills are some of the competencies that I have found are more important to the campus recruiter than to the experienced candidate recruiter. College recruiting is very much a long-term relationship business with the college clubs, career services staff, faculty, and other college administrators. I've found that these skills, combined with the sense of family or community in the campus recruiters, make for different expectations when hiring and evaluating campus recruiters.

Relationships and continuity are very important in maintaining a consistent college recruiting program. When speaking engagements or panel discussions become available on campus, career services professionals will call upon people they know and trust for these coveted opportunities. If the companies routinely turn over their campus recruiting staff, they may be missing out on some important relationship-building opportunities. While I have never stood in the way of promotional opportunities for my staff, some of the best and most passionate campus recruiters often have sampled life outside the college recruiting environment, and have come back to their former department or moved on to another company's college recruiting department.

The National Association of Colleges and Employers (NACE) serves as the natural affiliation for people in the profession, from the employer and career services perspectives. Regional associations of NACE also provide college recruiters with opportunities to network within the profession, become certified, hold office, and take on responsibilities beyond one's own organization. I have consistently encouraged all of my staff to take advantage of these professional opportunities, to network and befriend colleagues, and to get involved in association-sponsored activities and take leadership roles. Those who do often find the work and effort extremely fulfilling.

TREAT YOUR CAMPUS TEAMS
LIKE BUSINESSES

In my recruiting programs, our client-serving staff has always been willing to assist in our campus recruiting effort. I have also been fortunate to have the resources to adequately fund the campus teams. I have insisted, however, that the teams be accountable for their spending, and I have instituted a number of guidelines for each of the campus teams. Here are a number of suggestions to help organize your campus teams.

Hold Campus Kickoff Meetings
Late in the summer, each campus team should hold a kickoff meeting when roles are assigned, hiring goals are determined, budgets are allocated, and the strategy and calendar for the upcoming season are discussed.

Structure
Each of the national and tier-one universities—where you expect to spend significant amounts of time, effort, and resources to yield a minimum of 10 hires—must have a basic organization that includes:

- *Campus ambassador or campus executive*—Typically a vice president, essentially the CEO of the campus team.
- *Campus captain or campus manager*—Usually a senior manager, and tantamount to the chief operating officer (COO) for the team. He or she assigns the projects to team members, reviews the budget, and ensures that the various activities are fully staffed.
- *Events coordinators*—Designated leaders (as few or as many as you need) for the resume review team, career fair, interview day leader, or special events leaders (mock interview presentations, for example).
- *Diversity leader*—Helps ensure that you have a diverse applicant pool from which to choose. He or she is involved with a variety of diversity clubs on campus and diversity sponsorships.
- *Chief financial officer*—Develops and controls the team's budget.
- *Chief technical officer*—Coordinates databases developed by campus teams in order to maintain contact with team members and help everyone stay up-to-date on team activities, contact with candidates, candidate ratings, and most importantly, the status of each candidate.

Information flow and the development of a good database are critical to the success of campus teams.

- *Buddies or peer advisers*—Well-developed campus teams have assigned "buddies"—team members who routinely stay in touch with about 5 to 10 of the prospects after a career fair, an interview, or an offer. The buddies are generally alumni from the school (although not always), and can answer questions that the candidates were afraid to ask in an interview and review their status with them. Each biweekly contact with the candidates should also be entered into the team's database.

- *Chief fund-raiser*—Someone who helps promote the company's name at a particular event while helping meet the school's goal of raising money from the alumni. The chief fund-raiser may lend his or her name to soliciting funds for scholarships, for naming of rooms or labs, or for general funds, depending on the needs of the university. A solicitation on the company's stationery from a senior-level executive can be very persuasive.

Some campus teams are composed of as many as 80 employees. Recognizing their efforts and rewarding participation at performance review time are especially critical to the success of the teams.

Campus Debriefings

At the end of the campus recruiting season, I hold campus debriefings with each of the campus teams. We review statistics and discuss what worked well, what did not work, what the competition did, and other lessons that we take forward to the next recruiting season.

Suggestions for Maintaining a College Recruiting Program during a Downturn

You've obtained management support, selected targeted schools, developed a hiring plan, built your campus teams, secured adequate funding, and executed the plan accordingly. But an economic or industry downturn can quickly jeopardize your well-established college recruiting program.

In late 2000 and 2001, several events occurred simultaneously: The "dot-coms" became "dot-bombs"; the economy took a steep downturn; and the tragic events at the World Trade Center pushed the country into war and significantly affected the already battered economy. New layoffs were announced daily, which regrettably put some companies in a campus overhire situation; in short, they had promised to hire too many new employees. Companies recognized this problem at different stages and at different times of the year, further exacerbating a difficult situation.

When there are difficult economic times, we have seen the following reactions from companies:

- Layoffs and staff reductions, including the recruiting staff.
- Travel restrictions for all employees.
- Budget cuts for nonessential spending, including branding, advertising, and training.
- Reductions in the number of universities where recruiting takes place.
- Reduced philanthropy.
- Serious morale issues among the remaining staff.
- An increased focus on short-term return on investment.

As a result of the overhiring situation in 2001, companies responded in a variety of ways. Some immediately decided to rescind offers to candidates who had not yet started, a move that not only can deprive your company of some excellent hires but also can damage your recruiting efforts in the future. Here are seven options for dealing with an oversupply of campus hires:

1. *Defer or stagger start dates.* Some companies push out the start date for almost a year. This enables the company to buy time and hope that the economy will improve while keeping the candidates committed for future employment.
2. *Redirect the job.* When business circumstances dictate that a job or position is no longer available, a highly sought-after job candidate may well be just as qualified for another position.
3. *Change the geography.* There may be no openings in San Francisco, but the St. Louis office has vacancies that can be offered to your recruit.
4. *Accelerate the decision date.* Let the candidate know that he/she has until a certain date in order to make the employment decision.

5. *Offer salary reduction, four-day workweek, or furlough.* In order to save money and still meet hiring obligations, some companies have offered these alternatives to their existing staff and to their campus hires prior to their start dates.

6. *Help the deferred candidate financially.* You can bundle the sign-on, start, and relocation bonuses. Some companies have paid salaries or retainers for several months to provide the deferred candidates with some income.

7. *Cancel or modify the internship program.* Eliminating or reducing the time frame of internship programs can reduce costs.

Conclusion

Campus recruiting is a strategic process, one that takes more than a year from the planning stage until the recruited employee actually begins the job. In the best of times, campus recruiting requires careful planning, CEO support, budgeting, and strategic positioning both within the company and on the campus. If there is a sudden downturn or other financial events that cause companies to be in overhire situations, this will no doubt impact the company's ability to successfully recruit again on campus. How a company responds to these challenges and how it treats both its candidates and the college career services offices will determine how quickly the company can reestablish its campus recruiting efforts.

Work-Integrated Learning Programs: Proven Value for Staffing Professionals

Peter J. Franks

CEO, World Association for Cooperative Education, Inc.

A significant shift is occurring in the interface between the workplace and the classroom. While businesses and educational institutions have built fruitful alliances for many years, this arrangement has become more complex in the area of work-integrated learning programs that integrate undergraduate students into the workplace as part of their degree requirements. Such programs are also commonly known as work-integrated education (WIE), cooperative education, internships, or work-integrated learning in a broader context. Global economic pressures have impelled both parties to take a more critical view of these work/study arrangements, including those already in existence and others under consideration.

In times past, the situation was straightforward, following a regular pattern. For example, faculty coordinators—staff at an educational institution charged with the operation of co-op programs—would travel to a potential workplace and discuss placement possibilities with human resources and line managers. Then co-op student candidates would appear for an interview. Ideally, the job would complement the students' field of studies. If hired, they would effectively become "trial employees" for one or more work terms and receive salaries. All the while, the company could assess them as possible full-time members of its workforce after graduation.

In today's global economy, things have grown far less predictable. Because corporations operate multinational offices, their HR practitioners must recruit workers who speak different languages and live in societies with myriad cultures. They must find employees who are productive from the first day on the job, and recruit them at minimal cost to the business. How do they accomplish all this efficiently? Surprisingly enough, HR executives can still turn to educational institutions all over the world that offer work-integrated learning programs and hire talented students to fill both short- and long-term staffing needs. But beforehand, HR professionals need positive analytical proof that entry into such an education partnership will provide highly effective workers at minimal recruitment cost to their business.

Because of the changing economy over the past few years, there have been dramatic changes in the way that the university and the workplace interface in the realm of co-op student staffing. These changes are reflected in the following three HR issues:

1. What is the cost-effectiveness of using work-integrated learning as a staffing strategy versus recruiting nonstudent hires in more conventional ways? For years, colleges and universities have been saying that co-op student hires were more cost-effective than the others, but can this statement actually be proven on a quantitative basis?

2. The globalization of business offers new challenges in tapping work-integrated learning schools and colleges around the world. With so many models of work-integrated learning that now exist in different countries, how can HR staff make an analytical judgment as to what program is best for their company? There are almost as many forms of work-integrated learning as there are nations who participate in it. Most co-op programs require that the student be paid for work. Others, the majority of which are internships, offer no salary but intensive work experience.

3. Once work-integrated learning is adopted as a staffing resource, how do HR professionals access the global co-op labor pool? There are now at least 43 different countries that offer cooperative education in their educational institutions. Further complicating the matter is that co-op students cross borders to study and to work; they may remain in another country to fulfill all of their degree/work requirements, or they may return to their home country for part of their education and work.

The good news is that there are positive resolutions to all three issues, even in these challenging times. In fact, the current global climate makes the results even more important in reinforcing the ongoing success of work-integrated learning as a strong HR strategy. Let us examine the advantages of a work-integrated learning program.

Advantages of Cooperative Education from an HR Standpoint

Two years ago, the World Association for Cooperative Education, Inc. (WACE) launched an ongoing market study under the title of "Cooperative Education as a Source of Labor Supply to Firms in the College Labor Market." This study is being carried out by the Center for Labor Market Studies at Northeastern University, Boston, Massachusetts. Key collaborators are the Employment Management Association Foundation (EMAF), Camp Dresser & McKee, Inc. (CDM), and Northeastern University. The study, authored by Drs. Paul Harrington and Neeta Fogg, draws upon a database of close to 13,000 newly hired personnel with bachelor's or advanced degrees when they were hired by several U.S.-based multinational corporations. This personnel group was divided into three subcategories:

1. *New hires:* college graduates with a bachelor's degree or more who were hired during or after 1995.
2. *Co-op hires:* new hires with one or more co-op employment experiences with the firm, in addition to their bachelor's degree or more, prior to full-time employment at that firm.
3. *Non-co-op hires:* the remaining new group (total hires minus co-op hires).

Main findings of the study prove the value of hiring cooperative education students, using the benchmarks of occupational mobility, retention, performance appraisals, promotions, starting salaries, salary differentials, location of technical staff for IT and technology posts, and workplace diversity. In all cases, co-op hires surpassed their non-co-op counterparts as follows:

- They experienced significantly greater upward occupational mobility.
- They had higher retention rates.
- They received substantially better performance appraisals.
- They had many more promotions regardless of the length of their tenure at the firm.
- The mean starting salaries of co-op hires were somewhat lower than those of non-co-op hires. However, the gap between the two groups in these firms narrowed over time.
- After researchers applied statistical controls for several factors known to influence salaries (through regression analysis), sizable reductions were found in the salary gaps between co-op and non-co-op groups.
- Cooperative education and college recruitment were the most effective sources of labor supply for hard-to-fill engineering and information technology positions.
- Co-op was very effective in aiding the employer in hiring racial and ethnic minorities.

The cooperative education labor market study comes as a welcome development for practitioners of work-integrated learning, as well as its longtime advocates in the workplace. Up until now, no one had ever carried out this type of quantitative and qualitative analysis of cooperative education versus more conventional hires. For the first time, we can conclusively prove what we knew instinctively for years: that co-op students consistently outperform their non-co-op counterparts. When they are hired as permanent employees after graduation, they are fully productive from day one. Research from the labor market study will continue and draw upon data from other companies. It makes a powerful case for the worth of work-integrated learning programs in the marketplace.

Kraft Foods North America: A Corporate Case Study

For at least a quarter-century, Kraft Foods North America (KFNA) has seen the value of work-integrated education firsthand. College and university students can be found in all functions of the massive KFNA organization: both those on co-op assignments throughout the academic year, carried out in conjunction with a defined college curriculum, and others in off-term internship assignments outside a curriculum.

According to Carin Kaiser, director of staffing, work-integrated education at Kraft has now become an important means of identifying new talent for the company. "We had more than 300 WIE students working for us during the summer of 2002. The annual total is higher, as some functions have co-ops during the academic year."

Worldwide, Kraft Foods International consists of 61 brands in six groups: beverages, convenient meals, cheese, groceries, snacks, and beverages. Its revenue totals over $100 billion, with six brands over $1 billion.

Kraft maintains ties with more than 60 colleges and universities, plus the INROADS organization, to locate co-op students and interns. Both groups receive payment for their services. Regarding INROADS, a minority student recruiting association, Ms. Kaiser says that generally their students intern two summers at Kraft. "The INROADS program focuses on encouraging students to continue their education beyond high school with leadership development, business education, and career pursuits."

Work-integrated education students at Kraft are assigned to each of the organization's divisions and functions, including marketing, finance, information systems, and many others. These divisions each operate their own university relations programs, making contact with WIE colleges and universities.

Which academic disciplines are represented among the work-integrated education students hired by Kraft? Some of them include engineering, finance, information systems, business, liberal arts, and communications. Those students with a business and liberal arts background have multiple opportunities in such areas as marketing, service functions, human resources management, and compensation.

What happens to the students after graduation? Ms. Kaiser says that "the majority are offered and accept full-time assignments at Kraft, building upon their co-op and internship experiences. With on-the-job activity, skill development, and training, these well-prepared employees move into new assignments and/or are promoted within a few years."

Models of Cooperative Education around the World

Turning again to WACE, the organization draws its 1,200-member constituency from 43 countries. As of last year, the association began conducting the WACE Learning System, a regional training program tailor-made to the educational systems, employer needs, and cultures of different countries. Educators, business representatives, and government officials alike are welcome to attend. Recent Learning System programs utilizing international and regional experts have taken place in Thailand, France, Jamaica, Canada, and Germany.

Cooperative education is the most common title for work-integrated learning, used in North America, Europe, New Zealand, and Asia. In Australia, work-integrated learning—also encompassing lifelong learning programs—is used more often. The United Kingdom describes work/study curricula as "sandwich education," while France has adopted "stages." Students receive pay for many placements; however, the internship system of Japan and various other countries focuses on the work experience and does not offer a salary at present.

Which model of work/study is best for a particular company to adopt? HR practitioners encouraged WACE to develop a comparative study of the various forms in use today. The forms would be set out in such a way as to focus clearly on the respective advantages and disadvantages of each. Once convinced of the merit of adopting cooperative education, businesses could make an informed decision on which model best suits their needs. Other firms would also be able to expand or improve their involvement with work-integrated learning programs through the same guide.

WACE commissioned Dr. Rick Reeve of Canada, noted researcher in international work-integrated learning, to conduct the study and publish his findings. Providing funding support for the project was the education division of the General Motors Corporation. From the start, Dr. Reeve committed himself to producing a work that would be useful to global audiences, one free from any individual, institutional, or national bias. Further, it would be based entirely on the opinions of those currently involved in work-integrated learning activity.

The study led to the publication of the *Employers' Guide to Work-Integrated*

Learning in 2001. Information for the *Guide* was collected in two ways: an Internet-based survey and small group discussions of employers. A total of 385 companies from 12 countries completed the survey, and a further 45 were consulted in group discussions in New Zealand, Australia, the United Kingdom, Germany, Belgium, the Netherlands, and Sweden. Data collected included demographic information about the companies and the corporate function of the individuals filling out the survey form.

Of greatest interest to the study were the sections in which the companies identified the reasons they became involved with work-integrated learning programs in the first place; barriers they faced during implementation; and program features available to them that they considered most useful and important to their hiring needs. Another section enabled them to identify what they considered best practices in hiring students.

The *Guide* makes no attempt to judge which model of work-integrated learning is the best at meeting the needs of employers. Instead, the *Guide* helps employers make this judgment themselves by presenting the data in a graphic, easy-to-read form that lists the following information ranked according to level of importance in the workplace:

- The 20 most important reasons companies became involved with work-integrated learning programs.
- The 13 most common barriers companies faced when implementing a work-integrated learning hiring scheme or expanding an existing one.
- The 20 most highly valued program features (from a total of 55) available to companies through their collaboration with institutions offering work-integrated learning programs.
- The 12 most common best practices used by companies to optimize their hiring of students.

Some statistical analysis results are also presented, showing how responses in the survey differed between companies as a function of such factors as location, size, and sector, or between companies meeting different needs through their student recruitment. One interesting outcome of these analyses found that HR professionals attached higher value or importance to issues related to work-integrated learning involvement than did respondents from management or student supervisors.

A Web-Based System for Job Postings

WACE is the only organization that promotes, creates, and supports work-integrated learning internationally. It is now in the process of developing a Web job placement service for students enrolled in cooperative education programs. The WACE web site (www.waceinc.org) will link up with an Internet job placement site, to be announced in coming months.

Through this WACE site, multinational corporations will be able to hire well-qualified students for their domestic or international branches. The site will also benefit educational institutions, as they will be able to locate work-integrated learning positions for their domestic and international students. These assignments will allow students to advance in their education while providing them beneficial work experience. At this writing, WACE anticipates that the site will be up and running in the fall of 2002.

Some of the actions that WACE has taken in conjunction with establishment of the WACE job placement site include:

- Establishing a task force with corporate representatives and educators in Australia, Canada, and the United States, with Dr. Robert Nichols, vice president for enrollment management at Kettering University, United States, serving as chair. The task force reviewed issues of quality control, costs, content, ease of use, and marketing.

- Completing a survey of educational systems and employers. Even though the past year has been a turbulent one for the world economy, WACE continues its global commitment to expanding and improving work-integrated learning. This dedication remains stronger than ever among WACE's worldwide constituency. The WACE Secretariat continues to provide consultation to nations considering the adoption of work-integrated learning (Japan, Saudi Arabia, and the Caribbean region are some examples). WACE seeks to build consensus and support at the highest levels, so that fledgling programs meet the approval of the important stakeholders.

To reinforce its presence in Japan, WACE is exploring further collaboration with ILCC Co., Ltd., with offices in Tokyo and Boston. This respected consulting firm has taken a major role in the launching of Japanese work-integrated learning. ILCC has published the *Internship Handbook for Businesses and Universities* under the auspices of the Japan Regional Internship Consortium. Under the newest arrangement, ILCC would translate and market WACE research materials and promote WACE membership in Japan.

It is sometimes the case that existing work-integrated education programs founder. One major reason is that businesses do not provide meaningful work assignments for their students. It is essential that students have a clear job description, a mentor, a line supervisor, and an assignment that challenges them while it enhances what they are studying back in the classroom. WACE stands ready to assist businesses where cooperative work programs need reevaluation and reinforcement.

Outstanding work-integrated learning programs do not happen overnight. They require hard work and collaboration of both the HR community and educational staff to succeed. And when they do, the words of Dr. Reeve ring true: "Work-integrated learning is one of the most effective human resource development tools available today."

Appendix

The World Association for Cooperative Education, Inc. (WACE)
Suite 384, Columbus Place
360 Huntington Avenue
Boston, MA 02115-5096
USA
Telephone: 617-373-8885
Fax: 617-373-3463
E-mail: p.franks@neu.edu
Web site: www.waceinc.org

"Cooperative Education as a Source of Labor Supply to Firms in the College Labor Market": This study will continue for another year and will be published upon completion by WACE and the Employment Management Association Foundation (EMAF), a division of the Society for Human Resource Management (SHRM).

Reeve, R. S. *Employers' Guide to Work-Integrated Learning.* Boston: World Association for Cooperative Education, 2001. Copies may be ordered through WACE at the above address.

Optimum Source: The Military

Bill Gaul

President, The Destiny Group

The U.S. military service is not easy duty. For anyone who has ever been associated with the military—and even to those who have chosen to observe from the sidelines—it's very clear that the military is a difficult path to choose in order to obtain the goal of bettering oneself. To many, however, it is quite an admirable path, one that allows individuals to support themselves through school or enlist in the service and obtain money for a college education. Once this service commitment is completed, should employers reward this sacrifice by considering those who have served in the military as potential employees for our own organizational needs?

This essay presents the many advantages that are inherent when someone from the military is hired for work in corporate America. It includes a review of such factors as demographics and special talents, as a way to understand why companies find the military to be such a rich source of talent. And it concludes with a discussion of the strategies that can be used to recruit this military talent for the workplace.

Demographics

First, the military workforce is abundant. Around 200,000 people change uniforms each year, which means that one out of every six members of the military return to civilian life during any given calendar year. They are very young in relation to their extensive experience and training. In fact, 82 percent of departing military are between the ages of 18 and 34 years old. Most exit the service after completing their first enlistment or obligation (after three to five years). Those who retire from the military generally do so at the ripe old age of 37 to 38—still in their prime, anxious to learn new skills, and eager to apply what they have already experienced.

In addition, the military is a diverse group. Women enter the military at a rate of 30,000 to 35,000 per year. Within the past two years, minorities have accounted for nearly four out of every 10 new recruits into all military branches (38 percent). That compares to the entire U.S. minority population of 27 percent—a significant difference of 11 percent.

And organizations wishing to hire disabled applicants should consider veterans. Anyone discharged with as little as a 5 percent disability rating is considered a disabled hire, yet a fully capable prospective employee.

Training with Translatable Skills

The military does a lot of training—in just about everything. The current military is the most highly educated in history. More than 98 percent of all service members are high school graduates and over 46 percent have graduated from or attended college. Apart from college, there are numerous technical schools for almost any trade or skill. At the foundation of this training, applicants learn core values such as loyalty, personal responsibility, discipline, and motivation. From IT talent to vehicle repair, from engineer to truck driver, the military has it all. It helps to think of the military as a city with people who have varied educational and skill backgrounds to meet the needs and functions of the entire organization. There are engineers of all types, computer programmers, project managers, logisticians, system administrators, supervisors, electronic and electrical technicians, aircraft maintenance, machinists, general construction, and others. It is easy to see how these specialties would easily cross over into the military's civilian counterpart.

Proven Leadership

Granted, the military provides extensive technical training. But some companies may say they don't need technical people; they may need salespeople or business leaders. When looking at it from this perspective, the question is, "What has someone in the military really sold? What business operations experience do they have?" The answer may not be found on a militaristic resume, but in the character and experiences of the person.

That's why military applicants are prime prospects for supervisory and management positions. In fact, most situations demand a leadership style that empowers and motivates. A 1998 article written by U.S. Army Colonel Lloyd Mathews in the *Military Review* reveals that traditional military leadership ideals require that "leaders must always respect the innate human dignity of each subordinate. Leaders must recognize the status of U.S. service members as thinking individuals rather than mindless automatons, giving them opportunity wherever feasible to exercise initiative, shoulder responsibility, and employ their native ingenuity in accomplishing assigned tasks."

Many military candidates are leaders who can demonstrate that they can get the job done, under stressful conditions, and with limited resources. Could you use someone like that in your organization?

Flexibility

Adaptability is essential for a successful transition. This is certainly true when some candidates realize that they have not been trained for everything the civilian world has to offer (i.e. infantrymen, boatmen). Even with all the training and experience, this sometimes is the case for certain civilian job descriptions, or at least portions of work assignments. If so, candidates can be easily trained to help fill the gaps, or become "civilianized" on particular equipment or ways of doing business. Their ability to learn new things and adapt to a changing environment is crucial in meeting the demands of civilian reality.

Besides possessing such qualities as self-esteem, confidence, and discipline, military candidates have developed a desire to achieve and a mind-set of setting goals and working toward an objective until it is accomplished. Being flexible, learning new operations, and fulfilling new missions are all part of that objective in the entry-level civilian career.

Flexibility in choosing civilian work is another hallmark of military making the transition. In today's tight labor market, top civilian candidates call the shots for location and salary demands. In contrast, military candidates realize they have to prove themselves in the civilian world. They are eager and more willing to initially accept a less glamorous assignment, but one that could offer a rewarding and fulfilling experience. Shift work, remote locations, stressful work conditions, and average pay are the norm for these individuals in the military. Relocating every two to three years is typical for the military family, so moving to unknown territories is generally well received. In addition, free relocation benefits provided by the federal government to a new civilian hire make cross-country relocation a cost-savings win for the company.

Sourcing Strategies for Recruiting Military Talent

There are many sourcing strategies for recruiting military talent. Let's review a few of them.

OFFICIAL MILITARY BASE NEWSPAPERS

The base newspaper is circulated to active-duty personnel. Military media representatives can target advertising to specific bases or locations, identify bases with particular types of people (i.e., by occupation or experience), and provide information on other media vehicles such as billboards, ad racks, and radio and online advertising.

MILITARY CAREER SITES

The Destiny Group (www.destinygroup.com) (I am president and CEO of this organization); Military.com (www.military.com); and Armed Forces.com (www.armedforces.com) all offer worldwide job posting capability as well as resume searches. These web sites even offer a variety of special services that include unique audio/video profiling, job alert push technology, and nationwide job fair events. These services do not charge per hire, but by the service itself; companies may hire as many candidates as needed for one relatively low fixed cost.

GOVERNMENT-SPONSORED WEB SITES

The Department of Defense Job Search (www.dod.jobsearch.org), a part of America's Job Bank, is specifically targeted to those who are affiliated with our nation's defense. Employers have the ability to post jobs and "set up automated resume searches." You can even search by military rank and occupational specialty code. The Department of Defense Operation Transition (www.dmdc.osd.mil/ot) is another government-sponsored site that boasts more than 10,000 job want ads that represent over 30,000 jobs on average. The authority to operate such a service for departing military began back in 1991 with the passing of the Defense Authorization Act. Also known as the Transition Bulletin Board, (TBB), it was created in anticipation of a significant downsizing of the military and therefore has met a significant need for our servicemen and women. More than 24,000 employers who use the TTB—from small businesses to Fortune 500–size companies. The TBB also receives over 30,000 log-ins from job seekers each month.

MILITARY ASSOCIATIONS

You may wish to contact various military associations such as the Air Force Benefit Association, the Warrant Officer Association, or the Navy League. Each of these organizations runs its own Internet-based job board for its members, as well as maintaining a resume database that you can tap into very affordably. To access information on all military service organizations, the Office of the Secretary of Veterans Affairs has published an up-to-date Directory of Veterans Service Organizations, accessible online at www.va.gov/vso.

The Role of Staffing in Mergers and Acquisitions

John G. Kitson
Senior Vice President, FirstBank

Mergers and acquisitions have become an integral part of the business plans of many organizations. But the effects they have reach well beyond the organization itself. Mergers and acquisitions affect not only the people involved but also their jobs, families, and communities. Staffing professionals have a unique opportunity to address these effects in a way that helps ensure success and maintain a positive organizational image.

I've been involved in almost 40 mergers and acquisitions. From an operational perspective each has been unique, but all have had common issues related to people. How these people issues have been addressed from a staffing perspective has directly impacted the results achieved. Up-front, open, honest, and direct employee communication is of paramount importance. Effective planning is not enough to guarantee a successful merger and acquisition. Instead, effective planning *and* communication are two essential elements for the success of the staffing function's role in the merger and acquisition process. This essay outlines these essential elements and the steps necessary to carry them out.

From the Start

Once an organization to be acquired has been identified, human resources must begin conducting its own due diligence. A good place to start is by reviewing employee benefit packages, compensation practices, and employee relations. These are generally accessible and well documented. How well do the benefits packages align between the two organizations? Are pension and 401(k) plans properly funded? How do HR policies, procedures, and systems match up? Are there outstanding employment-related legal matters? These are just a few of the many questions that must be answered by HR in the due diligence process.

The staffing professional should start by looking at people. What will the combined organization look like? What are the skills required in the merged environment? What are the knowledge, skills, and abilities of the new people coming into the organization? These, again, are just a few of the many questions that will need to be answered as you develop a staffing plan. And you must determine whether the people working for the acquired organization have a bona fide interest in working for the new company. This is an important issue for the staffing professional to resolve and one that cannot be assumed. Making the wrong assessment about someone's long-term intent to work for the new company can have serious detrimental effects after the merger is complete. For this reason, open and honest two-way communication between the staffing professional and the acquired employee is critical to the success of staffing's role in the transaction.

Staffing is not an event but an ongoing process that ensures the right talent is in place to get the job done efficiently and effectively. Mergers and acquisitions create an incredible opportunity for the staffing professional to review talent requirements, assess employee skills and performance, and focus on retaining top performers. The obvious implication here is that you take a look at talent on both sides of the merger. Once you get started, you'll find that most of the work can be categorized into one of the following phases:

- Complete an organizational review.
- Begin communication and orientation.

- Conduct employee interviews and assessment.
- Create a staffing plan and review with unit managers.
- Implement the staffing plan.
- Measure success.

THE REVIEW

To begin, you must conduct a thorough review of the organization to be acquired in order to determine how and where its functions fit into your own organization and to establish a clear understanding of the staffing requirements needed in the merged environment. It's also important to learn about the culture of the organization and about the people who are key contributors to the organization's success. This will help you place people in jobs down the road. You have to understand the organization's human resources policies and practices and determine changes that will be made that affect people.

You'll want to have answers for questions employees have such as: Will I have a job? Will I lose my tenure? Will my responsibilities change? What will happen to my benefits? If I lose my job, will I receive severance pay? If you develop a clear understanding of the organization to be acquired, you will gain the perspective that allows you to answer these questions. And having a sense of where the merger and acquisition process is headed and what its impact will be before you start communicating with the staff will enhance your credibility throughout the implementation.

You'll also want to know a little about the organization's existing competitors. They will be out there, trying to take advantage of any opportunity they can to steal customers or key employees who may become disheartened by the mergers and acquisition activities. You will not want to lose either customers or employees. Be prepared to identify key talent and have a plan for retention throughout the merger process and beyond.

COMMUNICATION AND ORIENTATION

People want to hear from the new acquiring organization as soon as a merger is announced. I like to be on site within a day of the public announcement. That means my basic organizational review has to be completed beforehand. First impressions are so important. When possible, I conduct all-employee meetings—in shifts and in multiple locations if necessary—so that the entire staff can start seeing people from my organization and learn directly from us about our company and about the events that will take place as we complete the acquisition process. And I'm always prepared to answer, as best I can, the basic questions listed earlier.

Often, HR will not have the luxury of being able to conduct these first communication sessions in person. Of course, there are other ways to accomplish this—through print, video, or an online resource; some organizations establish web sites dedicated to merger-related communications. Whatever medium you choose, it's important to share information and try to ensure that people feel as comfortable as is reasonably possible about the changes that will occur. The first phase of communication is fundamental in nature. Since many employees will be surprised by the announcement of the acquisition, they won't necessarily be ready to hear a lot of detail or be of the mind-set to raise complex issues. However, as they begin to mull things over, they will develop a bigger appetite for additional information. Be prepared to provide it as appropriate. Ongoing, effective communication will become the foundation for success throughout the acquisition and merger process.

To help meet the desire for more detailed information, we've developed a special orientation program that is tailored to employees who join our organization by way of acquisition. In this orientation, we review our history, culture, policies, and procedures within the context of similar issues at the acquired company. This has helped employees better identify change and get immediate answers to their questions. For the customer contact staff, we prepare special product knowledge classes that compare our products to theirs and help them understand where we're heading so that they are well prepared to handle customer situations. Keep in mind that customers will only feel as good about the merger as the employees feel. Special attention must be given to customer contact staff so that they are prepared to answer customers' questions about the upcoming events with confidence and enthusiasm.

INTERVIEW AND ASSESS THE STAFF

Much can be accomplished by meeting individually with as many senior-level executives and line managers as possible as soon as possible. I like to begin by meeting individually with each member of the management team. The first meeting is much like an applicant's initial interview, because most frequently (whether it is discussed or not) we're both trying to determine whether there's a fit in the merged environment. There is one key difference, however.

In this situation, you have to remember that they are selling themselves and you are selling your organization—while trying to retain them in their current roles for at least some period of time. I can't over-emphasize the importance of this. Many mergers and acquisitions must go through some approval process before any transaction can occur. After that, there are significant milestones to be achieved before any consolidation of work can be realized. Both organizations must continue to operate effectively and efficiently during this period. The staffing professional must be careful not to discourage or scare off people who are needed during this process.

Once I have an understanding of the job responsibilities of the management team and have gained a sense of their skills and abilities, I develop a plan for interviews with every member of the staff from the organization about to be acquired. Every employee from that organization is assigned to a manager from the appropriate area in my organization. That manager will meet with them to establish their fit for and interest in our organization. From there, we begin to develop the staffing plan that will guide us through the remainder of the merger and acquisition process.

THE STAFFING PLAN

Once interviews have been conducted with every employee, you can begin to develop a plan. First, you have to determine the human capital requirements of each function within the combined organization. This will become your staffing model. Then, you must consider the qualifications and performance of staff from both organizations. This will be an excellent opportunity to address performance issues among existing staff members. Once you've determined the positions required and the number available for those coming in through the acquisition, you can begin listing their names in a way that will assist in future planning and communication. Your list might be similar to this:

- People whose positions will be eliminated.
- People whose positions will be eliminated but must be retained through a certain date.
- People whose positions will be eliminated but may be placed elsewhere within the organization.
- People who will be retained in their current roles.
- People who will be retained but in lesser roles or with lesser pay.
- People who will be retained and offered higher positions.

Being fair and consistent is obviously important as you develop this plan. Work with managers and supervisors to develop and approve this plan and provide them the support needed to determine the status of each employee and make selection decisions. Begin with senior management and work your way down, involving each new level of manager/supervisor in the process. Assign responsibility for communication, along with dates of completion.

For those who will be leaving the organization, you'll want to calculate the amounts of severance payments. Ideally, these severance payments should be made in exchange for a release of liability, reducing the risk of future charges of discrimination or wrongful discharge. You will also want to review the packages of key staff members—those critical to the success of the merger process. It may be necessary to add an additional incentive to entice them to stay as long as needed.

For those who will be staying, you'll want to establish job assignments and reporting relationships. Changes in pay and eligibility for benefits need to be identified, along with required training and development requirements.

IMPLEMENTATION

A well-thought-out staffing plan will make implementation considerably more effective. Keeping everyone on schedule and within the established time line is an important responsibility of the staffing professional. Everyone has been anxiously waiting to learn his or her status, and once the communication has begun, anxiety increases. Those who lose their jobs will display a mixed bag of emotions. Some will be expecting this news and may be relieved to be moving on. Others will be disappointed, even angry. You have to be prepared to deal with an array of emotions. How you handle the situation and the staff will say a lot about your organization and you as a staffing professional. Anything you can do to help employees move to another job opportunity will help diminish the negative affects the merger has on their loss of work. Many organizations offer outplacement assistance or workshops that help displaced employees prepare resumes, practice interviewing, and begin a job search. Some hold open houses, inviting other employers in to meet with workers whose positions will be eliminated. If nothing else, the staffing professional can always help someone develop a resume and offer a few tips for kicking off a job search.

It's important to focus attention on those who will be retained as well. They will be working for a new organization and will likely have a new boss. Keep in mind that these employees didn't necessarily choose to work for your company. They are eyewitnesses to what has happened to their coworkers, and they are watching how you treat them as they head out the door. Don't assume that people are pleased with the results of the merger simply because they have a job. Remember, your competitors are watching and ready to recruit those employees who may be less than enthused about the outcome of the merger. It will be necessary to address the concerns of those who will stay and gain their commitment to the new organization.

In Conclusion, Measure Results

As with all areas of performance management, it's important to measure the results of the merger and acquisition process. Results can be measured through employee opinion surveys or focus groups. Employee and customer retention rates can also indicate some measure of success. Occasionally, the unsolicited feedback you get from the employees involved in a merger or acquisition will help assess your results.

Measurement itself will help you improve your success in future acquisitions, allowing you to incorporate mergers and acquisitions as an integral part of the business plans of your organization.

Selecting High-Talent Professionals in the Competitive Global Marketplace

Kent Kirch

Global Director, Deloitte

How important is the concept of seamless, global service to your organization?

For most large multinational corporations, this is critically important—especially to their customers. Customers expect the same level of service whether they are in Chicago, Illinois or Sydney, Australia. How confident are you about your organization's ability to deliver consistent global service? If you are like most of us in the staffing business, you are no doubt concerned about your ability to deliver.

There are many variables that affect the quality and consistency of human capital. It all starts with how candidates are assessed and selected. Every company strives to attract and hire high-talent professionals. Having an effective global selection methodology is essential if you want to deliver consistent service through talented, capable employees in the global marketplace.

Implementing an "American" methodology globally is not the answer. In general, getting agreement on selection criteria and the approach to assessment of those criteria is a great start. Together, these create a baseline selection methodology. Each element must be adapted to the local culture. In many cases, they also must be translated to the local language to be used effectively. Most importantly, these elements must be owned by the project leader at the country level; in other words, the stakeholders in each country must believe in the need for a methodology and in the methodology itself. They must also be armed with the information and guidance to create the business case for their local business unit. If any of these criteria are not met, the likelihood of success is greatly reduced.

Developing an employee selection methodology includes determining the approach to be used and the selection criteria. One of the most common approaches to interviewing, for instance, is structured, behavior-based interviews. This is a process where questions that focus on past experiences are created prior to the interview. And there are a number of reasons for its widespread use. First, behavior-based interviewing is one of the most effective methods that can be used by an interviewer without specialized credentials to predict a candidate's future performance. Second, it is intuitive and requires only four to eight hours of training for someone to use it effectively. Third, this approach generates more and better data from the candidate than other types of interviews; it removes much of the inherent subjectivity from the process. And last, behavior-based questions provide real purpose and focus to an interview. If focused on the essential requirements of the job and used correctly, it also provides strong legal protection to employers in many countries.

In addition to the basic education and licensing requirements of a given position, key competencies are the most commonly used selection criteria. It is critical that competencies are carefully identified for each family of jobs. This is essential to making the right hiring decisions and, again, can have significant legal ramifications in many countries. Typically, the process to identify key competencies involves an evaluation of the most important requirements of a job by human resources professionals and both supervisors and incumbents of that job.

Once the approach and selection criteria are established, the selection process (process sequence) must be created; key concepts (competencies, rating systems) must be defined; tools (interview guides) must be created; and interviewers must be trained. If a large number of interviewers are to be trained, a "train the trainer" session is typically conducted to qualify a number of internal instructors who can then train hundreds or thousands of other employees.

Once implemented, the organization should be able to conclude that it is hiring highly successful and capable people. This can be measured through an analysis of new hire performance and retention. Studies have shown that the bottom line value of hiring a strong versus average performer is dramatic. Ultimately, the return on investment for a successful global employee selection methodology can be enormous, particularly for people-intensive businesses where employee performance and retention have significant implications.

In addition, most organizations find that they experience process efficiencies because second-round interview candidates have been more effectively screened. Companies have fewer second-round interview candidates, and a higher percentage of them receive offers. Acceptance rates increase because candidates understand more about the position they have interviewed for and believe that the employer thoroughly understands what they can contribute—due in large part to the volume and quality of the information shared during the interview process.

In conclusion, implementing a consistent, global selection methodology can pay enormous dividends, particularly for large employers. However, as with any project, the manner in which one moves through the process will dramatically impact results. Obtaining consensus on the approach and the selection criteria will create the consistency required for the desired results, while allowing enough flexibility for local adaptations. When done successfully, a consistent global employee selection methodology will help any organization win the escalating global war for high-talent professionals.

The Challenges of Staffing Overseas Operations

David Lowry

*Vice President, Freeport-McMoRan Copper and Gold,
and President, Freeport-McMoRan Foundation*

Globalization has brought many opportunities and also many challenges to multinational corporations (MNCs). Overseas operations open new markets for the sale of goods produced in a corporation's home country and enhance operational growth. For many companies in the developed world, overseas operations in developing countries also allow core manufacturing to be done in places where costs can be minimized. In addition, extractive industries, which have already exploited deposits in the more developed parts of the world, often find it necessary to develop mines and oil fields in developing countries—both for their own future and to supply the resource needs of the developed and developing world.

In this essay, I will address some of the staffing issues that multinational companies face when they open overseas operations. The most complex issues are those that companies face when they move into less developed areas to do manufacturing or, in the case of extractives, move into substantially underdeveloped areas to mine or drill for oil and gas. I will address these issues in depth, focusing mainly on managerial and technical staffing. Recruiting, training, and retaining processes for these highly skilled employees are most difficult and most crucial for the success of MNCs.

There are three reasons why multinational corporations operate overseas:

1. To sell more products, by opening overseas markets.
2. To manufacture more inexpensively.
3. To extract natural resources.

In some cases, companies will have all three of these as goals; in others, one of the three goals will dominate. The most general rule about staffing an overseas operation is that the larger the operation, the more complex it is, and the more remote it is, the more difficult the staffing challenges will be. For that reason, selling products internationally will have the fewest staffing challenges and the extractive industries will bring the greatest challenges.

Where to Start? Company Values and the Workforce

Building a workforce starts with corporate values and the articulation of those values. Corporate values should be in place wherever a corporation works. There should not be one set of values in the corporation's home base and another at its remote operations in a developing country. Since cost control is an important issue for companies working overseas, there can be a temptation to chip away at corporate values to save as much money as possible in every area of overseas operations—including salaries, benefits, and training of workers. This is a mistake, because loyal employees are essential to success, especially in foreign operations. In addition, it is a mistake because globalization of industry is being paralleled by globalization of information; even before multinational corporations can get their internationally produced goods to the international markets, workers, often supported by a network of international nongovernmental organizations (NGOs), can get the word out about how employees are being treated. One need only ask the garment, shoe, and toy industries about international labor and employment issues to know that the flow of information around the world is both efficient and potentially damaging to the reputations of corporations. Conversely, enlightened treatment of employees in overseas operations can greatly enhance corporate reputations. So start international staffing with clearly articulated corporate standards that are normative everywhere the corporation operates.

Obviously, salaries and benefits will vary from location to location. But the standard of paying a living wage—one that at least matches the minimum wage required by the country and region where a multinational operates—should be the absolute minimum that a company pays. In addition, the company should provide benefits to employees at overseas operations that reasonably parallel those that are offered to comparable employees in the company's home location. Some will object, saying that the reason for operating overseas, and especially in developing countries, is to minimize costs—and that certainly is important. However, if minimizing costs can only be done at the price of dissolving a company's core values and exploiting workers, the argument can be made that the business is not worth doing—at least not in that way or in that location.

Expatriates and International Staffing

It may seem perverse to begin an essay on international staffing with expatriates. However, most international operations of multinational corporations begin with expatriate management—and too many operations still have many expatriate managers many years into the operation. The success of the corporation and the expatriates who set up and manage the new operation will determine whether the operation nationalizes its workforce while still adhering to the corporate ethos as set by the corporation for its operations worldwide. Corporations that work successfully in a variety of countries hold to core values while being sensitive to cultural differences and find ways to integrate local culture into core values. This sounds sensible and relatively easy to do—that is, until one tries to do it in the real world, where it can become a most difficult task.

Success in setting up and staffing a foreign operation begins with the selection and training of the expatriates who form the first management/operational team in the new location. Many companies (including those that have numerous overseas operations) believe that any good manager from the home office can do just fine walking into a foreign operation and can make it work just like a domestic operation. Sometimes this is true; more often it is absolutely untrue. Most expatriate managers who are sent to open new offices are hard-driving, young managers who are on their way up in the organization. They see that the way to get further ahead in their organizations is to have both experience and success in establishing or enhancing an overseas operation. They want to quickly prove their management competence in the international field and get a ticket back home. The home office wants the same. Therefore, niceties such as language and cultural training are either omitted or so cursory that the expatriate must approach the establishment of the foreign operation as if it is an extension of a home country operation. The expatriate staff feels pressured to get the operation up and running as quickly as possible, with few "hiccups." To accomplish this they either do all the work themselves (assuring hard times for the operation when they leave the country) or they try to recruit national employees who are willing to manage like expatriates. This is, I would suggest, a short-term fix with long-term negative consequences.

The other option that companies sometimes choose is to look for an "old country hand" expatriate (à la Paul Scott's novel *Staying On*, about expatriates in India after Indian independence). Such expatriates usually speak the local language and are well immersed in the culture—but most often they do not understand the culture of the company that is opening the operation and, since these expatriates have no pressing desire to return to their home country, they tend to create a perpetual need for their presence at or near the apex of the national office. These expatriate managers want to build a staff to support the expatriate's employment goals rather than build a national management staff that can fulfill the MNC's vision and goals.

Clearly, neither of these expatriate staffing solutions is optimum. What is needed, I would suggest, is a much more carefully formulated plan for staffing international operations with clear indicators of success (and at times failure), a plan that is transparent to expatriates as well as the national employees. That would include language and cultural training for expatriate employees and a realistic time frame for expatriate managers to transfer their positions to well-trained national managers. Equally, a training and succession plan needs to be created both for expatriate-filled positions and for national employees. Many multinational corporations will want to keep a home office oversight individual or team in place to make certain that corporate core values remain in place in foreign operations. This is a perfectly reasonable option, provided that the oversight individual or team does not interfere too regularly in the national management of day-to-day operations.

Some may object that few, if any, start-up, expatriate managers will become sufficiently talented in the language where an operation is being started to be able to do business in that language (unless Spanish or French is the language spoken where a business is located and companies have a native or near-native speaker to send overseas). That is true, but not really the point. Most international business is done in English, at least at the management level; few managers, in spite of intensive language training, should try to do business in a newly acquired language. However, to be able to carry on middle-level conversations with fellow employees in their language is a skill that should not be dismissed. With national coworkers trying hard to keep up with expatriates in the expatriate's language, those times when expatriates work at dealing with coworkers in their language become very special and important.

Culture and International Business Success

Culture is equally important for business success. Most companies going into an international business setting subscribe to the belief that there are certain cultural taboos that a business should avoid—such as extending your left hand to a Muslim or sitting with your legs crossed in Asia and your foot pointed at another person in the room. These cultural faux pas certainly need to be avoided. However, a successful business needs to understand culture at a much deeper level to make an operation run as smoothly as possible. People understand life (and work) in the context of deep and ingrained cultural patterns. Over the past few decades, Western business may have been remarkably more successful than other business in other parts of the world (although not long ago we in the West were desperately trying to find out how we could do business more like it was done in Japan because Japanese business culture seemed so much better than that in the West). Western business culture may or may not be the best in the future— that remains to be seen. At the moment, because the Western business model (culture) is most successful, Western businesses working in other parts of the world desire and sometimes demand that Western business practices be the norm for the operation. Imposing an outside culture, no matter how superior one may think that culture is, is fraught with danger.

Let me give an example. I have had the opportunity to work for well over a decade in and around Indonesia. Indonesian culture is remarkably multifaceted, which is exactly what one might expect from a country made up of 14,000 or so islands (at low tide, at least). The dominant culture in Indonesia is Javan culture, and Javan culture is very rich and textured. It is also very much indirect. What you see when dealing with Javan culture is not what you get. In Javan culture, shadow puppets known as *wayang kulit* are very popular. In *wayang kulit*, one sees the puppets, but the real meaning of what is going on is in the shadows behind the puppets. People from Java understand life much like they understand the shadow puppet plays. There are things that are immediately seen, but most often they are not the ultimate meaning. Compare that with Western life and Western management. Most often we like to think that what you see is what you get. When I say something, that is exactly what I mean. But we know that's not always true and when it isn't true we accuse people of "passive-aggressive behavior," which we see as a fault rather than a virtue. In managing in Southeast Asia in general, and in a place like Indonesia most specifically, expatriates have to be aware that what you immediately see is probably not what you should be looking for and that if you follow your Western instincts, you will probably get the matter wrong. Therefore, some of the cultural skills that Westerners need to accept and understand are looking in the shadows, listening ever so carefully, making judgments more slowly rather than more quickly, and watching for indications that what you think as a manager to be true may not really be true.

Obviously, there is a converse to this. Effective management means that native employees, in this case Indonesian employees, must learn a little about the Western mind and the Western way of doing things, and there has to be a meeting of those two cultures. Neither culture will be obliterated, but both will be softened and the barriers between those two cultures will be blended somewhat if there is to be successful management.

There are literally thousands of examples like this in the world of international relationships and international business. This study cannot begin to categorize all of those. But if there is one point to be made, it is this: To manage successfully, all parties have to understand themselves and each other. One cannot assume that Indonesians are going to manage like Americans, nor can Indonesians assume that their expatriates from the United States are going to immediately manage the way they do. There is a process through which both parties have to go, which is a process of cultural understanding. It is a difficult, complex, and ongoing process that needs to be respected.

It is certainly true in Asia that one should not sit with your legs crossed and toes pointing toward a fellow worker, and it is certainly true that handing out business cards with the left hand will be taken as an affront. But mastering those simple issues will not assure the type of cultural sensitivity that is necessary to manage difficult situations. As stress increases, and doing business internationally is a stressful business for all parties, one tends to go back to immediately accustomed behavior. That is, Westerners become more Western and Easterners become more Eastern. When the difficult decisions need to be made, it is most challenging to find the type of cultural understanding and appreciation that will allow for good decisions to be made and for them to be implemented correctly.

Recruiting and Training a National Staff

The backbone of an operation in a country other than the home of a multinational corporation is the recruitment and training of a national workforce. In this section, I wish to build upon the discussion of finding a cultural middle ground between the ethos of a multinational corporation based on the culture of the home country and the ethos of a national workforce based on the culture of the host country. Obviously, a multinational corporation would like to fill its entire national staff with people who understand issues and solve problems in the same way that a workforce would in the corporation's home country. It is equally obvious to any who have worked internationally, and especially those who have worked in developing countries, that this is impossible. So what can realistically be done to recruit a workforce that will be as successful as possible in an operation that must bridge cultures? Let us start with those who will serve in management positions. The first and most obvious candidates for positions in management will be those who have good language skills in the tongue of the home of the multinational corporation. Most often this will be English. An added benefit would be to hire host country nationals who have already worked in an operation in the home country of the corporation, or who have worked with an American country in their homeland. Clearly, this is a limited number and one cannot build a large managerial staff from such limited numbers. In addition, a corporation starting an overseas operation must be careful not to be seduced by proficiency in English and previous background. All too often, expatriates become enamored with someone's proficiency in English, only to discover that while they have a staff they can understand, the staff does not manage matters of business or personnel well. It sometimes becomes desirable for their own home office needs to send young and fast-charging expatriates into the field. These go-getters have little if any desire to do the patient teaching and mentoring that is required to develop a national workforce. They tend to be insensitive to different cultures, often failing to learn the language of the country in which they work and expecting the national employees to intuitively understand what they, as managers, want employees to do. This often leads to failure—both for the manager and for the development of local employees. Frustrations mount, and all too often the expatriates return home, sensing their own failure. And the company finds itself in a position of having to continuously send expatriates to manage operations.

Clearly there is a better way to do this. Expatriates need to be carefully chosen, and often the young, hard-driven junior executive is the wrong choice. Equally, a person who is desirous of staying on indefinitely is a wrong choice.

Recruiting, Integrating, Training and Retaining a National Workforce

It is obvious that recruiting, integrating, training, and retaining a national workforce are the real issues that a corporation must face in making an overseas operation successful. The expatriate managers and technical experts are crucial in starting the operation. But one could argue that they are even more important when called upon to put in place a national management team that will be able to direct operations and a workforce that will (1) fulfill the needs of the multinational parent company and (2) be sensitive to the culture of the national workforce they will most directly manage. These responsibilities are great, crucial, and difficult—not to mention carried out while mediating between two groups that are as apt to be in conflict as in concert (namely, foreign management and national workers). Special sensitivity and training are needed for and by expatriates in foreign assignments. Equally important, national senior managers need this training, too. But where would a company find such national managers, and how should they be trained?

In essence, there are two potential answers: recruit experienced managers from other multinational or national corporations, and/or recruit college and university students and train/educate them to manage exactly as the parent company would want them to manage. Business necessity suggests that a company do both. Managers with experience in national or multinational enterprises in their home country bring the type of hands-on experience that is invaluable in an operation; they can guide expatriates through the reality training that is often necessary to address the issues that bedevil start-up operations of multinationals. However, these national professionals may have habits that the expatriate managers will find (possibly) helpful at the beginning of an operation, but which are quickly found to be counterproductive in the long run. How often these exasperated expatriates will hear their senior hands argue, "But sir, that is the way we do things here." Peace (and even productivity) is kept for a time, but in the end the way "we do things" is not the way the company wants things to be done—and habits, good, bad, or indifferent, are hard to change.

That leaves the second option, which one chief executive I know calls the "growing your own tomatoes" option. This technique involves creating scholarship programs for high school students; bringing them to the multinational corporation's home country; having the students do work-study in a corporation's headquarters, regional office, and/or operation in the home country; giving them internships in the multinational's operations in their own country; and then working to recruit them for full-time employment. The benefits of this system are obvious: The student knows the culture and the work culture of the multinational; the student has worked in operations in both the student's home country and the home of the parent company; and the management of the home country has been able to evaluate the potential of the "home-grown tomato" to do the work home-office management wants done. However, there are downsides as well. When students spends four (or often more) years living and working in a country other than their own, they become more like a foreigner than a native. While nationals tolerate some of the traits of expatriates, they are more unforgiving of their nationals who seem more expatriate than national. The displeased employees know that almost all expatriates will eventually leave; they fear that their "expatriatized" nationals will stay forever (and often they will!). There are other problems as well. Long-term students in overseas locations, and especially those who do work-study, experience and come to expect to receive salaries and benefits that they received as student workers overseas. This can become a serious problem when the relative salaries and the exchange rate between countries makes it appear that a former student and now a regular worker in his or her home country is being paid less than when he worked as a work-study or internship participant. There is no easy answer to this dilemma. A foreign work-study participant cannot be paid less than any other work-study participant. Yet the foreign work-study participant needs to be prepared to work in his or her home country at a rate of pay and with benefits that are reasonable and competitive with other similarly situated workers.

For multinational corporations, this raises the issue of whether they are compensating all their workers in foreign operations fairly. As foreign-national workers are prepared for employment and/or given training during employment at operations or at the corporation's headquarters, they begin to sense whether they are being treated reasonably in their home country. This is especially true when a large amount of the multinational's revenue stream comes from the same country as the foreign national.

There are other special challenges that the foreign-educated national manager faces. One is that workers from the home country have not had the opportunity for the type of education and training that the foreign-educated manager has had; they resent the opportunity that the "home-grown tomato" has had. This jealousy is often turned into manager-worker problems that can be most vexing. I have even seen this type of jealousy among older workers who have worked hard to get their children into foreign scholarship programs and then resent having similarly situated people manage them.

All of this raises an important general cultural point. Few of us like being managed by people younger than we are; and many Western men don't like being managed by women. In the West, however, that is becoming a some-time reality—and our society is no longer traditional. In many countries where Western multinationals are operating, very traditional cultures still exist. The insertion of a Western-trained young manager and possibly even a young female manager can be a very unsettling experience and can desta-bilize operations. I am not arguing that the education and training of young nationals—who in the eyes of expatriate management are more flexible and can better understand Western management goals and styles—should no longer be the core of operations management in foreign locations where multinationals operate. I only point out that it would be naive to expect that the imposition of a substantially changed management style—with dif-fering personnel than the workforce has been accustomed to—would be easily accepted within any group. Within more traditional groups, it is even more difficult to integrate.

Implicit in the recruiting, educating, and training of managers in the multinational's home country—and expecting them, to some extent at least, to implement Western personnel and management practices—is the desire to move toward performance-based evaluation of employees for promotions and compensation. The corporation looks at potential, demonstrated skills and job performance as the *individual* traits that are necessary to move forward in the workplace—and wants nationals to understand and enforce this type of human resources management. All too often, managers find strong and un-compromising resistance to such value-based schemes of human resources management. There are several reasons for this. First, many cultures frown upon actions that cause anyone to publicly lose face; when someone with age and longevity is passed over for a promotion, it's a losing-face experience.

Second, there is an expectation in many countries that those who were hired together will advance together irrespective of performance. To overcome these points, adoption to Western management styles must be done with care, forethought, and sensitivity—but it can be done.

A Special Case of Extractive Resources

At the beginning of this essay, I suggested three reasons why multinational corporations operate outside of their home countries. The first was to expand the market share of their sales by opening up new markets. The second was to manufacture goods at a lower cost by using less expensive human resources. And the third was the need of extractive industries to go to the places where minerals and oil and gas could be found. I now wish to focus on the special case of human resources development and staffing with respect to extractive industries. Extractive industries have always operated at the geographic outskirts of development. Outside of the main areas of a population, people explored for the natural resources that the more developed parts of a country would need for economic growth. Today the extractive industries are searching further and further afield for the resources to develop. With regard to staffing of international operations, natural resource development has the greatest challenges. Sales are done in the most urbanized areas and, for that reason, companies involved in expanding their sales have the greatest number of well-educated and well-trained individuals available for their workforce, and especially for their management. Manufacturing has many more challenges, especially with regard to management; most manufacturing sites in overseas operations are focused on areas outside of the most urbanized centers, where it is less expensive to procure land for a manufacturing operation. Because of the distance from the most urbanized centers, staffing manufacturing facilities with competent managers is somewhat more difficult than staffing sales offices (although in a number of cases, management functions are relatively centralized within urban areas rather than being located in the plants). Therefore, the recruitment of management staff for representative and sales offices and most manufacturing facilities is relatively easy. And it's much more difficult to find staff for the natural resource development operations.

There are a number of reasons for this. First, natural resource development has historically taken place on the peripheries of human development, far from the centers of civilization. Seldom does one find oil and gas and mining operations in the midst of urbanized centers. Throughout history, though, many centers of urbanized life have been located where extractive industries operated many years previously, and the extractive industries created the basis for growing urbanized areas. When an operation is located far from urban centers, it is most difficult to recruit and retain a management staff. There are two reasons for this. First, the level of education, work experience, and work skills among those who live around the natural resource site tend to be minimal. Second, those who have a high level of management skill and experience tend to live far away from the remote natural resource site, and many of the most qualified managers would not wish to relocate for an extended period of time to a remote location to manage a natural resource operation. These special staffing demands must be taken into account by multinational corporations in setting up their natural resource development operations.

Further complicating this situation are the demands of those who live around the place where the extraction of natural resources takes place—the residents often known as "indigenous peoples." The demand for employment includes not only lower-level positions, but also management positions. Companies would no doubt find it easier to bring in outside management, whether expatriate or national, from among those who have the greatest experience in these management fields, and often that is a necessity for the start-up of an operation. However, along with that start-up, extractive industries must have a very clear policy and program in place for the development of the local population if they are to assume positions of responsibility and trust within the operation. When this does not happen, the relationship between the extractive operation and the local population disintegrates over the years, and increasing tension as well as demands for reparations are put upon the extractive industries. This is being seen throughout the developing world in the most remote areas where extractive industries operate. This also reflects part of the world's demand that extractive industries be responsive in some way to sustainability. In other words, how can the extraction of natural resources, which is by nature not sustainable and renewable, bring sustainable benefits to local populations? Obviously, the creation of long-term infrastructure, sustainable business development beyond the natural resource, health care, and education are crucial for this process of sustainability if you are dealing with a nonsustainable natural resource. However, employment opportunities, including the training and education necessary to be able to manage ongoing operations in natural resources or in other areas, becomes a reasonable expectation of populations whose lives are impacted by extractive industries.

Over the past decade, many of the large extractive corporations have begun to look at this entire question of sustainability. A good number of those companies have created positive employment atmospheres for local people who wish to work for those corporations; in many cases, governments have been unable to provide proper education for employment of local and indigenous peoples. Companies have stepped into that process. This is a long-term commitment, and we are only beginning to see how these company initiatives will benefit the overall well-being of communities. Already a number of local people are graduating into management positions because of the commitment of companies and others to provide such opportunities. A number of multinational extractive-oriented corporations are providing scholarships for students to study, both in their native lands and in the developed world, to gain knowledge and skills necessary to assume management positions in multinational corporations. These programs are the foundation for truly indigenous management of operations and a local workforce. The benefits will be realized by the extractive resource corporation as well as by the local community. It is, in the best sense, a win-win situation.

Pulling It All Together: Summary and Conclusions

In this short essay, I have tried to raise some of the most important issues that a variety of corporations operating throughout the world would face. I have focused my comments more specifically on developing nations rather than looking at the relatively simple task of operating in countries that are developed in a similar way to the home country of a multinational corporation. However, that does not mean that some of the same challenges and potentials are not found when an American company opens an office in Great Britain or vice versa.

Every operation needs to find the proper way to operate in its given local, national, and international context. No one answer will fit all. I only hope that I have raised a sufficient number of questions and given at least some tentative suggestions of how to deal with those questions. Perhaps managers of multinational corporations who are looking at staffing operations overseas will have a somewhat greater insight into the issues they face when they venture into a new country and culture.

The Challenges of Recruiting for Those in Creative Enterprises

Cheryl Fry

Vice President, BBDO Worldwide

What makes a creative enterprise creative? After all, in the evolving new age of business, many organizations are aspiring to be more creative and innovative. Stating the obvious—that the nature of an enterprise's work or product is creative—is an oversimplification. Each organization may define and measure creativity differently.

The business concept is simple. Successful creative enterprises, regardless of their product or service, hire creative people into organizations that allow them to be creative. These organizations have built a culture that encourages and enables talent and ideas. Routine is not routine. The conventional is unconventional. How people work is as critical as what they do. The challenges of recruiting, therefore, cannot be separated from the challenges of managing and retaining talent in a creative enterprise.

Advertising has traditionally been considered a creative enterprise. In advertising, hiring and retaining the best talent has always equaled having a competitive advantage. The so-called information age, where intangible assets and intellectual capital are the new inventory of corporations, has always been the milieu of advertising. Knowledge and ideas have always been the currency. High-performing talent has always been the primary asset.

Most of the corporate world is now fully engaged in the war for talent, a battleground where ad agencies have wrangled with each other for years. Industry high performers have always been widely known and in constant demand. The workforce is mobile, driving a continuous hunt for talent with the "right stuff."

As experienced soldiers in the war for talent, advertising recruiters and HR professionals have gained some insights into the effective hiring and managing of talent in a creative enterprise. They can be loosely grouped into three key areas:

1. The organization should strive to define and clearly understand its talent and culture.
2. Locating and engaging top creative talent require a strategic approach that goes beyond traditional recruitment techniques.
3. A special breed of human resources and recruitment professionals is necessary.

Defining the Talent and Culture

Since talent truly does drive the business in the creative world, an organization must be able to define its talent. Creativity is a subjective area. How does your perception of creative talent differ from that of your competitors? How will you recognize high-performing talent? How will you measure success?

It's important for the organization to understand its core competencies—to determine how and why top performers produce outstanding results, so that the performance can be replicated throughout the company. In a creative enterprise, competencies may include creativity and innovation, or an entrepreneurial mind-set. Clearly, these competencies may not be commonplace in the so-called traditional corporate world.

In any business environment, core competencies can be acquired or developed. The knowledge and skills components of a core competency are usually easy to measure and develop. They are evident on a resume and are visible "above the water line." The greater value of core competencies lies below the water line, in the behaviors and motivations of an organization's top performers. These are less obvious and very hard to change or influence. They should be acquired through effective recruitment and selection.

All interviewers should have highly developed skills in competency-based interviewing, with questions defined to assess for creativity and innovation, an entrepreneurial mind-set, or whatever the appropriate competencies are.

And as everyone knows, making the right hire just begins the process. The challenge then becomes managing and retaining a creative workforce. An effective, engaging orientation program will build bonds to the organization, working to retain employees from their first days of employment. The culture must support ideas and the people who produce them. The environment should encourage innovation, risk taking, and challenging the status quo. "Out-of-the-box" thinking is critical for business success. It will win new accounts, secure existing business, and drive new and better ways to work.

In most creatively driven organizations, policies, and procedures work best as guidelines—not cut-in-stone requirements. The reality is that a highly creative workforce will sometimes march to the beat of a different drummer, and effective talent management may require addressing individuals rather than groups.

The focus in any creative enterprise is on achieving business results. Breakthrough work rarely comes out of a rigid system with a focus on policies. The creative experience usually offers the opportunity to work with some extraordinary talent, to do work you're passionate about, to work as an individual, and to have fun along the way.

Sourcing and Engaging Top Talent

How do we source the best creative talent? Like most industries, we do utilize the Internet for sourcing candidates—although we rarely run traditional recruitment ads. And we utilize the career pages of our corporate web site as a tool for building our employment brand and differentiating our workplace from those of our competitors.

Successful hires in a creative enterprise are often the result of a strategically driven, exhaustive search for the right talent for the organization. We may have spent months—or even years—nurturing and protecting a relationship with the candidate, waiting for the right opportunity to present itself. We have worked to sell an employment experience and create a compelling opportunity for the best applicants.

We rely heavily on competitive intelligence. Like the entertainment business, the stars in advertising tend to be well known. Recruiters know who they are, where they are, and how likely they might be to make a change. We endeavor to build a personal relationship with the best talent, one that will be sustained until we can make the hire.

Employee referrals are often utilized, both formally (with rewards for successful hires) and informally (through networking discussions with friends and connections). We follow up on all leads, wherever they may take us.

The industry recognizes that talent can come in any package, so nontraditional backgrounds in education and experience are explored and pursued. A recruiter in advertising might source candidates from the military, entertainment, law, marketing, or retail. And if they have the right core competencies, most of them can quickly and successfully morph into advertising professionals.

We focus on marketing the company, on building a strong employment brand that is aligned with the corporate brand. In advertising, an agency's image as a major player—including the ability to attract high-profile employees, to win prestigious industry awards for its work, and to acquire new clients—plays a significant role in its ability to attract talent. Some good PR happens naturally as agencies win awards and new accounts, but some of it is actively driven by pursuing opportunities for our leaders to speak at industry events and to serve on advertising committees. We encourage all employees who are involved in education programs and charitable events to seize the opportunities for networking inherent in those activities.

Most ad agencies are willing to rehire ex-employees when the circumstances are right. In almost any market conditions, top talent will receive calls about employment opportunities from competitors or external recruiters. People will usually explore a new opportunity, and sometimes that means that good employees leave. We understand that. We endeavor to keep in touch with our alumni and track their progress. If there is an opportunity for rehiring, the organization will often move to acquire proven expertise—with little or no training time required, for little or no recruitment costs.

In a creative-driven, talent-based workplace, companies may have to be willing to break the rules to successfully close the deal when hiring. It may be necessary to treat candidates as individuals with unique needs and wishes. In this business, one size rarely fits all.

We invest in talented high performers with nontraditional compensation and customized career packages. We offer some flexibility in how and where people work, as well as lifestyle benefits. We let our people know that their own commitment and contribution will determine their future. Value creation will drive success.

Providing HR Leadership in a Creative Enterprise

Doing successful human resources in a creative enterprise provides its own set of challenges. Providing HR leadership in a nontraditional work environment is not for the faint of heart! Those who revel in policy manuals and a by-the-book approach need not apply. All the planning and strategizing that goes into hiring top creative talent also goes into recruiting HR professionals who are results—not process—focused.

The traditional HR paradigm is about conformity and uniformity—in other words, policing those who break the rules and fitting employees into the boxes defined by job descriptions. However, for our creative enterprise HR pros, "outside the box" is a normal place to be. Job descriptions are only reference tools. Every employee's real job is to build the business. The reality is that the next big idea can come from anywhere.

HR must look beyond a resume and a candidate's external packaging to see talent. We do interviews with applicants who run the gamut from spiked green hair to corporate blue suits. When we've located top talent in the recruiting process, our HR teams will often endeavor to make job offers on the spot. Those offers will include a focus on the nonmonetary aspects of the job. We've learned that the best people will usually focus on the long-term impact of the job, rather than the short-term implications of the financial package.

Understanding the nature of the business is paramount for HR. Our job is to engage talent on the front line, to convince them that we can offer an opportunity beyond our competitors. If we can't do that successfully, candidates won't make it through to the hiring managers. So HR markets the organization from the initial contact, and presents the business case. We might show a reel of commercials in an interview, or talk about the company's performance at a recent awards show. We'll present success stories of current employees. And, yes, we'll proudly parade the best of our HR employment practices to attest to the quality of our workplace.

Recruiting the right HR people for a creative enterprise is a challenge. They must be comfortable with ambiguity and dealing with the unexpected. They are rule breakers and risk takers, who are not afraid to fail. Our HR pros are open to new ideas from unexpected sources. HR must be creative and be able to assess creativity.

Obviously, even within the same industry, companies vary greatly in their approach to business. A worldwide network may be very centralized, with a strong corporate identity and uniform HR practices. Or alternatively, networks may be only loosely connected, with local management given the autonomy to set their own operating guidelines. Whatever the corporate structure, HR must ensure that it is aligned and positioned to meet the global and local objectives of the business. HR's job is to provide the organization with an ongoing competitive advantage through its people.

Conclusion

Historically, hiring and managing talent in a creative enterprise has required an approach that has been somewhat of an anomaly in business. Now, as the knowledge-based economy drives up the value of talent, most of the corporate world is moving toward a more creative approach to attract, hire, and retain top performers.

Talented people equal competitive advantage. Hiring and managing talented people requires long-term strategic planning, tied to the business needs of the organization. This is not just a job for HR. All managers should be accountable for the effective management of talent.

Organizations—creative and otherwise—will need to present a compelling employment opportunity that offers:

- Satisfying and challenging work.
- Career development, with success based on an employee's contributions and impact.
- Strong leadership, operating with a sound business strategy and a persuasive vision.
- Flexibility and lifestyle benefits.
- Competitive and often customized compensation.

In creative enterprises we have already established what the rest of the business world is discovering. It's all about talent. Organizations that do the best job of hiring and retaining top talent will outperform their competitors.

Management Recruitment: Current and Future Models for the Service Industry

Raj Gnana-Pragasam

Vice President, Compass Group

Overview

Compass Group is one of the largest food service providers in the North American market. Since 1994, the North American division of Compass Group has grown from 18,000 associates to greater than 116,000 associates. In terms of importance to the cost structure, labor is directly on a par with food and beverage purchasing; however, it receives a fraction of the attention. While we invest enormous resources in the way we buy food, the supply chain for labor remains as fragmented as ever.

Recruitment is—at a basic level—the cultivation of relationships to match candidates with appropriate opportunities. The Internet is ideally suited to such tasks. Clearly, the application of Internet technology for recruitment is not news. Online recruitment agencies are proliferating; however, most are fragmented start-ups that will never achieve the critical mass required for success. When you examine what it will take to be successful in this market, it is clear that the changes in technology and the recruitment market provide a major opportunity for the largest recruiters—such as Compass Group's Resource Network—to knock the existing players out of the marketplace. This essay explores the differences between the current and the future industry models for management recruitment.

Current and Future Models

As shown in Figure 36.1, key characteristics of the current model are:

- Operations partners (or hiring managers) contact potential employees through a combination of bricks-and-mortar agencies, job centers, media advertising, and walk-ins (at retail units).

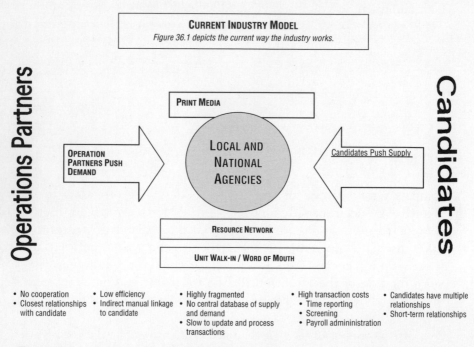

Figure 36.1   Management Recruitment Model.

- Agencies collect and hold databases of potential employees. Employers hold no central record of who has been contacted, nor do they know of the candidate's employment intentions. There is no knowledge of how timely the database is unless you control it.

- Enormous advantages to scale exist in building and exploiting databases of employees. Employees prefer to target whoever has the largest list of opportunities, while employers want to target whoever has the largest list of available employees. However, agencies have required significant investment in highly visible, local physical offices to achieve this scale.

- The labor market is artificially fragmented into temporary and permanent markets. This distinction is becoming increasingly blurred and irrelevant. The recruitment process (including application, screening, etc.) is labor intensive, and agencies are frequently exploiting the temporary placement database for permanent placements. But what they are doing is compromising the quality of the permanent staff. Temporary placements have different perceptions of the future and of their responsibilities, and do not share the permanent placement's commitment to vision and value. The model does not easily allow employers to contact employees. Both have to push their interests to central intermediaries (media ads, agencies, etc.), which inefficiently match supply with demand.

- In reality, the labor markets fail both employers and employees. Employers are forced to use a variety of fragmented intermediaries to source labor (even the largest agencies can supply only 50 percent of the demand put on them) and employees frequently register their interest in work with multiple agencies. This adds costs to all the parties.

As shown in Figure 36.2, key characteristics of the future model are:

- Technology automates matching and improves previous cost-intensive processes.
- Tracking performance history could allow for more timely hires.
- The resource network will act as a liaison between candidate and operations.
- Commitment from operations partners is required to post their jobs through the channel.

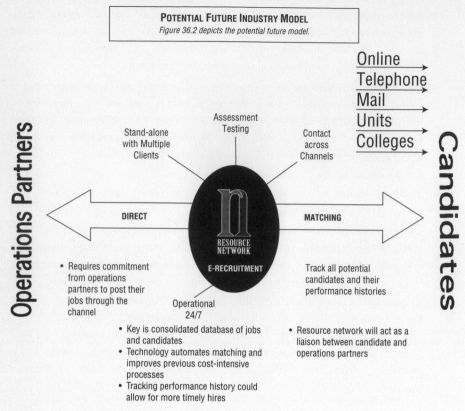

Figure 36.2   Management Future Recruitment Model.

In many ways, the principles of the future model are not significantly different from those of the present. Indeed, the basic feature of scale advantage will remain as important as ever. However, technology will revolutionize the processes through online applications, assessment testing, and a job posting system. The recruitment experience will, therefore, look and feel very different in the future model. Traditional agencies and print media advertising will be replaced by a "labor exchange" managed by the resource network. At Compass, our "Resource Network" is actually a model for our consolidated, integrated management recruitment service that manages cost and quality and networks all resourcing opportunities within the company. HR executives and recruiters run it.

There are a number of key reasons that explain why a technology-based model will succeed over the long term. Those reasons are:

- The database of jobs and candidates is key. To maximize value, the information must be centralized (although this does not mean that the recruitment process should be centralized). The advantages to scale in the database are enormous. The closer the market gets to all job seekers being able to register in one place and all employers to look in one place, the more efficient that market becomes.
- The quality of the technological infrastructure and the information it contains is crucial. It should allow the resource network to apply its own selection criteria, approved by the operations partners in order to identify qualified candidates.
- Technology can enable or undertake most of the key recruitment processes—matching jobs to candidates, testing for basic aptitudes, employee administration (payroll, etc.), temporary scheduling, and time reporting. Each of these processes is currently labor and cost intensive.
- The intermediary market will be unbundled into its constituent components:
  - Matching supply and demand.
  - Screening.
  - Payroll and employee administration.
  - Training.
- A technology-based model will not necessarily require employees to be online. Currently, the online penetration of our employee base is low (except those who are already in our networked units). While direct online access by employees would be a theoretical ideal, the basic principles of the model would allow employees to access via multiple channels—for example, registration by e-mail, telephone, or postal mail. Some of the existing agencies are beginning to use technology.

Assets Required for Success

The two most important assets for success are:

1. Owning the demand for labor—demand.
2. Relationships with potential employees—supply.

These requirements create enormous barriers to entry for independent start-ups and tip the balance of power from existing intermediaries to the largest employers. Many large employers have begun to understand the cost efficiency of the internal cost function.

OWNING THE DEMAND FOR LABOR

Developing a business of this type is a classic virtual circle—the greater the stock of jobs, the more incentive for employees to register with the business. The more employees who register, the more incentive there is for employers to put their vacancies through the business. Getting momentum into this virtual circle is the single biggest barrier to enter into the market. The cost of customer acquisition, the investment required to attract employers and employees, will almost certainly break (or exclude) the majority of businesses positioning themselves to enter this business.

Compass Group has an enormous asset at its potential disposal—our own demand for labor. Consolidating demand (in the form of the largest food service organization) is far easier than consolidating supply. Three to four U.S. employers could put out one end of 200,000 potential job openings into a single marketplace. Trying from scratch to consolidate 200,000 job seekers per year would be enormously expensive. As one of the largest food service employers in the U.S. and other markets, our demand could make or break a business entering this market. The implicit choice is whether to harness that demand to create value for our own business or to allow it to remain fragmented and be used to make profits for others.

Internally, this may be the biggest hurdle. Success will depend upon the operations partners and the resource network team working together; however, power will come first by consolidating our demand in one place.

RELATIONSHIPS WITH POTENTIAL EMPLOYEES

The other element of the virtual circle is a relationship with the potential candidate. This manifests in the form of databases and recognition in the industry as a good place to find jobs. Currently, the best databases (which are far from perfect) and recruitment brands sit with intermediaries (Addeco, K-force, Eden, or Target). Fundamentally, this makes no sense. Employers should have the most comprehensive knowledge of the candidate pool (names, addresses, administrative details, capabilities, etc.). However, as the industry currently works, employers fragment their knowledge (even single organizations) and, in effect, spend large amounts of money trying to reestablish contacts with potential candidates. Even then, the results are poor and slow, and the costs are high.

The vision for a recruitment business of the future should be to create a single database for food service candidates worldwide. The business should be one with which the candidate builds a long-term relationship beyond individual job searches. The key sell for the candidate would be this: By being registered, they would be considered for all suitable jobs within Compass Group. The organization's prestige and the integrity of the system will help to draw and maintain the interest of quality candidates.

Competitor Activity

There are a number of comparable businesses emerging in different recruitment sectors—H-careers.com, Addeco, and so on; however, none have shown any indication of targeting the food service and hotel sector.

In summary, there is plenty of activity on the Web surrounding food service recruitment; however, none appears to go beyond using the Web as a virtual posting board acting as an online version of traditional employment intermediaries. Also, none has created a focused contract food service brand. Critically, the principle of direct, electronic matching (letting employers and candidates find each other) has not been exploited.

In today's employment marketplace, it is becoming more and more difficult to identify quality future associates. By developing a streamlined one-stop shop, the resource network can help to centralize processes and alleviate the time-consuming recruiting efforts currently being used by the operations partners.

General Management Perspective on Staffing: The Staffing Commandments

Gail Hyland-Savage

Chief Operating Officer, Michaelson, Connor & Boul

S taffing is absolutely critical to the success of every company. To be competitive in today's economy, companies need the best people to create ideas and execute them for the organization. Without a competent and talented workforce, organizations will stagnate and eventually perish. The right employees are the most important resources of companies today.

Staffing begins with the acquisition of talent—the actual recruiting process designed to hire the best employees for your organization. But this is only the first step in the overall staffing process. To maximize the positive impact that staffing can have on an organization, the entire process must include the areas of retention and development of human capital. By bringing all these disciplines together, an organization benefits not only from hiring the best people but also from developing and growing their staff and keeping their employees satisfied and productive.

An ongoing, flexible staffing process is the lifeblood of every growing and changing organization. Staffing requires constant attention and involvement from the entire management team—from front-line supervisors to senior executives and every level in between—and from every employee in the organization. Unless everyone in the organization believes in the company's values and mission, there will be a disconnect in the overall staffing process. As staffing professionals, you must provide your company's senior management team with the right support and information to ensure that the staffing function continues to play a critical role in the strategy and growth of your entire company.

As you look at your staffing function, whether it has been in operation for decades or is just under development, there are several key factors that will ensure its success. From my general management perspective, I would even describe these critical factors as The Staffing Commandments. They can be viewed in one of two ways: (1) what your CEO and entire senior management team expects from your staffing operation or (2) what the senior team needs to know to appreciate how and why the staffing function supports the goals of the entire organization. It's important to remember that staffing functions within human resources must always be vitally aware that they contribute to the overall strength or bottom line of the organization. This is how your CEO and senior management will ultimately evaluate the success of your staffing operation.

These five Staffing Commandments provide a guideline to staffing professionals. Use them to help you establish, evaluate. and change your operation as needed.

The Staffing Commandments, or What Your CEO Wants to Know

1. Staffing is an integral part of the company mission and values, as well as the company's strategic and operating plans.
2. The staffing plan is designed to achieve short- and long-term needs.
3. The staffing operation measures and evaluates its processes and is held accountable.
4. The staffing process nurtures relationships with hiring managers and all employees because every employee is a recruiter.
5. Your company brand is an integral part of your staffing efforts, every day.

Let's examine each commandment to see how it applies to the staffing process.

Staffing Is an Integral Part of the Company Mission and Values, as well as Strategic and Operating Plans

To be effective, staffing strategies must support the organization's mission and values, and be integrated into its long-term strategic plan and short-term operating plan. When the staffing process is connected to the company's goals, you are providing the right human capital to operate effectively, be innovative and creative, grow revenue, and generate cash flow for the entire operation.

Take a look at your company mission statement. If your mission is a meaningful statement that your employees successfully use to make decisions in their day-to-day activities, it probably already has a component that speaks to the value of your employees. If your mission statement doesn't focus in any way on your company's valuable human capital, change it. Remember: Your people are a critical differentiation for your company, and your mission statement must reflect this.

Once a company has determined its mission and values, the strategy and operating plans follow, in that order. At this juncture, the staffing function should be integrated into the organization's strategies and day-to-day operations. The staffing and overall human resources strategy must provide direction to assist the organization in achieving the corporate mission. The staffing strategy must identify when and where employees are needed, how they will be recruited, and the types of training and development programs the organization needs. To do this, the staffing operation also needs its own strategic and operating plans, which are a part of the human resources plan and the enterprise-wide plan for the organization.

Remember: Your CEO needs to see evidence that staffing is connected to and supportive of the company's mission, strategy, and day-to-day operations.

The Staffing Plan Is Designed to Achieve Short- and Long-Term Needs

The staffing plan is flexible and evolving, while it supports the corporate strategy to either expand, transition, or contract the organization.

If a company is poised for growth, the staffing plan focuses on recruitment, training, career pathing, and promotions. Companies that are putting new processes or technology in place—or involved in mergers or acquisitions—are in a transitional phase; in this case, staffing is accomplished through transfers, cross-training, and retraining. And when a company must reduce its workforce, staffing responsibilities shift to plans for attrition, early retirement, layoffs, outsourcing, and part-time positions.

Short-term staffing plans look at the needs of the organization within the next 12 months. Long-term plans generally encompass one to three years in today's fast-moving economy. But even when focused on immediate needs, it's critically important that the staffing plan give a nod to longer-term goals that keep the company mission and values at the forefront. In addition, staffing professionals are always presenting the company's image to external candidates (whether hiring or going through staff reductions); this image needs to be put in the perspective of long-term needs so the company can attract the best talent. One example of a short-term plan that also focuses on long-term needs would be a company in a downsizing mode that continues to train and promote valuable employees. The company is containing costs while laying a foundation for future growth.

Remember: Your CEO needs to know that the staffing plan is flexible, one that allows the company to achieve its current operating plan with a focus on longer-term strategic needs.

The Staffing Operation Measures and Evaluates Its Processes and Is Held Accountable

Why measure? Because if you don't measure your staffing operation performance, it won't be important to you or to others in the organization. You won't know how the staffing operation is functioning, what programs are working, or what needs to be changed or replaced.

Staffing metrics are increasingly important to a company's senior management teams. With today's drive for profitability, all departments must be held accountable to standard measurements. Different metrics are needed in various parts of the company—ranging from metrics that track revenue for sales, reducing errors for manufacturing, brand awareness for marketing, or cost per hire for staffing. By measuring its staffing functions, human resources is being held to the same standards as other departments that play an integral role in the company's strategy and operations.

To measure your own performance, collect and report on meaningful staffing data that is readily available within your department. Then review what additional information you and the senior management team need for operating the business, measuring your success, or benchmarking your operation with other companies.

If you are already using staffing metrics, make sure you communicate the results to your organization, both within your department and throughout the company. And don't forget to benchmark your results with other similar operations to learn how you measure up.

If are not measuring your staffing processes, start immediately by collecting your available data and planning for future data collection. You may choose to consult similar companies to learn how they use staffing metrics. You can also refer to a number of professional associations that provide data and guidelines on staffing metrics, including:

- The Employment Management Association (a professional emphasis group of the Society for Human Resource Management dedicated to furthering the staffing profession), found online at www.shrm.org/ema.
- Staffing.org (a Web-based nonprofit organization dedicated to gathering, organizing, and presenting data on recruiting practices and performance) at www.staffing.org.
- The Saratoga Institute, the benchmarking and measurement arm of Spherion, at www.saratoga.org.

Remember: Your CEO will hold the staffing function accountable for its successes and areas that need improvement. You need to measure and communicate.

The Staffing Process Nurtures Relationships with Hiring Managers and All Employees

I have always viewed the staffing process as a partnership between staffing professionals and hiring managers. The process achieves the greatest success when these groups work hand in hand before, during, and after the actual hiring. When the human resources managers and hiring managers work closely to develop retention programs, companies successfully hold on to more of the right people in the organization. And working together to develop human capital brings the greatest benefits to the organization. As I mentioned earlier, our people are what make the difference in our organizations. They are our only true, competitive advantage.

Nurturing relationships between staffing professionals and others in the organization increases the success of the entire staffing function. One way to do this is to plan in advance for hiring, retention, and development needs and to understand up front what successful programs look like to all involved. Focus on the key drivers and the time-sensitive issues—and then develop the metrics you need to report back on performance.

Each and every day, every employee is an ambassador for a company among customers, business colleagues, professional associations, and even friends and families. What people say about their workplace is critical for attracting new talent to the organization. If employees report that they work for a great company that values their employees, this message will be remembered when someone is in the market for a career change. What employees say about their work is also a reflection of the company's mission and values, sending a clear message to potential recruits.

Remember: Your CEO will have a clearer understanding and respect for the staffing operation if all employees line up with its goals and strategies.

Your Employer Brand Is an Integral Part of Your Staffing Efforts

When it comes to the staffing process, the concept of branding is becoming increasingly important to any successful human resources operation. Branding is an image, a means of identifying and differentiating a company, product, or service. In fact, an employer is actually a brand. If managed correctly, your employer brand provides a strong, competitive advantage to your organization.

What creates an employer brand? An employer brand is a company's products and services, intermingled with its employee commitment, capability, and values. Our employees are clearly the most powerful image creators any organization can have—much more powerful than advertising, press releases, or public relations. If your company's staffing process includes all the right elements to grow its employees—namely, recruiting, hiring, development, and retention—they will no doubt be a reflection of the brand you want to project.

Your employer brand is really reflected in everything your company does—through product advertising, consumer instruction manuals, and even events or conferences your employees attend. It's important that your employer brand be reflected appropriately and consistently in all contacts with potential job candidates. And be certain that the brand works with your long-term staffing plan; to accomplish this, your staffing professionals must have a close working relationship with all departments within your organization, especially marketing and public affairs. Nurturing relationships with all employees in these areas plays a critical role in achieving these goals.

Remember: Your CEO needs to see evidence of the staffing function's connection and support of the overall employer brand for the organization.

Conclusion

Staffing is the most important function in an organization—and that has never been truer than in today's ever-changing and competitive business environment. The slowing economy, industry consolidation, global competition, and changing workforce demographics all contribute to the challenges facing today's staffing profession. But I am convinced that we have more opportunities than ever before to be successful within our organizations and to hire, train, and retain the best people.

As I complete this essay, I am embarking on a new career as chief operating officer for a fast-growing real estate services company, located in Southern California with operations around the country. After years in publishing, I am changing industries but I will continue to focus on what has made me successful as a general manager. Without a doubt, any success I have had depended on the acquisition of talent and the development and retention of the company's most important resource—human capital.

As I look ahead to evaluating a new staffing operation, these five Staffing Commandments will serve as a guide to what is critically important to the staffing process, and remind me what my new CEO needs to know and understand about the staffing operation.

Financial Impact of New Human Capital Acquisition Technology

Yves Lermusiaux

President, iLogos Research

What are the true factors of the financial performance of an organization?

Financial models as we know them have their limits. And today, with often more than half of the market capitalization of a firm based on intangibles, interest goes toward understanding underlying new principles. This essay details how the new economy and technology have created new principles of human capital, and why any organization must understand and internalize these new principles in order to be a leader. This essay reviews all five principles of human capital, but concentrates on the first principle of human capital and the financial benefits a corporation can realize from implementing human capital technology.

Understand New Principles of Human Capital

There are five new principles of human capital management:

1. A skilled workforce as a cash multiplier.
2. The ubiquity of skills demand.
3. The automated matching of supply and demand.
4. The recruiting supply chain.
5. Human capital management as a systematic process.

For each, we identify the consequences for large corporations and provide some actionable recommendations for an enterprise to become human capital-centric.

Principle 1: A Skilled Workforce as a Cash Multiplier

The new economy is often called the "knowledge economy." Emerging from an industrial age, this new economy distinguishes itself by having a large amount of the value of the company residing in the head of the employee instead of in the tangible assets of the company.

This realization was made very clear by a 1999 *Business Week* article showing that the valuation of Microsoft was superior to GM, Ford, Boeing, Lockheed-Martin, Deere, Caterpillar, USX, Weyerhaeuser, Union Pacific, Kodak, Sears, Marriott, Safeway, and Kellogg. Yet, the only value at Microsoft resides in the heads of its employees!

Another way to show the intrinsic value of intangible and human capital is to look at the historical evolution of the ratio of the S&P 500 between the market value and the book value. The ratio of market value to book value was approximately 1 in the early 1980s. By 2000, it had risen to about 6. Among those companies, current employees are now perceived as a key element in their valuation, along with the ability to attract new talent and retain existing one. Faced with this issue, many academics started to review and suggest some new models to give a better account of a corporation's worth.

Fortune magazine's "Best Company to Work For" is also a sign of the times, showing more emphasis on human capital importance. But the distinction is more than a tool to attract twice as many applications and make the front page; it has also been shown that those corporations exhibit better financial performance than other companies.[1]

---

[1] *Are the 100 Best Better? An Empirical Investigation of the Relationship between Being a Best Employer and Firm Performance.* Hewitt Associates LLC, March 2000.

The challenge to any corporation for the recruitment and retention of outstanding talent has never been more profound. High-performing employees are the key for corporate success. At the individual level, a study from McKinsey & Company showed how high performers generate more results than average performers; corporate officers they surveyed believe the difference in impact for sales positions is as high as 67 percent.[2]

As mentioned on a corporate level, studies from Hewitt and Watson Wyatt have shown that recruiting excellence brings positive financial results. The Human Capital Index Survey demonstrated that organizations with excellent practices in recruiting have been linked to a 10.1 percent return in shareholder value. Human capital management strategies make a clear impact on the corporate bottom line.

The key consequence of a true understanding of this principle is an emphasis on a quality workforce. The definition of quality is the ability for an individual to increase the corporate value. Although the discussion of the legitimacy of this definition is beyond the scope of this paper, the strategies to achieve better quality can be understood and applied.

In light of this first principle, it is paramount for organizations to understand and be able to articulate the basis for a sound human capital acquisition investment. To illustrate, we will outline a quick framework for understanding the business case for best-of-breed staffing automation technology based on ROI (return on investment).

HUMAN CAPITAL ACQUISITION ROI FRAMEWORK

A 2000 study by the Gartner Group found that 80 percent of HR decision makers from global corporations were not able to state the ROI of a given project—in the study's case, an employee self-service portal. This situation is not well tolerated by CEOs and CFOs; substantiating ROI is no longer an optional step in project planning, but a mandatory one.

Let's review the basics of ROI for human capital acquisition from a selected summary of work from iLogos Research (www.ilogos.com)—an example that has helped many HR professionals present their cases successfully to their companies.

In order to show how a particular course of action is a sound investment,

---

[2]*The War for Talent*, McKinsey and Company, September 2001.

it's important to be comfortable using the language and reasoning of business: Everything must be assigned a dollar value, and a good decision is one in which the benefits derived from it outweigh its costs. A return on investment is the reward gained over and above the cost of the investment. If every dollar invested returns $1.01, the reward represents a return on investment of 1 percent. The length of time it takes for the investment to pay for itself is referred to as the payback period, after which any additional reward represents a return on investment.

HARD SAVINGS

The savings that result from reducing expenses are sometimes referred to as "hard-dollar savings." All companies pursue hard-dollar savings—producing the same results with fewer resources—since such moves have a tremendous effect on a company's profitability. Consider that a company with a 5 percent profit margin would need to increase revenues by $100 million per year to have the same impact on profitability as a $5 million per year cost savings.

SOFT SAVINGS

By contrast, so-called "soft savings" are not as readily apparent or as easily measured, since they do not manifest themselves as dollars remaining in a budget. Here we may be addressing the use of time and levels of productivity, from the HR or IT departments or the hiring managers. Savings won't be realized in dollars spent but in increased productivity resulting from automation and process improvements. If the time saved can be applied to other important projects, the savings clearly have meaning. Good metrics that calculate time, labor, and process are needed to quantify these savings accurately.

COST OF CAPITAL

It is also important to understand the basic financial concepts of the cost of capital. To take our previous example, $1 invested today at a 10 percent cost of capital will have to generate a $1.10 return to only offset its depreciation. So a flat return is not a sign of success. Accordingly, the $1 investment that generates a $1.11 return has a 1 percent return for a 10 percent cost of capital.

COST OF DELAY

The last metric is cost of delay (see Figure 38.1). In a sense, the cost of delay is the flip side of the ROI calculation. Every month of inaction or delay costs the enterprise the value of the delayed benefits for that month. If you multiply this by 12 and adjust for the cost of capital, you can estimate your annual cost of delay.

MEASURING ROI OF HUMAN CAPITAL ACQUISITION SOLUTION

Direct Savings

The implementation of a human capital management technology solution can make a positive financial impact on a company in two ways: directly, through direct cost savings or bottom line impact; and indirectly, through an improvement in the top line. Here are three examples of staffing management technology solutions, and how they result in savings:

1. Staffing management solutions allow recruiters to manage ongoing relationships with candidates. Candidate relationship management reduces the reliance upon outsourcing spending in order to find

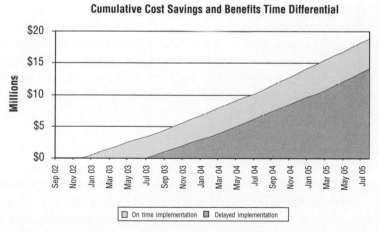

Figure 38.1   Cost of Delay.

candidates each time a hiring need arises. The hard savings may appear in a reduction in the advertising budget, a reduced dependency on search firms, or in the fewer number of job fairs attended.

2. Staffing management solutions store resumes digitally and often automate the routing of information between recruiters and hiring managers. Hard savings would result from a reduction in the material costs associated with the handling and filing of paper, and a decreased reliance on administrative support staff.

3. By automating many low-value administrative tasks, staffing management solutions can help recruiters handle a greater workload of requisitions. The hard-dollar savings resulting from this increase in recruiter productivity is derived from savings in salaries and compensation, because the same workload requires fewer full-time equivalent recruiters.

Indirect Benefits

Indirect benefits from implementing a staffing management solution may include a streamlined process and higher-quality hires. Here are just three significant gains to understand: increase in the speed of the staffing process, increased productivity, and Equal Employment Opportunity Commission (EEOC) exposure reduction.

1. Decreasing hiring cycle time is advantageous in a number of ways. The additional speed in responding to applicants will result in productive employees sooner. It will also increase the overall quality of the workforce, since top performers will not be lost due to quicker reactions by competitors. Better recruiter efficiency means more jobs will be filled in a given time, resulting in increased staffing levels, which will also directly increase the ability to develop innovative products and increase product development speed. The reduction in time to fill can also be translated into lower opportunity cost for an open position. Opportunity cost of open positions can be very expensive: Imagine the impact when an unfilled sales job results in an unachieved quota, or how a lack of nurses for a hospital may cause it to refuse patients (not to mention the compromised quality of care given to patients).

2. Systematic staffing processes (such as the ACE Staffing Best Practice of Recruitsoft) has shown a more consistent approach to talent management and a qualitative increase in the workforce deployed. Although those are hard to quantify, even the most conservative leap in productivity and reduction in turnover (due to better fit and quality of the human capital acquisition and deployment) translates into a sizable impact, as we have seen in iLogos studies with Fortune 500 companies.

3. Equal Employment Opportunity Commission (EEOC) compliance is of extreme importance to many corporations. Staffing processes must be designed to provide all necessary documentation to limit potential liability to the corporation. Fines for noncompliance are steep, as are costs in time and resources to undergo an EEOC audit. Mitigating this exposure is valuable, and surely merits a line item when calculating ROI for a staffing management solution. One indirect yet powerful benefit of implementing a staffing management solution may be realized in the reduction of legal exposure through implementing a standardized, consistent digital process with built-in centralized documentation and reporting along with EEOC data gathering.

COMPLETE THE BUSINESS CASE

When implementing a staffing management solution, itemizing the expected benefits is only half of the business case. On the other side of the equation are the expected costs. Only with a complete picture of both costs and benefits can one then assess whether a decision to implement makes sound business sense.

When contemplating an IT purchase, it is clear that the invoice does not represent the real cost the organization will eventually pay. Total cost of ownership, or TCO, is a concept used to represent the true costs of owning enterprise software. A TCO analysis seeks to measure all of the expenses, both human and technical, behind a given technology initiative. It includes all costs related to the life cycle of the technology, including procurement, deployment, maintenance, and support. Thinking in terms of TCO helps the understanding and management of the budgeted and unbudgeted, direct and indirect costs incurred for acquiring, maintaining, and using an enterprise computing application.

TOTAL COST OF OWNERSHIP (TCO)

Direct, budgeted expenditures that relate to the solution itself include costs for the software. In some cases, there will be substantial additional costs for the hardware and IT infrastructure necessary to run the application. A staffing management solution from an application service provider (ASP) greatly simplifies a TCO analysis, since it does not require the purchase of hardware or upgrades to a typical company IT infrastructure. In essence, the company does not own the software; it pays a usage fee, though many such providers will place the source code in escrow if requested. If you do not license the application from an ASP (which generally provides technical support), be prepared for stiff charge-backs from the IT department to support and maintain the hardware infrastructure necessary to run the application behind your company firewall, as well as the maintenance fees covered below.

The second component of direct costs is labor—including consulting, technical support, operations, and administration. Support and training make the system work for users, and the price of those services must be factored into the TCO analysis. Combining the financial and human resources necessary to run and support the business application will give you a sense of the TCO for a particular staffing management solution.

For direct costs, it is helpful to break the TCO analysis into initial and ongoing costs. Initial costs include the software licensing fees and professional services fees for implementation and training. Direct costs also include internal staffing costs for implementation and support, as well as the cost of pulling people off of regular duties for training.

Ongoing costs include maintenance fees and the cost of major upgrades. Here again, costs come from the vendor for the IT infrastructure maintenance and upgrades, especially if the staffing management software solution is not delivered via the ASP model. Remember the human side: tech support, ongoing training, system administration, and staffing costs. There is a cost to each. Resources are being dedicated, when they could be applied elsewhere.

Indirect costs are a more difficult aspect to quantify, but they can often add significantly to the TCO. Indirect costs include unproductive end-user time, troubleshooting, and system downtime. Examine every area of cost or effort, particularly at key milestones in the life cycle of the solution.

RETURN ON INVESTMENT (ROI)

Once each of the line items outlined earlier is calculated, you can make the ROI estimation. The ROI equals the projected savings minus the total cost of ownership, less the cost of capital: ROI = (Savings – TCO) – Cost of capital. As you build your business case, also remember to place value on the cost of delaying a project's implementation time frame. Identify benchmarks from your company or the industry to use as a point of reference. Use the resources from outside experts to help you understand the ROI for your company and to support your position. By articulating the ROI of your staffing management solution choice, you will substantiate the case that excellence in the hiring and deployment of human capital assets is key to corporate success.

Principle 2: Ubiquity of Skills Demand

The second principle of human capital is the ubiquity of skills demand. The best way to understand this principle and its implications is to describe the dynamic between supply and demand in the workforce arena. If we look at the demand side, we see organizations in demand of skills or talents to perform the tasks to deliver value to the marketplace.

The theory of supply and demand in economics has been widely publicized. In summary: In any market, there is equilibrium between demand and supply that will set a specific price point.

However, every economist knows the limitation of this theory. For instance, if I am a corporation looking for a specific skill to perform a task, I demand it by using traditional recruiting methods such as advertising and a referral system. The limited reach of the demand broadcast creates its own limitation: limited supply. The reason for limited access to supply is called friction, or a lack of perfect communication between the suppliers and the buyers (in this case between the employers and the job seekers).

Digital communication has been a great tool to reduce friction and enable better equilibrium. Today's online marketing techniques enable job seekers and corporations to bridge the gap between supply and demand, and reduce friction.

Let's consider some data and online tactics. In 2002, as Figure 38.2 shows, job seekers could access job opportunities of 91 percent of Global 500 companies online at any time, from anywhere. This increased from 29 percent in 1998. This contrasts well with the traditional unique source of employment opportunities available quasi-exclusively through newspapers as it was only a few years ago. This first shift in availability or ubiquity of data is called by iLogos ubiquity of demand—which means every job opportunity is available anywhere at any time.

Figure 38.2   Corporate Web Site Recruiting.

Other techniques are available for corporations to market their opportunities to candidates in a timely fashion. One is job agents, an extension of the permission marketing concept. The candidate can leave a personal e-mail address to receive automated notification of future matching positions. Job agents build ongoing relationships with job seekers, stretch marketing budgets further, and require no resource allotment from recruiting staff. In 2000, only 6 percent of Fortune 500 companies benefited from this powerful functionality,[3] perhaps because their hiring management systems did not provide the necessary profiling and automation.

The consequences of this new principle of ubiquity of skills demand are multiple. The first one is to give the job seeker the ability to shop more for opportunity and be more in a decision-maker role: "I know what is available out there and what I am worth." Today, many salary surveys are available online and give the job seeker control over his or her own career.

The second consequence of this principle is an increased flow of supply

[3]*Best Practices for Fortune 500 Career Web Site Recruiting*, iLogos Research, 2000.

for the corporation. This translates simply to an increased volume of applications and the issue of quality. To address this fully, it is important to understand the third and next principle of human capital management.

Principle 3: Automated Matching of Supply and Demand

The ubiquity of skills demand, brought about by the shift in availability of data, is a great step forward. Nevertheless, it is also a limitation and often creates a fair amount of unqualified supply. If the network that created the Internet is the basis of the second principle, the computers that are linked by this network are the enablers of this third principle.

To explain the "automated matching of supply and demand" principle, we have to dissect the content of the communication delivered in this transaction. For years, the content holder for such transactions has been the resume. The resume has been the best tool to summarize the competencies and skills a candidate can bring to a new position by highlighting abilities, certification, and experience through descriptions of past positions, diplomas, and employers. The resume has been the best tool at the time to try to make a match between a task and an individual.

The process of finding the best individual to fulfill a given task has been highly manual and paper-intensive, with very little automation. Why? Because a fit for a position is not reducible to a computer algorithm. However, although the final fit of the position with the individual cannot be based on a computer-made decision, the first set of selections based on minimum criteria can be. A final decision should and will always be based on individuals working together and having to meet and to know each other.

Let's review and understand what is done when a department of a large company needs additional resources. Employees fill out a request form that is called a requisition, go through the approval process, and create a job description. The job description will be used to match the candidates with the tasks for them to achieve. In fact, it is the job description that will be matched to the resumes of the candidates. (See Figure 38.3.)

This matching of two unstructured documents is done by individuals who (most of the time by applying highly unsystematic and subjective criteria) make the first selection, called prescreening. This activity not only has been highly inefficient and very time-consuming, but also very ineffective. The criteria used to select candidates do not ensure systematic results.

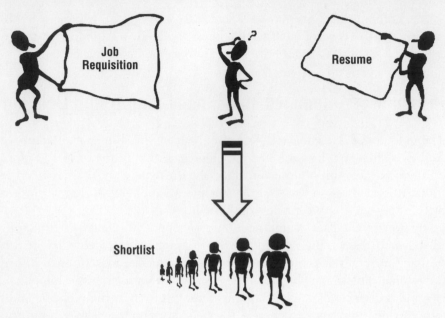

Figure 38.3   Manual Prescreening.

Yet, manual prescreening was the best and only option available at the time. It was better than recommending a candidate for hiring simply because he or she is the first on the pile.

Today, the Internet combines the connectivity of the phone and the processing power of the computer. The Internet is the common medium of communication between talent supply and demand. To enable automated talent matching, what is required is a common platform for both the job description and the resume. Job descriptions (talent demand) and resumes (talent supply) can be reformulated in terms of a common currency—skills. The corporation defines corporate-wide standard skills, which are then systematically attached to job descriptions. (See Figure 38.4.) Talent supply then aligns itself to meet the new standards, reaching a new equilibrium. This new possibility has been created only by the widespread acceptance of the computer as a new communication device for job applications externally and as a portal for redeployment internally.

The ubiquity of skills demand and the matching of supply with demand have an important impact at the macroeconomic level. A more efficient process for matching talent supply with demand will reduce the base level

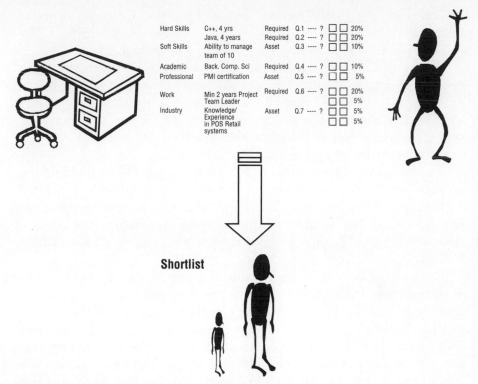

Hard Skills	C++, 4 yrs	Required	Q.1 ---- ?	☐ ☐	20%	
	Java, 4 years	Required	Q.2 ---- ?	☐ ☐	20%	
Soft Skills	Ability to manage team of 10	Asset	Q.3 ---- ?	☐ ☐	10%	
Academic	Back. Comp. Sci	Required	Q.4 ---- ?	☐ ☐	10%	
Professional	PMI certification	Asset	Q.5 ---- ?	☐ ☐	5%	
Work	Min 2 years Project Team Leader	Required	Q.6 ---- ?	☐ ☐	20%	
				☐ ☐	5%	
Industry	Knowledge/ Experience in POS Retail systems	Asset	Q.7 ---- ?	☐ ☐	5%	
				☐ ☐	5%	

Shortlist

Figure 38.4   Automated Talent Matching.

of unemployment called friction unemployment. Friction unemployment is the residual level caused by the inefficiency of the communication between corporation and individual. Moreover, real-time access to a pool of candidates does more than impact the economy globally and help redeploy resources in a downturn; it also creates a positive productivity boost in corporations that can identify needs, translate them into a common language, and fill positions in a timely and quality fashion.

Principle 4: Recruiting Supply Chain

Recruiting can be seen as a succession of steps in a process with several providers. Traditionally, providers and processes—such as hiring managers, recruiters, and candidates, as well as the processes of background checking,

EEO data gathering and reporting, job board posting, and so on—operated independently for the most part. Today, they can be brought together. The Internet has allowed recruiting to function at a much higher level.

The recruiting flow can now be seen as a supply chain and thought of in terms of inventory. The importance of the supply chain principle applied to recruitment is the just-in-time (JIT) philosophy. When we start to see the individuals performing the tasks as inventory, and we see the opportunity cost of undone tasks, we recognize the importance of a readily available workforce or redeployment efficiencies.

Consider: The opportunity cost is typically computed by dividing the revenue by the number of employees, which gives revenue generated each year by each employee. We then divide this number by the number of working days in order to calculate the opportunity cost per day. So every day saved by providing an on-time inventory does have a financial impact.

The importance of thinking in terms of inventory and supply chain enables two other consequences. The first one is to push human resources to think more in financial terms and the complete business impact on corporations. This shift has already transpired in the language used to describe the practice itself: Human resources is often described today as human capital. The second consequence is to be able to upgrade from a tracking system to a work flow. This distinction is more than just a semantic one; it is the difference between a simple date stamp system and a push process that drives next steps in order to speed up the final result.

Principle 5: Human Capital Management as a Systematic Process

Today, human capital management is regarded as a true business differentiator for any successful business. The principles detailed in this essay mean that corporations can now begin to think about human resources as a true process, not as something that is hard to grasp and is mostly an art. If all business is a combination of science and art, human capital has been the area in which the proportion of art has been way above its level in the other disciplines. New technology can help to give more balance and at the same time more efficiency.

The birth of an infosphere called the Internet has allowed the second principle, the ubiquity of demand, to become reality. Technology had enabled the third and fourth principles—the automated matching of supply and demand and the recruiting supply chain. However, only the leaders of organizations will mold human capital management into a systematic process. It is the increasing amount of evidence from the first principle—a skilled workforce as a cash multiplier—that is pushing them to act now.

Preparing to Take the Next Step in the Utilization of HR Technology

Nick Scobbo

Mitre Corporation

The process of sourcing, selecting, and hiring employees to staff your enterprise is a critical function. And as with many critical and complex business functions, effective staffing requires a wide array of organizational competencies and technical systems. HR departments have years of experience in many of the functions that comprise staffing, such as interviewing, branding, generating competitive offers, and assimilating new employees. However, one unique aspect of the staffing function, due to its relative youth, is the assimilation and use of technology.

Staffing is no stranger to technology. Many departments have purchased and employ a variety of technical solutions. Up to this point in time, these systems' main purpose has been to improve existing processes. However, the potential value of staffing and HR technology goes beyond simply streamlining staffing transactions.

While many of the HR departments who made investments in technology have seen some improvement in key time-to-fill or other important metrics, the true value of the utilization of technology lies much deeper. In order to extract the most added value from the enormous array of sophisticated software technologies available for purchase or internal development, it's time for staffing to look beyond streamlining of processes as the only desired result.

Within the past five years, the proliferation of HR technology product offerings has been extraordinary. Organizations of all sizes have embraced Enterprise Resource Planning (ERP), applicant tracking systems (ATS), and other systems in the HR domain. This staggering proliferation has ridden on the wave of technologies that were once very uncommon to the HR world. When many of today's staffing managers were learning their trade, there was no emphasis on how to utilize corporate intranets or how best to integrate disparate systems. Today, however, extracting the most value out of the staffing function means coming to terms with the technology that defines the everyday tasks of a recruiter. In order to get the most productivity out of recruiters, they must understand every detail of the systems they use. Getting the highest return on the significant investments already made in these systems means staffing must utilize them to their fullest extent.

I believe that there are three distinct areas in which staffing can improve to ensure a higher return on technical investments. Existing systems need to be better integrated, the use of metrics must be institutionalized and their aggregation automated, and staffing personnel need to embrace technical and analytical skills.

The standard set of tasks that recruiters performed 10 years ago is only a subset of those tasks required today. Not only does a recruiter have to be excellent selling the company's image or showing off the finer points of a high-impact job to a potential candidate, recruiters now must also know how to utilize the costly systems installed on their desktops. In order to achieve the maximum value from recruitment systems, technical knowledge in the recruiting function must be honed to the point where a recruiter can mine the corporate ERP to provide clients with workforce analysis. Dealing with busy hiring managers and selecting the right person from a huge database of candidates is only half the staffing services HR should be providing. The other half lies in being able to proactively and definitively provide strategic staffing solutions to the enterprise.

In many HR organizations, the job of data mining and analysis is not part of the recruiting function. This has the potential to create problems and inefficiencies in servicing internal clients. Clearly recruiters (or generalists in a distributed model of HR) should know the business situations facing their clients. However, those HR staff typically asked to perform metric, efficiency, and forecasting analysis are often too far removed from line management for their analysis to be timely and relevant. This can often lead to underutilization of core HR technology investments and poor analytical contributions to the set of services HR can deliver.

Another contributing factor to underperforming investments on HR technology is the inability to easily link disparate systems. The recruiting function has begun to leverage HR technology in many areas, but often failed to link each system to a central core data source. For example, an ATS may not be properly communicating with the ERP. In such a case investments in both systems are made less effective, as functionality in each system may not be properly utilized, leaving excess capacity and no single source of recruitment data.

With the proliferation of ERP systems, HR has become increasing reliant on a single vendor for all of their technical infrastructure needs. Having complete reliance on a single vendor is a dangerous situation leaving HR with little or no leverage in demanding compatibility among suppliers. It is therefore crucial to select recruitment system vendors that will provide seamless integration to the ERP in order to receive the most return on investments in both the ERP and the recruitment system. Influencing vendors to provide integrated services at a reasonable cost will be major challenge to HR, and the recruitment function in particular. Standards bodies such the HR-XML Consortium are working to meet this challenge. However, such efforts will only succeed with the dedicated efforts of experienced and influential leaders in corporate staffing.

The third area of concern in the adoption of HR technology is in metric aggregation and reporting. Very few successful business functions can be run efficiently and effectively without measuring their contributions to the enterprise. HR and staffing are no exception. Measuring staffing's contributions to clients is a requirement of a productive staffing function, and one that should be smoothly handled by a strategy of integrated HR technology.

HR technology should be optimized to perform much of the dirty work and number crunching that metrics programs require. In any staffing transaction, there is contained enough information that can be used to extract meaningful metrics. The key is for existing systems to be able to track what pieces of data make up a meaningful metric and extract that data on the fly as transactions happen.

For example, some of the information that may be captured during a staffing transaction may be interview dates, interview reports, date of the open requisition, date of hire, starting salary, any bonuses paid, and source code of the new hire's resume. Chances are that somewhere in the process of hiring an employee, this information, and more, is captured in one or more internal or application service provider systems. Imagine the power and added value if HR systems were configured in such a way as to extract meaning from this data on a transaction-by-transaction basis. Upon completion of hiring the employee, the recruiter and hiring manager could receive a receipt of sorts with metric information about the hiring process, such as time to fill, compensation recruited, and any other metrics the organization feels are important.

Now imagine a complete database of each staffing transaction updated in real time upon completion of each transaction. Each data field can be easily aggregated to report standard metrics over any time period. Management would always have a clear, accurate, and up-to-date picture of the performance of the staffing function. Storing all of this data can also lead to much simpler extraction to third parties for benchmarking purposes. Extensible Markup Language (XML) and Web services can then be used to transmit aggregate metric data to the third party and back again for use in any applications or analysis of staffing performance metrics.

The technology for both automatic metric aggregation, as well as systems integration, exists today. However, few HR departments are taking advantage of these opportunities. In my experience this is generally due to the restrictive costs of system integration. However, these costs will not remain high indefinitely. Both technology suppliers and HR departments will realize the value that can be achieved through proper systems integration.

To serve as a guide to getting the most return out of investments in staffing technology, I have laid out the following points of emphasis.

Determine the goals the staffing group would like to accomplish. This may seem a simple task, but it will be the most difficult one facing HR in the near future. The staffing function will have to decide if they really have the desire to move to the next level of technology utilization. To do so, staffing must have a clear idea of what services it can provide and how those services can spur business growth for their clients.

Make sure that the necessary data to meet these requirements is being captured accurately and completely. It is very difficult to generate on-the-fly staffing metrics reports if the data needed for these reports is not being systematically captured. It is extremely important that standardized controls be set up to guide the precision, accuracy, and extent of data capture. It is this step that many times will lead to customization of commercial off-the-shelf systems. While most systems engineers would recommend that customizations always be kept to a minimum, I would add that they are sometimes a necessary evil. It may be more worthwhile to create some customization headaches if the data captured in those customizations is central to achieving staffing's desired objectives.

Integrate all the disparate systems and sources of data. This is, in my experience, the most important step to achieving the most return on any investments made in HR or staffing technology. In an informal survey I performed with the HR-XML Consortium, approximately 50 percent of deployed HR systems had no integration whatsoever with other HR systems, and over 80 percent of HRMS systems were not integrated with other key HR systems. This lack of focused integration is the source of frustration and lost return on investment in HR technology. Proper integration is the most important priority in taking the next step in technology utilization. There are more costs to be reduced and more value to be added in the staffing function by moving beyond utilizing technology to simply streamline processes. Systems integration is the key to providing incremental, real value to clients of the staffing function.

A single source of information can be used to add analytical value to any business function, staffing included. Many areas of enterprise support have adopted data warehouses and portal systems to provide integrated systems and services to their clients. Staffing must step up to this challenge in an environment where continual pressures are being placed on support organizations to cut costs and improve performance.

Measure your performance and contributions. By this, I do not mean simply counting the number of people hired per year, but rather the effectiveness and skill in which that number was achieved. Any staffing group, both internal and outsourced, can hire people. What data can be shown that your group does this more effectively and efficiently?

Integrated technology solutions employed in HR should be able to collect, monitor, and report on key metrics. Automating the metric collection and aggregation process should free up valuable resources to study and analyze metric data, looking for trends and opportunities to forecast. When metrics are valued in staffing and their collection is automated, a greater level of service can be provided to staffing clients.

Make sure recruiters have the skills and are empowered to utilize HR technology to its fullest. As I have said before, the technology for complete integration and metrics reporting exists today. However, one of the stumbling blocks that organizations encounter is a recruiting function that does not embrace technical and analytical skill sets. The best HR technology strategies can quickly go to waste if the recruiting function does not have the skills necessary to best utilize these assets.

The staffing function has come a long way toward embracing technology; the many new companies and products that target the staffing industry are testament to this. However, it is time for staffing to take the next step. It is time to truly get the most productivity out of the function by careful planning and integration of existing systems and improved focus on technical and analytical skills in the profession.

The Human Resources–Security Relationship

Harvey Burstein

Professor, Northeastern University

O ver the past several years, security in the workplace has moved to the forefront of many corporate agendas, and the focus has largely been on dealing with terrorism. The importance of coping with terrorist activity cannot and should not be minimized, let alone ignored. From a management perspective, however, it is no less important to keep in mind the fact that the vast majority of businesses and institutions are not realistic terrorist targets. In this respect it is far more important to have a better understanding of what security really is, or should be, and the relationship between human resources and security functions.

In its purest form, security protects individuals and businesses from loss. With the exception of natural disasters, all forms of loss are attributable to the actions of people. This is true whether the losses are due to crimes, mistakes, accidents, waste, or unethical behavior. Equally true is the need for people to be involved in preventing those losses. Consequently, the importance of preemployment screening and the orientation of new hires can significantly contribute to all loss prevention efforts. No less important is the need to provide employees with a suitable and safe work environment and to always protect them as they go about their work. While these objectives are consistent with security function goals, in reality their execution is a human resources function—one that can have a positive impact on the total workplace environment.

Background

No business or institution is immune from losses. Size, location, and type of activity are immaterial. For-profit organizations, with goals of optimum profits, certainly do not want losses. Even nonprofit institutions cannot survive indefinitely if sizable losses are sustained. Not all need—or can justify having—security departments as such; but in the interest of operating efficiency and profitability, there must be someone to whom the responsibility for security is assigned.

Part of the problem in developing security policies and accountability has always been related to a failure to fully understand what security is really all about. There has always been confusion between the security industry and security as a business function. Let's start by reviewing security in these two respective roles.

The security industry consists of those for-profit businesses that sell a variety of services and equipment to buyers. These services include everything from security system hardware to computer security software and security personnel positioned at the front desk. Security as a business function makes use of some aspects of the industry, but concerns itself with much more than safety; the business functional side of security is concerned with loss—not merely crime—prevention. To achieve this goal, security needs to be fully integrated into all phases of an employer's operations. If there are separate security departments, there is a tendency to think of them as a form of private policing designed to prevent crime; in this division, other forms of loss are not considered part of security's role, and they should be, because in reality, the terms "security" and "loss prevention" are synonymous.

One can see a relationship between security and an organization's law department or outside counsel. This is based on the premise that there is no other business function that is affected by the law as much as security. Equally true, one can understand a relationship between security and risk management. Although focused on preventing losses, security knows some are inevitable and thus it tries to minimize them to the greatest extent possible. Risk management tries to minimize losses through the purchase of insurance.

What, then, is the relationship between human resources and the security function? The answer becomes clear once there is an appreciation of the sources of possible loss that security must deal with. Security tries to prevent losses attributable to crime, but it is also responsible for preventing losses that result from such disparate sources as accidents, waste, mistakes, and unethical behavior. With the exception of possible losses resulting from natural disasters, all of these losses can be traced to some form of human behavior.

The Security Function

In an effort to prevent losses, cost-effective security programs approach the subject from two different perspectives. And both involve the human equation.

On one hand, security programs are obliged to protect the organization's assets in terms of its real and personal property. This is done through appropriate security hardware; the development, implementation, and oversight of security policies; procedures to ensure compliance; and operating systems and procedures that incorporate controls and accountability with business operations.

On the other hand, there is an equal obligation to protect employees. If they feel unsafe or insecure while at work, production will suffer and so will the employer's profit picture. The need to do everything possible for the protection of employees must be extended beyond the confines of the workplace in those instances where business travel is required. This is done by providing guidance and advice to those who travel in order to minimize the possible risk of any known or unknown endangering events.

Human Resources, Preemployment Screening, and Security

Keep in mind that the ability to achieve the security function's goals is not dependent only on a security department's existence. Rather, security and human resources share a security interdependence that's based on the human resources department's understanding of how certain security principles related to preemployment can help prevent losses, and how they need to be applied. Consider the preemployment screening process. Some employers feel that in-depth inquiries are a waste of time and money; others base the extent of their preemployment screening on the type of position for which an applicant is being considered. In reality, security considerations need to be given to individuals who will have access to assets, including sensitive information, or whose work may have an impact on the employer's reputation. Minimizing the importance of preemployment screening can be costly in various ways—including the risk of litigation that alleges negligent hiring.

The foundation for building background inquiries is the application for employment. Therefore, step one in the process lies in the application's adequacy. It obviously must avoid asking questions that are prohibited by law. Nevertheless, within those parameters it should be as searching as possible into an individual's history. For example, questions need to be directed around licensing issues, which can vary from state to state. Completion of an application should be required even if an applicant has submitted a resume.

Next, care must be exercised in examining the application. Where a resume has been submitted, the information provided on each application should be compared. Look for unexplained voids in time, frequent job changes, and leaving one job for another where the pay is less and the commute is considerably longer; check job titles, the names of supervisors, and the names and addresses of personal references.

If the position being applied for has academic requirements, the names and addresses of the schools, dates attended, and degrees awarded need to be stated. Do not be impressed by the efficiency of applicants who offer copies of transcripts; insist that the school mail them directly to human resources. If the position requires a license to practice, find out if the person practiced his or her profession or trade in any other jurisdictions.

If a resume is submitted and comparing it to the application reveals some discrepancies, it does not necessarily mean that the person is being intentionally deceptive. Remember that resumes are designed to make the best impression possible. On occasion, they offer an inflated picture of the applicant, especially when it comes to such things as job titles or responsibilities. Applications are usually more concise, and the forms applicants must complete are usually written within a relatively short period of time on the prospective employer's premises.

Sometimes, the initial meeting between an applicant and human resources representative is devoted more to convincing the job seeker that the prospective employer's place of business would be a good place to work—not necessarily learning as much as is permissible about the applicant. Ideally, this first meeting is the time for the human resources representative to examine the application (with or without an attached resume) in the applicant's presence; if any parts of the application need clarification, this is the time to ask questions. Consider a few examples of what can happen when these simple procedural steps are not taken:

- School bus drivers with felony convictions were employed because a permissible question was not asked on their applications.

- When the director of recruiting for a major technology company died, his employer learned not only of his prior conviction for embezzlement but also that he had lied on his employment application.

- A customer service representative in jail for robbing a supermarket had been imprisoned for three years before being hired. The human resources representative had ignored the fact that he failed to answer a question about felony convictions on the application and that he failed to account for those three years on the application.

- A security manager was hired on the basis of his having been a police officer for nine years. His early retirement from the police force was due to an injury that reportedly required the constant use of medication; his subsequent inability to hold any one job for more than six months and gaps in time between jobs were ignored by human resources. The security manager was involved in the theft of precious metals from his employer in order to help pay for his drug habit.

Obviously, to get information is one thing; to verify it is another. Although background checks and obtaining employment information are akin to an investigation, it is conducted by the human resources department. Former employers should be contacted to verify dates of employment, job titles, salaries or wages paid, supervisors' or managers' names, and reasons an applicant left a job. It's not always easy. For instance, one prospective employer learned that a capable and qualified applicant nevertheless had embellished her resume by conveying the impression that she had held a much higher ranking in her former employer's hierarchy, and had been given more responsibility than had been true. It's important to remember, however, that many former employers will be reluctant to provide details regarding terminations; at the very minimum, they must be asked if they would consider the applicant eligible for reemployment. It is unfortunate, and unfair to subsequent employers, that those who hesitate to report wrongdoing fear that they could face litigation, when in fact they can avoid liability as long as they limit their remarks to proven facts.

Among the legitimate concerns of the security function is the protection of an organization's reputation. Certainly, recent events that highlighted corporate governance and related issues have shown how reputations can be severely damaged when questions of unethical behavior are raised. Consequently, as part of the preemployment screening procedure, prospective employers could benefit from posing ethically related hypothetical questions to applicants—in an effort to learn their perceptions of right versus wrong where ethical behavior is an issue.

It's important to contact personal references. Do not succumb to the notion that applicants give only personal references who will report favorable comments. While this is true from their perspective, it is equally true that a personal reference might offer a commendable trait that could possibly influence a prospective employer's hiring decision. For instance, a hotel seeks to hire a man whose application suggests that he is an ideal candidate to be the hotel's chief engineer. A personal reference is contacted and cites all of the applicant's favorable qualities—including the fact that he deserves a lot of credit for trying to deal with his drinking problem. Does the hotel want to risk hiring someone whose reliability may be in question without further consideration?

New Employee Orientation

All new hires should receive orientation. A good orientation session will cover fringe benefits, time allowances for breaks and lunch, and the employer's paid holiday policy. But it will also make the new hire aware of the employer's ground rules, including its attitude toward loss prevention, related policies and procedures, and its ethical standards. Depending on the nature of the employer's business, orientation is a perfect opportunity to discuss how patent agreements and/or conflicts of interest statements should be executed. If employers have security/loss prevention departments, a representative of that department should present the security phase of the orientation program.

Injecting the subject of security into a new employee's orientation program can serve a dual purpose. It obviously lets new employees know the employer's attitude with regard to loss prevention. However, it also may help avoid subsequent labor-management problems. The latter can arise in the event that employees are disciplined for having done or not done something—yet the root of the problem can be traced to the fact that the employer's way of doing business was never fully explained when they were originally hired.

In some organizations—especially large businesses and institutions—HR departments have special training programs for newly hired or promoted supervisory and management personnel. The subject of security/loss prevention needs to be incorporated into the curriculum of these programs, which can serve two purposes. One, as with new employees, it makes them aware of the importance of loss prevention. Two, by hearing about examples of how actual problems were dealt with, the newly hired or promoted supervisors and managers are more aware of their responsibilities and the best ways in which to deal with them.

Protecting Employees

The Occupational Safety and Health Act (OSHA), first passed by Congress in 1970, calls upon employers to provide their employees with a safe and healthful workplace. It also makes it clear that employees have a role to play by complying with the employer's safety program. However, there are other aspects of employee protection that are no less important. Two security issues that are directly related to the human resources function are workplace violence and sexual harassment.

Workplace violence is not merely a case of forbidding employees from having weapons at work. It means providing guidance to employees so that they recognize telltale signs that may indicate a problem; offering counseling to employees who may have problems regardless of whether those problems are work or home induced; and above all, emphasizing the importance of the "human" aspect of human resources in dealing with people.

Sexual harassment may not involve physical violence, but its impact on a victimized employee can be traumatic. Employers need to have clear-cut policies with regard to this kind of activity. Complaints of sexual harassment should be taken seriously and thoroughly investigated; if substantiated, appropriate action must be taken with those guilty of such conduct.

An additional aspect of employee protection concerns those who work for an organization where either domestic or international travel is required. When traveling on business, employees should be given guidance in general, especially if they have to visit countries where small- or large-scale terrorist or anti-American activity is not uncommon. One bit of advice worth heeding, regardless of where they may be going, would be to follow the United States government's policy relative to hotels. Federal employees traveling on business are not supposed to stay in hotels that do not have sprinklers and smoke detection systems. Otherwise, room reservations should be for a hotel's lower floors since fire department ladder apparatus often cannot be extended beyond the tenth floor in case of evacuation. Employees should be instructed to take advantage of safe-deposit facilities; securing personal and business assets, including information and laptop computers, should be mandated.

Multinational employers should be aware of information provided by the United States Department of State and Federal Bureau of Investigation with respect to countries that are unfriendly to American businesses or where there are other forms of political unrest. Employees traveling to such countries should be made aware of the importance of keeping a low profile. If there is political unrest, every effort should be made for them to stay at hotels that are not controlled by the government or local politicians; they also need to be told to avoid restaurants, bars, and places of entertainment frequented by government officials, especially those in the military or law enforcement.

Some organizations, especially larger ones, often are concerned with executive protection. Those covered by the program should be lectured on the importance of not becoming creatures of habit, especially in terms of travel to and from work. In the interest of their own security, it also may be wise to forgo some of the perquisites normally associated with executive travel, either here or abroad. For example, executives should be picked up at the airport only by people they know; they should not engage in activities that draw attention to themselves. At the same time, companies that have executive protection programs also need to consider their responsibilities to the executives' immediate families, especially if there are children living at home.

Security's Place in a Table of Organization

In an organization, establishing security's role in preventing losses can be done without the presence of an established security department. However, there also are many businesses and institutions whose size, assets, and a host of other considerations make it advisable, if not absolutely necessary, to have one. Under some circumstances, the rank-and-file security officers may be proprietary; in other cases, they may be obtained from a contract agency. In either event, the organization is best served if the department head is an employee of the company rather than a representative from the contract agency.

When security departments do exist, a question that often arises concerns where they belong in a table of organization. Although it is not unusual for them to report to the head of the human resources department, in reality this arrangement has the potential for a conflict of interest. The end result can be damaging to either good labor relations or the loss prevention program. For instance, unhappy employees rightly should voice their complaints to those to whom they directly report. Absent satisfaction, they then should go to human resources. Unfortunately, albeit only on occasion, the conduct of security personnel can be the basis upon which a complaint will be lodged. For instance, security may become involved in an altercation with an employee who wants to enter a building without valid identification.

In this case, the reaction from the human resources department can be critically important. If it sides with the complaining employee the impression will be that the security department and the loss prevention program are of no real consequence and can be ignored—thus undermining the entire effort. If HR supports security, though, there is an equal risk that employees will conclude that they cannot get a fair hearing. This obviously can have an adverse impact on labor relations.

Conclusion

No business or institution wants to suffer losses. Any organization needs programs that will help prevent them or at least minimize their impact. Whether or not an organization can justify the need for a security department—and many cannot—is not as important as understanding the security function and its relation to that of human resources. Understanding this relationship is the one constant in all meaningful loss prevention efforts.

Comprehensive and Effective Relocations

Laura Herring

President and CEO, The IMPACT Group

In today's business environment, human resources is considered as accountable for the company's business success as the operations and marketing areas. Managing human capital to produce the highest return on investment is truly a mantra of today's business leaders. Nowhere is that truer than in the staffing function. And many of today's staffing concerns reflect the issues that come up time and again when staffing includes employee relocation.

This essay reviews why companies that address the issues that arise as workforce demographics evolve are the very companies that are destined to succeed in the war for the best talent. With the concern for quality of life and balance increasing worldwide, companies that provide support services before, during, and after relocation will no doubt find it easier to attract and retain their top candidates.

Recruiters and Their Relocation Dilemma

A recruiter's job description? "Bring me the best and brightest, and I will then sell them on the company and tell them you want them to relocate 1,500 miles from family and friends—and make them happy about it." Today, as in the past, the job of staffing is dependent on knowing and addressing the needs of the business as well as listening and responding to the needs of those recruits who are most likely to meet the organization's goals. Hence, the recruiter's role increasingly becomes that of listener, the one who meets everyone's needs, and the person who bridges gaps between candidates and the corporation or agency. And all the while, the recruiter must demonstrate a solid return on investment in the process.

What happens, however, when the prospective employee does not verbalize his or her true needs, but rather perfunctorily goes through the interview process, responding to background and accomplishment-related questions but concerned that the recruiter is asking the "sensitive questions" regarding his/her personal and work needs?

What usually happens is that the recruit turns down the opportunity with a general statement, such as "This isn't a good time" or "It's not a good fit." Translated? "It's not good for me personally or for my family" or "I'm interested but I don't/my family doesn't want to relocate." The variations on this theme go on and on.

Worse, sometimes the recruit accepts the offer hoping that things will work out, but leaves the organization when personal or family needs conflict with the job demands. The Transition Management Institute in 2001 reported that employees who relocate leave companies at more than three times the rate of those who don't, with annual employee turnover rates at 12.3 percent for relocated employees compared to 4 percent for nonrelocated employees. Factoring in recruitment expenses and hiring a replacement, the cost to the company is between $100,000 and $200,000.

Both costs and turnover are even higher in the international staffing arena. According to a 2001 Global Relocation Trends Survey, 26 percent of international transferees leave a company within two years. And since nearly half of the companies surveyed do not track attrition rates for expatriates, the figure is probably much higher, a troubling possibility since an international assignment's cost, including relocation, often tops $1 million.

Staffing professionals need to be aware of the impact that changing demographic trends have on the recruitment process. Organizations no longer are recruiting individuals. They are "recruiting" spouses, partners, families, extended family members, lifestyles, and much more.

The Special Needs of Relocation

Many times, a recruitment offer involves a relocation, either immediately or in the near future. At this point, the situation typically is turned over to the "relocation department" (internal or external), whose specialties often are household goods movement, real estate transactions, policy administration, and relocation expense tracking/management. Seldom is the relocation department in a position to pave the way for a successful recruitment by providing an impartial ancillary set of ears to identify the full "human side" of the recruitment process. And yet it's important to acknowledge these critical personal and human factors from the very beginning.

The IMPACT Group developed a program that takes the human side of the recruitment process into account. It's called Recruitment Plus. Once an offer has been made, recruits are provided the opportunity to speak with an experienced career/family consultant. The consultant explains that he/she has been asked to assist the recruit in identifying and addressing any personal or professional roadblocks that might stand in the way of accepting the offer.

The consultant, trained in listening and probing, explores any nuances of the offer that might be barriers to acceptance. Issues that often surface can be related to a spouse/partner's career concerns, community/geographic resource availability, or children's or elders' special needs. These open a dialogue that results in the consultant providing research and information to address these issues, along with skilled decision-making guidance. The consultant gives the recruit and family the tools to make a fully informed decision about relocation, rather than one based on assumptions or fears.

In one recent situation, a food service company was trying to recruit an executive to accept a position that would have meant a relocation to an urban area that the family was unfamiliar with. In an initial conversation, the executive's spouse explained to the consultant that she had done a lot of Internet-based research and had significant concerns regarding crime rates and the safety of the schools—two major considerations for the family.

From this early contact, the consultant was able to allay many unfounded concerns by describing the wide range of public and private school options available within an easy commute of the executive's future office. The consultant also was able to answer many questions about the destination city's cultural climate and recreational opportunities. Each of these areas then became the subject for follow-up research to provide the family with the specifics they felt they needed in order to make their decision.

Without proactive support that allows the candidate to fully consider the impact of the move on all involved, the results can be less successful. A financial services company recruited a sales management executive to move halfway across the country to accept a position that was being tailored around his particular area of expertise. The match was a wonderful one for the sales manager, but little, if any, thought was given to his wife, who had been a very prominent and active community volunteer in their previous location. Early on, she devoted her energies to getting her daughters through their final years of high school and decorating the home, which was much larger than they previously had been able to afford. But these activities wore thin, especially after the older daughter left for college. Within two and a half years of accepting the opportunity, the sales executive resigned to return to work for a competitor in their former area, largely at the urging of his increasingly unhappy wife.

Addressing Relocation Concerns

What steps should take place in the recruitment process to ensure that potentially unspoken needs are addressed?

It is important that an objective third party be able to consult with the candidate/transferee and/or family members to surface information they may need. The topics are as varied as families are today: schools, child care, health-related special needs, cultural/ethnic resources, religious institutions, professional associations, family member employment opportunities, and any other issues that might be seen as vital to ensuring the emotional or physical well-being of the recruit/family. Proactive contact throughout the decision-making process and potential move builds a familiarity and trust to uncover and address needs as they arise, as well as provides emotional support that so often is needed during those crisis phases that occur in many a relocation.

This process, when handled well, uncovers hidden needs that might be barriers to the acceptance of the offer. And it also allows the recruit to have a level of comfort, having fully and openly explored the pros and cons of the overall situation. This results in a feeling of control over the process, and a commitment to the ultimate decision. The information that is provided may not always be what the recruit hopes to hear, but it does help set realistic expectations so that a truer picture emerges. The advantage of this holistic approach also can save the sponsoring company many dollars.

A retail organization called upon The IMPACT Group to assist a management-level employee who was considering a job offer. The offer was one that would have relocated him from a small East Coast community with a fine school system, in reasonable commuting distance of his office, to a West Coast urban area with fewer options for commuting. The manager had stringent requirements for the quality of the schools in which his children would be enrolled. Unfortunately, The IMPACT Group's research revealed that new area's school options that met his requirements were located in communities where the real estate costs were not affordable, given the salary the company was willing and able to pay. The offer was declined, but the sponsoring company nevertheless was happy with the outcome. The staffing manager stated that if the offer had been accepted with an expectation that "things would work out," she believed that the manager's tenure with the company would have been short—a failed relocation that would have cost the company $80,000 to $100,000.

Another example: A software engineer and database developer for a consumer products company accepted a transfer, but did not tell her employer that her husband and children would not relocate until the husband was able to find a comparable job in the new location. The area where she was relocating was experiencing many layoffs and had a surplus of qualified workers—which made the husband's job search quite challenging. Fortunately, her company assisted her husband with his job search by retaining the services of The IMPACT Group; the family endured the difficulties of a six-month separation, and is now once again happily reunited.

Working with the recruiter, a relocation transition assistance support company like The IMPACT Group plays a critical role in finding a win-win solution for all those involved.

Understanding the Relocation Needs of Today's Recruits

It is important to understand the needs of today's recruits who are asked to relocate. An article in *Work/Life Today* from June 2002 identified four key areas of concern for relocating employees: balance, the spouse's career, adjustment of children, and elder care. These are not comfortable discussion items during a recruitment interview, but nonetheless should be accounted for, given the following demographics of the workforce:

- Twenty-two percent of corporate transferees are women.
- Sixty-five percent of corporate transferees are dual-career.
- Sixty-two percent of corporate transferees have children under the age of six.
- Nearly one in four adults currently cares for an elderly loved one.
- Approximately 1 in 10 American households with one or more persons aged 30 through 60 are comprised of dual-earner, sandwich-generation couples.

According to the 2000 U.S. Census, only 23.5 percent of American families fit the nuclear family mold of mom, dad, and a couple of kids. Yet a 2002 Roper poll revealed that nearly 70 percent of workers said that "family" is their top priority, however that term is configured.

Challenges of sandwich-generation workers are particularly compounded during a relocation. Consider this example: A transportation company manager repatriated to the United States from the Philippines with her six-year-old son and her ailing mother, who had been taking care of the boy during an international assignment. The grandmother, who suffered from emphysema, was having trouble keeping up with the bright youngster. The son, who had no memory of having lived in the United States, had significant acclimation problems. His acting out included ordering items from a television home shopping channel and calling 911 to see what would happen (the police came!). The recruiting company consultant researched camps and other worthwhile activities for the mother in order to relieve the strain on the grandmother, to better direct the boy's energies, and to allow the employee to focus her attention on her new job's responsibilities.

Currently, approximately 45 percent of Fortune 500 companies offer some form of employee/spouse/family relocation transition assistance, according to a 2001 article in *Mobility* magazine, a publication of the Employee Relocation Council. As with the Recruitment Plus program described previously, an experienced consultant from outside the employer company assesses the needs of the transferring employee. Whether the transferee is single, a single parent, part of a dual-career household, the sole breadwinner in a traditional family, or moving with aging parents, the needs of the transferee are identified; counseling and customized research, tailored to the specific issues of the individual, are provided.

In comprehensive programs, the consultant also proactively follows up with the family on a regular basis to address the shifting needs of the family during the move and reacclimation process. This can take as long as a year or more, depending on the circumstances of the relocation and the family dynamics. Internationally, acclimation support may be required throughout the assignment. Every recruit or transferee should be given the opportunity to receive company-sponsored transition assistance, to provide a sense of comfort and privacy to assess independently the need for and benefit of the assistance for themselves and their family.

Having assessed the needs of nearly 100,000 recruits/transferees, The IMPACT Group has learned that 65 percent to 80 percent of those who relocate desire some type of transitional support. And this includes those who are single. Single transferees typically are thought of as not having significant needs; but singles, including college recruits and new hires, are highly vulnerable to relocation failure. Moving to a new location separates them from family and friends. Having uprooted themselves once, they are reasonably likely to succumb to the lure of a competitive offer or a desire to resign in order to deal with a personal or extended family situation.

A single transferee with a major pharmaceutical company approached her promotion and related relocation to a new location with the comment, "I don't think this move is going to work out!" However, through a series of conversations with her IMPACT Group consultant, they brainstormed ways that would help make an uninviting, unfriendly, disappointing community into one where the transferee wanted to live. Ultimately, she was inspired to take her own reaction to the community as a challenge to help others in similar situations. She started a singles group that in the first three months grew from 20 people to more than 50 people, meeting monthly to establish friendships and provide one another with support.

Summary

Top-tier, talented individuals are attracted to companies that recognize their personal and professional developmental needs. In this era of changing demographics, staffing professionals need to remain aware that personal needs that were not recognized 10 years ago do exist. Unless personal as well as professional needs are met, corporations will spend millions of dollars each year recruiting and relocating talented employees, only to find them exiting prematurely.

The hiring company benefits in other ways as well. A 1998 study reported by the Society for Human Resource Management (SHRM)/HR News Online showed that workers who believe their basic needs are being met are 50 percent more likely to achieve customer loyalty and 44 percent more likely to produce above-average profits. And perhaps as a result, employers supporting their employees' basic needs experienced 24 percent more profitability, 19 percent higher revenue, and 10 percent lower turnover. These are all worthy goals of any HR organization seeking to bolster its company's return on investment.

CHAPTER

42

Business and Workforce Environment

Garrett Walker and Elizabeth Hoane
IBM

Most business leaders will state that the employees of their companies—their human capital—are critical to their business success. In the next 10 years, the source of any sustainable competitive advantage for many businesses will increasingly focus on optimizing the talent within the organization. Indeed, a key dimension of business success will be the ability of an organization to manage, grow, and measure the human capital contributions to their business results.

Today's challenging business and workforce environment foreshadows these needs. Demanding customers, rapidly changing markets, multiple potential suppliers, and a declining world economy require organizations to be more focused than ever before on effective execution of business strategy under tight expense controls. The employer-employee relationship continues to rapidly evolve: Employees are less likely to remain long with a single employer, specialized talent remains difficult to retain, employees expect more work/life balance, and talent within the organization continues to have diverse interests and needs.

With respect to the future, the increasing need to improve employee performance with flat or decreasing business investments requires human resources to lead with creative and high-impact solutions—solutions designed to deliver business results while balancing the individual needs of an organization's talent. In today's environment, human resources has the opportunity to provide business leadership in part through a major strategic shift in organizational learning strategy, investment, and direction. The foundation for this shift is the Strategic Learning Plan. To realize the optimal business benefit from the business investment in employee learning, a clear plan is required to align learning priorities with business priorities.

Strategic Learning Planning

A Strategic Learning Plan (SLP):

- Ensures that learning is used effectively and cost efficiently to drive business performance.
- Provides a framework for learning that is flexible and customizable for unique business requirements across the units.
- Is completely integrated with the business strategy process.
- Reports back to the business the value received.

Measuring the results of the SLP provides business and financial information targeted to add additional profit to the bottom line by showing the HR/learning team how to optimize the learning in order to achieve greater business impact.

How important is an SLP strategy and execution in your organization? Properly executed, a learning strategy aligned with the business strategy could make the difference between average performance and truly achieving a sustainable, competitive advantage through human capital management. But in many organizations, learning strategy implementations fail more often than they succeed. Why? Because these organizations have not developed the techniques, process, or infrastructure to translate business strategic goals into meaningful human capital learning action plans that can be executed by HR and line management. Nor have they developed the ability to track and report to the business on the real value delivered by key learning programs. As a result, strategic organizational learning remains primarily theoretical, and businesses cannot effectively align their organizational learning goals with business performance objectives.

Alignment of Business Strategy and Learning Objectives

IBM's Strategic Learning Plan process enables the organization to overcome this challenge. At IBM, the SLP couples leading-edge strategy management techniques (that have been executed well within general management functions of a business) with a highly effective learning design process and automated operational/financial management technology for aligning learning investments and measuring the impact on business performance.

Designed to plan and quantify strategic learning impact and organizational execution, IBM's Strategic Learning Plan process is a human capital management solution that identifies business objectives and measures performance across multiple perspectives such as financial, customer, internal operations, and learning. We identify learning focus areas based on the critical business objectives across these perspectives. Key performance indicators strategically align and provide better assessment of current and projected learning contributions to business performance and establish feedback loops for improved organizational effectiveness. Using the principles of a strategy-focused organization developed by Dr. Robert Kaplan and Dr. David Norton, the SLP process is deployed within a consistent framework applied within each business unit—beginning with business strategy mapping (Figure 42.1) and drilling into each aspect of essential business execution. This provides a clear line of sight for critical learning requirements. The organizational learning process is integrated with core business value chains and ensures efficient alignment of investments and resources. (See Figure 42.2.)

To be effective, learning strategy must be communicated in terms that make it relevant and doable for everyone in our organization. The SLP process makes it easy to cascade business objectives and learning strategy

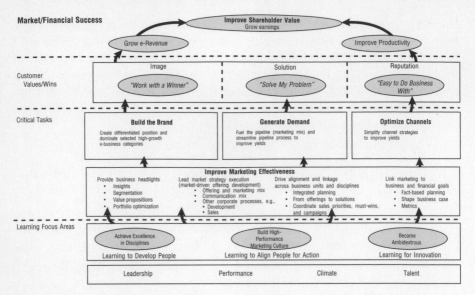

Figure 42.1   Strategy Map: Linking Learning Directly to Business Strategy and Critical Objectives of the Business.

	Step 1 Validate Business Priorities	Step 2 Translate Business Priorities into Strategy Map	Step 3 Identify Strategic Measures	Step 4 Identify and Prioritize Learning Interventions	Step 5 Implement Strategic Learning Plan
Activities	Assemble strategy documents Review business plans Identify critical priorities and cause-and-effect links Identify key line executives for validation	Identify specific business issues and objectives Determine strategic themes Validate strategy map Highlight critical issues to be addressed by learning	Identify key measures Align existing business measures to objectives from strategy map	Identify learning interventions Review list of proposed interventions Apply prioritization process Validate with BU leadership	Develop and deploy learning interventions Develop reporting and feedback mechanisms Develop communications plan
Deliverables	Understanding of business plans	Strategy map	Selected business measures Measurement plan	Prioritized learning interventions	Finalized strategic learning plan
Roles	Corporate learning Executive sponsor Learning contact Subject matter experts	Corporate learning Learning contact Subject matter experts	Corporate learning Learning contact Subject matter experts	Corporate learning Executive sponsor Subject matter experts	Corporate learning Executive sponsor Subject matter experts

Figure 42.2   Steps in Developing a Strategic Learning Plan.

through the organization, from business line to the production and service line. High-level business strategies and objectives are broken down into lower-level business learning metrics with clear objectives that support the organization's overall business strategy. Individuals then understand how to align their actions to achieve those objectives. Armed with specific and relevant performance information, we adjust and proactively manage our response to the changing business environment.

As it helps us manage and execute the learning strategies, the SLP:

- Provides a cross-enterprise view of learning performance and business impact.
- Identifies common initiatives to better leverage synergies and drive integration.
- Prioritizes learning programs in a consistent framework based on the expected level of business impact.
- Builds collaboration between business strategy development and analysis of learning contribution.
- Communicates strategic learning goals and performance across the enterprise.

At the core of the SLP is the ability to plan and report the value of learning in terms of specific business value delivered. In addition, the IBM SLP process and supporting technologies provide general value to our businesses in the following ways:

- Drives specific business objectives by designing learning programs to fill critical gaps.
- Organizes strategic thinking and performance management/measurement.
- Translates the business strategy into a focused, executable model.
- Clearly communicates strategy and measures of success across the business.
- Aligns behavior and increases organizational focus on key business priority initiatives.

- Delivers business intelligence coupled with human capital management data to the desktops of line executives.

Integrated Environment

The SLP operates in an integrated environment to develop, report on, and analyze learning strategy. We leverage the Human Capital Information Warehouse, Finance Information Warehouse, and business intelligence systems along with IBM analytic business applications. A single model for developing business strategies is used across the business and forms the basis of the SLP. This high-level infrastructure and integration enables the SLP to drive investment planning and optimize critical learning impact for business results.

Additionally, human resources professionals now have strategic tools with simulation and forecasting capabilities that can be applied to create a forward-looking analysis in support of learning optimization. This framework provides the context business leaders and line managers need to make well-informed decisions. Our executives and line managers get at-a-glance qualitative and quantitative information about the strategic performance of their business and the alignment of their learning initiatives across business lines and the enterprise. An example of the Web-based e-learning executive dashboard is shown in Figure 42.3.

Challenges and Trends

A core challenge we face within human resources is communicating and reinforcing the linkages between HR actions and business results. Most businesses have clear strategies with targeted business results and objectives. What is often missing is a human capital strategy directly linked to the needs of the business and expressed in terms of specific people imperatives.

As we continue to more directly link our learning initiatives to business results, we see certain key areas of value recognized by the business. Areas of specific interest to the business are:

- Justify the cost of training before deploying it.
- Convert learning expense into an investment.

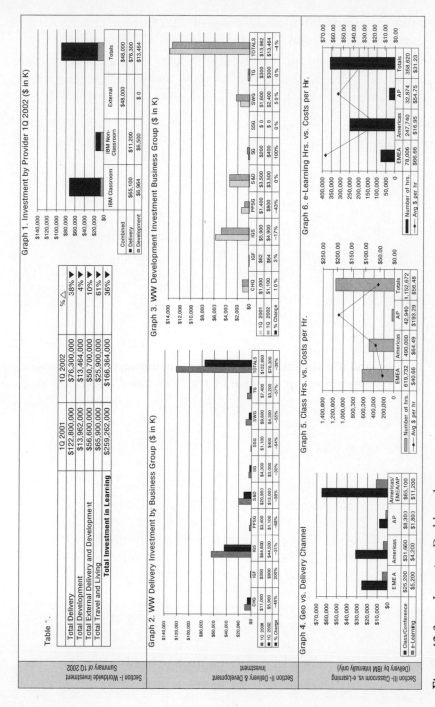

Figure 42.3 e-Learning Dashboard.

331

- Validate learning as a tool to cause beneficial business change.
- Establish the optimal training configuration based on specific constraints such as performance factors, budget, and location, enabling employees more flexibility, control, and access, and reducing time away from job.

Conclusion

The Strategic Learning Plan process provides a consistent way to clearly link learning to the key objectives and requirements of the business. Development of the SLP clearly positions learning to drive increased value to the business. And execution of the process ensures that the business receives the best return on its learning investment.

Use of the SLP process has changed the focus of learning in IBM from skills development to a critical strategic success factor. The framework depicts how learning can be a key element in the organization's success story. We speak the language of the business, using terms and metrics that are familiar to the line executives. And we show how properly aligned learning can help them achieve their goals.

43

Elusive and Critical: The Role of Group Dynamics in Recruitment and Retention

Lawrence J. Quartana, Ph.D.

Staffing operations have historically focused on matching the knowledge and skill requirements of the job with the knowledge and skills present in the candidate. Methodologies such as behavioral event interviewing have been developed to help recruiters and hiring managers determine whether the knowledge and skills a candidate claims to possess have actually been demonstrated and used successfully in previous settings. After all, past performance is taken as a reliable predictor of future performance. Add a series of good impressions with key people and it's possible to establish a satisfactory candidate match.

This scenario often results in a "good hire"—someone who is productive over the long term and fits well within the organization. Yet it is also often true that promising candidates, even those whose knowledge and skills had been confirmed, end up either being unproductive and disappointing or leaving after a short period, or both. Everything seemed right, but the fit just was not there.

"Fit"—a concept familiar to all staffing professionals—is difficult to define, though most claim to know it or, more tellingly, feel it when they see it. But the critical need for skilled workers and the costs associated with turnover have both contributed to the urgency to understand fit beyond the level of a gut feeling. Staffing professionals need the resources to understand the dynamics that contribute to employees fitting in, and the role these dynamics play in successful recruitment and retention.

Dr. Susan Wheelan, a researcher at Temple University in Philadelphia, has spent the past 20 years conducting meticulous research on how groups work and develop, and she has produced a simple, accessible model of developmental processes in groups. Dr. Wheelan's model bears some resemblance to the familiar "forming, storming, norming, performing" model. But it is distinctive because it is the only model of group development that is validated by research: Systematic observation by dedicated researchers has demonstrated with great confidence that groups really do go through the developmental sequence described in the model and exhibit all the characteristics associated with each stage.

Candidates do not get recruited into a job only; the job exists in a social context that is defined by the dynamics of the work group. An awareness and understanding of a work group's developmental issues would be a critical consideration for staffing professionals as they fill positions within work groups. A brief overview of Wheelan's model is presented here, followed by implications for staffing practice.

Wheelan's Four-Stage Model of Group Development

A complete treatment of the four-stage group development model can be found in Dr. Wheelan's *Group Processes: A Developmental Perspective* (Allyn & Bacon, 1994).

STAGE ONE: DEPENDENCY AND INCLUSION

Major characteristics of a stage one group include:

- Personal safety, inclusion, and acceptance are primary concerns of group members.
- Rejection by the group is a major fear.

- Communication tends to be tentative and polite.
- Compliance is high.
- Overt conflict is minimal.
- Goals are not clear to members, but clarity is not sought.
- The leader is seen as benevolent and competent.
- Members expect the leader to provide safety and direction.
- The leader is rarely challenged.
- Members act as though they need directive leadership.

Stage one groups can be misinterpreted as highly effective groups because of high compliance among members and the lack of overt conflict—"Everyone gets along in that group." However, absence of conflict is not a reliable indicator of group, or leader, effectiveness. Ultimately, groups must develop beyond this stage to reach their optimum effectiveness.

STAGE TWO: COUNTERDEPENDENCY AND FIGHT

Major characteristics of a stage two group include:

- Disagreements about goals and tasks emerge.
- Increased feelings of safety allow dissent to occur.
- Clarification of goals begins.
- Conformity decreases.
- Attempts to manage conflict emerge.
- Trust and cohesion begin to build if conflict resolution is successful.
- The leader is challenged by members.
- Benevolence and competence of the leader is no longer assumed by members.

This stage is often the most difficult for group members. However, as Wheelan has observed, "Trust comes from fighting, not hugs." Every group has to get to a point where it can openly discuss the issues it is experiencing and successfully resolve them. This stage cannot be skipped; every group must come to terms with its issues. Urgent needs to become a high-performing team immediately are not possible; groups, like individuals, must develop, like it or not.

Trying to skip this stage is rather like an individual saying that he or she is going to skip adolescence and go right to adulthood. It simply cannot happen.

If a group is able to recognize its differences and build effective conflict management into its operation, it will then be free to move to stage three. If conflict is dealt with in a manner that leaves individual members feeling injured, then the group will revert to the dependency of stage one, setting up a cycle of dependency followed by counterdependency that can go on indefinitely. Conflict resolution is thus not simply a matter of "making everyone feel better." It is a necessity for business success.

STAGE THREE: TRUST AND STRUCTURE

Major characteristics of a stage three group include:

- Cohesion and trust increase.
- Conflict continues to occur; conflict management is more effective.
- Individual commitment to goals is high.
- Communication structure is flexible rather than centralized through the leader.
- Member satisfaction increases.
- Roles and tasks get adjusted to increase the probability of success.
- The leader becomes less directive and more consultative.

There is an unstated belief that groups can behave like this kind of a group simply by deciding that they want to do so. However, the research is clear: There are no shortcuts. The level of functioning exhibited by stage three groups comes only after the group has developed through stages one and two. Moreover, Wheelan has found that development to stage three can take up to six months or longer from the group's inception. Weekend team-building sessions with trust walks and feedback sessions cannot accelerate group development. Team building can be a useful part of a group's development, but true group development is carried out within the pursuit of the purpose and goals of the group.

STAGE FOUR: WORK AND TERMINATION

Major characteristics of a stage four group include:

- Members are clear about goals and agree with them.
- There is an open communication structure in which all members participate.
- The group spends time planning how it will solve problems, committing the time needed to do so effectively.
- Voluntary conformity is high.
- The group expects to be successful.
- The group is cohesive and members are cooperative.
- Effective conflict management is in place; conflict happens, but is dealt with effectively.
- Interpersonal attraction is high; members like being part of the group.
- The leader adopts a consultative role.

Achieving stage four requires the efforts of the entire group, not just the leader. In fact, the leader alone cannot drive group development; it is an initiative that must be wanted and pursued by all members. Ownership for the group's success must be resident in all members, not just the group leader.

Implications for Recruiting and Retention

The stages of group development offer some insight into the concept of fit as used by staffing professionals. Fit can be understood, at least in part, by how well the new hire is dealing with the dynamics of the group into which he or she has been placed. A new hire may be seen as argumentative, but this could be the result of being placed in a stage two group. Another new hire who is placed in a stage one group may be observed to be dependent and compliant and, consequently, wrongly assessed as "not strong enough to be a leader." Similarly, a new hire in a stage three or stage four group may be seen as "a strong team player"; but if this person is in a stage two group, he or she would be argumentative and conflict-oriented.

"Fit" can thus be understood as how well the new hire is adjusting to the dynamics of the work group into which he has been placed. Can a hard-charging person have the patience to sit in a stage one group and help the group develop, or will she get frustrated and angry and blame the group for preventing her from doing her job? Can a manager with a preferred leadership style of consultation operate in a directive way with a stage one or two group? Can a manager with a high need for control lead a stage four group by getting out of the way of the members? Many other similar questions can be imagined.

Beyond having the prerequisite knowledge and skills, candidates must be able to function within the social dynamics of the work group to which they will be assigned. It thus becomes incumbent upon staffing professionals to understand the dynamics of the various work groups they serve and to take these dynamics into account when placing new hires into these groups. Here are some questions that can help staffing professionals do this:

- What are the observable dynamics of the group where you are placing a new hire? What stage of development does the group appear to be in?

- What can you tell the candidate about the dynamics of the group?

- What can you ask the candidate in order to determine if he or she has functioned in a similar group in the past?

- Given the dynamics of the group, what are the candidate's chances of being successful in the group environment?

- If hiring a manager, is the manager prepared to exercise leadership that is compatible with the developmental stage of the group?

- Can the candidate for a management position provide evidence of successfully leading groups at different levels of development?

- Will your organization tolerate behavior by managers that is compatible with the developmental level of the group they are leading? (For instance, if conflict is seen as a sign of poor leadership, then anyone who is leading a group at stage two will be seen as ineffective.)

Summary

The dynamics of groups are, of course, a field of study unto themselves. These few questions only begin to address questions of group development considerations in recruitment and retention.

But it is important that staffing professionals begin to incorporate the dynamics of work groups into their professional practice. Reliance on elusive concepts like fit is no longer adequate for today's staffing professional. Those who do not feel they have the necessary expertise to diagnose group functioning can make use of consultants with this expertise. After all, human capital is the critical variable for success or failure for any organization. Staffing professionals must make use of validated models grounded in sound research to predict success for potential new employees, and thus improve recruitment and retention.

Measured Employee Development and Verification of Core Expertise

Richard A. Swanson
University of Minnesota

Elwood F. Holton III
Louisiana State University

Overview

"If you can't measure it, you can't manage it" is an old management dictum that is usually greeted with approving nods. But when this adage is focused on measuring employee development, approving nods often switch to puzzled looks. Measured employee development has a good beat, but is hard to dance to. Even so, organizations and consumers of human expertise want to know that employees have the expertise that is required of the situation, not that they simply have work experience or have attended workshops and seminars.

While basic information on the psychometrics of measuring knowledge and expertise is readily available in professional literature (Swanson & Holton 1999), not many organizations measure employee development or verify that employees have the expertise required to perform. When the development of expertise is measured, it is generally done in situations where lives can be lost (e.g., medicine), in dangerous occupations (e.g., chemical handling), or in highly specialized technical tasks (e.g., certified public accounting).

Some argue that measuring employee development and certifying employee expertise should be considered for all people who work in core business processes. Those who hold this perspective generally view workplace expertise as the fuel of an organization. Herling (2000) characterizes human expertise as a complex and multifaceted phenomenon.

Human expertise is displayed behavior within a specialized domain and/or related domain in the form of consistently demonstrated actions of an individual that are both optimally efficient in their execution and effective in their results (Herling 2000, 20).

Developing and maintaining workforce expertise—connected to organization goals and core work process requirements—are fundamental challenges to organizations. To measure and verify employee expertise in contemporary organizations requires a variety of approaches. The approaches described in this chapter include and go beyond the traditional job and task analysis view of expertise into a contemporary performance-improvement approach.

Objectives, Strategies, and Process

The objective of measured employee development is to have valid and useful assessments of the worker expertise required by the employing organization. Three general strategies, or approaches, include (1) traditional job-task approach, (2) competency approach, and (3) work process approach.

TRADITIONAL JOB-TASK APPROACH

Organizations have, for the most part, embraced the job- and task-oriented approaches to defining workplace expertise and have relied on multiple analysis procedures to do this work (Holton 1995; Swanson 1996). These approaches are familiar to most human resources professionals and are in many cases driven by federal laws. Essentially, they all contain these basic steps:

1. Develop a list of job tasks performed in a job.
2. Verify the task list as a valid representation of the job.
3. Analyze precisely what a person needs to know and do to meet a specified performance standard for each task (basis for the development, assessment, and certification).
4. Structure and deliver a program to develop the expertise in employees to meet the required performance standards.
5. Measure employee development in terms of their attainment of the expertise required to meet the required performance standards and certify those meeting the standards.

Fundamentally, job and task analysis methodologies address the appropriate unit of analysis—the work task. In practice, existing job structures, current work practices, and current employees are used as the frame with which to determine work task requirements. The outcome is employee development expertise, management, and verification grounded in the present world. In stable environments, this approach works well. What happens, however, if jobs, work tasks, and task expertise are not stable and are rapidly evolving? In today's fast-changing world, job responsibilities and requirements can shift quickly.

COMPETENCY APPROACH

Competency assessment is one approach to overcome some of the limitations of traditional job and task analysis (DuBois 1993). Competencies are generally defined as some underlying characteristic of an employee that enables him or her to perform the job or task. Because competencies are underlying characteristics and one step removed from the tasks themselves, this method is viewed as a more flexible approach that can be used to select and develop employees across multiple jobs. The limitation of this approach (namely, being one step removed) creates a disconnect between more general competencies and specific job requirements and expertise.

Competency models generally proceed in the same fundamental steps as the job analysis approach. The difference is that work tasks are analyzed for underlying competencies as opposed to task-specific knowledge and expertise. In some cases, steps one and two of the traditional job-task approach are skipped and experts are used to directly specify the competencies. The key point is that competency models are also job-based; therefore, they operate under a number of the same assumptions outlined earlier and are subject to the same criticisms raised about job-based methods. To the extent that competencies are more likely to be stable than are job tasks, they are an improvement. But they still fall short for all situations, particularly in the realm of defining the specific expertise (not general competencies) required to perform.

WORK PROCESS APPROACH

In this approach, the focus is on a core work process and the workforce expertise required to optimize the work. This approach is often pursued in the context of revising an existing work process.

The core method of documenting the work process is to: (1) meet with a select group of employees, managers, and support personnel, then verify and expand upon any previously drawn-up task lists; (2) create a first draft of the integrated flowchart; (3) coordinate visits by a lead person to multiple sites to observe employees carrying out their work; (4) require the lead person to then create a second draft of the integrated flowchart; and (5) give the integrated process flowchart to the select group for review, revision, and approval.

The integrated process flowchart of how the work is to be done is used as a basis for measuring employee development (see Swanson and Holton 1998). Steps in the work process, and the job roles of those working in the process, are specified. The final analysis work can be through a face-to-face work session, with each expert-participant having a draft of the integrated flowchart prior to the session. As each work step is reviewed, along with the job roles contributing to that step, improvement revisions can be entertained, evaluated, and acted upon by the group.

Given the improved process, the process steps can then be clustered into tasks attributable to one or more of the job roles within the process. In some instances, a single process step can be a task; in most instances, several highly related steps are clustered into a process-referenced task. These descriptions are fundamental in connecting work tasks to core work process—something regularly missing in organizations and a source of major performance disconnects in organizations.

Success Stories

Measuring employee development and verifying worker expertise require orderly thinking and methods. Two useful tools that we developed and successfully used in a Fortune 100 insurance company named Insurance Inc. are presented in this section. The first is a Measurement Standards Data Sheet, designed to guide the establishment of process-referenced task performance, knowledge, and expertise. The second is a functional model of an employee certification and development process.

Insurance Inc. was facing a serious business problem. Even though the company had many extraordinarily capable people, the largest accounts were increasingly being captured by the competition. Sales were down. An analysis revealed that the company needed to revise a core work process and the way people did their jobs. In all, the people working in nine job roles within a specific realm of the firm were required to develop new expertise and a new working relationship.

MEASUREMENT STANDARDS DATA SHEET

Establishing measurement standards for employee development (performance, expertise, and knowledge) is essential work in measured employee development. Expertise standards for each task include the establishment of (1) a performance "measure and standard," (2) the "must know" knowledge, and (3) the "must do" expertise. In doing this work, the data sheet is used to record decisions (Figure 44.1).

One critical timesaving aspect to this effort is to identify existing documentation and sources of knowledge, expertise, and measurement. Participants in this process were asked to attend a work session with in-house experts; they were told to bring along all readily available documentation relevant to the tasks that were under consideration for review. During this work session, so many good ideas came out so fast from the group that it was critical to have an official recorder of information so that no information was lost.

Task #   Take from integrated flowchart

Task Name   • Unique and discrete
                          • Intermediate and reasonable size
                          • Action verb and object of action

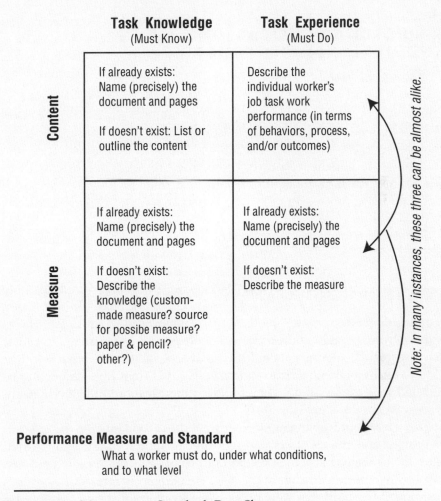

	Task Knowledge (Must Know)	**Task Experience** (Must Do)
Content	If already exists: Name (precisely) the document and pages If doesn't exist: List or outline the content	Describe the individual worker's job task work performance (in terms of behaviors, process, and/or outcomes)
Measure	If already exists: Name (precisely) the document and pages If doesn't exist: Describe the knowledge (custom-made measure? source for possibe measure? paper & pencil? other?)	If already exists: Name (precisely) the document and pages If doesn't exist: Describe the measure

Note: In many instances, these three can be almost alike.

Performance Measure and Standard
        What a worker must do, under what conditions,
        and to what level

Figure 44.1   Measurement Standards Data Sheet.
Source: Swanson and Holton (1999), page 224. Used with permission.

This highly charged session at Insurance Inc. yielded critical, basic information in the realms of performance standards, basic knowledge, and unexpected sources of expertise and related training materials. The group discovered that two particular employees produced exceptional proposals for customers; the team requested copies to use as core training aids and employee development measurement tools.

EMPLOYEE CERTIFICATION AND DEVELOPMENT PROCESS

By linking the process of front-end analysis to the knowledge and expertise assessment techniques, an effective employee development and certification system was implemented at Insurance Inc. (see Swanson 1996). The power of this system started with organizational performance—not jobs or subject matter—in order to define expertise and knowledge requirements of the company in selected critical areas. Specifically, the measurement of employee development was transformed into a powerful process for certifying expertise to perform within core organizational processes.

The measurement and management of expertise at Insurance Inc. was limited in scope to selected critical jobs having high impact. After the establishment of the measurement standards for the selected critical jobs, Insurance Inc.'s training professionals put together field-based learning modules for those employees. The learning objectives, field learning guides, and support materials were produced to develop the required knowledge and expertise. In addition, tests were developed and administered to certify knowledge and expertise on a task-by-task basis.

Individuals working in these Insurance Inc. positions were required to be certified in each job task. The employee certification and development process is illustrated in Figure 44.2.

The strategic management of expertise at Insurance Inc. proved to be efficient and effective. A significant portion of the activity was in uncharted territory for the company. While the individual elements appeared rational and at times routine, the overall perspective of directly connecting business goals and the expertise of individuals was radical.

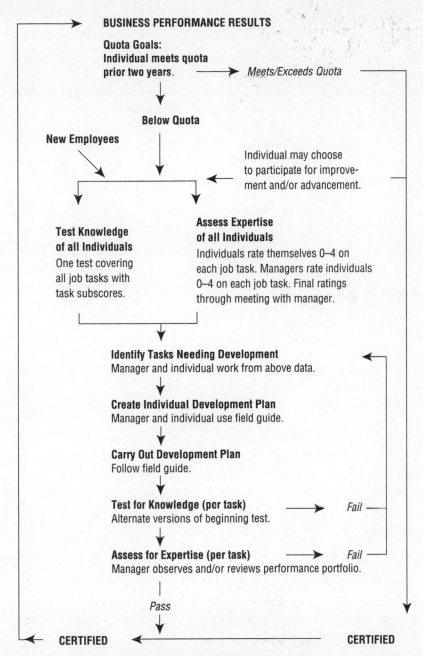

BUSINESS PERFORMANCE RESULTS

Quota Goals:
Individual meets quota
prior two years. ─────▶ *Meets/Exceeds Quota*

Below Quota

New Employees

Individual may choose
to participate for improvement and/or advancement.

Test Knowledge
of all Individuals
One test covering
all job tasks with
task subscores.

Assess Expertise
of all Individuals
Individuals rate themselves 0–4 on
each job task. Managers rate individuals
0–4 on each job task. Final ratings
through meeting with manager.

Identify Tasks Needing Development
Manager and individual work from above data.

Create Individual Development Plan
Manager and individual use field guide.

Carry Out Development Plan
Follow field guide.

Test for Knowledge (per task) ─────▶ *Fail*
Alternate versions of beginning test.

Assess for Expertise (per task) ─────▶ *Fail*
Manager observes and/or reviews performance portfolio.

Pass

◀─ **CERTIFIED** ◀─────── **CERTIFIED**

Figure 44.2 Employee Certification and Development Process.
Source: Swanson and Holton (1999), page 226. Used with permission.

Challenges, Developments, and Trends

Strategically, many organizations need a new system for identifying, measuring, and certifying employee development expertise. Ideally, this system is anchored in the more stable components of the organization; is flexible as it relates to job structures; separates work expertise and individuals from job structures; and addresses organizational, process, and individual levels of performance that can be used strategically, not reactively.

This strategic management of expertise (Swanson and Holton 1998) is fundamentally different from traditional approaches because it addresses the aforementioned points. In this approach, organizations manage strategic goals, core processes, and core competencies *and* expertise. Employee development systems are focused on expertise, not jobs. Job structures emerge as a final step in the process, but have no real role in the planning—which means that jobs can be reorganized without affecting the planning for expertise. Jobs are expected to change frequently, as expertise is redeployed to achieve strategic goals. This integrated planning process links expertise to core business processes that are in turn linked to customer needs (see Figure 44.3).

This planning process has many implications. But for employee development measurement purposes, our interest is in how it can lead to more effective identification of expertise needed to achieve organizational goals, and how it can be used to develop standards to certify employee expertise.

The basic premise of this approach is that expertise should not be linked to jobs—which are inherently unstable—but to core business processes for accomplishing organizational goals. Results assessment then takes on a strategic role by certifying core expertise. By linking expertise to business processes instead of jobs, organizations have:

- A more flexible expertise structure that allows jobs to be reorganized to encompass different process tasks without requiring new job analysis.
- Expertise that is more focused on organizational goals.
- A certification system built on process functions, rather than positions.
- Expertise that is clearly linked to organizational processes.

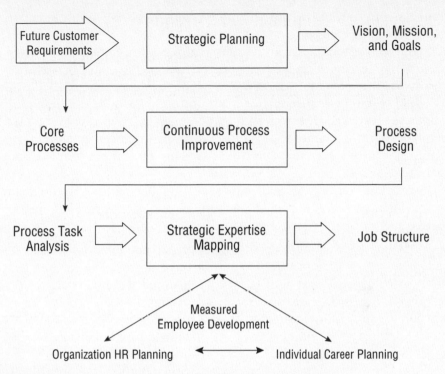

Figure 44.3 Strategic Management of Expertise Flowchart.
Source: Swanson and Holton (1999), page 215. Used with permission.

Conclusions

Measured employee development can be focused on employees who build a portfolio of certified expertise that is linked to core organizational processes. Measured employee development needs to become performance- and future-oriented while being closely linked to core business processes and critical strategic goals. With valid development and measurement systems in place, employees can begin to manage their careers based on expertise, rather than jobs. Jobs will then become temporary places for utilizing expertise.

Employees should be selected both for the expertise they bring with them and for their capacity to develop new expertise as needs change. Especially in high-technology arenas, today's expertise may well be obsolete in a short time. In the midst of change, the capacity to develop is just as important as current expertise.

Similarly, organizations can become partners with employees to determine future expertise and development requirements. The organization clearly has the most strategic view and needs to be sure that development will lead to business performance in the future. However, the individual employee is often the first to realize that changes are occurring in the marketplace that will require new expertise. In many instances, employees recognize the need for new business practices and innovations before management does.

In conclusion, managers and employees should be partners in the realm of development—with measured employee development providing the objective anchor for the transactions.

References

DuBois, D. 1993. *Competency-based performance improvement.* Amherst, MA: HRD Press.

Herling, R. W. 2000. "Operational definitions of expertise and competence." In R. W. Herling and J. Provo (Eds.), *Strategic Perspectives on Knowledge, Competence, and Expertise.* Thousand Oaks, CA: Sage.

Swanson, R. A. 1996. *Analysis for improving performance: Tools for diagnosing organizations and documenting workplace expertise.* San Francisco: Berrett-Koehler.

Swanson, R. A., and E. F. Holton. 1998. "Process-referenced expertise: Developing and maintaining core expertise in the midst of change." *National Productivity Review*, 17(2): 29–38.

Swanson, R. A., and E. F. Holton. 1999. *Results: How to assess performance, learning, and perceptions in organizations.* San Francisco: Berrett-Koehler.

Retention—The Key to the Human Capital Cycle

Joe Bosch

Chief People Officer, Pizza Hut

If you ask a roomful of people about the worst job they ever had, chances are that you'll hear about a horrible first day or week in which they were not made to feel welcome, appreciated, or important. And the chances are even higher that during this ill-fated first day or week on this brand-new job, the new employee also started to think about leaving.

When we talk about the human capital cycle, we're usually most focused on input—the people coming into the organization. But more and more companies are realizing that managing the retention of those people can be even more important. An environment that doesn't nurture and welcome a new employee from day one can cost a company millions of dollars a year—all because of turnover. And yet businesses are loath to measure the culture of an organization—an element that has a tremendous impact on retention—because it's difficult to measure.

The restaurant industry is a great example of an industry that struggles with this issue on a daily basis. It's a high-churn, fast-paced business plagued by a reputation for institutional instability. We have managers who think it's impossible to operate at less than 150 percent turnover. Yet we also have endless examples of managers who have less than 50 percent turnover—and in almost every case, their overall performance is higher because of it. In the restaurant industry, many find it difficult to imagine having turnover so low that the quality and consistency of work are at a premium. But it can happen. If you hire the right kind of people—and then create an environment in which they want to stay—you'd feel less at the mercy of your workforce and more indebted to the way you've trained your team members to treat your customers.

Suppose we could engineer out all parts of the process that might interfere with a great restaurant experience? After all, we often say that the goal of all our HR systems is to bring stability and reliability to an inherently unstable business. Certainly we can create foolproof systems, such as cooking equipment to increase food quality, inventory tools that ensure the right supply of menu items, or drive-through window procedures that speed up customer orders and wait times. But that moment of truth still awaits when a customer meets a team member: Did he smile at you? Did she remember the catsup for your fries—or did you drive off without it? Did the delivery driver find your house before your pizza got cold? The only thing that might take all the potential points of failure out of the system would be a vending machine! And we know what that food tastes like.

A restaurant is a great model for the entire business cycle:

1. Raw materials come in the back and are inventoried.
2. Customers place orders.
3. Order takers communicate them to the kitchen (or the plant).
4. The kitchen staff prepares, cooks, and assembles the finished product.
5. A service person delivers the finished product to your table at the restaurant or to your home.
6. Finally, payment is collected.

Consider the points in this cycle where a customer meets a team member; these represent a lot of potential success or failure points! Think of your own good or bad restaurant experiences—what makes the difference? It usually comes down to service, which really means it comes down to the people. Since we can engineer out some but not all of the variability, we inevitably depend on individuals to make the right decision at that moment of truth: namely, when a customer's unanticipated need or a breakdown in the process requires an individual to exercise individual judgment and discretion to satisfy the customer.

At Pizza Hut and YUM! Brands, we have been working on creating performance management systems and processes that drive performance and help individuals know exactly what to do at that moment of truth, when the decisions they make can determine whether the customer has a good or bad experience. We are fortunate that we have systemwide support for the components of our performance management system—such as balanced scorecards, bench planning, and internal promotion processes and selection systems. Through the use of these components, we can demonstrate a direct correlation to business results.

For example, we know that bench planning has created a way to proactively manage the churn or turnover of employees in our restaurants. With bench planning procedures, we plan for churn and continually add managers-in-training in order to minimize job vacancies at restaurants and eliminate the potential daisy chain of movement created by the loss of one manager. We also know if we can just keep the same manager in the same restaurant for one full year, it is worth two margin points on the P&L statement. Likewise, we know that an externally hired manager takes three years to reach the same level of productivity—profit—as an internally promoted manager. When you're armed with these facts, it's easy to get line managers to spend time on bench planning and preparing people for internal promotions.

Our four-tiered balanced scorecard measures (1) profit, (2) sales, (3) people, and (4) customers, and has helped our managers make trade-offs between what they sometimes perceive as conflicting priorities. We have engineered the scorecard to ensure you cannot truly succeed without being at least somewhat successful in all categories. This has given our managers a clear road map to building a successful restaurant. Most importantly, we believe that a manager cannot be successful without getting the people component right.

Recently, we began to connect the dots from the overall work environment to the leader's behavior. A few years ago, we began asking our restaurant team members to complete the annual Voice of Champions culture survey. It gives our team members the opportunity to relay what it's like to work in their restaurant and for their manager. Similar to a 360° feedback report, Voice of Champions clearly demonstrates that culture does drive performance—up or down. For example, we did some simple correlations that show how our best-performing restaurants score higher than poorly performing restaurants (see Table 45.1). While this makes good, logical sense, it gives us the opportunity to explore and coach around what a leader needs to do to create a great culture. Our best-performing managers:

- Set clear standards.
- Talk to the teams about goals for improving their restaurants' performance.
- Recognize people for their contributions.

What is equally interesting is that the managers who exhibit these behaviors set a true atmosphere of trust. Trust has two important ramifications in a labor-intensive work environment.

First, the workforce has a real sense of equity. What is fair? Is the allocation of work and scheduled hours on and off fair? Is my manager fair and equitable in how he/she treats me? Does everyone pull his or her share of the work? The perceived validity of fairness in the workplace is a key determinant to whether people stay with you and feel committed to give their fair share of effort.

Table 45.1   Best-Performing Restaurant versus Poorly Performing Restaurant

Standards	Top 10%	Bottom 10%	Difference
• People in my restaurant usually come to work on time.	78	46	32
• When it slows down, the first thing we do is clean.	85	48	37
• I am proud of how clean the restaurant is kept.	96	63	33
• When it starts to get busy, our restaurant is organized and ready for customers.	94	62	32
Recognition			
• My manager recognizes me when I do a good job.	98	67	31
Communication			
• I know what goals my manager has for improving our restaurant's performance.	97	69	28
• My manager talks to us about our restaurant's performance.	97	69	28

Table 45.2 Manager Trust Factor in Best-Performing Restaurant versus Poorly Performing Restaurant

Trust	Top 10%	Bottom 10%	Difference
• I trust the people I work with.	92	64	28
• I trust my manager.	93	64	29
• I am satisfied with my work schedule.	89	63	26
• Everyone in this restaurant does their fair share of the work.	78	40	38
• People on our team help out even if it's not their job.	71	38	33

Second, in a customer/labor-intensive business where millions of transactions occur, there can be huge ambiguity and uncertainty. Service is intangible, because what each of us expects can vary widely. Trust reduces uncertainty. As a team member, I know I am trusted to make anything right for the customer.

The workplace culture—one where trust is evident and competencies are valued—can make a significant difference in business. But is this something we can really measure? Yes, without a doubt. A company's culture is created from an organization's mission, capital, governance, and founders, all the way down to an individual supervisor or worker's behavior. Granted, measurement of culture is difficult, and businesses are hesitant to spend time on measuring the value of culture. That doesn't mean we shouldn't focus on it, though.

Why? Look around at local and national listings of "best companies." Even with a degree of subjectivity, these companies are recognized because of the investments they've made in their people. Winning companies have distinct cultures that their people—their human capital—choose to belong to. The growing labor shortage and lack of employee commitment have brought the issue of company culture to the forefront. Even Wall Street recognizes the importance of human capital—its loss or inefficient use has become a key component for valuation. Subsequently, more and more companies have begun to talk about their ROI on human capital.

However, even with new awareness, corporations need more real progress. Convincing line management to tend to their culture—to nourish it and shape it—is the most important contribution a human resources function can make to the long-term success of any business.

It's Time for a Strategic Approach to Retaining Talent

Barbara Mitchell
Millennium Group

Introduction

Employee retention has for years been discussed and debated in American businesses. Much of what has been discussed, however, seems to focus on doing more to keep employees happy so that they won't quit. It's time to develop a strategic approach to retaining talent, one that will serve the organization well over time.

Everyone seems to agree that recruiting and retention are strongly linked. The argument can be made, in fact, that one of the key players in any retention strategy is the organization's recruiter or recruiting function, and that one of the key elements in any retention strategy is the premise that you have to start with the right people. And it's important to remember that retention is everyone's responsibility. Everyone in an organization owns retention. It cannot be the responsibility of just the recruiter or HR or the CEO. Granted, some people play a greater role than others do, but each and every person in the organization plays a role in retention.

Developing a retention strategy involves several important steps:

1. Knowing the kind of talent your organization needs to be successful.
2. Finding out what those people really value at work.
3. Providing leadership so that the strategy can be implemented.

Implementing these steps is not always easy. In fact, everyone knows that it's a lot harder to ensure that your managers know how to provide excellent feedback to their staff than it is to buy a pool table for the employee lounge. And when all else fails, organizations desperate for a retention Holy Grail will steal ideas from each other without any regard for whether or not the same ideas will work in their own culture.

Consider this scenario and see if you recognize yourself or your organization:

You are the vice president of HR for a medium-sized organization where turnover is a major issue. You arrive at work on Monday morning and find an e-mail from your CEO: "This weekend, I came across this article about a great retention strategy." He wants you to read the article and get to work on making these same ideas happen in your organization. So you start making calls to set up the fruit-and-cheese trays for Fridays and you call vendors for pricing on fighter-pilot training for your sales staff. But before you get through the morning, there is a call from your CEO, the one who sent you the e-mail. Only this time, he wants you to "forget about what I told you in my e-mail. I have an even better idea. On my way to work today, I heard the greatest thoughts on the radio, and here is what we should be doing to stop our people from leaving. . . ."

Okay. So maybe this is bit extreme. But from my experience, there has been a lot of similar extreme retention scrambling going on in American businesses over the past few years. Call it "trying the latest and greatest" or "management by magazine" or whatever, but it is a deadly way to approach retention issues. Why? Because retention must be approached strategically in order to have long-term impact on your organization. And the key to a successful retention strategy is knowing what is going to work for your employees.

Developing a Retention Strategy

To start your strategic approach to retaining talent, I recommend that you first collect demographic data. You need to know the facts about your employees—why they accepted a position, why they leave—in order to develop solid retention strategies for your workforce. Exit interviews, while not perfect, can provide valuable information. If existing employees are asked well-crafted, open-ended questions, they will usually share what's on their minds. However, if you find that you are not getting good information from exit interviews, try calling the exiting employees a month or so after they have left and see if they are willing to talk more freely and share more information.

Next, analyze your turnover rate. How does your organization compare to others in your industry? How much of that turnover could be controlled by the organization? How much was due to personal situations out of your control, such as moves related to the relocation of a spouse or changes in family circumstances like a new baby, divorce, death in family, or illness of a parent.

Now, determine the individuals in your organization whom you simply can't live without. A critical element in understanding your organization is to know who you positively must retain in order to stay in business and/or be successful. This is the talent pool that is critical to your success. Realistically, not everyone in your organization fits into this group; there are people and positions that could be replaced. If you don't know who your superstars are in your organization, take the time to find out. If the organization has recently lost any of these employees, take a close look at the reasons why, and ask yourself this important question: What could have been done to keep them?

And last but not least, find out why people stay with your organization. Most organizations focus a great deal of attention on asking people why they are leaving, when they would be much better served by asking talented employees why they stay. When you focus on why people stay, your retention strategy will be easy to follow. How? You'll simply do more of what they are telling you they like! This information is best collected in personal interviews. But if you aren't comfortable having these types of discussions with employees, consider doing an employee satisfaction survey and/or a 360° assessment to gather data on what people like about your organization.

A recent study called "What Do Employees Really Want? The Perception vs. Reality," conducted by the Center for Effective Organizations, Marshall School of Business, University of Southern California, found that employees most valued:

- Work/life balance.
- Job security.
- Financial rewards.
- Influence/autonomy.
- Professional status.
- Career advancement.
- Pay for performance.

But a word of caution. No list, even one that's well researched, is going to be the perfect list for your organization or the secret to retention. You need to find out what your employees value at work—not what you *think* they value! When your organization knows what your employees value at work, you can begin to plan your strategy.

Retention Strategies in Action

I spent a good deal of my HR career with the Marriott Corp. At one point, Marriott was in the fast-food business and the employee turnover rates were extremely high. The company could have said, "Our turnover is no worse than anyone else's in the fast-food business," but instead we undertook a major study to see if we could positively impact the numbers.

A task force was assembled with representatives from human resources, marketing research, and strategic planning. Interviews were conducted with current and past employees and with people who would be in the target market for us to recruit but who had never worked for the fast-food division of Marriott.

The data was collected and analyzed. And we determined that there were some very interesting patterns that then formed the basis for our retention strategy. We had to make some painful decisions about which employees we could keep and those employees we could not keep for long. For example, we found that if people were solely working for their paychecks, they were vulnerable to an offer from a competitor. Since we were not prepared to make counteroffers, we determined we would not include that group in our retention strategy. And we agreed that we would do our best not to recruit people who were motivated only by a paycheck and by nothing else.

Many employees told us that they valued such things as promotional opportunities within the corporation, training and development, the chance to do interesting work, good working conditions, excellent and affordable benefits, and so on. These were things we could work with and enhance— and make a part of our recruiting and retention strategy.

Unit managers were asked to review our research, and some participated in developing solutions. Employees saw that the organization was really committed to understanding what they wanted and needed, and they could tell that we were really listening to them. Turnover was reduced significantly in the next 12 months and continued to decline thereafter as the organization improved some of its processes and systems.

As your retention strategy begins to unfold, you will learn things that can be used both in recruiting and in orientation of new hires. You will gradually come to know a lot about who is successful and what those people value at your organization. This information should be folded into your competencies so that recruiters can use it during the hiring process. And it should be shared with your managers in the performance review process.

Market Important Elements of Your Retention Strategy Internally

A good retention strategy has some marketing elements to it. I am sure that your organization focuses a great deal of attention and money on its external marketing efforts to attract and retain customers. Most likely, your organization focuses much of its HR budget on attracting new employees. The missing elements are the time and resources needed to market key elements of your company to your existing employees—especially your superstars. We can't stop marketing to our employees just because they work for us. They constantly need to be reminded of why they joined us in the first place.

Consider how you can market your organization's strengths to your current employees. For instance:

- Be sure your current employees know the good things you are doing in the community (hopefully you are!).

- Let employees know of awards and successes that are acknowledged in the press or by professional associations.

- Celebrate your sales, your wins, and your accomplishments and do it publicly so that your employees continue to be proud of where they work.

- Don't overlook the importance of involving your employee's family, if applicable.

A major food service company tells the story of a top sales employee who was injured in a non-job-related accident. The company did more than just send flowers; senior executives visited him in the hospital. Food was sent from the company to the home. They didn't just mail him information on his disability insurance; a representative from the benefits department went to the hospital and walked him through it. Cards and food continued to be delivered even after he was home recovering. A while after he returned to work, he told his wife he was considering taking an offer from a competing company that would pay significantly better. His wife and children reminded him of how well the company had treated him when he was injured and strongly urged him to stay where he was appreciated.

Having an internal marketing strategy is what the authors of McKinsey and Company's *The War for Talent* call the "Employee Value Proposition." They describe an Employee Value Proposition (EVP) as "the holistic sum of everything people experience and receive while they are part of a company— everything from the intrinsic satisfaction of the work to the environment, leadership, colleagues, compensation, and more. It's about how well the company fulfills people's needs, their expectations, and even their dreams."

If you have an employment brand, use it internally as well as externally. Use it to remind your employees about what sets you apart from your competition and what makes your culture strong.

Key People Can Make a Difference

Most organizations completely overlook one of the most important elements of a sound retention strategy—the role of the manager. "People don't work for companies as much as they work for other people," Ruth Branson, a vice president for Shaw's Supermarkets, once said in *The Wall Street Journal*. Translated? Your organization can have all the right values and opportunities, but if your first-line supervisors and managers don't know how to do the basics, you will continue to have retention problems.

I have a niece who graduated from college a few years ago and spent a great deal of time researching where she wanted to work. She looked at an organization's mission and values. She evaluated the company's benefits programs as well as its rewards and recognition structure. The company she joined is a major corporation that is frequently cited as a great place to work. After she had been there for an exciting year, she told me she was thinking of quitting. I was surprised and said, "I thought you loved your company!" She replied, "I do love the company. I've met the founders and I really believe that they are managing a great company. But my manager is a jerk!" I learned a lot from that conversation.

Here's my advice: Train your managers on the basics of management. Do they know how to provide feedback—both positive and negative? Can they do a performance evaluation? Do they know when to praise? Can they coach an employee to reach greater levels of achievement? If your managers aren't good at these basics, then part of your retention strategy must be to provide management development. If you do, rest assured that you are focusing on the things that can make a difference in the daily life of your employees!

And remember this: Talent attracts talent and talent retains talent. Your outstanding people attract others who want to be part of something special. However, if your organization tolerates substandard performance, you stand a greater chance of losing your superstars. They will not want to be a part of an organization that does not discipline substandard performers or develop them into better performers.

The Future of Employee Retention

Many people have recently predicted that retention issues were no longer as critical to organizations. After all, with the economic slowdown and the failures in the dot-com world and other economic pitfalls, they figured that the employee shortage was at an end.

I am sorry to report that nothing could be further from the truth.

Yes, there are many more people looking to fill each available position. More and more resumes arrive daily. The job boards are jammed with people who are looking for positions. However, the talent shortage lingers and demographic studies predict that this shortage will exist for another 10 to 20 years. And this dire prediction doesn't even take into account new businesses, new technologies, and new products that will be coming along.

Which leads me to my final point: Talented people are always in demand. Talented people are no doubt those you identify as your superstars—the people your competition knows about and covets. It is critical to your organization's success and growth over the next few decades that you have a strategy for retaining your talented workforce. It's clear that a well-defined retention strategy is even more important than ever.

Conclusion

It is time for a strategic approach to retention. Developing a solid and effective retention strategy to retain talent is not an easy task, but it has the potential to provide definite rewards for your organization. Certainly, your company will realize financial savings when you have a successful plan to retain more of your superstars; studies have clearly shown that employee turnover is one of a company's highest costs. But there are additional benefits to retaining employees that have nothing to do with the corporate bottom line: companies with fewer turnovers and more satisfied employees have better morale and increased productivity. When your current employees are happy, they turn around and become valuable recruiters. Granted, you can't keep every employee forever. But if you develop a retention strategy that is built on what is most valued in your organization, you can keep your superstars just a little bit longer. And that alone is significant.

The magnitude of having a successful retention strategy is perhaps best summed up in this quote from Scott McNealy, CEO of Sun Microsystems: "Hiring, retaining, and developing great people is the biggest challenge and single greatest key to the success of any business."

I couldn't agree more.

Metrics Are Everything— Why, What, and How to Choose

Kim Burns

Executive Director, Staffing.org

It's intimidating. Metrics, those staffing equations and measurement devices that seek to measure human capital performance, are everywhere. Virtually every HR article or presentation includes metrics. Once an industry buzzword, "metrics" has moved from a monthly exercise to a weekly priority. An overreaction perhaps, but both the business and popular press are reporting that the demand for organization performance data is continuing and dramatically increasing. And it's not just more numbers that are in demand, but also the details behind these numbers called metrics. Indeed, the practice of pitching staffing numbers like breakfast cereal is over. Everyone—analysts, the market, the government—are all going to be a lot more careful and demanding.

To date, however, there's been at least one very obvious problem: Though every product or service touts them, almost all human capital performance metrics come with their own definitions and formulas. And that's confusing. At Staffing.org, a nonprofit organization devoted to human capital performance measurement, we frequently hear the following questions about metrics:

"Every number seems to be a metric; which ones are most important?"
"Which metrics should I start with?"
"Is ROI the most important metric?"
"Which staffing/HRIS providers have the best dashboards?"

This essay will address these questions, and attempt to unscramble the tangled landscape that surfaces when the mere word "metrics" is mentioned. Granted, most organizations are already behind in their ability to measure and understand human capital, which presents an extra challenge for HR leaders. But at Staffing.org, we believe that the challenges of human capital performance measurement are totally worth embracing. To begin, here are some tips that will enable you to respond to the challenge of metrics.

- Don't get caught up in the "measure everything" frenzy; just make sure that you're measuring what is important to your customers and that your human capital metrics are directly tied to organizational objectives. For example: Retention—keeping the people you want to keep—is more important than turnover data.
- Focus on measuring desired outcomes rather than negative statistics. For instance, measure new hire quality rather than the cost of turnover.
- Make sure the numbers are right. Check them yourself and then ask someone else to review them. Over 70 percent of the reported HR performance data that we have analyzed are incorrect.
- Exploit your existing systems to collect data even if you have to manually calculate the metrics. Use general ledger data for any financial input; don't keep your own records. You know the data is accurate and it will fit with any accounting reports.
- If you're acquiring a new staffing or HRIS system, demand that it calculate real performance metrics before signing the contract. The "metrics" that most of these providers are marketing, in the words of a CFO we know, "are just a bunch of HR numbers."

Metrics Q&A

Every number seems to be a metric; which ones are most important?"

Every number is not a metric. The most important metrics are the ones that are most important to your customers. Recruiting has received the most attention of all the human capital performance metrics, probably because the acquisition of human capital is both resource-intensive and critical to organizational success.

"Which metrics should I start with?"

Just start measuring what you're doing now. As the famous Nike ad admonishes, "Just Do It." Don't wait another day, because measuring—just the very act of measuring—improves performance. It also gives you hard data to report. It's important that you first validate the objectives of an assignment or project and then determine the best metrics to measure those objectives.

For example, if your goal is to increase the sales force by 20 percent, two associated metrics are the number of sales hires and the retention of sales employees. The associated metrics then help to clarify what you need to do to get the performance you want.

Understanding candidate flow—applicant-to-interview, interview-to-offer, offer-to-acceptance, and acceptance-to-start ratios—are important activity indicators that will help you to drive sales hires. Retention is generally more complicated. But recruiting to retain—what Staffing.org adviser Lynn Nemser calls "sticky recruiting"—and focusing on retaining the employees you want to retain are activities that will help drive the desired retention metric.

"Is ROI the most important metric?"

Although a fundamental measure, ROI is neither a metric nor an activity indicator. Simply put, ROI is the return/investment or benefit/cost. The more associated costs and benefits that are identified for the same time period, the more accurate and therefore telling the ROI. The ROI should be the key factor in evaluating any notable expenditure or change.

"Which staffing/HRIS providers have the best dashboards?"

The proliferation of proprietary dashboards crammed with data is of great interest to those obsessed with measurement. Just remember that the dashboards themselves are less important than the data they report, so make sure you understand what is being tracked and the basis of the formulations.

Remember, too, that metrics should measure outcomes and results associated with specific objectives. Although much of the dashboard readouts are actually activity indicators, they can be incredibly helpful in providing data to monitor performance so that positive trends can be exploited and negative ones addressed before they undermine performance.

HR Measurement: Why Are We Just Starting to Get Serious?

"Why now?" people often ask about metrics and the sudden interest in measuring. Understanding why HR is just beginning to address HR metrics will help us to do a better job, both now and in the future. Here are some of the reasons that human capital performance and HR haven't been measured until now:

- *We didn't have to.* Senior executives accepted HR as a "soft," unavoidable cost of doing business that managed executive compensation, handled employee processing and support, and, hopefully, prevented lawsuits.
- *There was no sound "metric" starting point.* Although head count, HR staff per 100 employees, and cost per hire were considered common HR "metrics," they don't stand up to hard business questions and challenges. These early metrics ironically helped to reinforce the belief that HR couldn't be measured.
- *You can't measure strategy.* HR became obsessed with becoming strategic in the 1990s. Although the shift was positive, most of the metrics initiatives that followed tried to measure strategy. Metrics should measure outcomes and results associated with objectives.
- *They are too complex.* Many of the HR metrics formulations were just too complex to allow ongoing measurement.
- *There are too many of them.* Some of the first organizations to measure HR tracked more than 100 different HR metrics.
- *There is a lack of standards.* Most HR metrics were developed by competing and proprietary consultants and firms. Although they have certainly all done very good work, the expense and exclusionary nature of working with them has not fostered ongoing HR measurement.

Core metrics should address customer-defined objectives. They should be standard and easy to compare regardless of geography, industry, or size. The right metrics actually drive continuous staffing improvement. Staffing.org is working very closely with academics, companies, and metrics providers globally to further define core human capital performance measures.

That said, just start measuring. The core metrics proposed by Staffing.org allow you to do just that.

Core Metrics

NEW HIRE QUALITY METRIC

The first and most important staffing metric is new hire quality. The standards for new hire quality should be determined by the hiring manager before recruiting is initiated, and the quality measures taken within the first 90 to 180 days of employment. This is after the easiest and hardest periods of new hire assimilation, and also before organizational influences significantly impact the rating.

ACTUAL/CONTRACTED TIME-TO-FILL METRIC

How often are you approached by a hiring manager with an open requisition who needs the position filled yesterday? How often do you, as a recruiter, feel that you are doing your best to get the position filled quickly and with quality candidates, yet you sense some disappointment from the hiring manager in terms of how long it's taken you to get the position filled? This metric addresses these issues.

The "actual" time is the number of days between when recruiting is initiated and when the new employee starts. The "contracted" time is the number of days between the date that recruiting is initiated and the date that the recruiter and hiring manager mutually agree that the position will be filled.

The contracted Time-to-Fill Metric:

- Allows for the fact that some positions take longer to fill than others.
- Encourages and/or requires recruiters to plan before the search begins.
- Lets recruiters set realistic expectations with hiring managers.

- Helps create shared ownership of the process with the hiring manager.
- Provides incentive for recruiters to focus on the quality of the hire in addition to the time required to fill the position.
- Does *not* provide incentive to fill all positions as fast as possible.

By initiating a conversation with the hiring manager regarding the contracted time to fill, you are moving from the role of order taker to business partner.

CUSTOMER SATISFACTION

How many times have you reviewed a job description and wondered which of the many requirements were the most important to the hiring manager? Then, after the hire is made, how many recruiters have gone back and evaluated whether the candidate truly met these qualifications? The customer satisfaction measurement tool allows you to do just that. It provides critical, easy-to-track data to determine the hiring manager's preferences before recruiting is initiated, and then to evaluate staffing performance post-hire. It fosters a professionalism and shared responsibility for filling positions, where the recruiter is viewed as a business partner rather than an order taker.

STAFFING COST RATIO

The staffing cost ratio is a simple, straightforward calculation that:

- Takes into account that in most cases, the higher the pay, the more costly it is to fill a position.
- Reflects the correlation between compensation and candidate supply and demand.
- Allows for an assessment of staffing efficiency for a broad mix of positions.
- Establishes a benchmark to determine external fees.
- Is the best measure of staffing efficiency.

The staffing cost ratio is calculated by dividing total staffing costs by total compensation recruited. This ratio addresses all of the difficulties associated with the cost-per-hire metric. It reflects the correlation in compensation variations in market, level, industry, and geography (i.e., more difficult markets will require higher compensation to secure a candidate).

Total staffing costs include:

- *Internal recruiting costs.* These are your fixed or overhead expenses, comprising everything from recruiter compensation and benefits to office and technology expenses. These operating expenses are defined as virtually all costs required to maintain a staffing operation.

- *External recruiting costs.* These expenses are also referred to as sourcing costs and include advertising and agency and search fees, as well as the costs associated with Internet postings. External recruiting costs include virtually all expenses involved in identifying and recruiting candidates. Sourcing costs are usually incurred for a specific position or positions, but they can also include general initiatives such as employer branding.

Total compensation recruited is the sum of the base annual starting compensation of all external positions filled by staffing operations. For seasonal and part-time hires, this should be the total compensation they would be expected to earn in one year.

Table 47.1 indicates the value of the staffing efficiency ratio as compared to cost per hire and is based on actual examples.

If only cost per hire is considered, it appears that the recruiter of customer service reps is performing better than the recruiter of software engineers. However, by calculating the staffing efficiency ratio of each recruiter, you can see that each recruiter is operating at the same level of efficiency; that is, each is incurring the same expense to their organization to bring in the same amount of compensation.

Table 47.1   Value of Staffing Efficiency Ratio Compared to Cost per Hire

Positions Filled	Average Compensation	Number of Positions Filled	Traditional Cost per Hire	Staffing Efficiency Ratio
Customer service reps	$20,000	500	$2,000	10%
Software engineers	$60,000	100	$6,000	10%

Advancing on Several Fronts

Now that we're really getting serious, the metrics movement is advancing on several fronts. Data standards will make HR measurement much easier if not ubiquitous, and the HR-XML Consortium has taken on this important and daunting challenge.

Also a nonprofit, HR-XML is dedicated to the development and promotion of a standard suite of specifications to enable e-business and the automation of human resources–related data exchanges. The mission of the Consortium is to spare employers and vendors the risk and expense of having to negotiate and agree upon data interchange mechanisms on an ad hoc basis. By developing and publishing open data exchange standards based on Extensible Markup Language (XML), the Consortium provides the means for any company to transact with other companies without having to establish, engineer, and implement many separate interchange mechanisms.

Two projects are currently being considered by HR-XML are:

1. Developing a very generalized schema to support the interchange of metrics data.
2. Developing a catalogue or taxonomy of core HR performance metrics.

In addition to data standards, advances in HR measurement are proceeding on three other fronts:

1. Human capital performance metrics research.
2. Education and training.
3. And the most important, starting to measure.

In 2003, everyone is looking forward to fresh starts and hoping for a better economy. Change is prominent on every organization's to-do list: agencies, recruiting firms, and even systems if the funding can be justified. And although rarely at the top, we're glad to see that "measure better" or "better measures" at least made most lists. Our goal is to see human capital performance metrics on all HR lists in the future, providing staffing measurement that is neither intimidating nor confusing.

48

How to Make Trends and Influence Strategy: Becoming an Effective Leader of the Recruiting Function

Dan Guaglianone

Senior Director Recruiting, Merck's Research Laboratories

W hen talking about trends in recruiting, many industry observers tend to focus on a single issue within the discipline, such as recruitment technology, employment branding, Internet recruiting, or trends in workforce demographics. It's important to understand these issues and their impact on recruiting. And, in fact, this is what many of us are charged with every day: to become experts for a particular area and make the best decisions that relate to that area.

But mastering a single issue does not guarantee that you're in step with your organization's business objectives. And it rarely yields a world-class recruiting function.

As recruiters, we must also understand the interrelationship between the various recruiting practices, as well as the strategies of the business and the influences of the market. Recruiting tools and tactics change regularly. And so do the trends and objectives that affect business strategy. As recruiting professionals, it's critical that we forecast those changes and prepare strategies to address them before they occur.

By stepping up to such challenges, recruiting professionals will be in lockstep with the business and lead innovation in the recruiting field. Organizations will soon find that they can attract a more effective pool of talent, keep talent acquisition costs low, streamline the discipline for greater efficiency, and perhaps even realize new opportunities for generating revenue.

What Is Good Leadership?

In the past, being a good leader meant having your finger on the pulse of the latest trends in recruiting. Leaders would know which classified ads yielded the best candidates, which sourcing firm to partner with, and which professional organizations provided the best networking opportunities.

Times have changed. In an economy that is increasingly service-driven, and with price comparisons via the Internet driving down margins on many products, organizations must work harder than ever to control overhead costs. CEOs now place value on a function by how it impacts the bottom line. HR professionals, including recruiters, are pushed to demonstrate how they add value to the business by increasing revenue, decreasing expenses, or helping the organization make the best use of all available resources.

This is not to say that tactics are not important. But where tactics were once driven by past experience—and perhaps a little intuition—today they must be driven by the needs of the organization. Recruiting leaders are focusing less on where to advertise open positions and which technology has the best functionality, and more on what skills the organization needs in the long term and what systems best streamline the overall recruiting process.

To be such a leader, you must know the goals of the organization and understand the drivers of corporate strategy. You must be able to relate how recruiting can facilitate the strategy and enhance business results. And this means being invited to the table when the strategy is being formulated and discussed.

Managers of all disciplines continuously struggle to get to the table, to be seen as valuable contributors and innovators. But there's no magic formula or secret handshake for achieving this level of recognition. Quite simply, you must develop new ways for your discipline to create value by:

- Understanding all of the practices of recruiting and how they work together under various conditions.
- Comprehending the vision of the business.
- Being aware of external trends in recruiting and your industry, and then projecting how they will have an impact on talent acquisition in both the short and long term.
- Communicating challenges, solutions, and results in a way that's meaningful to the senior management team.

Let's take each in turn to see how they can help recruiting add value to your organization, and help you become an organizational leader.

Getting Your House in Order

The first step is to get a complete picture of the various practices within the recruiting function in your organization. Create a model that depicts these practices and how they interrelate. With this model, you can begin to spot synergies and analyze challenges.

As you craft this model, understand the difference between a practice and a tool. A practice is an important activity that drives the recruiting cycle. A tool is an enabler that facilitates greater efficiencies or effectiveness within one or more practices.

For example, candidate sourcing is a practice. Internet-based recruiting and job board strategies are tools that support the candidate sourcing practice. Knowledge management (managing information about active and passive job candidates) is a practice. Applicant tracking and recruiting automation software are tools that support the knowledge management practice.

It will be tempting to see technology as a separate practice. But technology alone does not make you an innovator or a thought leader. Rather, the way in which you use the technology to solve a business problem is what differentiates you from others. And that differentiation must be your focus.

Exhibit 48.1 shows the model we developed for the Unisys recruiting discipline. The cycle begins with forecasting, with each practice feeding into the next. Each practice is centrally managed to ensure coherency and to recognize synergies. All of our recruiters, regardless of their individual responsibilities, play a role in supporting each of these practices.

When the business is faced with a new challenge, we analyze that challenge against the model. From that analysis, we create a plan for taking advantage of our strengths and overcoming our weaknesses.

One such challenge was a shift in the Unisys recruiting strategy from 2001 to 2002, moving from recruiting large numbers of employees with midlevel IT skills to small numbers of employees for business-leader positions.

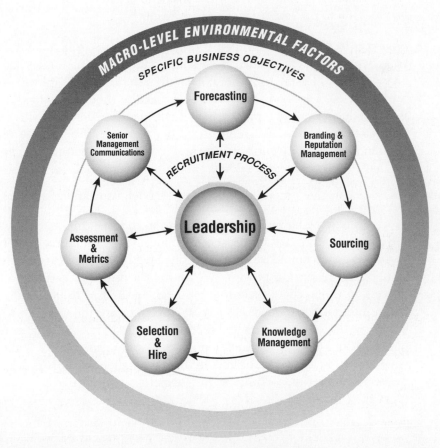

Exhibit 48.1 Model for Unisys Recruiting Discipline. (Reprinted with permission.)

We began with an analysis against this model, and developed a holistic strategy based on differences we saw in:

- *Forecasting.* In 2001, it was difficult to forecast exactly how many IT workers we needed, or which skill sets we required. Often, these decisions depended on new contract wins or the extension of existing contracts. In 2002, forecasting was more defined, dependent on the business's strategy for growth in predefined market segments.

- *Branding and reputation management.* In 2001 we worked to build our brand to inform candidates about what Unisys was and what it had to offer to employees. In 2002 we shifted our communications strategy, recognizing that our new business leaders would be the brand going forward, that they would shape the Unisys reputation in their given markets.

- *Sourcing.* In 2001 we often identified job candidates from a database of active job seekers gleaned from traditional recruiting tactics such as job boards, classified ads, our corporate web site, and employee referrals. In 2002 we had to actively seek out the thought leaders in a given industry and determine how their expertise matched the requirements of Unisys. We reorganized our recruiters into an internal sourcing team to help control costs and optimize the recruiting talent we had. We continued to focus on employee referrals as the best source for job candidates.

- *Selection and hire.* To attract industry leaders, our selection and hire process had to be far more hands-on than in the past. In addition, we recognized that we had to create a mechanism that would require our recruiters—and our executives—to demand high-end skills as the start of the recruiting process. We utilized a principal certification process by which these incoming business leaders had to be certified by an internal Unisys board of experts before beginning work for the company. Because managers and recruiters wanted to be sure that candidates would pass the certification process, they spent a great deal of time and effort ensuring the quality of the candidates. This practice drove down the time to hire for these experts and increased the quality of the candidates.

By using this model for this and many other types of analyses, we've not only realized greater operational efficiencies but also found several opportunities for cost control. By the end of 2001, Unisys was realizing a time to fill of just 45 days, while our cost per hire was approximately half the IT industry average.

Understanding the Business Strategy

To get a true, big-picture view of your organization's strategy and its vision for the future, you must look at the organization from as many different points of view as possible. But first you must educate yourself in business theory and terminology. Some of the most ambitious recruiters go back to school for an MBA, but in most cases a simple dedication to educating yourself on business issues is sufficient.

Start by looking at your organization's earnings statement. Do you know what all of the terms in that statement mean? How do results for the current year compare with past years? What do analysts think of the organization's performance?

Listen to what the president or CEO says about business drivers and the organization's strategic direction to both internal and external audiences. How do those messages compare and complement one another? What do industry observers think of the overall vision? How does that vision compare with what competitors are doing?

In addition, build your own network of contacts within the company at various levels and across disciplines. Talk with these contacts about how the organization is internalizing the vision and how they are working to execute against that vision. Listen to what they predict for the future; those in the field often can spot emerging trends before those at headquarters.

As you gain insight into the business strategy, think creatively about how talent acquisition and management can help the organization achieve its goals. For example, if your organization plans to launch a new product line or enter a new area of business, how will that affect required skills in the long term? How can you begin preparations for growth or a strategy shift now?

When Lawrence A. Weinbach became the chairman, president, and CEO of Unisys in 1997, he presented his vision of Unisys, then a technology company specializing in high-end hardware, as a services business that would provide expertise in networking, systems integration, consulting, and outsourcing. That affected not only what skills we looked for, but also our ideas on compensation, recruiting tactics, employee education, and employee retention and development. Five years later, we're now seeing a shift in customer needs from implementation services to ongoing management and services. Recognizing such shifts enables us to get the skills we need early, helping the business enhance customer service and realize opportunities for revenue growth as quickly as possible.

Recognizing External Trends

Understanding and supporting business strategy makes you a valuable partner in the organization. But what sets you apart as a thought leader both internally and externally is how well you can recognize and react to external trends.

There are several factors that will have a significant impact on talent acquisition in the long term, including the shrinking workforce, development of new technology, and shortage of math and science teachers.

THE SHRINKING WORKFORCE

Trends in demographics reveal that organizations will continue to have a smaller workforce pool from which to hire. According to the U.S. Census Bureau, by 2035 there will be approximately 60 million people in the United States 65 years and older. The United Nations expects that by the year 2050 there will be nearly 2 billion people in the world 60 years and older.

As a result, organizations around the world are wrestling with new strategies for recruiting and retention. Some are looking for ways to attract retirees back into the workforce. Some are reevaluating the organization's benefits and compensation offerings. Some are intensifying their recruiting efforts overseas, while others are examining the potential of outsourcing noncore disciplines. As a leader, you must define a strategy that will best meet the needs and capabilities of your organization.

DEVELOPMENT OF NEW TECHNOLOGY

There are myriad tools and processes available for attracting job candidates. New software packages can monitor the level and quality of traffic from individual job boards and search engines to help you refine your online strategy. Applicant tracking and communication tools can speed the hiring process while making the experience more fulfilling for the job candidate. You must be aware of the technologies, as well as how these technologies can improve your own operations.

SHORTAGE OF MATH AND SCIENCE TEACHERS

Today's organizations rely heavily upon technology for generating revenue and effectively managing the business. But such dependence requires skilled workers to manage and enhance technology now and in the future. Without a strong educational infrastructure to encourage future generations to enter technology-related fields, organizations will find it increasingly difficult to attract and retain the technology workers they need.

Keeping up with the latest trends and determining which are relevant to you requires diligence and active communications with experts in your field. Read HR trade publications and publications related to your organization's industry and talent needs. Read the leading business publications to see what trends they believe are important. Attend HR and industry conferences; if possible, talk one-on-one with thought leaders at those events. Network with your peers at every opportunity to see what trends they're watching. Finally, when you see a trend that you believe will have a significant impact, become an active participant. Join task forces, advisory councils, and other organizations that are working to influence the future.

Of Communications and Metrics

One key skill of recruiting leadership is managing the expectations of senior managers. Work with them to understand their recruiting requirements, and inform them of what they can reasonably expect.

Exhibit 48.2A is a model I use to help managers understand the implications of their demands. Each side of the triangle represents recruiting time, cost, and quality, respectively. The goal in recruiting is always to get the highest-quality candidate for the organization. But that quality will be influenced by how much time and money you are willing to invest to find and attract the candidate.

For example, if a manager demands high-quality hires in a short time frame, costs will increase (see Exhibit 48.2B). If a manager must keep costs low and hire people quickly, it is likely that the quality of hires will be

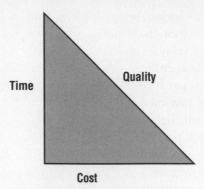

Exhibit 48.2A   Model of Implications of Manager Demands. (Reprinted with permission.)

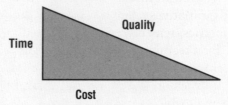

Exhibit 48.2B   Impact of High-Quality Hires in Short Time Frame. (Reprinted with permission.)

compromised (see Exhibit 48.2C). Using graphics like these facilitates understanding, and sometimes even greater cooperation, from executives of other disciplines.

Once you begin to see the challenges, solutions, trends, innovations, and successes of your discipline, you must be able to communicate these effectively to senior managers. This means telling them of your successes in terms to which they can relate. It also means having strong metrics that are meaningful to them.

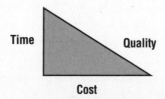

Exhibit 48.2C   Impact of Low Costs and Quick Hires. (Reprinted with permission.)

Recruiting, like all industries, has terms and measurements that are meaningful to its practitioners. People outside the industry, however, often do not understand the relevance of these terms.

For example, in the recruiting profession we tend to use metrics such as "time to fill" and "cost per hire" as measures of recruiting effectiveness. But to a CEO, these are just measures of how recruiting is keeping its costs down. That's important, but not as critical as how well the function is able to get the skills the business needs or how it is helping the company generate revenue. We know anecdotally that getting the right people and skills on board at the right time leads to greater business success. But how do you back it up with objective proof?

Getting to this level of measurement is not easy, and there is no clearly defined process. HR thought leaders are working to design effective metrics that show how HR initiatives relate to workforce productivity.

Regardless of metrics, remember to stay focused on the single most important objective for a recruiter: to attract the highest-quality candidates in a way that will yield the best benefit for the organization. Whether we can or cannot accurately measure our success today in this area, it is the single most important way in which we impact revenue, because people with the right skills who are the right fit for the organization will work to drive it forward. Anything less will compromise its capabilities.

The Future of Recruiting: The Human Capital Marketplace

John Sumser

Founder, Interbiznet, Inc.

Recruiting in a New Environment

A relationship is a sequence of emotional experiences. Given a slow-growth economy and a growing distrust in large corporate institutions and their promises, recruiting is increasingly about the development and execution of trustworthiness in emotion-laced relationships.

Now, more than ever, effective recruiting will focus on the 20 percent of hires who produce 80 percent of the results. These critical hires are not best handled with automated sourcing methods, but depend on successful mastery of time-honored search techniques. Like other acquisition disciplines, the most valuable assets can only be purchased through diligent negotiation and the pursuit of win-win outcomes.

Although the figures are impressive, only half of the population uses the Internet for any form of job search. For the most part, the important

20 percent are not a part of this universe. Automated support systems that resemble customer relationship management tools are essential for acquiring this most critical talent. The front end that provides source information, however, will not come from job boards or other Web traffic/surveillance methods.

This suggests a window of opportunity for traditional search firms—and a number of development possibilities for the incumbent vendors of recruiting software. Essentially, there is a market for solutions that directly treat the question of the hard-to-find candidate. This essay explores that issue.

Emergence of Relationship Management

In spite of the sluggish economy, demographics-caused labor shortages are a fact of life in some professions and regions. More than any other factor, the labor shortage and its consequences are driving the rapid adoption of both workforce planning and Future Employee Relationship Management Systems (FERMS). While alumni management tools (Select Minds, Aptium) provide audience tailoring for one subset of the FERMS market, most offerings currently resemble work flow templates as a subset of an applicant tracking system (ATS).

Although Hire.com introduced the idea of talent relationship management in the late 1990s, almost all ATS companies offer some form of FERMS tool. However, Hire.com continues to lead the industry. The essential difference between the Hire.com offering and other tools lies in the objectives of the system. While most FERMS facilitate the tracking of a variety of activities and documents (correspondence, meetings, interviews, and credentials), the Hire.com system is designed to produce interested and available candidates. As a result, the work flow prescribed by the system is fundamentally different and goal-directed. Interestingly, when coupled with a nonautomated front end, the Hire.com tool set appears to be more useful than other systems as a solution for the hard-to-find candidate.

Surprisingly, recruiter training plays a key role in the effective development of relationships that can be readily converted into useful "inventory." The coming years will include a heavy focus on the development of conceptual aids and the broad base of competencies required by recruiters who attempt to build relationships as the key to guaranteeing labor supply availability.

The Industry Matures

The revolution is over. After nearly a decade of development, electronic tools and recruitment automation are no longer novelties that need evangelical sales efforts. Although there is a significant market of late adopters, sales techniques are maturing to focus on return on investment and more strategic benefits.

Maturity suggests that new, industry-oriented institutions are about to emerge. With a clearly observable network, the infrastructure required to maintain and improve a solid professional performance will come. We anticipate the arrival of professional accreditation, training, and development in the near term. Associations that meaningfully add to the overall growth and development of the industry and its customers are not far behind. The last remnants of nonprofits designed to compete with industry players will have short lives.

Sophisticated professionals in the human capital marketplace will have skills in procurement, network development-maintenance, partnership development, outsourcing, design trade-offs, and process optimization.

In *keiretsus* (co-prosperity partnerships), corporations will transfer staff among themselves for better cultural, career, or job fit. Experienced managers will similarly let OEMs and VARs hire away staff who desire more focus on specific (noncore) functions (e.g., Unix system administration and Visual Basic programming), and hire from these same partners project leaders, sourcing managers, and strategic planners. Some of the best sources of future employees can be found within a firm's value chain, including clients.

The next step in industry maturity will involve tools that manage staffing throughout the value chain.

The Industry Is a Network

It appears that there are network-related principles that underlie the structure of biology, electronics, human personality, social environments, power grids, and physics. Bridging complexity and fractals, network science, which is in the earliest stages of development itself, suggests that many phenomena can be explained by looking at the nodes and links that comprise some form of underlying network.

The Internet itself gives substantial credence to the idea.

There seems to be a number of repeated patterns involving the development of linkages between sites and relative market dominance. Rather than the first-mover advantage that was proclaimed so heavily in the dot-com days, it appears that market leadership is a function of connectedness (traffic plus inbound links) and fitness (suitability and reliability for a specific task).

In niche after niche (think Yahoo!, Google, and AOL), we see a player with traffic and revenues that are 4 to 10 times those of the closest competitor. Generally, there is a cluster of operations at the second level. The third level is composed of 20 to 1,000 businesses that are generally one-fourth to one-tenth the size of the second level. This distribution, known as a power curve, is symptomatic of an industry that is a network. Dominance is traffic, revenue, and inbound links. Maintaining dominance involves continuing to be the fittest for the task. The dominant players currently appear to be Monster.com, Salary.com, Recruitsoft, RecruitUSA, Adecco, Brainbench, and a few others, each in its own niche.

For the second-level players, there are two choices (none of them include price wars): expansion of the dominance characteristics (larger sales forces, advertising, and linkage development) or radical improvement of their suitability for the task. Movement between levels in a network requires significant investments in user benefits, name recognition, and traffic development. The incumbent niche dominators have a virtual lock on the top slot unless their challengers step up to radical improvements. The dollars per percentage of market share calculation is a steep one.

Google displaced all of its earlier competitors by focusing on fitness and customer experience. This is the approach pursued by IIRC, Hire.com, and, we think, Manpower. It is well worth reading up on Google's various initiatives as it displaced the first-mover incumbents.

Not all is lost for the second- and third-level players. The notion that each niche contains a dominant player does not eliminate the alternatives. Rather, it means that the effort required to topple an incumbent dominant player is quite extraordinary.

It is entirely possible to build a handsome, profitable modest-growth company based on a firm grasp of the second or third level. It takes superhuman effort to displace the market dominators (although some second-level players are closer than others). A clear understanding that market dominance is tied to customer satisfaction (both at current levels and at beyond-the-current-market levels) is essential to any strategy that supposes to unseat one of the dominant players.

Job Hunting Online

Fifty-two million Americans have looked online for information about jobs, and more than four million do so on a typical day.

Overall, these figures represent a more than 60 percent jump in the number of online job hunters from March 2000, when we first asked about the subject. We found then that 32 million had used the Internet to check out jobs. Moreover, there has been about a 33 percent hike in the daily traffic related to job searching. On a typical day in March 2000, about three million Internet users were searching for job information.

These figures come from a 2002 Pew Internet Project survey of 2,259 Internet users. The margin of error is plus or minus two percentage points. Among those who are the most likely to do online searches for jobs:

- *Young Internet users between the ages of 18 and 29.* Some 61 percent of them have looked for jobs online, compared to 42 percent of those ages 30–49 and 27 percent of those ages 50–64.
- *Men.* Some 50 percent of online men had sought job information, compared to 44 percent of online women. On a typical day, twice as many online men are job hunting as women.
- *The unemployed.* About 51 percent of those who do not currently have jobs have Internet access. On a typical day, a tenth of the unemployed with Internet access are online scouring job sites, compared to 4 percent of the wired Americans who have full-time jobs.
- *African-Americans and Hispanics.* While 44 percent of whites have done online job seeking, close to 60 percent of African-Americans with Internet access and online Hispanics have sought job information on the Internet.
- *Those in sales-related jobs.* Some 55 percent of those with Internet access who currently hold media sales jobs have looked for new job information online, compared to 44 percent of the online executives and professionals, and 49 percent of the wired clerical and office workers. However, on a typical day online the most active job searchers are online office workers. Skilled laborers and service workers are the least likely to have done job hunting online.
- *Those in higher income brackets and with high education levels.* High socioeconomic status is correlated with online job searching. Those who

live in households with incomes above $75,000 are more likely than others with lesser incomes to have done job searches online, and those with college or graduate degrees are more likely than those with only high school diplomas to have explored the job classifieds online.

The findings clearly reflect two broad trends: First, Internet use is growing, especially for important types of information searches. Second, there has been turmoil and tightening of the job market. As of May 2002, the U.S. Department of Labor reported the current unemployment rate at 5.8 percent, or 8.4 million people.

It is not surprising, then, to see that nearly half of all Internet users have looked for information about a job online.

Market Consolidation

The earliest attempts to organize the human capital (HC) marketplace focused exclusively on the labor end of the equation. It is no accident that the form that emerged in both medieval guilds and early twentieth-century labor unions was a combination of regional and professional interests. In the HC market, the issues are cultural, political, and professional. As a result, the market has a native tendency to revert to these structural dynamics.

The dot-com land rush introduced thousands of companies with national and international ambition to the market. Throughout the buildup, pundits and analysts consistently forecasted a radical shrinking of the overall number with a final market consolidation featuring two or three key players. Many of the largest competitors, from CareerBuilder to BrassRing, based their strategies on the assumption that consolidation was inevitable.

Indeed, more than a third of the Internet-inspired initiatives went out with a whimper during the protracted economic downturn. What is surprising is the solid number of firms that survived the so-called consolidation. Relying heavily on the fact that the HC market is intensively niched, companies scaled back their expenses, moved to organic growth, reduced unnecessary development costs, and focused on the fundamentals. Rather than a massive retrenchment to a few players, the industry emerged from the consolidation process as a tiered structure.

With the revolutionary rhetoric gone from the marketing literature, it is becoming easier to discriminate among the choices available to human resources and recruiting professionals. Like politics, human capital is a lo-cal phenomenon with a national component.

Workstream Rolls Up an Anticyclical

Led by Mike Mullarkey, a former Sony Consumer Products executive, Workstream (WSTM) is a classic roll-up company. At the very bottom of the market, Mullarkey was busily acquiring a series of companies (including job boards, Web design firms, and workforce management operations) to supplement an existing portfolio of HC-related operations.

By combining outplacement and career management services with tradi-tional HC product lines, Mullarkey hopes to develop a company that will be able to avoid the traditional boom and bust cycle associated with the HC market. Although it may seem like a solution to last year's problem, the company *is* built around a team of solid and experienced managers who know how to stick to the fundamentals.

Although we cannot be certain that HR buyers will understand Work-stream's vision, the organizational design is a logical choice. Like ADP and other HR service providers, a model that accounts for the ups and downs of the labor market should have staying power. The firms that lost the most ground during the downturn were those that had a method for collecting revenue only during times of employment expansion.

Workstream operates by taking advantage of the down cycle in the in-dustry. Difficult investments made by entrepreneurs and their backers plowed the ground required to build the industry into its current state. Un-fortunately, those early investments did not produce much in the way of protectable intellectual property. Hopefully, future business models will in-clude an emphasis on the necessary research and development required to move the game forward.

Monster.com Achieves Market Dominance

As mentioned elsewhere, 50 percent of all job hunters spend time looking for work at Monster.com's web site. The company owns 40 percent of in-dustry revenue and 40 percent of traffic, and has four times the number of paying customers of any competitor. As it is with other key hubs in the on-line arena, the firm is a huge iceberg in the middle of a tranquil harbor.

Monster manages to accomplish this feat while carrying the rest of the holdings of its Monster parent firm. The challenges for the other firms in the arena are simple:

- How to offer services that clearly complement Monster.com's offerings.
- Whether or not Monster.com intends to enter or defend in their space.

Clearly, Monster.com will have to reassert its prowess as a growth-oriented operation. Like all of the other players in the game, the recession eliminated growth as a consideration. The firm chose to expend its resources on the improvement of customer satisfaction and has built a powerhouse operation that exceeds customer expectations. By doing so, it has solidified its brand with paying customers and poses a serious threat in adjacent niches.

Building a robust and profitable business in the HC industry need not be hampered by the fact that a single firm is dominant. Rather, as it has been historically, smaller, more agile firms simply navigate around the iceberg. The only problem comes if their growth ambitions include dominance.

We're betting that sort of scenario will be minor during the coming years. As accounting scandals and bad business practices, spawned by the fever of the late 1990s, continue to surface, buyers will show some preference for small ethical companies. In a way, the biggest meaning of Monster's dominant position is that not all companies should become multibillion-dollar enterprises. That's a good thing.

Meanwhile, as the industry leader, Monster is more vulnerable to the fitness question than other players. It is traditional for the industry leader to demonstrate leadership. While we do argue that the firm is setting the standard for excellence in customer service, the areas of standardization, ethics, professional education, and conceptual expansion are currently wanting. We expect Monster to move into these responsibilities over the coming year.

Identity Management: Disruptive Technology

It will not be long until every software application uses some form of identity management technology to recognize users and their preferences. A stand-alone application hosted on the corporate mainframe requires simple levels of security management. But when all computers are essentially connected to all other computers, the question of levels of security, preferences, and interoperability drive identity management out into the open.

In the past, it was adequate to control this information in a database. They weren't really users; they were "access permissions." As the demand for identity services grows, however, so do questions that reach across classes of users so that policies may be applied, but individuals still experience uniqueness.

It's not going to be a fancy revolution with a lot of new gee-whiz technologies. It will be a singularly disciplined and large market research project. The only way that identity management schemes can work (and therefore save us from endless tweaking of endless systems) will be if identity management companies can come up with a manageable set of categories and classes that can be used to achieve the conflicting objectives of customization and policy. Once solved, however, they provide a fascinating foundation for a reorganization of the human capital marketplace. It is as simple as the fact that much of the profiling done in personnel-related matters is the very same profiling that will be accomplished by identity management firms.

Likely to have a deeper relationship with their customers (because they are not only in the game during job searches), the identity management firms will have their hands on a technology that is disruptive in our market.

Population Growth and Labor Markets

For employees, the first decade of the twenty-first century will be a time of unparalleled opportunity. On average, there will be 2.6 new jobs created for each new person who enters the American labor market. The competition to acquire new employees and retain existing personnel will reach dimensions that are unthinkable in today's environment. By the end of this decade, the overall labor shortage, measured in unfilled jobs, will be 21.3 percent, according to the federal government. And its statistics on the subject are usually very conservative.

Surprisingly, white-collar, college-educated workers will not be the category with the greatest shortages (although 1.5 out of 10 of those desks will be empty). Lower-level service and production jobs that require little formal education but a degree of on-the-job-training (OJT) will be harder to fill, sooner. This implies that the first wave of impact will involve watching professional and managerial employees cleaning their own offices and doing the landscaping after they have finished loading the trucks.

Already, we are witnessing sustained shortages in retail, hospitality, and health care. The immediate future will bring additional shortages in transportation, agriculture, and low-end manufacturing. The white-collar (or "talent") shortages are still another couple of years away.

Interestingly, there are clear and simple-to-execute methods for developing labor availability forecasts that can be readily combined with retention program management to more effectively optimize the efforts of a given firm in a given labor market. With a realistic forecast in hand, the correct investments in acquisition and retention can be argued like any other business decision. The data is readily available from federal and local government sources.

Shifting Compensation Paradigms

With nearly 500 sites broadcasting the compensation information provided by Salary.com, a sea change took place with little or no notice. Today, any employee, with a few simple clicks, can obtain a ballpark estimate of their market worth. For an additional $20, they can receive a detailed, substantial report on their value in the local and national markets.

For the first time ever, this places employers at a distinct disadvantage in the negotiation process. Formerly, the person negotiating on the company's behalf always had the upper hand in salary conversations. Now, that person must be prepared to deal with a fully informed partner in a negotiation. In terms of the equity of the transaction, it moves things to a more level playing field. In terms of competence, everyone charged with these important negotiations now requires more formal training.

Workforce Management and Optimization

The notion that the members of a company's team could be deployed more effectively is the holy grail of productivity improvement projects. Limited discipline in the human capital acquisition process, coupled with even less postacquisition follow-up, makes the process of considering the right person for the right job seem impossible. However, like capital equipment utilization in a manufacturing environment, the question is as simple as understanding individual capacity and overall corporate needs.

During the past five years, the level of HR automation has rapidly increased—to the point of data overload. Much is measured, although it is rarely the right thing. Although some effort has been made, the automation of the acquisition process is still disconnected from the rest of the organization. HR remains a silo.

Workforce optimization is as simple as matching a detailed inventory of human capital against a detailed analysis of work requirements. More suited to complex engineering environments in its early evolution (because of engineers' insistence on detailed task definitions), the technique is slowly migrating toward broader usage.

Slowly at first, workforce optimization will become the rallying point for broad enterprise-level integration of the various silos of information technology. The combination of financial, technical, and human capital measurement makes first-line decision making simpler and executive decision making more powerful. We anticipate several interesting moves in this arena from the large HR outsourcing operations who, in order to manage the risks of their contracts, will be more or less forced to seek deeper integration with the rest of the company's IT infrastructure.

Outsourcing: Exult, Inc.

Jim Madden founded Exult, Inc. in 1998. Designed to provide complete HR outsourcing, the firm is poised to take advantage of the traditional pendulum swing toward the outsourcing of HR functions. The company achieved powerful momentum in its start-up phase. With revenues rapidly closing in on the half-billion-dollars-per-year mark, Exult is clearly the fastest-growth firm in the HC industry.

Outsourcing human resources departments can be a good idea. Although the responsibility for actually gaining market advantage from employees cannot be delegated, many of the traditional HR functions are tedious and distract from the real business of running a company. Typically, however, outsourcing has been used to clean house in HR; a temporary outsourcing project over a couple of years allows senior management to eliminate the obstacles that accrue from a function that yields little enduring value. Perhaps the best feature of the idea is that accountability and measurement are necessary components of a subcontract, while they can be nearly impossible to execute within the existing environment.

Over the long haul, outsourcing the acquisition, development, and disposition of human capital will be understood as folly, however. This is the core expertise of any company. The outsourcing phenomenon, we predict, will be finished within five years, for this cycle of the pendulum at least.

Marketing Alternatives Post–September 11

A significant component of the fallout from September 11 is the virtual failure of the industry trade show. Although there was always a question of the performance of an investment in these operations, me-too marketing dominated the industry's mind-set. In the months following the disaster, the marketing and advertising techniques and investments have flowered powerfully.

Rather than building a booth designed to compete for attention with hundreds of others, the most sophisticated companies in our industry are focusing heavily on specific customers and effective online advertising. The two initiatives of improvements in customer satisfaction and explicitly targeted advertising are proving to be far more powerful than a paid speaker's slot at a trade show. Since paying customers are no longer traveling, getting their attention means giving them something that they need.

Monster.com, the industry leader in customer satisfaction improvement, has reorganized its entire operation so that customer satisfaction receives the highest priority in all functional decisions. Hire.com, the consistent leader of the technical development arm of the industry, has taken the question to heart as well. Their thought leadership program sets standards for moving the ball forward well beyond the bounds of our industry.

On a tactical level, all successful vendors in the industry have mastered the delivery of "webinars" and other electronic outreach. Coupling effective online advertising with useful information is the key to building long-term value-based relationships with customers.

Gone are the free cocktails and key chains of the trade show era. In their place are solid programs that directly benefit customers in their jobs. It is an important trend.

Viability of the JAD Marketplace

The job board, classified advertising, and corporate employment page component of our industry is often referred to as the "sourcing" end of the business. In reality, it is a slightly more complex version of the area that advertising agencies used to manage and bill as "media planning." The job advertising distribution (JAD) companies are those firms that derive their revenues from helping customers target their Web (and increasingly other forms) advertising and distribute job ads around the Internet.

Advertising, unlike various other forms of commerce, is a very elastic product. In other words, it is terribly hard to identify the 50 percent of your advertising expenditures that you know are wasted. As a result, the sourcing market will always have room for a large variety of small players who offer access to regional and professional niches.

The JAD companies handle the inherent complexity of the market by offering customers the opportunity to use and measure various services under a single invoice program. From HodesIQ to RecruitUSA to IIRC, these companies have weathered the economic hard times and validated the value of their service in the most difficult of circumstances. As the economy returns to warmer times, these firms will produce a significant volume of real market leadership. Their task, in the short term, is relative differentiation. That will be accomplished through a range of additional services.

Role Shift for Enterprise Software

Most of the major enterprise software vendors (i.e., Oracle, Lawson, PeopleSoft, and SAP) view the HC acquisition market as an environment for transactions they can claim because they are on the desktop. In other words, the offerings from these vendors are limited by the imaginations of their management. While the approach guarantees that a customer will experience the marketplace as risk-free, enterprise software tends to choke off the possibility of process innovation. As a result, the leading software firms are beginning to deploy more responsive systems.

Retention: Understanding the Pull Factor

Human capital flows through an organization. To further refine that notion, you could say that social network nodes link to some network; when a company acquires a new worker, that node becomes, over time, increasingly linked to the company network (some obviously more than others). At a later point, the node goes through some form of transformation and becomes linked to yet another organization.

It is now possible to understand that final step. A clear answer to the question "Where do people go when they leave our company?" has eluded most organizations. As a result, retention programs focus on putting up fences rather than a potentially more proactive approach.

Where do people go when they leave our company?

The answer is available by mining the data in a resume database that contains 20 million (or so) resumes. Much smaller and you lose the possibility that the data is scientific. At 20 million, the possibility that the data is valid looms high on the probability scale. Of course, the answer is a network map that might even include a subset question (i.e., "When do they return?").

This simple example points out that in the labor supply, there is a flow toward other networks. A deep analysis should show that some "next stops" in the flow have a great deal of influence on the process even though they are small consumers in volume terms. Large resume database houses will be offering products like this over the coming years.

Assessing Future Recruitment Trends with The New York Times Job Market Confidence Index

Carl Haacke
Economist and Consultant to The New York Times Job Market

The need for useful, insightful information is in great demand today among human resources professionals who must continually gauge the hiring trends that affect their companies' bottom lines. While many of today's available economic indicators hold great value, they report on past performance of the economy. For example, the unemployment rate is a month old by the time the government announces the figure. The gross domestic product (GDP), the core measure of the strength of the nation's economy, is three months old by the time final figures are announced, and even then they can be subject to revision.

As a result, it is often challenging to make business decisions about the future while relying on data from the past. Solid information and research are critical to making effective planning decisions, so the better the information available, the better the decisions.

In February 2002, The New York Times Job Market, the print and online recruitment services offering of *The New York Times*, introduced the Job Market Confidence Index to provide the human resource community with insight into *future* hiring trends in the metropolitan New York market.[1] The forward-looking nature of The New York Times Job Market Confidence Index provides key measures to help identify recruitment trends in a perpetually changing economy. The Index provides insight on changes occurring in New York area recruitment activity because it surveys perceptions of employers and job seekers about what they see occurring, what they expect to happen in coming months, and what they plan to do about it.

For example, the results of The New York Times Job Market Confidence Index can help predict when employers are likely to plan hiring again. It can help predict when they might lay off, whether they believe their staff levels are sufficient for their current workloads, what their plans are for salary increases, the salary expectations of job seekers, and other key determinants of market conditions.

The New York Times Job Market Confidence Index has three components:

1. *Topline data.* The Index's topline data provides an overview of the level of confidence that employers and job seekers have in the job market. (See Exhibit 50.1.) To get these results, employers are asked questions about their intended plans to hire or lay off staff and about current vacancies within their company. Job seekers are asked questions designed to reveal their perceptions about the availability of jobs in the marketplace.

2. *Current conditions.* The Index also analyzes current employment conditions through a set of questions that probe employers' and job seekers' perceptions about the status of the *current* job market. (See Exhibit 50.2.)

3. *Future expectations.* The Index collects data on expectations of the *future* job market. These are drawn from questions designed to determine companies' expected hiring activities in the coming six-month period. (See Exhibit 50.3.)

---

[1] The New York Times Job Market, the print and online recruitment services offering of *The New York Times*, provides employers and job seekers with comprehensive resources to streamline the recruitment process. The New York Times Job Market, its Confidence Index, and its other research are not affiliated with the editorial operations of *The New York Times* newspaper and do not reflect the views of the newspaper or its journalists.

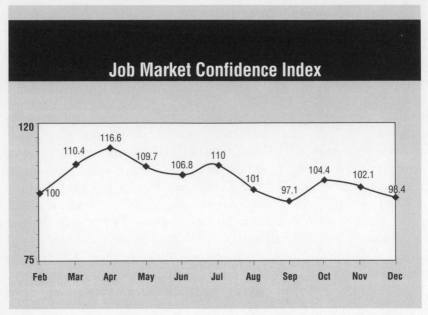

Exhibit 50.1   Job Market Confidence Index. (Reprinted with permission.)

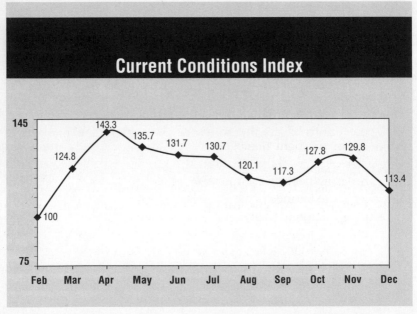

Exhibit 50.2   Current Conditions Index. (Reprinted with permission.)

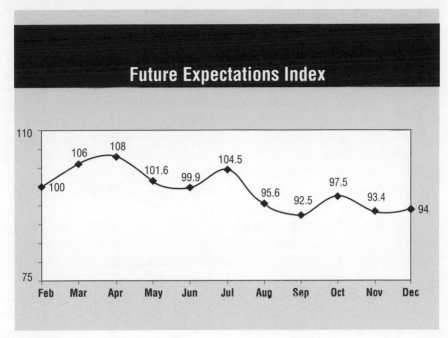

Exhibit 50.3 Future Expectations Index. (Reprinted with permission.)

The contrast of the current conditions and future expectations data provides a sense of employers' confidence in the current job market compared to what they believe lies ahead.

In addition to these data, a battery of questions is tracked over time to get a specific picture of trends in the job market, and their causes. One of the most interesting questions tracked is whether employers have too many, too few, or about the right number of people to handle the current workload. Questions on workload conditions provide critical insight into whether businesses believe their staff is stretched beyond capacity and, thus, whether those businesses may start hiring again.

For instance, between August and September 2002, the percentage of employers who said that they employed *too few* people to handle their current workload rose from 24.1 percent to 30.2 percent. Firms were not hiring; they were trying to do more with less. But they were also reporting that this was not sustainable. This would imply that employers would need to start hiring soon to meet the needs of their current workload. And in fact, in the next period between September and October 2002, there was an increase in the percentage of employers (from 33.5 percent to 39.3 percent) planning to hire for newly created positions.

To gain insight into the challenges employers face in the economy, the survey also asks what needs to change in the economy or in their business before they will resume hiring. Do they need to see improvements in their company's sales, or an uptick in the stock market or in business investments? Insight derived from such questions sheds light on two issues: the bottlenecks that may be affecting recruitment activity and the impact that employers' and job seekers' perceptions, expectations, and planned hiring activity have on the New York recruitment landscape.

One of the innovations of The New York Times Job Market Confidence Index is its measurement of *perceptions*.

In the past, economists established theories based on the assumption that all people behave rationally. However, we know this is not an accurate portrayal of the real world. In fact, our perceptions dramatically affect the decisions we make, and our view of the economy plays an important role in defining economic reality. In a word, psychology matters. Slowly some economists are beginning to acknowledge this. The best sign of progress in the field is seen by the awarding of the 2002 Nobel Prize for economics to *psychologist* Daniel Kahneman of Princeton University (shared with an expert in experimental economics).

Psychology was a powerful driving force in our nation's economy during the booming 1990s and the bust of 2000. Many consumers and businesspeople in the United States were swept away by the euphoria of the Internet and the promise of the "new economy." How did this psychology operate on a practical level, day to day? The answer is that when people are optimistic about the future, they tend to spend more money. And when people spend more money, businesses do better. And when businesses do better, they hire more people and pay higher wages. Finally, when more people are employed and earning more money, they spend more money. This kind of economic growth is cyclical.

Historically, the most important measures of this kind of psychology are the Conference Board's Consumer Confidence Index and the University of Michigan's Consumer Sentiment Index. Wall Street follows these numbers intensely, and the markets often swing dramatically depending on the results. During recessions, Wall Street watches these figures even more closely for signs that consumers may slow down their spending and further threaten a stalling economy. These two indexes are also among the key indicators used by the Federal Reserve Board when deciding to increase or decrease interest rates. Retailers watch these figures for signs of future sales. Economic studies show that forecast models that include the Consumer Confidence Index are more accurate at predicting economic growth than models that don't. These measures focus on consumer behavior. But the same dynamics also hold true for the job market.

By incorporating the human element into an analysis of the job market, The New York Times Job Market Confidence Index provides great insight into the economy and can help people make more informed decisions. Through benchmarking and trend analysis, the Index attempts to uncover the drivers of today's workplace trends, and provides those involved with human resources planning with timely and practical information.

You can register at www.nytimes.com/jobmarket to receive a monthly report of The New York Times Job Market Confidence Index.

Biblical Boats, Medieval Spires, and Cesium Clocks Have More in Common with Staffing Than Meets the Eye

Gerry Crispin
SPHR

The 50 essays chosen for *On Staffing: Advice and Perspectives from HR Leaders* were written, principally, by practitioners for practitioners. This collection of thoughts from hands-on contributors serves many purposes, but taken together, they provide a point of departure for what will arguably become the most critical human resources discipline. Because this is the first serious effort at redefining the size and scope of staffing.

After reading articles like Barry Siegel's description of outsourcing or Dan Guaglianone's discussion about staffing leadership, it is easy to envision just how broad a view of staffing we might aspire to along with all the challenges, obstacles, and opportunities this entails.

What we can't lose sight of is the fact that the landscape of staffing is continually evolving. And, in part because of these changes, it often appears as just a jumble of random possibilities—shifting scenes viewed from a speeding train littered with fabulous ideas, tools, technologies, systems, techniques, and strategies. How do they all go together? Are we to patiently wait for a collection of interconnected Lego kits with detailed contents and suggested building plans? Are we locked into an eternal struggle to get any two random pieces to fit together? *On Staffing* offers insights into these questions and, at the same time, suggests what we'll need in order answer them effectively.

Learn from the experience of the professionals who have contributed here by keeping in mind three basic principles shared by all staffing disciplines: internal consistency, best practices, and common standards.

Internal Consistency

In biblical times, you couldn't go to Home Depot and buy a yardstick. Measurement was up close and personal. A foot-rule was the length of a man's foot. No matter that it might differ by half a "foot" from one individual to the next. Fortunately, common ratios existed in body measurements (they still do). Dividing a foot by 12 approximated the width of a thumb, an inch. The distance from the tip of a man's nose to the end of his outstretched arm was approximately three (of his) feet, or a yard. Twice this distance, a man's outstretched arms became a fathom. Half a yard was a cubit. Half a cubit was a span, which was the also the distance from the tip of the thumb to the tip of the pinky when the fingers were spread out as far as possible. Got all that? Now, go build a boat.

A couple of problems might have occurred to Noah while building the Ark:

1. Planks measured by any two people with slightly different body parts would produce vastly different boats.
2. Even one person might produce different results if exercise, diet, temperature, and (many) other factors were not held constant over time.

Folks still built pretty good boats in those days, although I'll bet most of them leaked. It is unlikely, though, that the best boat builders ever lost sight of the importance of internal consistency. They had to have the discipline to measure the same way every time. (Yardsticks came much later.)

Are we as disciplined in staffing? The language of staffing is no more consistent than an "inch" was in biblical times. Does the "number of hires" seem like an idea as basic as an inch? Over what period of time would you measure these hires? Does that include internal movement? All locations? Temporary and contingent hires? All levels? Are we measuring from the "offer acceptance" or the "start date"? Would every stakeholder in our firm get the answers correct?

To automatically assume that a fundamental understanding of what we do in staffing reflects the same reality for each person in our own firm (let alone externally) will only ensure that the boat you build has seriously mismatched planks and leaks like a sieve. If "number of hires" lacks internal consistency, how is it we would agree on cost per hire, quality of hire, source of hire, or behavioral interview? Would any two people in the same firm define applicant tracking the same way? First and foremost, a firm must carefully define its internal staffing processes—then adhere to them even as you measure the results, and do it the same way every time. It goes without saying that attending to the basics is a prerequisite for sharing best practices.

Best Practices

The medieval masons were the masters of best practices. They learned their discipline through apprenticeship, despite the fact that few could read or write. Their knowledge included material selection, geometrical proportions, load distribution, architectural design, and much more. They devised a way to share their knowledge before there was a science; indeed, they knew little of formal mathematics. Their discipline, however, consisted of jealously guarded but successful proportions that resulted, for example, in the spire on the eleventh-century cathedral at Strasbourg that towers more than 40 stories. No other buildings reached that height until 100 years ago (and the masons did it without steel or concrete). A pair of dividers was their standard, but it was a shared knowledge about what works that resulted in buildings capable of lasting a millennium.

Do we even know the learning we expect staffing professionals to absorb at our firms? Can we relate the practice of that knowledge to specific results (like a building that doesn't fall down)? Firms that can consistently define what staffing is and what it must accomplish will have a competitive edge in sharing and teaching best practices. They will also be positioned to leverage their knowledge to establish industry standards.

Common Standards

There are almost no commonly accepted standards in staffing—despite the fact that in almost all other areas, the world literally couldn't run without standards. In Australia, for example, until only a few years ago, different states had different standards for the width of their railroad tracks. Railroads were simply not used to ship many goods, and no one noticed or cared very much. Imagine loading your shipment of goods in Sydney, having it travel a hundred miles to the border of New South Wales, and then having to unload it and load it all over again on another train. Inefficient or just dumb?

So consider how many Fortune 500 firms have multiple divisions—with each using a different system (even multiple systems) for tracking employment-related data. Unload, upload. (Some would argue, though, that most of these systems do employ common "data standards.")

Getting people to agree on a standard system is not without its problems. The French government adopted a new system of standards called the metric system more than 200 years ago. The meter was originally conceived as one ten-millionth part of the distance from the North Pole to the Equator when measured on a straight line running along the surface of the Earth through Paris. Perhaps if the line were drawn through Washington, D.C., the metric system might be the standard in the United States today. Instead, we have to teach every schoolchild how to divide inches by 2.54 in order to speak with the rest of the world. Unload, upload.

There are notable exceptions. Take a minute, for example. Actually, just take a second. All we really have to know in order to have exactly the same time as anyone else in the world is to click "yes" when a Microsoft "wizard" asks if you want your internal computer clock to be updated live. Your time will be so accurate that it would take a million years for an error of one second to creep in (not that you'll really care after a million years). Behind the scenes and beyond the technology is an underlying implicit agreement that one second is always (operationally) exactly 9,192,631,770 oscillations of a particular cesium atom. This standard is measured, observed, communicated, compared, and integrated worldwide. Yes, we still have to adjust for the date line and daylight saving time. Still, no one argues over what second it is. Staffing has no such fixed agreements, and for tens of thousands of years neither did time. Few cared what time it was elsewhere when the only concern was when to plant or when to harvest.

Times have changed. Companies are now concerned with cost of acquiring the competencies they need to succeed, the impact these collections of competencies make, and the investments required to retain them.

Common standards—including those that measure human capital in general and staffing in particular—are destined to follow a similar evolutionary path. Cost, quality, time, productivity, and efficiency can all be determined; we only lack an agreement on how to treat the differences among us.

If we are willing to describe our staffing processes, measure them consistently, share what works with others, and agree on the underlying standards that govern their operation, then we will have truly created a staffing discipline. *On Staffing: Advice and Perspectives from HR Leaders* is a step in the right direction.

Index